BATMAN® & the Justice League

VOL. 2

STORY AND ART BY

SHIORI TESHIROGI

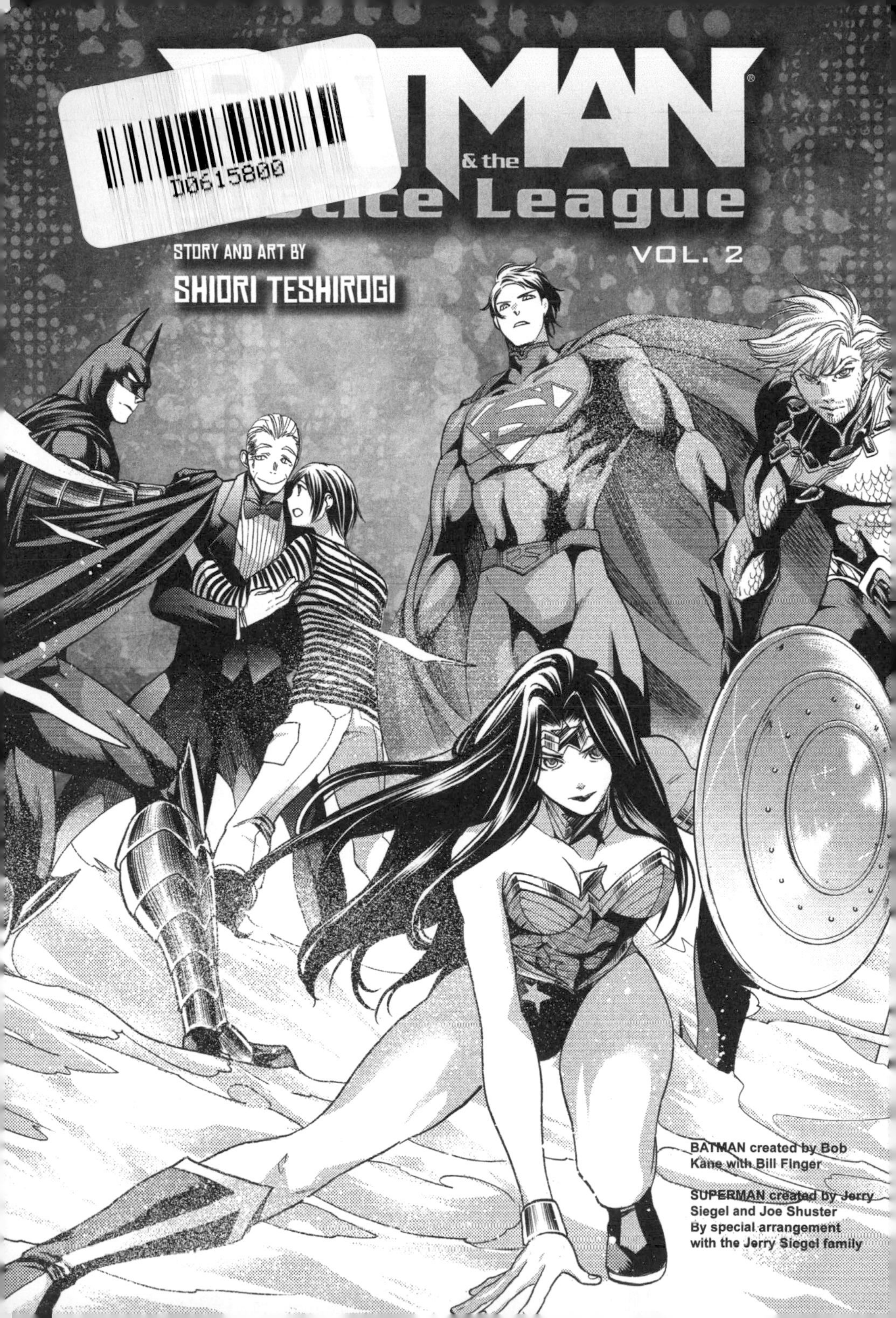

BATMAN created by Bob Kane with Bill Finger

SUPERMAN created by Jerry Siegel and Joe Shuster
By special arrangement with the Jerry Siegel family

SHELDON DRZKA Translation
STUART MOORE Adaptation
DERON BENNETT Letters

JIM CHADWICK Group Editor – Collected Edition
KRISTY QUINN Editor – Collected Edition
LIZ ERICKSON Assistant Editor – Collected Edition
STEVE COOK Design Director – Books
LARRY BERRY Publication Design

BOB HARRAS Senior VP – Editor-in-Chief, DC Comics
PAT McCALLUM Executive Editor, DC Comics

DAN DiDIO Publisher
JIM LEE Publisher & Chief Creative Officer
AMIT DESAI Executive VP – Business & Marketing Strategy,
Direct to Consumer & Global Franchise Management
BOBBIE CHASE VP & Executive Editor, Young Reader &
Talent Development
MARK CHIARELLO Senior VP – Art, Design & Collected Editions
JOHN CUNNINGHAM Senior VP – Sales & Trade Marketing
BRIAR DARDEN VP – Business Affairs
ANNE DePIES Senior VP – Business Strategy, Finance & Administration
DON FALLETTI VP – Manufacturing Operations
LAWRENCE GANEM VP – Editorial Administration & Talent Relations
ALISON GILL Senior VP – Manufacturing & Operations
JASON GREENBERG VP – Business Strategy & Finance
HANK KANALZ Senior VP – Editorial Strategy & Administration
JAY KOGAN Senior VP – Legal Affairs
NICK J. NAPOLITANO VP – Manufacturing Administration
LISETTE OSTERLOH VP – Digital Marketing & Events
EDDIE SCANNELL VP – Consumer Marketing
COURTNEY SIMMONS Senior VP – Publicity & Communications
JIM (SKI) SOKOLOWSKI VP – Comic Book Specialty Sales &
Trade Marketing
NANCY SPEARS VP – Mass, Book, Digital Sales & Trade Marketing
MICHELE R. WELLS VP – Content Strategy

BATMAN AND THE JUSTICE LEAGUE VOL. 2

Published by DC Comics. Compilation and all new
material Copyright © 2019 DC Comics. All Rights
Reserved. Originally published in Japan as
BATMAN AND THE JUSTICE LEAGUE in
Champion Red 12, 1, 2, 3, 4 by Akita Shoten.
Copyright © 2017, 2018 DC Comics. All Rights
Reserved. DC LOGO, BATMAN, THE JUSTICE
LEAGUE and all related characters and elements
© and ™ DC Comics. The stories, characters and
incidents featured in this publication are entirely
fictional. DC Comics does not read or accept
unsolicited submissions of ideas, stories or artwork.

DC Comics, 2900 West Alameda Ave., Burbank, CA
91505. Printed in Canada. 3/22/19. First Printing.
ISBN: 978-1-4012-9059-7

Library of Congress Cataloging-in-Publication
Data is available.

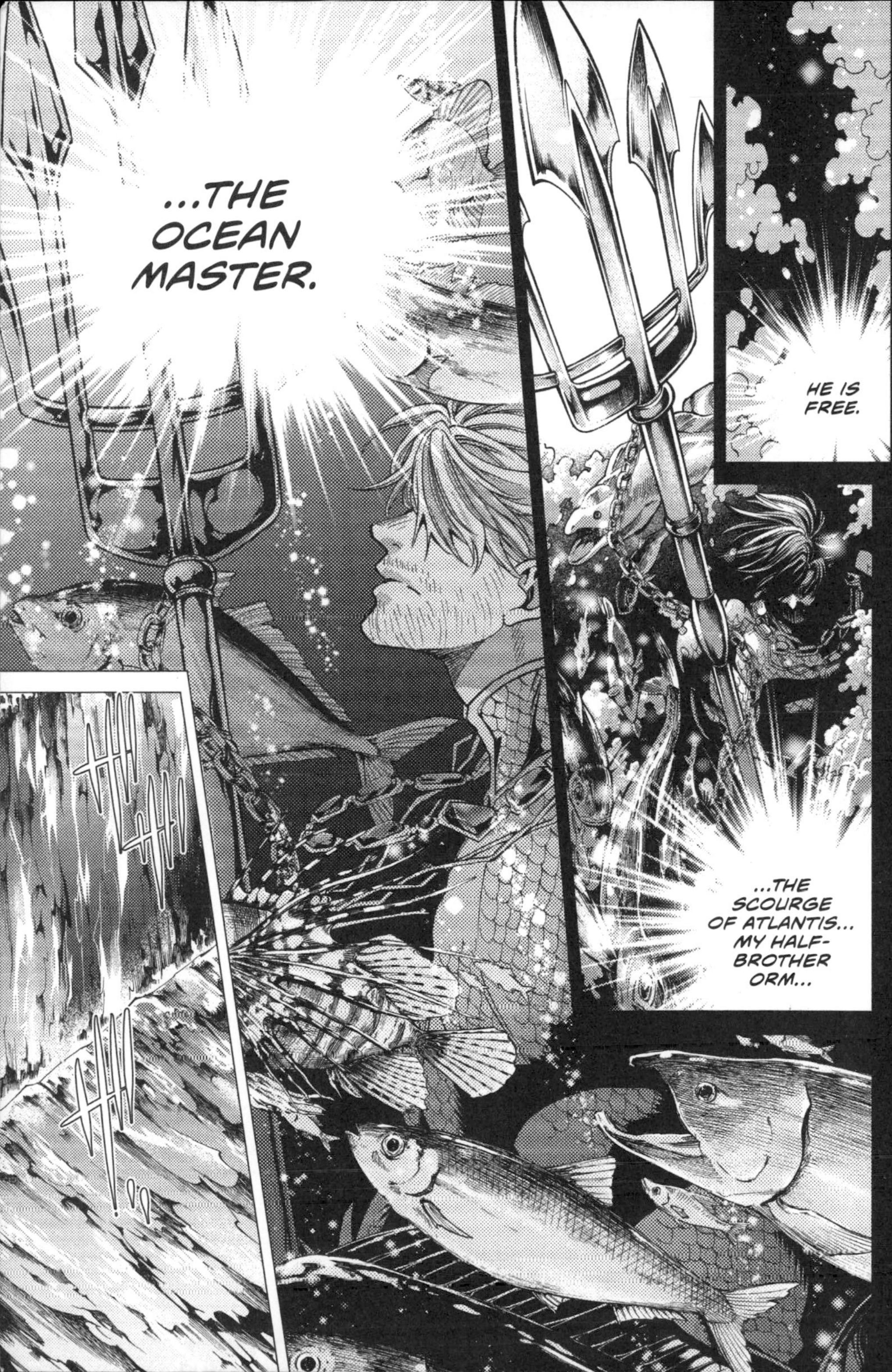
HE IS FREE.
...THE SCOURGE OF ATLANTIS... MY HALF-BROTHER ORM...
...THE OCEAN MASTER.

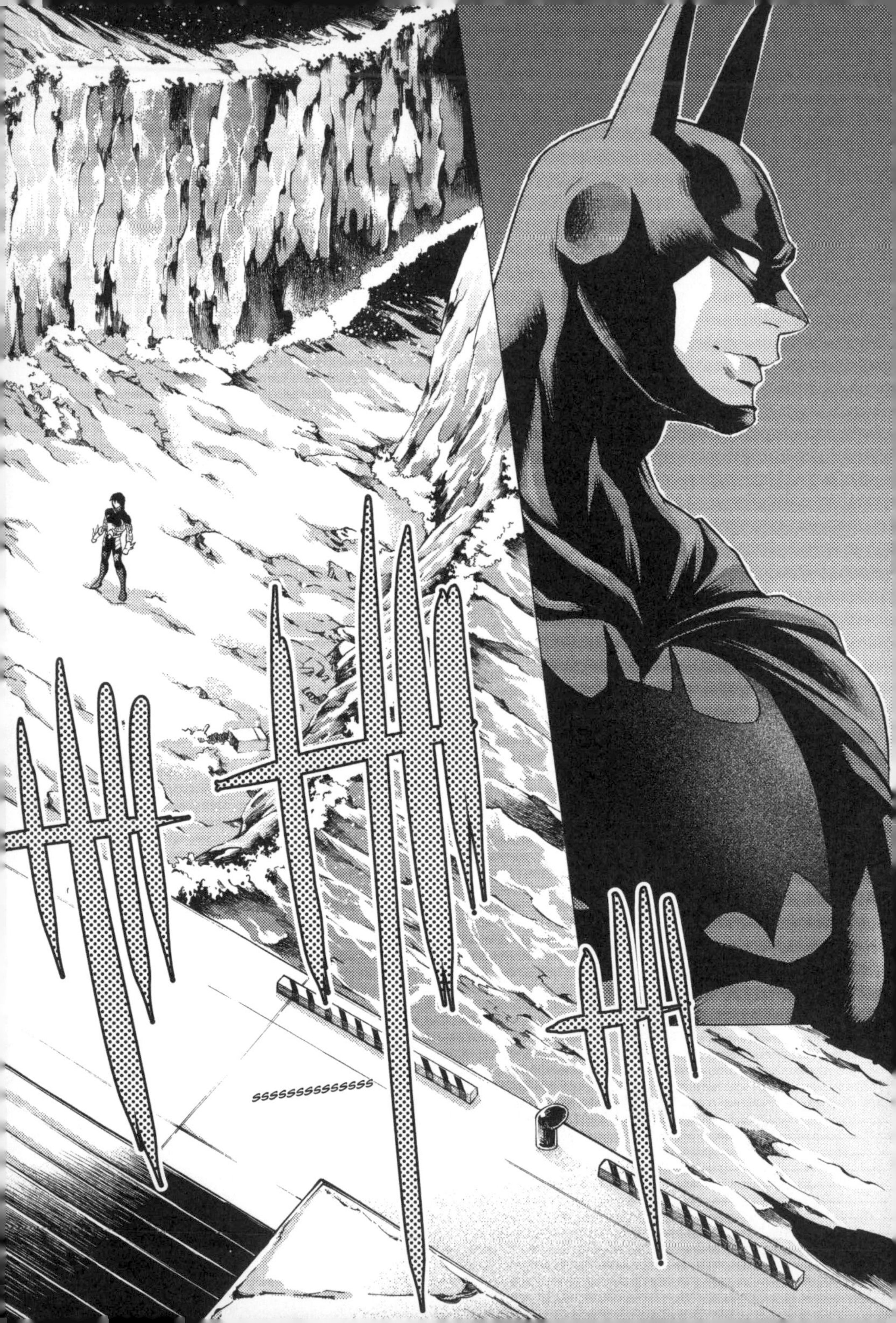
SSSSSSSSSSSSSS

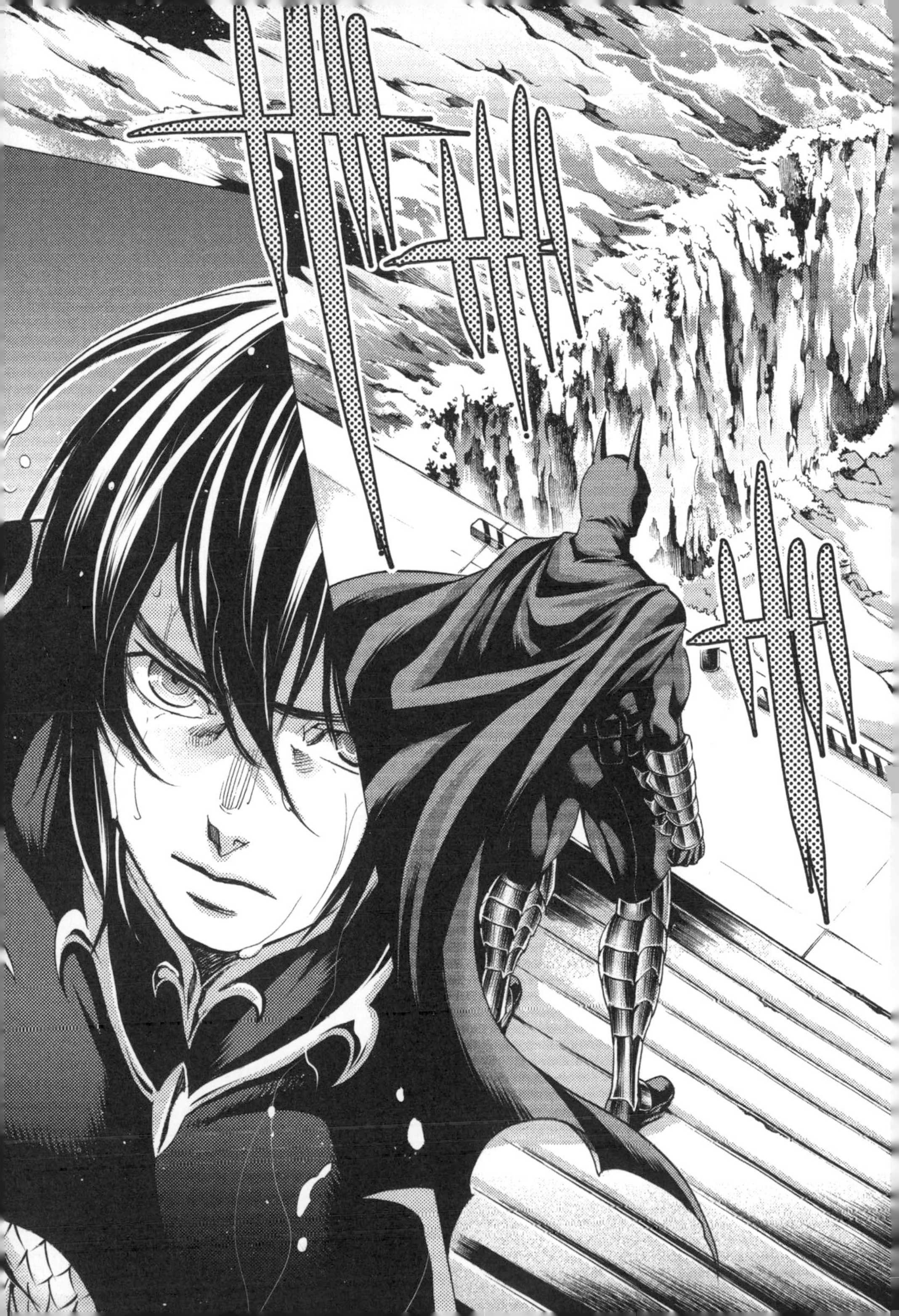

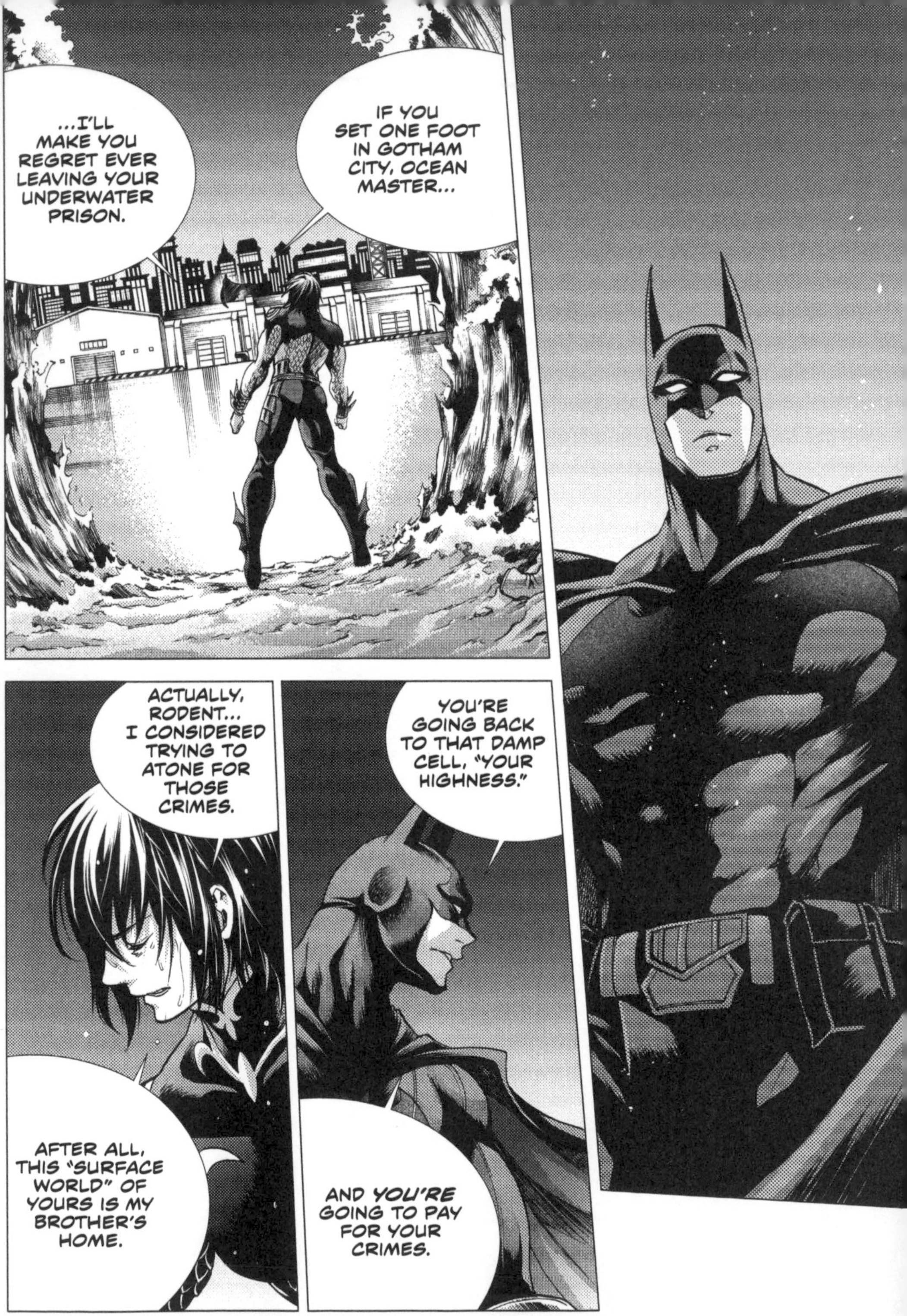
IF YOU SET ONE FOOT IN GOTHAM CITY, OCEAN MASTER...
...I'LL MAKE YOU REGRET EVER LEAVING YOUR UNDERWATER PRISON.
YOU'RE GOING BACK TO THAT DAMP CELL, "YOUR HIGHNESS."
AND *YOU'RE* GOING TO PAY FOR YOUR CRIMES.
ACTUALLY, RODENT... I CONSIDERED TRYING TO ATONE FOR THOSE CRIMES.
AFTER ALL, THIS "SURFACE WORLD" OF YOURS IS MY BROTHER'S HOME.

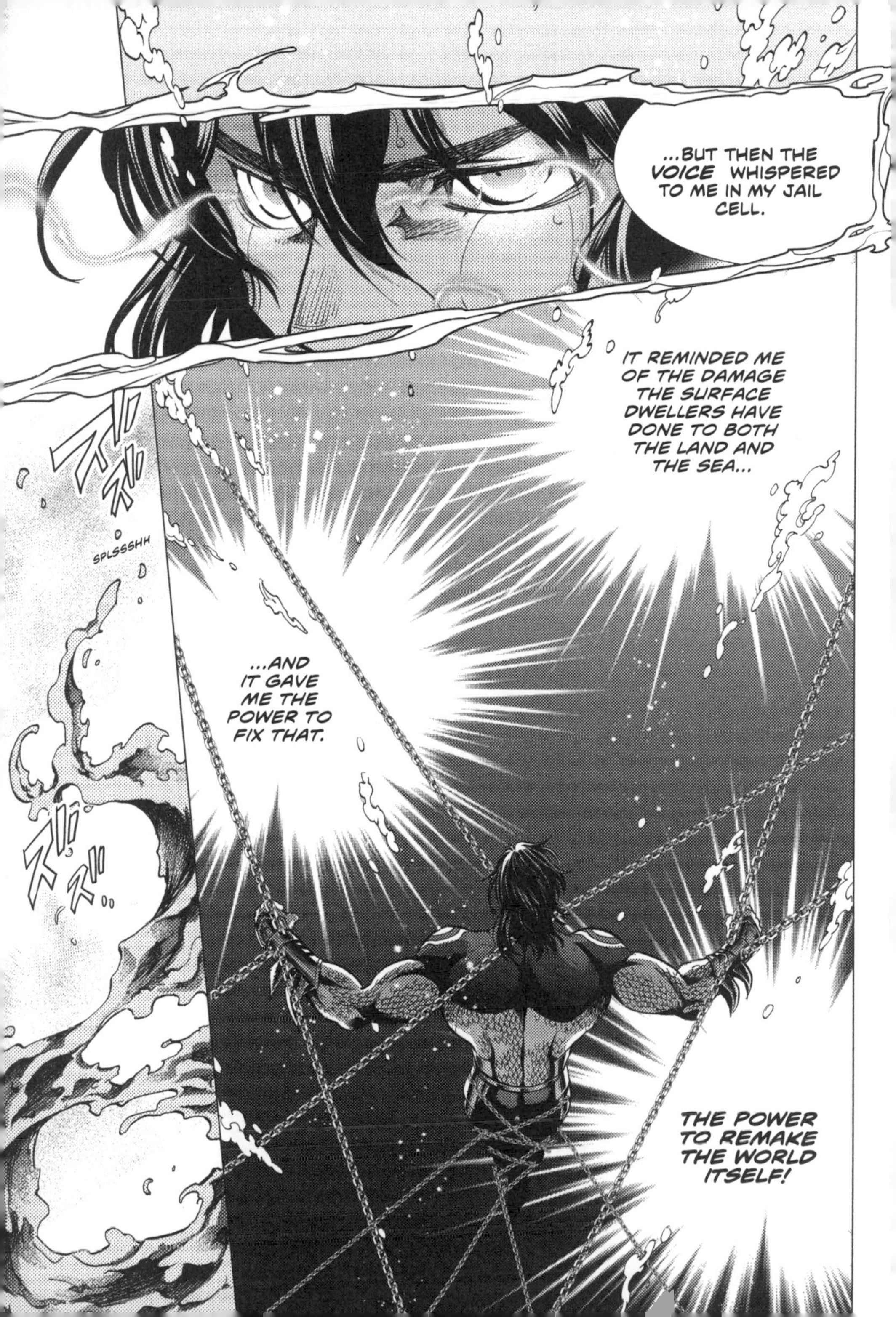
...BUT THEN THE *VOICE* WHISPERED TO ME IN MY JAIL CELL.
IT REMINDED ME OF THE DAMAGE THE SURFACE DWELLERS HAVE DONE TO BOTH THE LAND AND THE SEA...
...AND IT GAVE ME THE POWER TO FIX THAT.
THE POWER TO REMAKE THE WORLD ITSELF!
SPLSSSHH

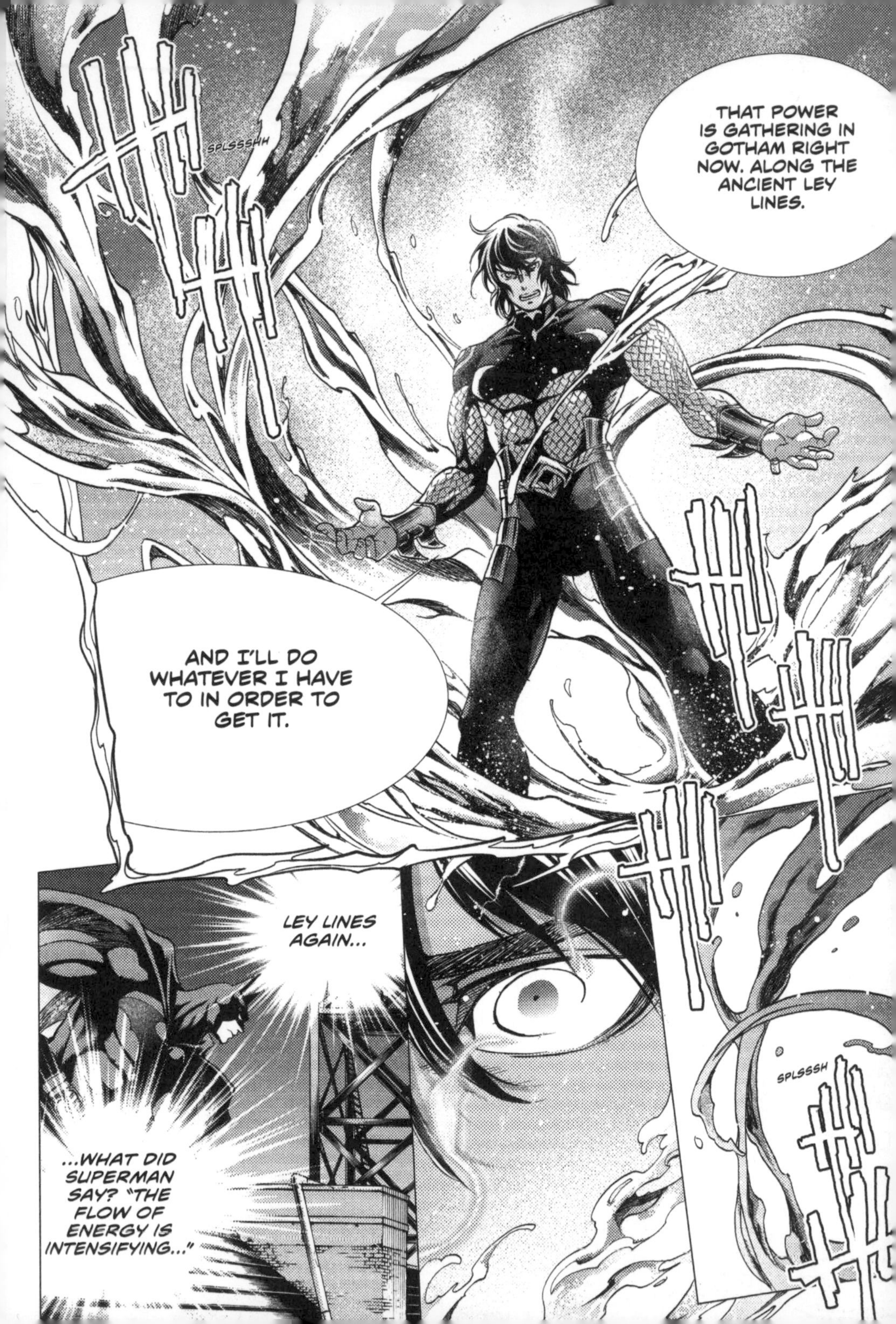
THAT POWER IS GATHERING IN GOTHAM RIGHT NOW. ALONG THE ANCIENT LEY LINES.
SPLSSSHH
AND I'LL DO WHATEVER I HAVE TO IN ORDER TO GET IT.
SPLSSSH
LEY LINES AGAIN...
...WHAT DID SUPERMAN SAY? "THE FLOW OF ENERGY IS INTENSIFYING..."

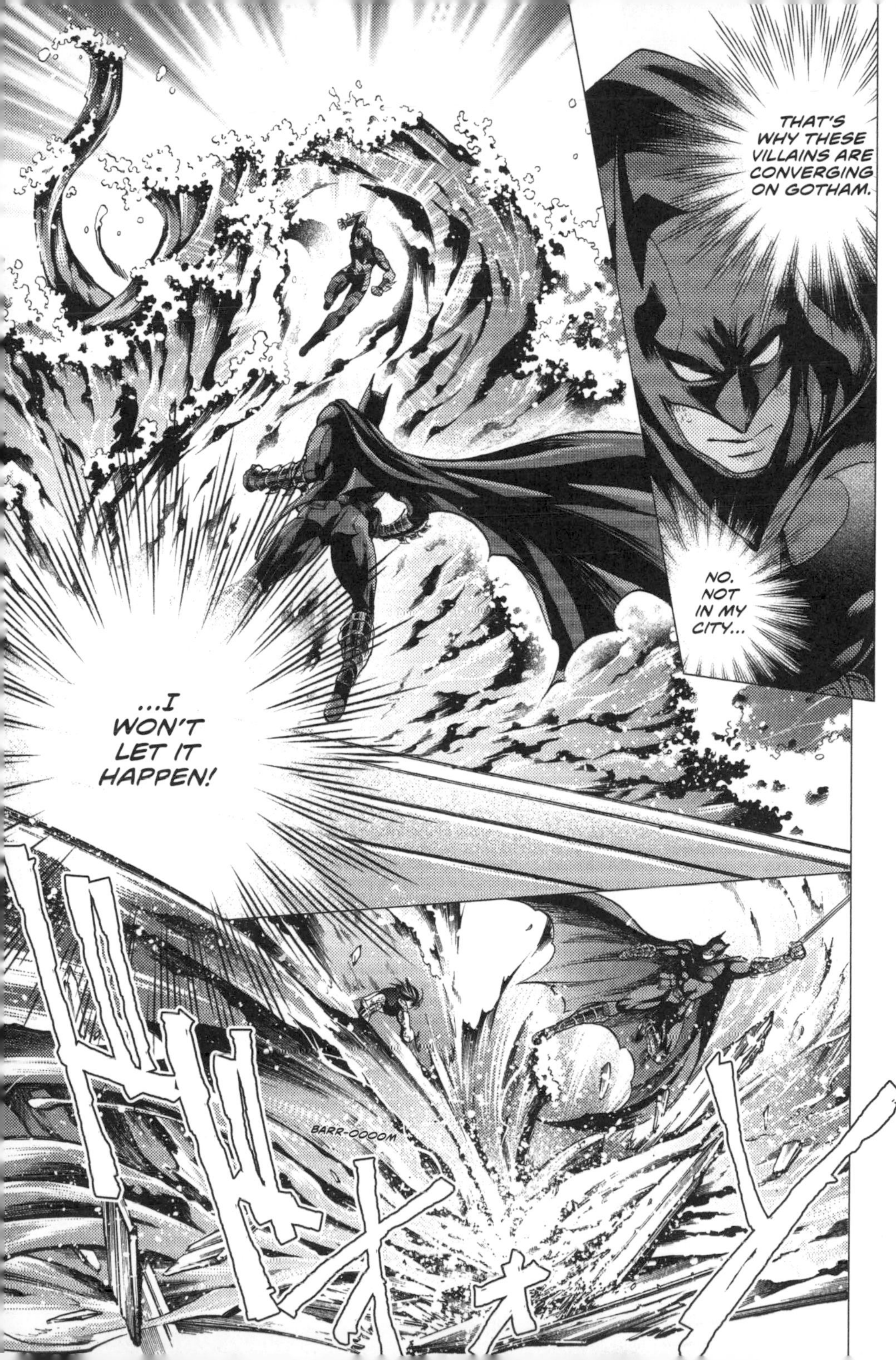
THAT'S WHY THESE VILLAINS ARE CONVERGING ON GOTHAM.
NO. NOT IN MY CITY...
...I WON'T LET IT HAPPEN!
BARR-OOOOM

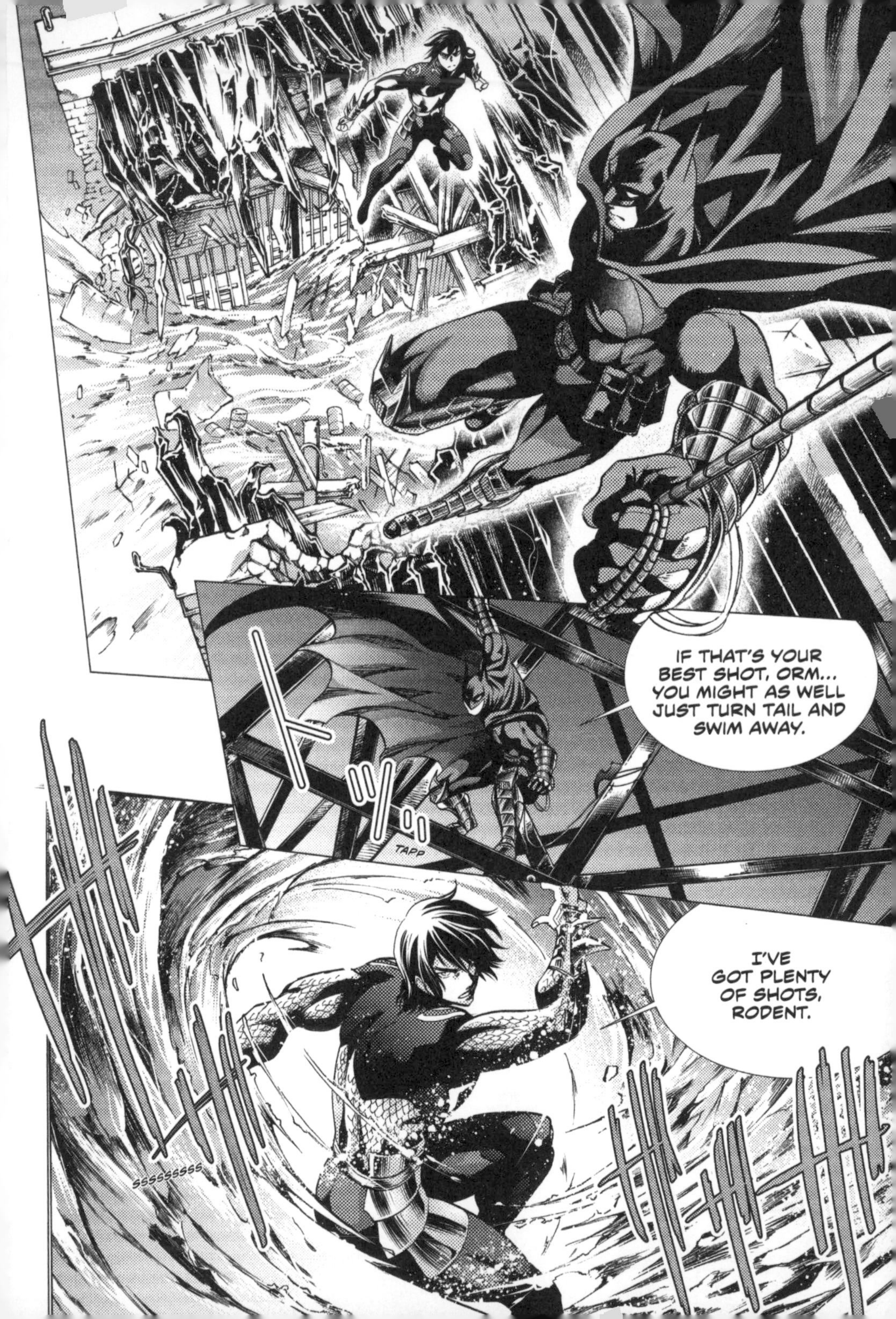

IF THAT'S YOUR BEST SHOT, ORM... YOU MIGHT AS WELL JUST TURN TAIL AND SWIM AWAY.
TAPP
I'VE GOT PLENTY OF SHOTS, RODENT.
SSSSSSSSSS

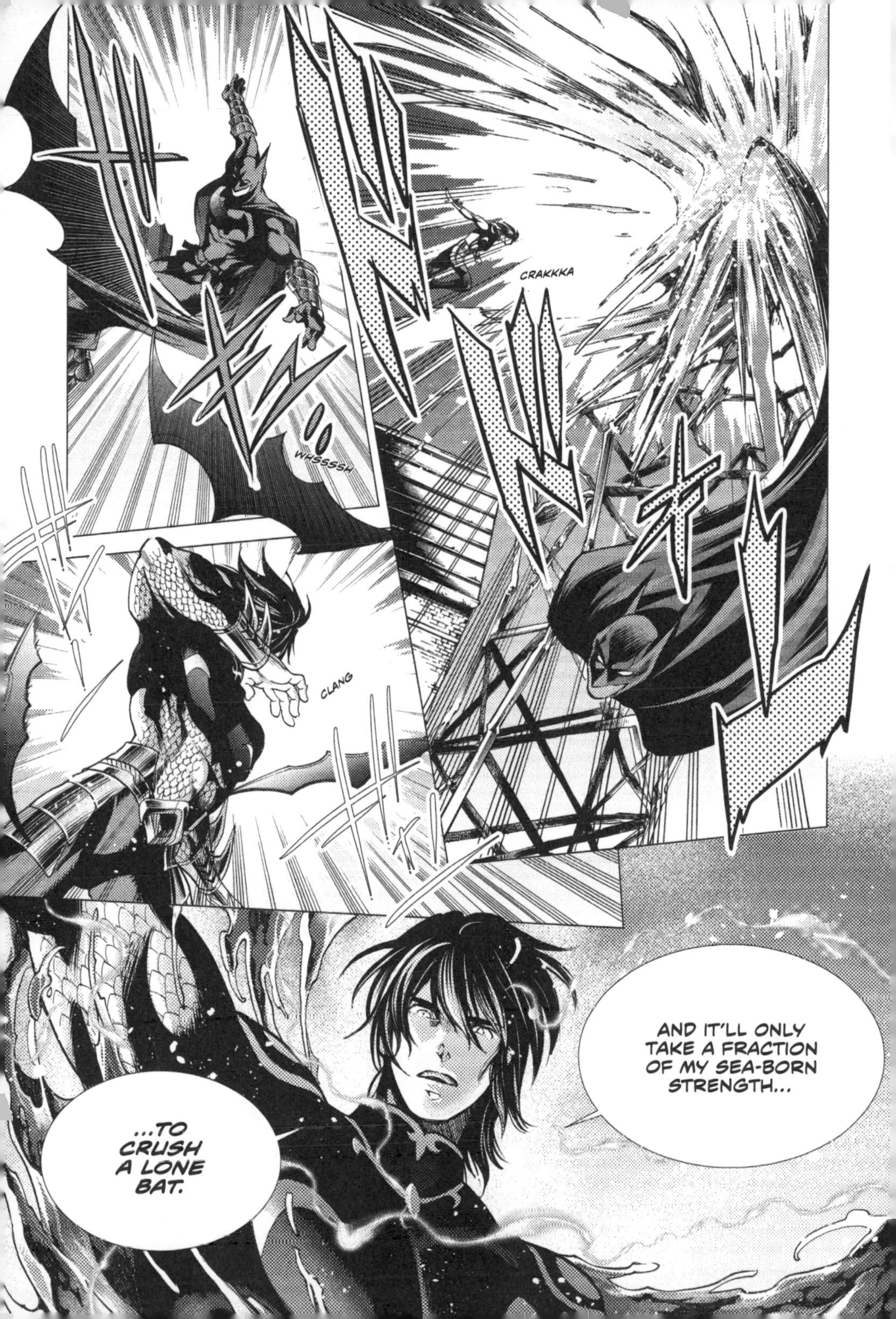
CRAKKKA
WHSSSSH
CLANG
AND IT'LL ONLY TAKE A FRACTION OF MY SEA-BORN STRENGTH...
...TO CRUSH A LONE BAT.

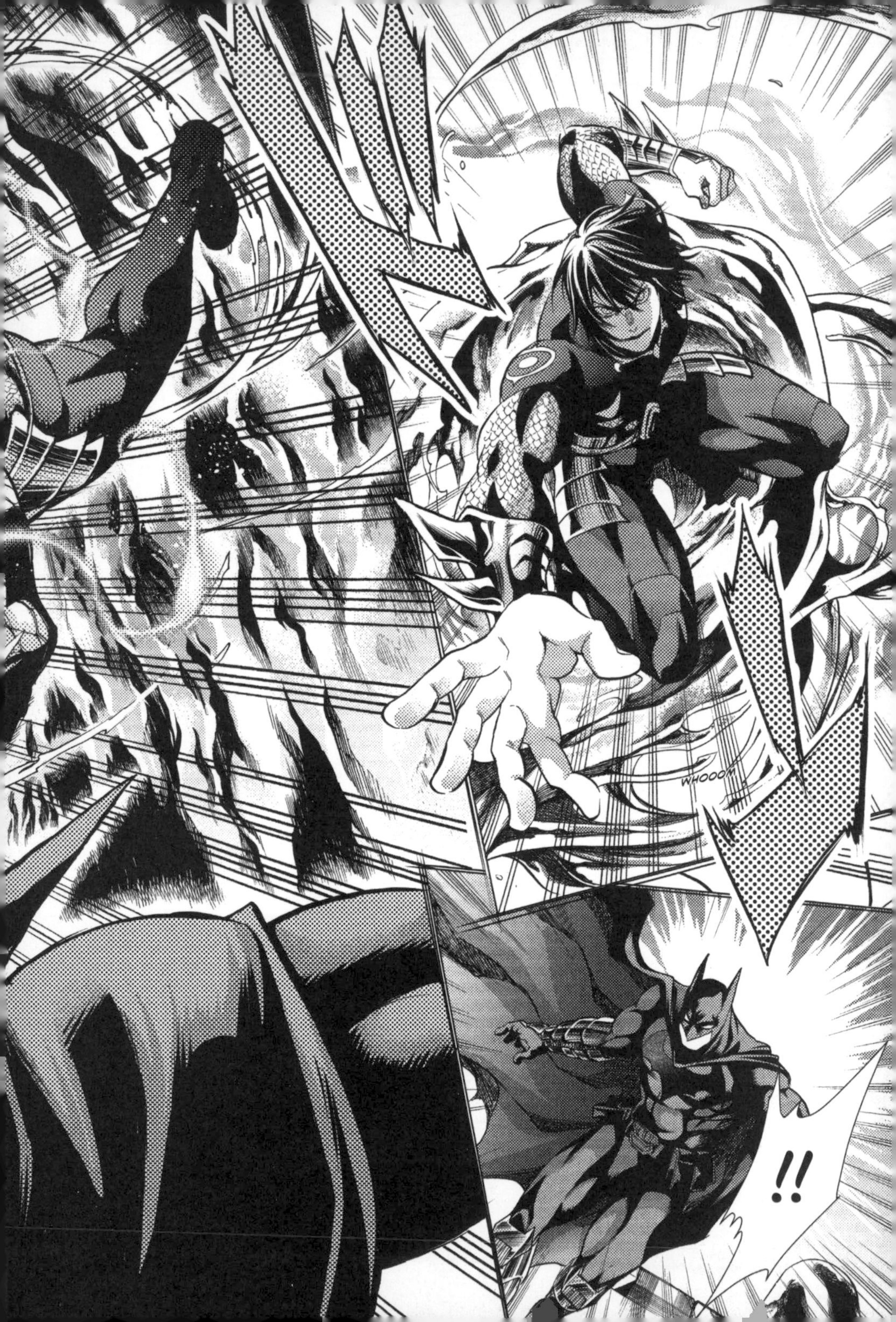
WHOOOM
!!

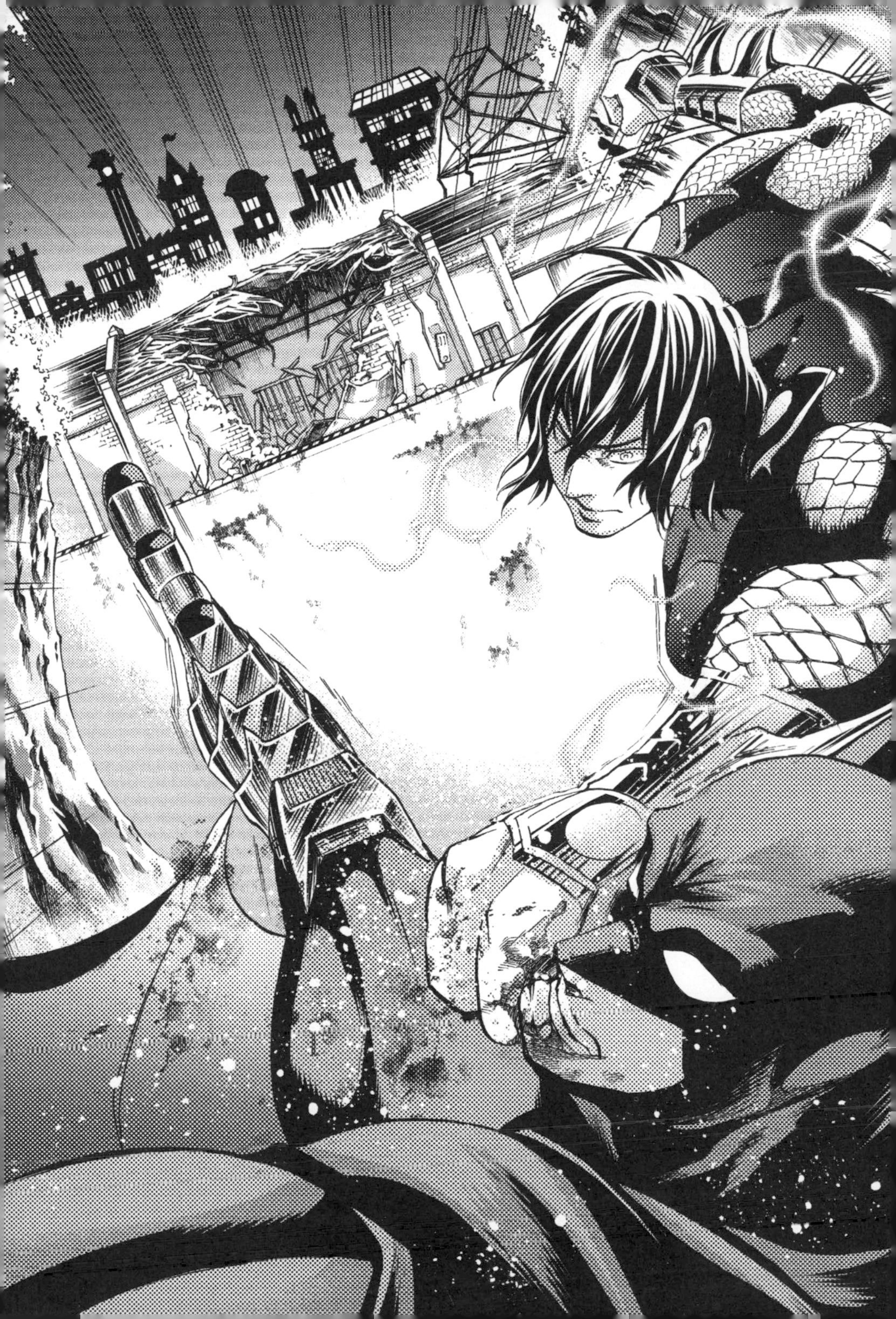

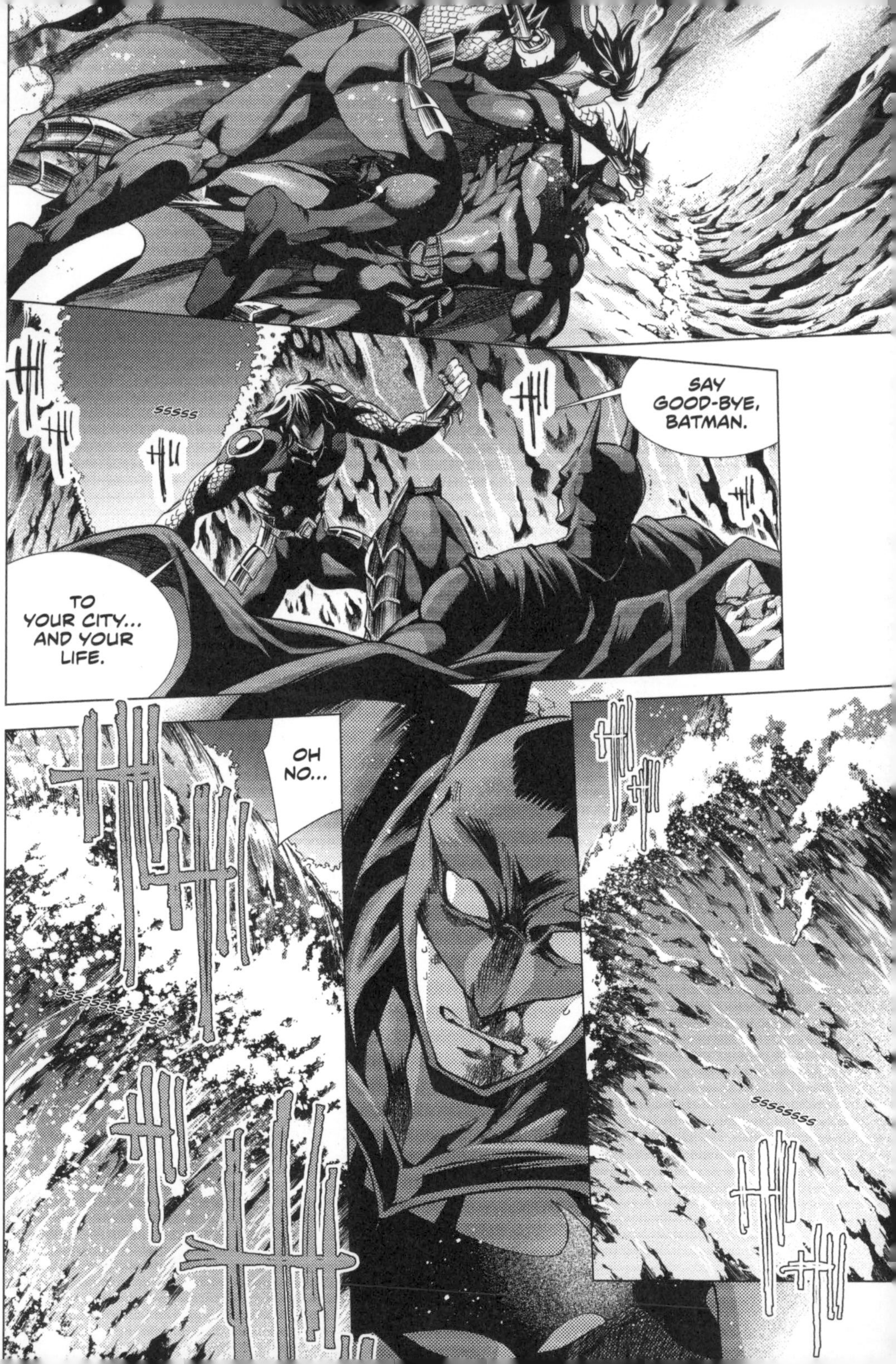
SAY GOOD-BYE, BATMAN.
SSSSS
TO YOUR CITY... AND YOUR LIFE.
SSSSSSSS
OH NO...
SSSSSSSSSSSSS

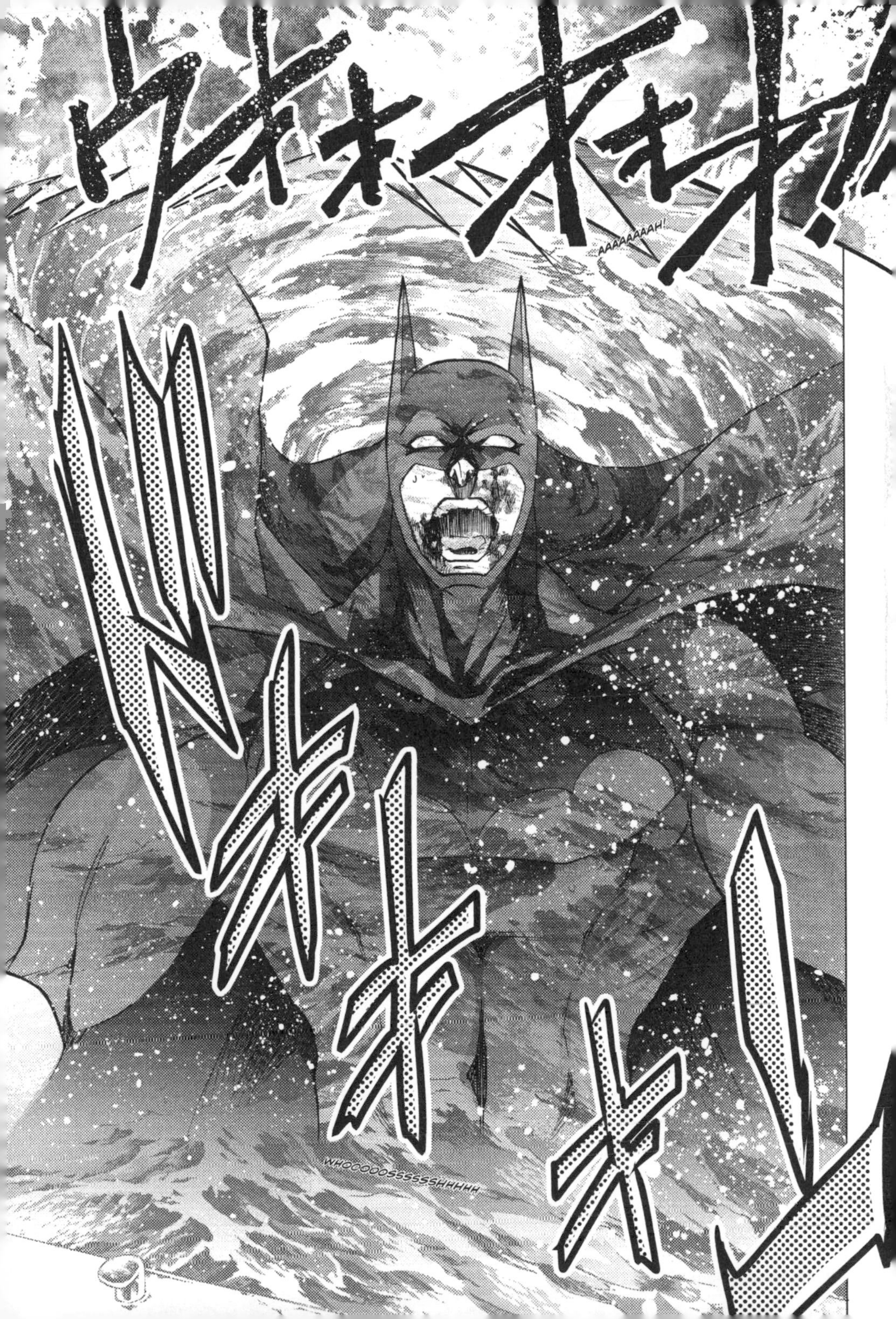

ウオオーオオオ!!
AAAAAAAAAH!
WHOOOOOOSSSSSSSHHHHHH

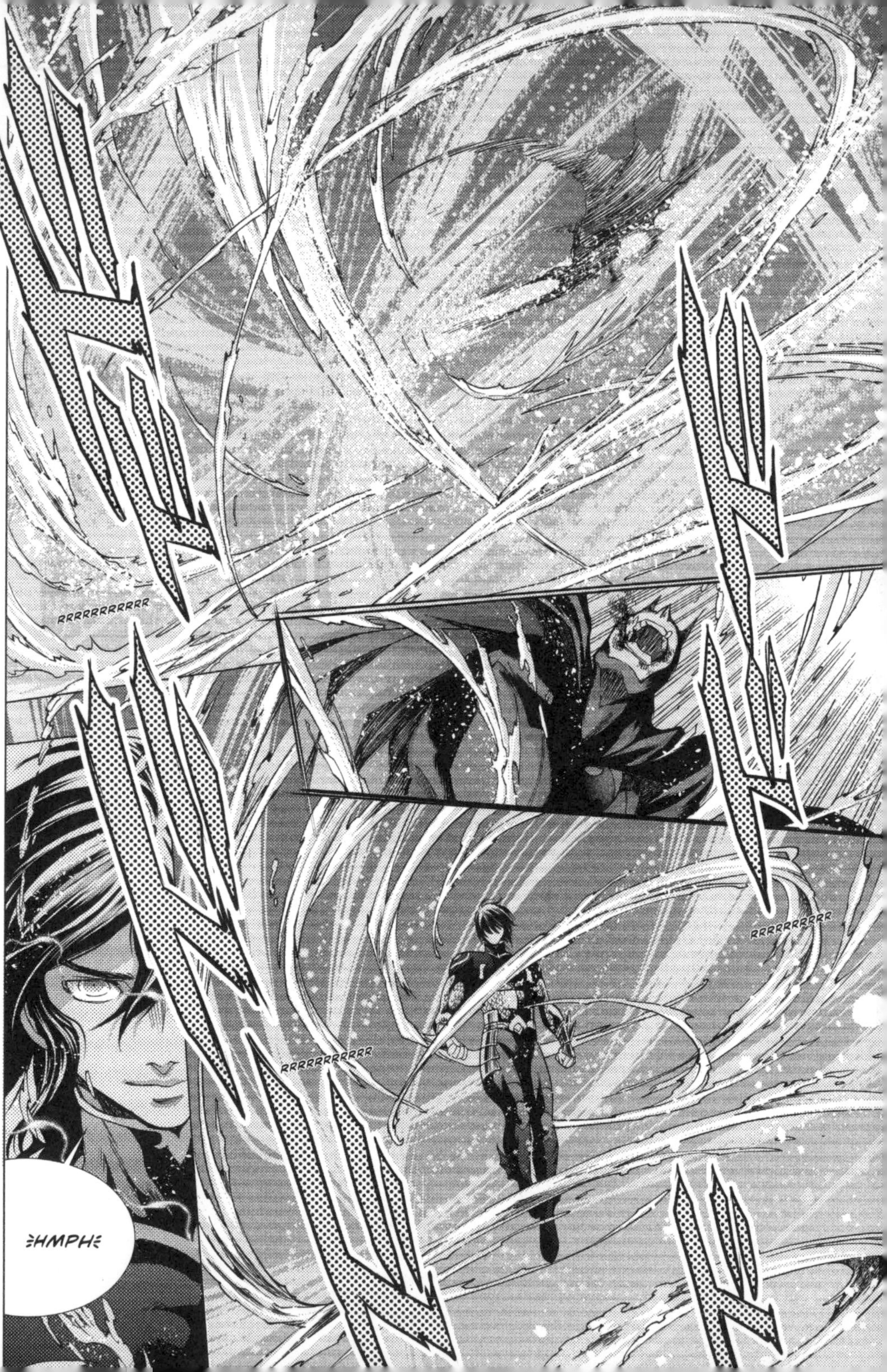
RRRRRRRRRRR
RRRRRRRRRR
RRRRRRRRRRR
HMPH

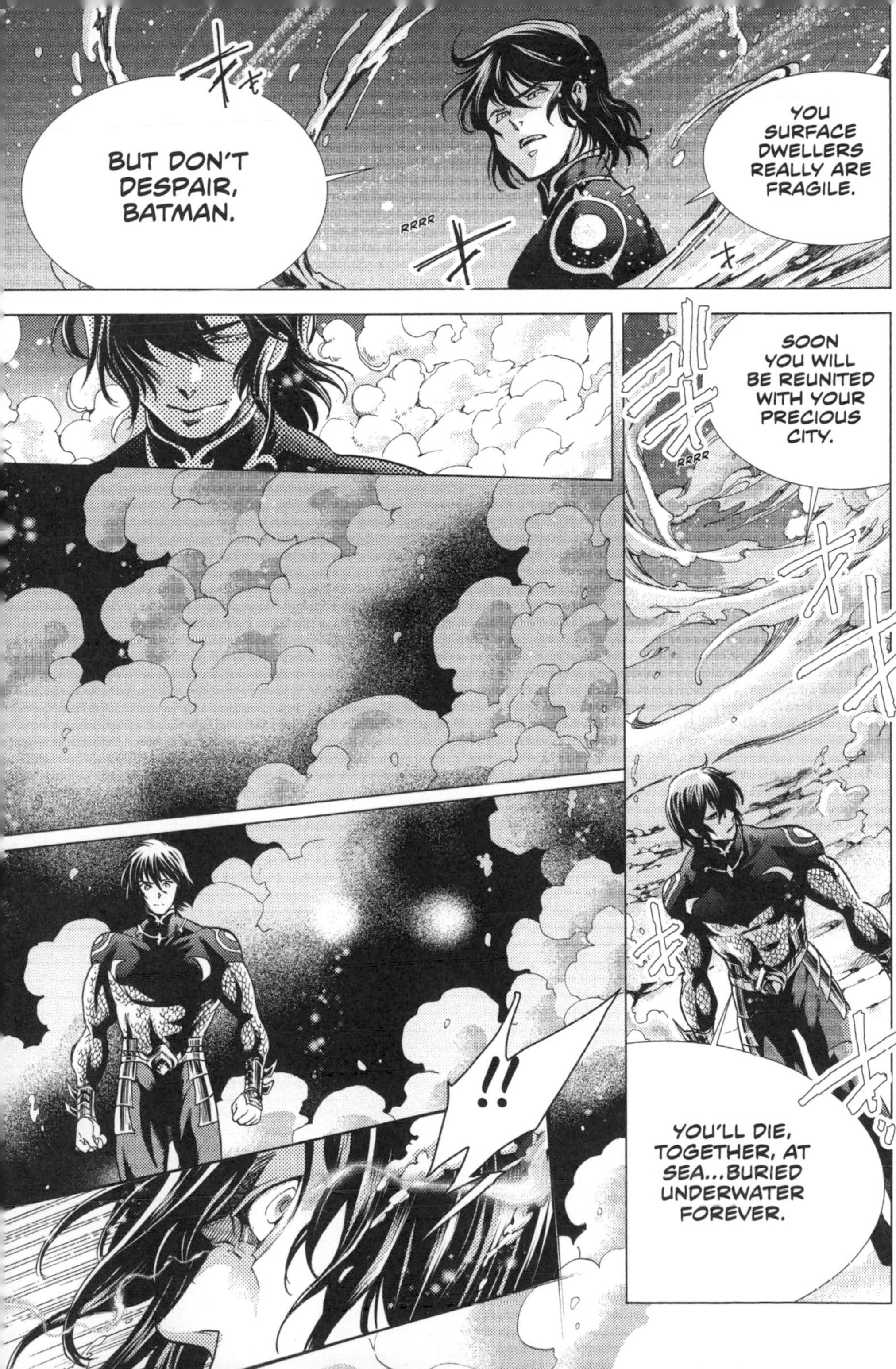
YOU SURFACE DWELLERS REALLY ARE FRAGILE.
RRRR
BUT DON'T DESPAIR, BATMAN.
SOON YOU WILL BE REUNITED WITH YOUR PRECIOUS CITY.
RRRR
YOU'LL DIE, TOGETHER, AT SEA...BURIED UNDERWATER FOREVER.
!!

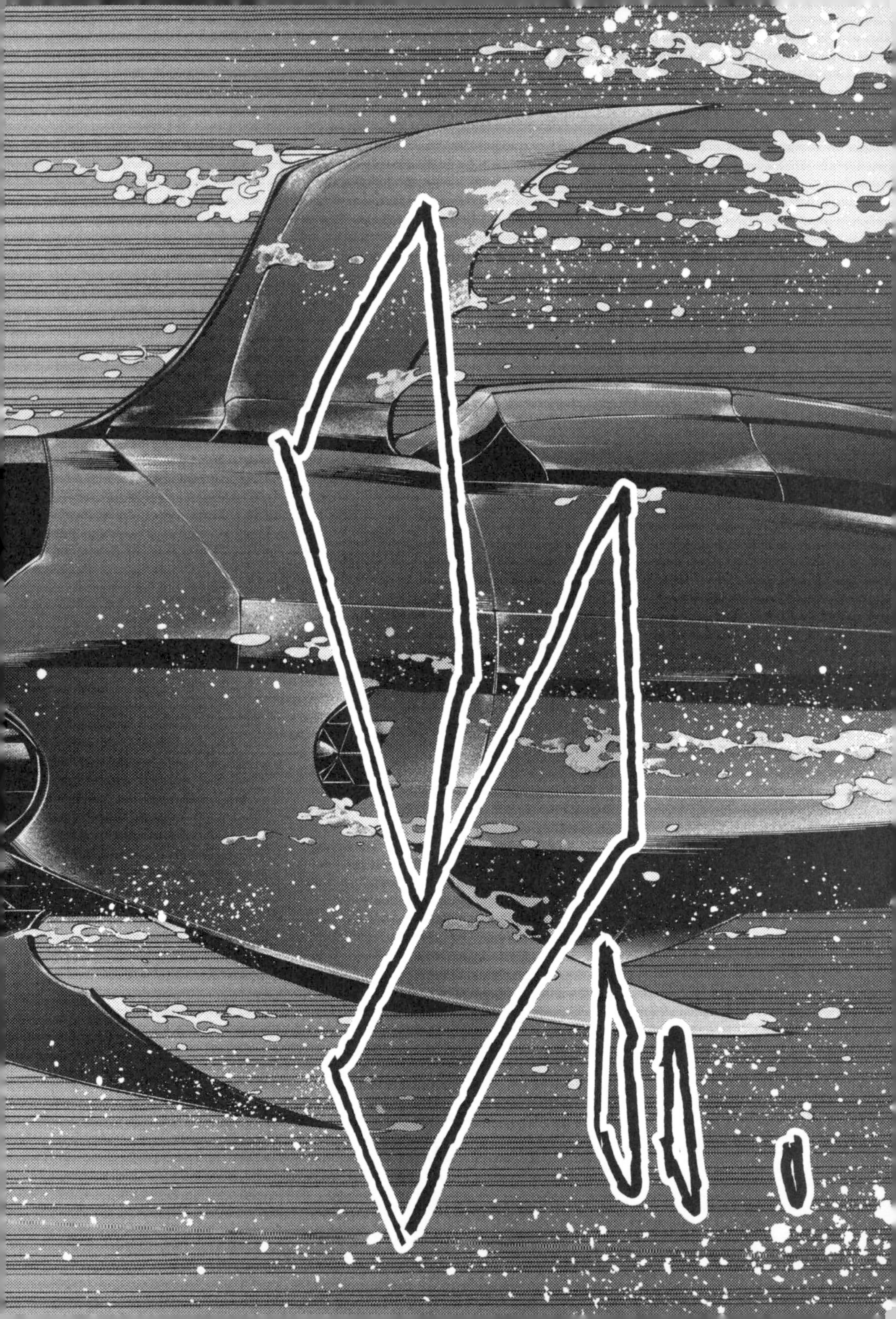

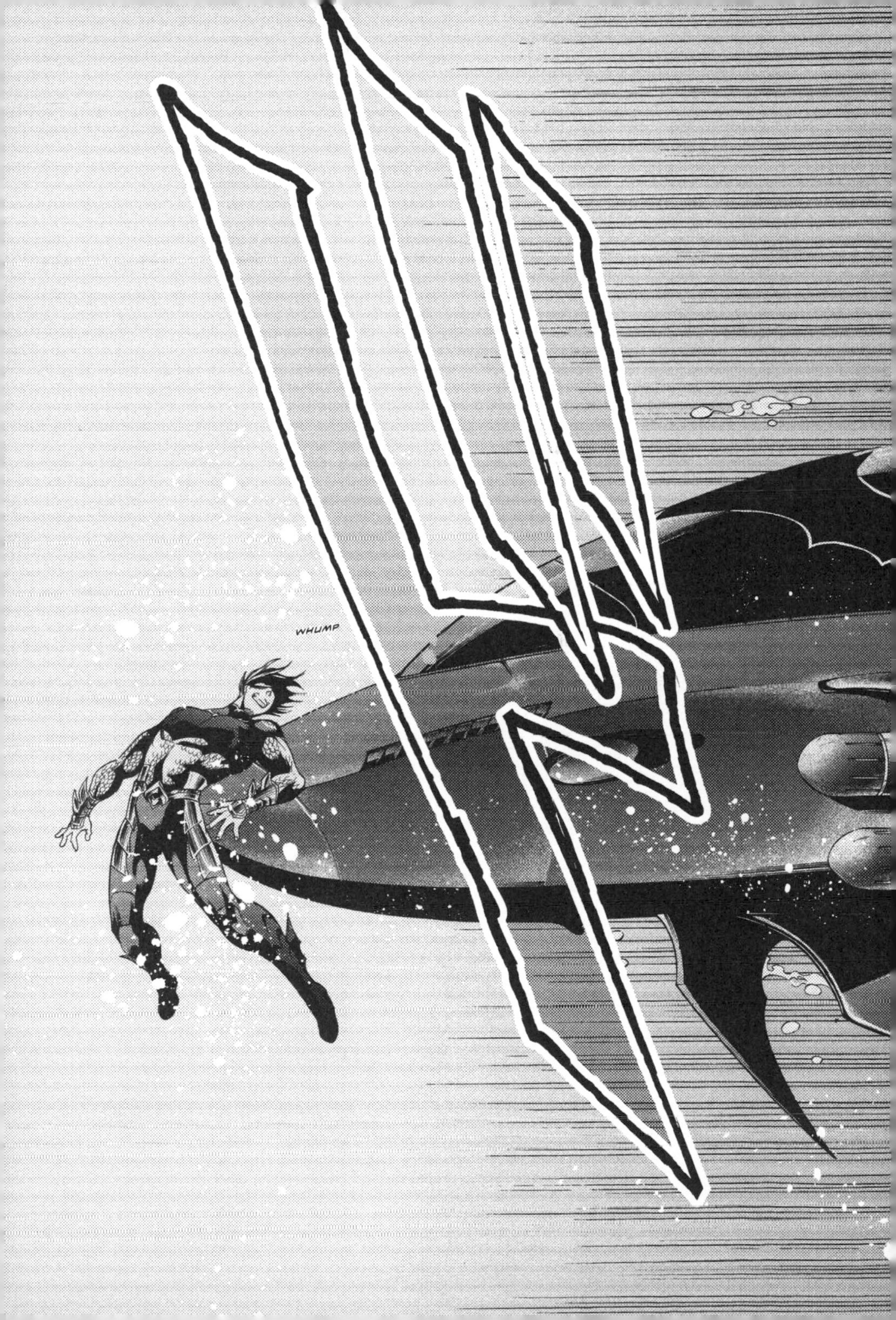
WHUMP

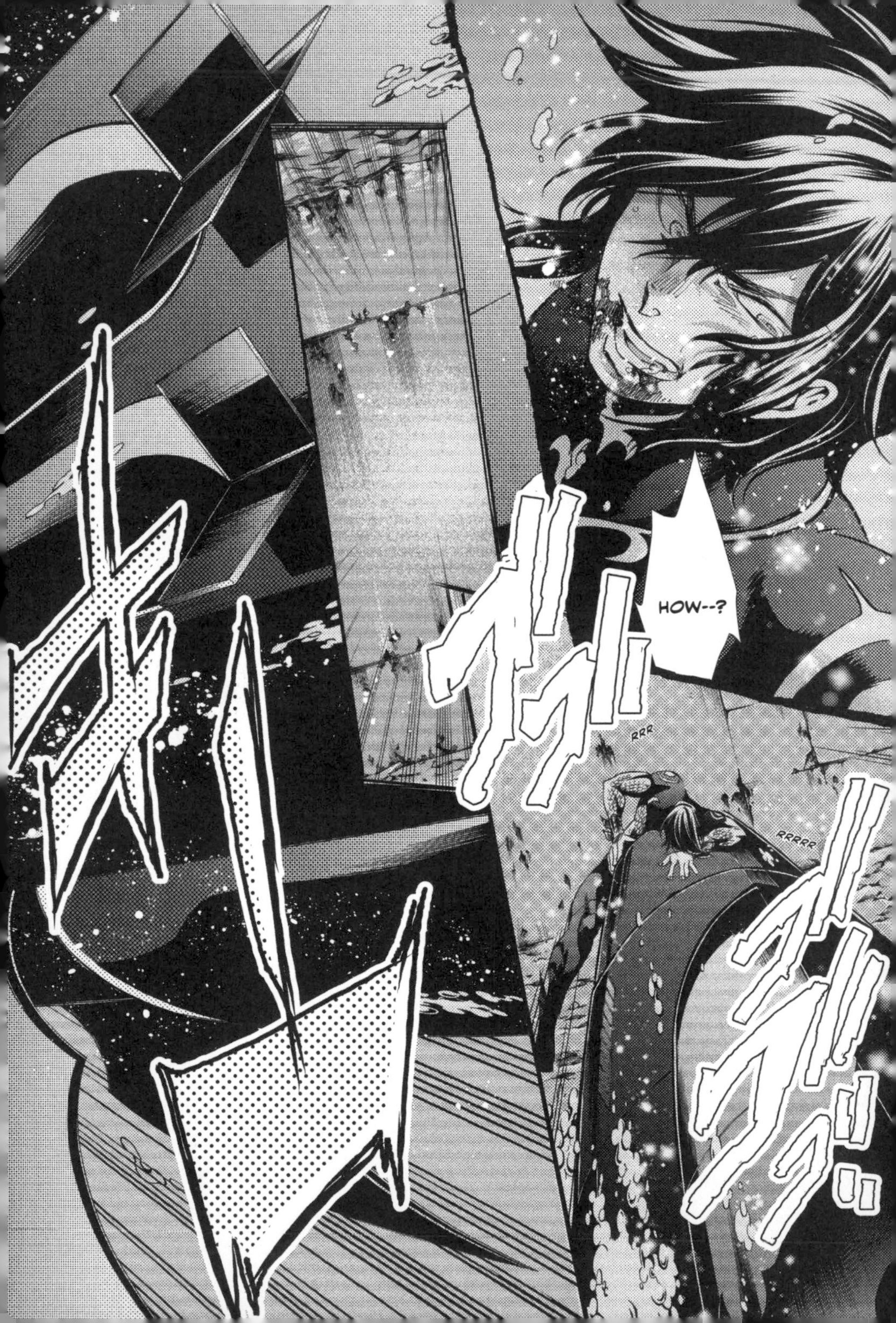
HOW--?
RRR
RRRRR

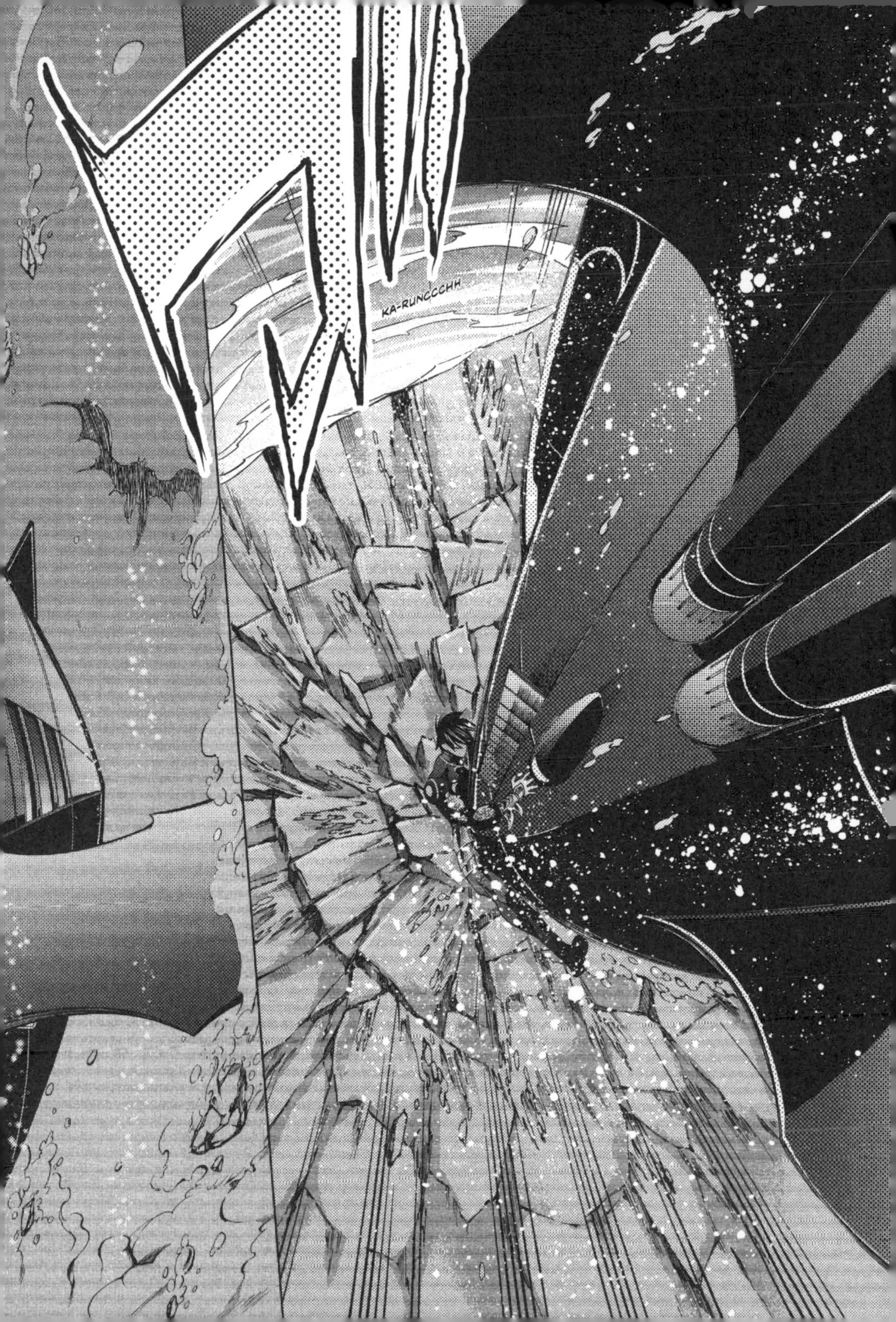
KA-RUNCCCHH

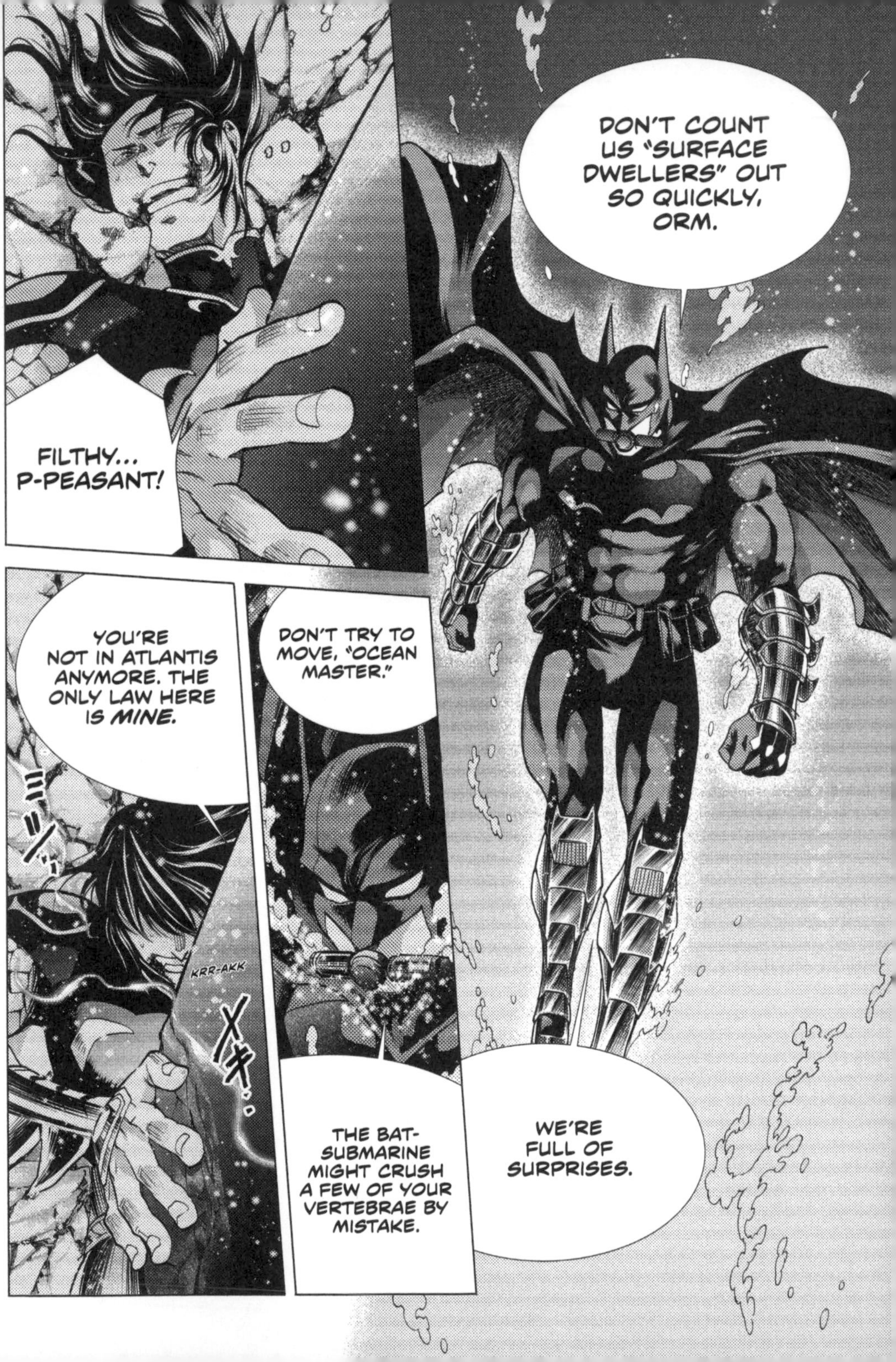
DON'T COUNT US "SURFACE DWELLERS" OUT SO QUICKLY, ORM.
WE'RE FULL OF SURPRISES.
FILTHY... P-PEASANT!
DON'T TRY TO MOVE, "OCEAN MASTER."
THE BAT-SUBMARINE MIGHT CRUSH A FEW OF YOUR VERTEBRAE BY MISTAKE.
YOU'RE NOT IN ATLANTIS ANYMORE. THE ONLY LAW HERE IS *MINE.*
KRR-AKK

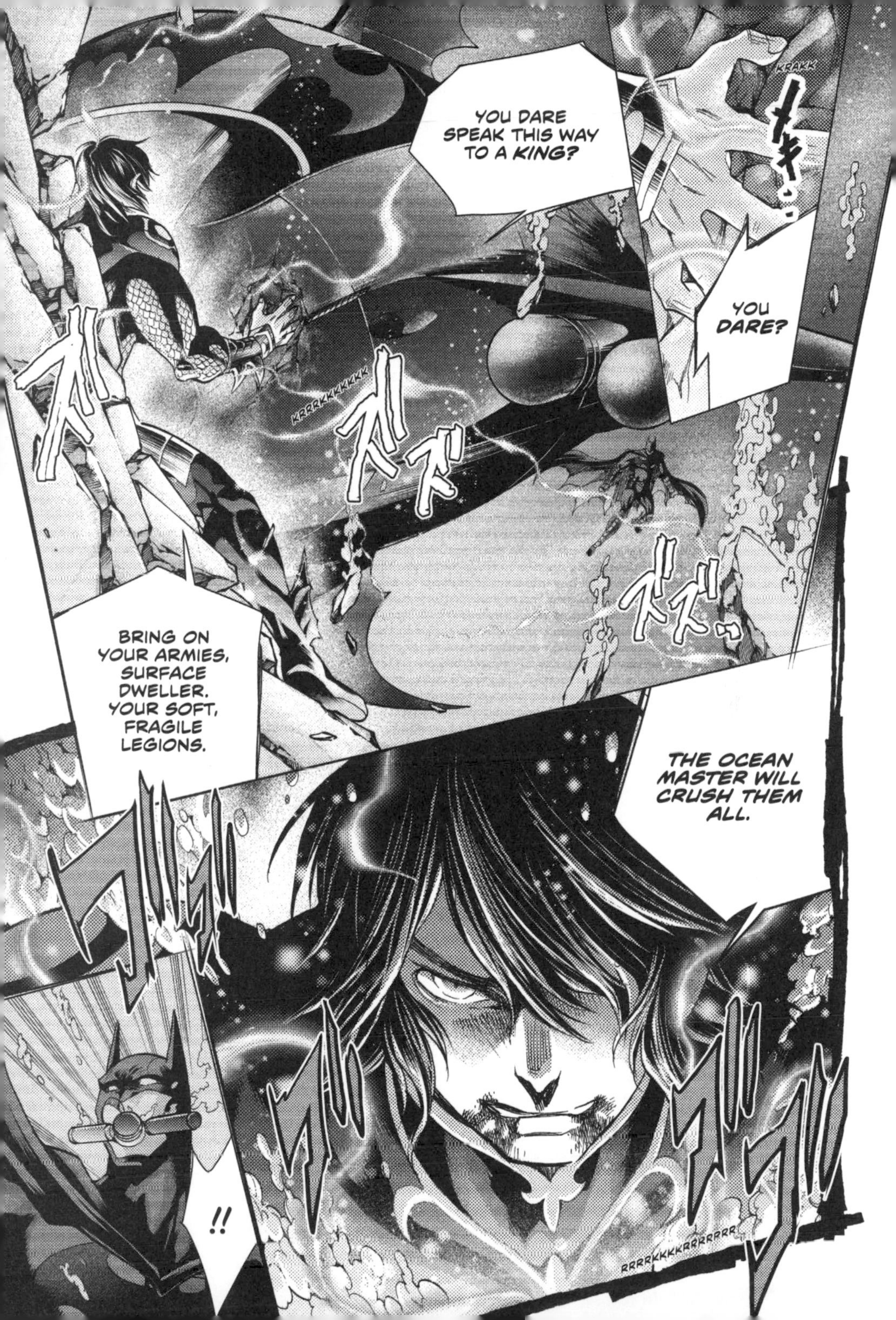
KRAKK
YOU DARE?
YOU DARE SPEAK THIS WAY TO A *KING?*
KRRRKKKKKKK
BRING ON YOUR ARMIES, SURFACE DWELLER. YOUR SOFT, FRAGILE LEGIONS.
THE OCEAN MASTER WILL CRUSH THEM ALL.
RRRRKKKKRRRRRRR
!!

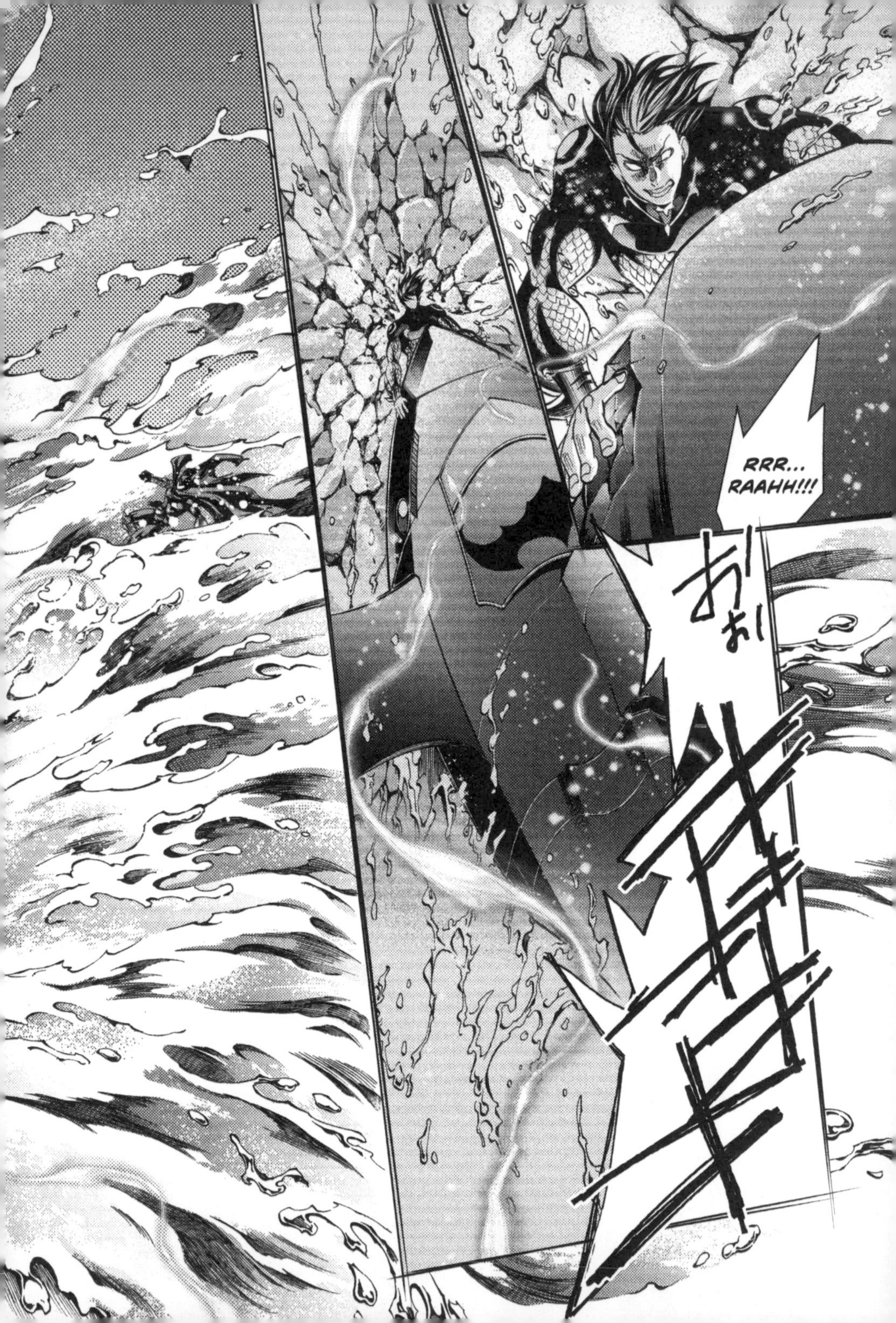
RRR... RAAHH!!!
あぁ

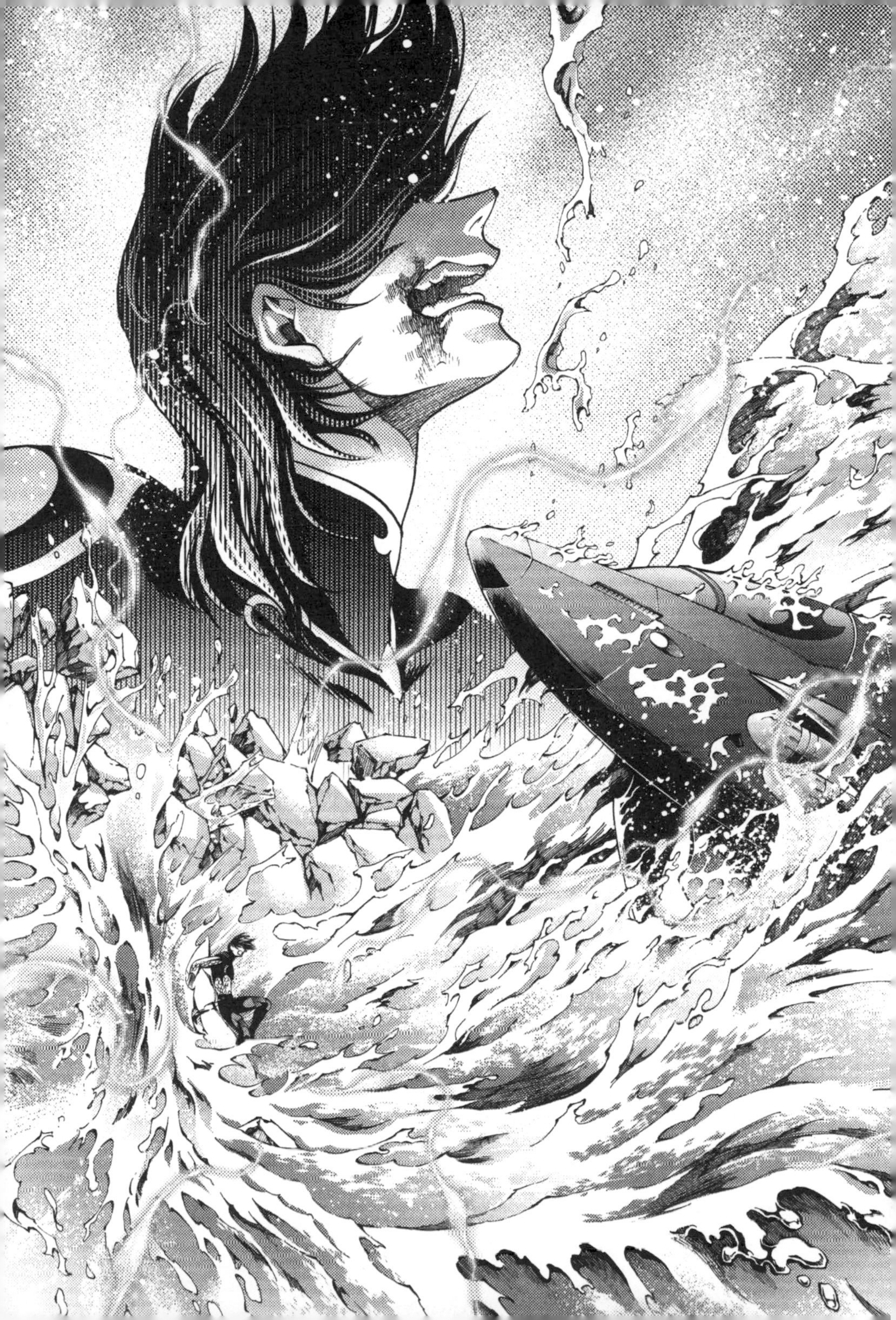

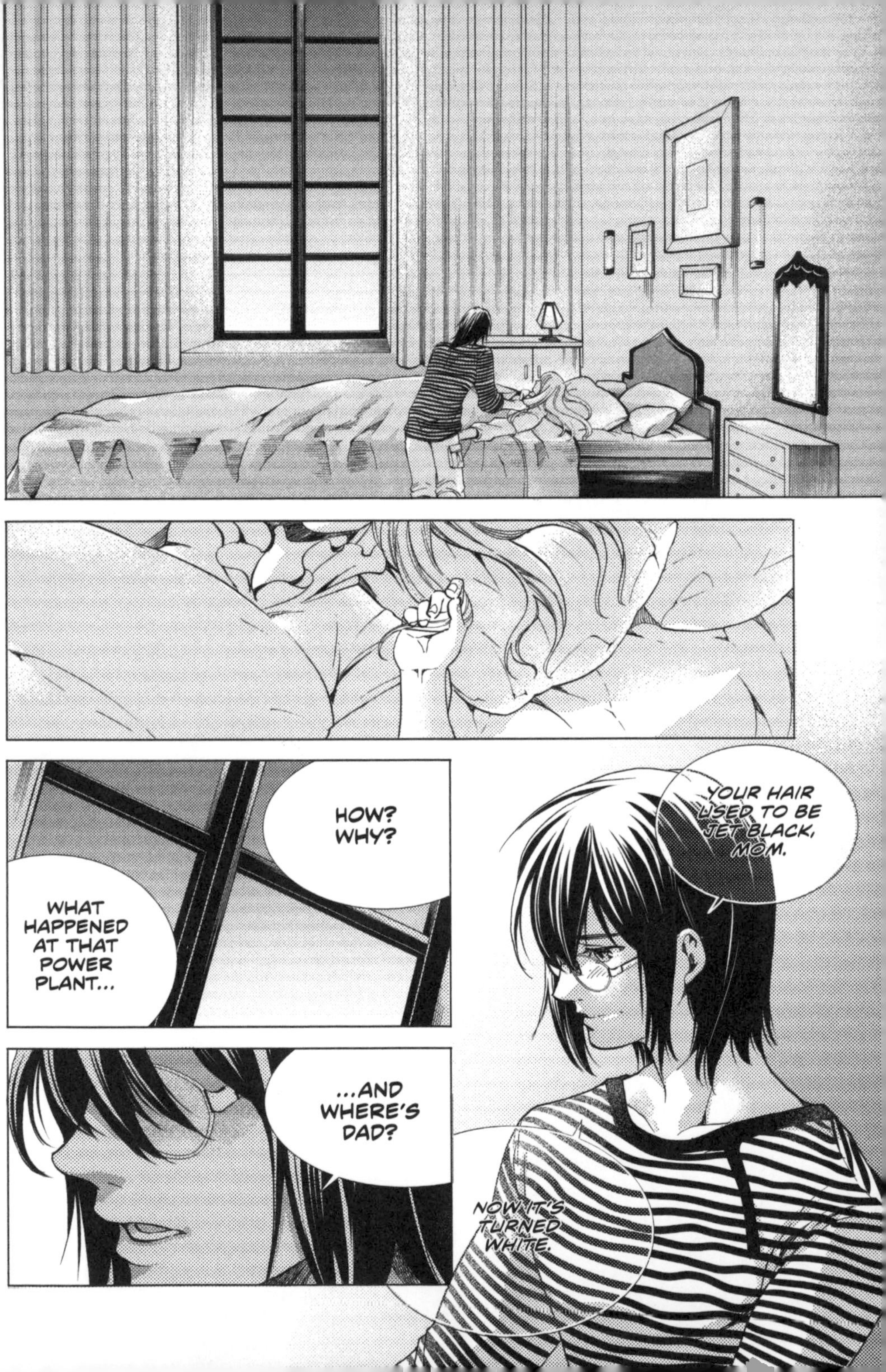
YOUR HAIR USED TO BE JET BLACK, MOM.
NOW IT'S TURNED WHITE.
HOW? WHY?
WHAT HAPPENED AT THAT POWER PLANT...
...AND WHERE'S DAD?

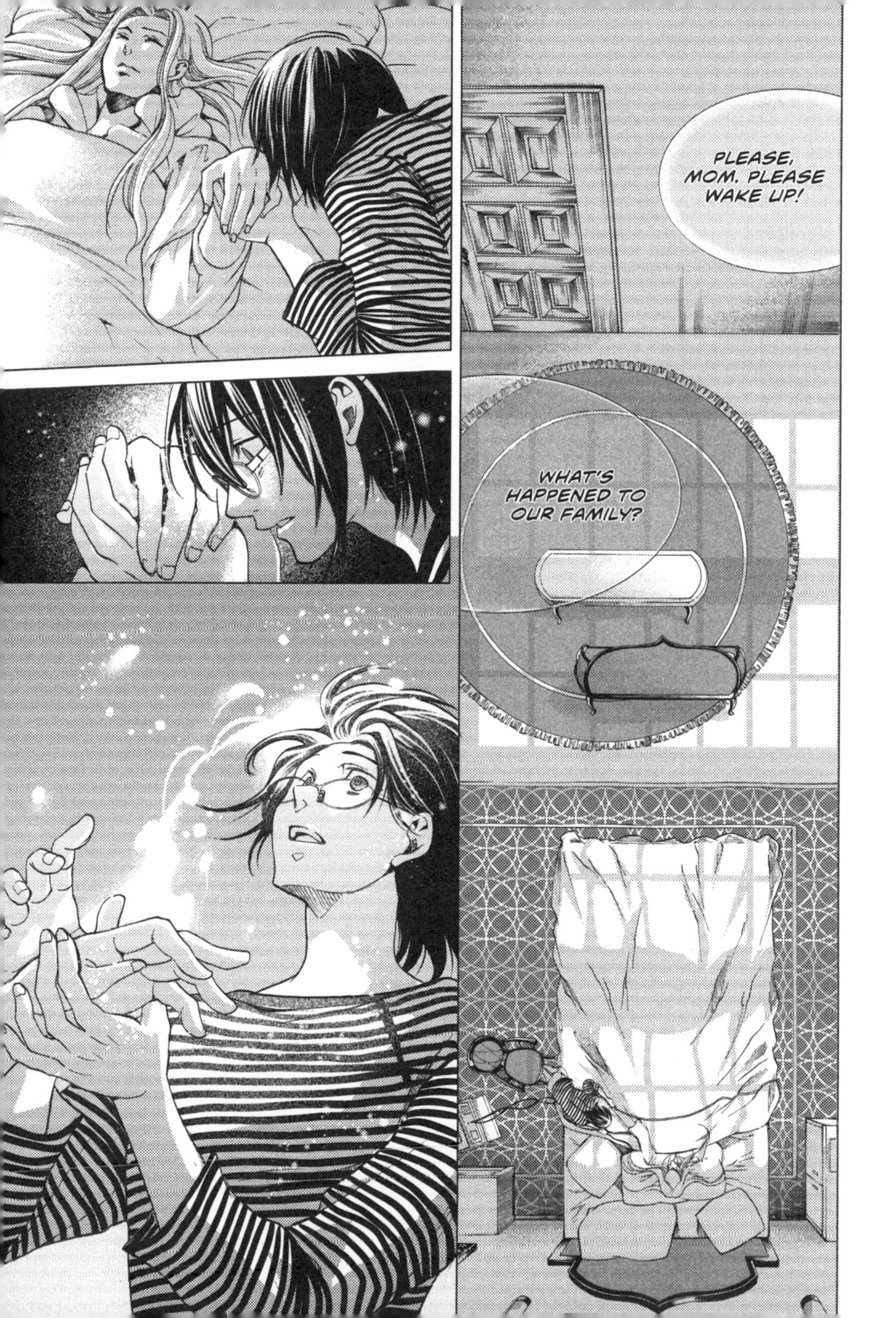
PLEASE, MOM. PLEASE WAKE UP!
WHAT'S HAPPENED TO OUR FAMILY?

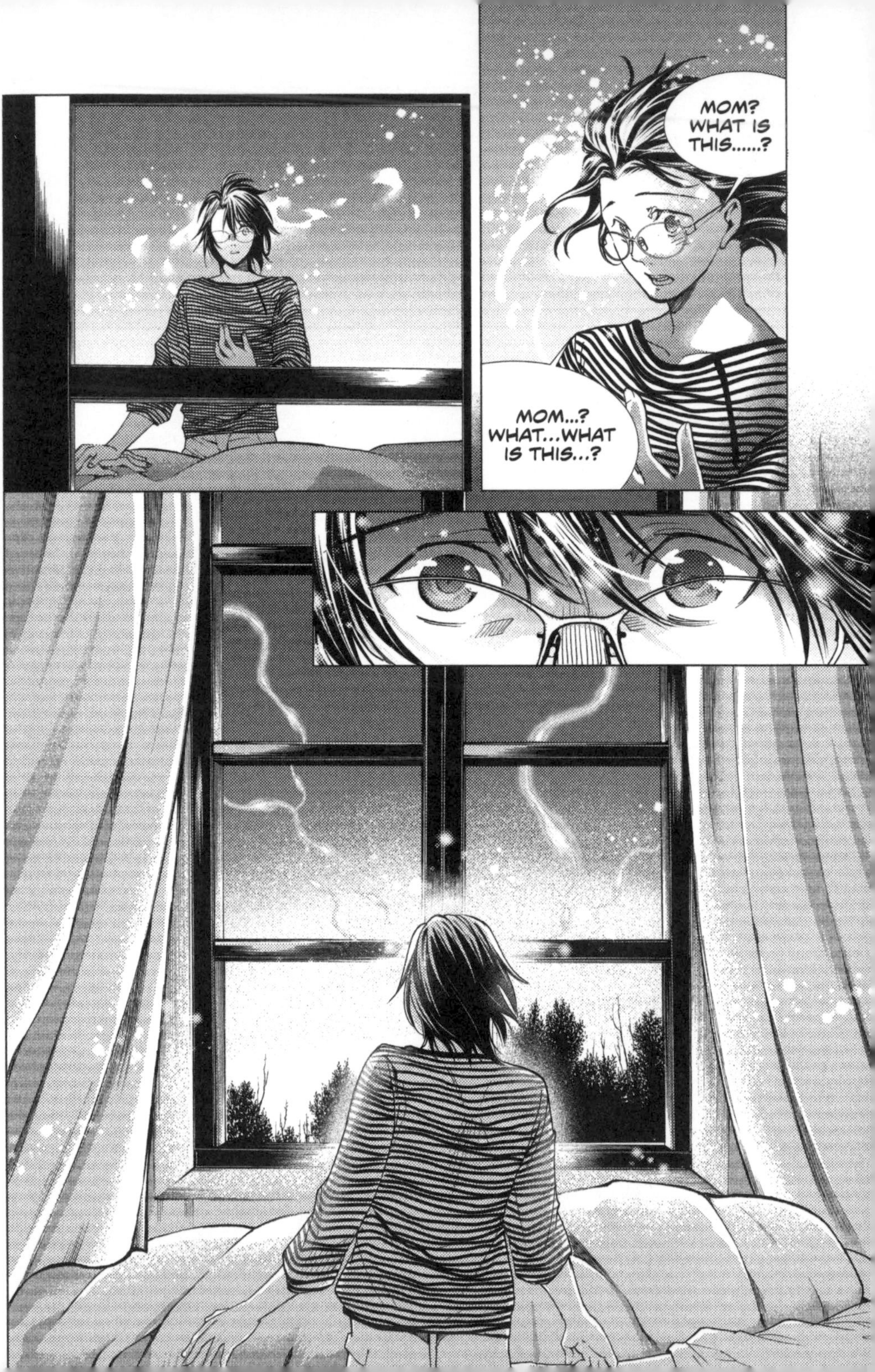
MOM? WHAT IS THIS......?
MOM...? WHAT...WHAT IS THIS...?

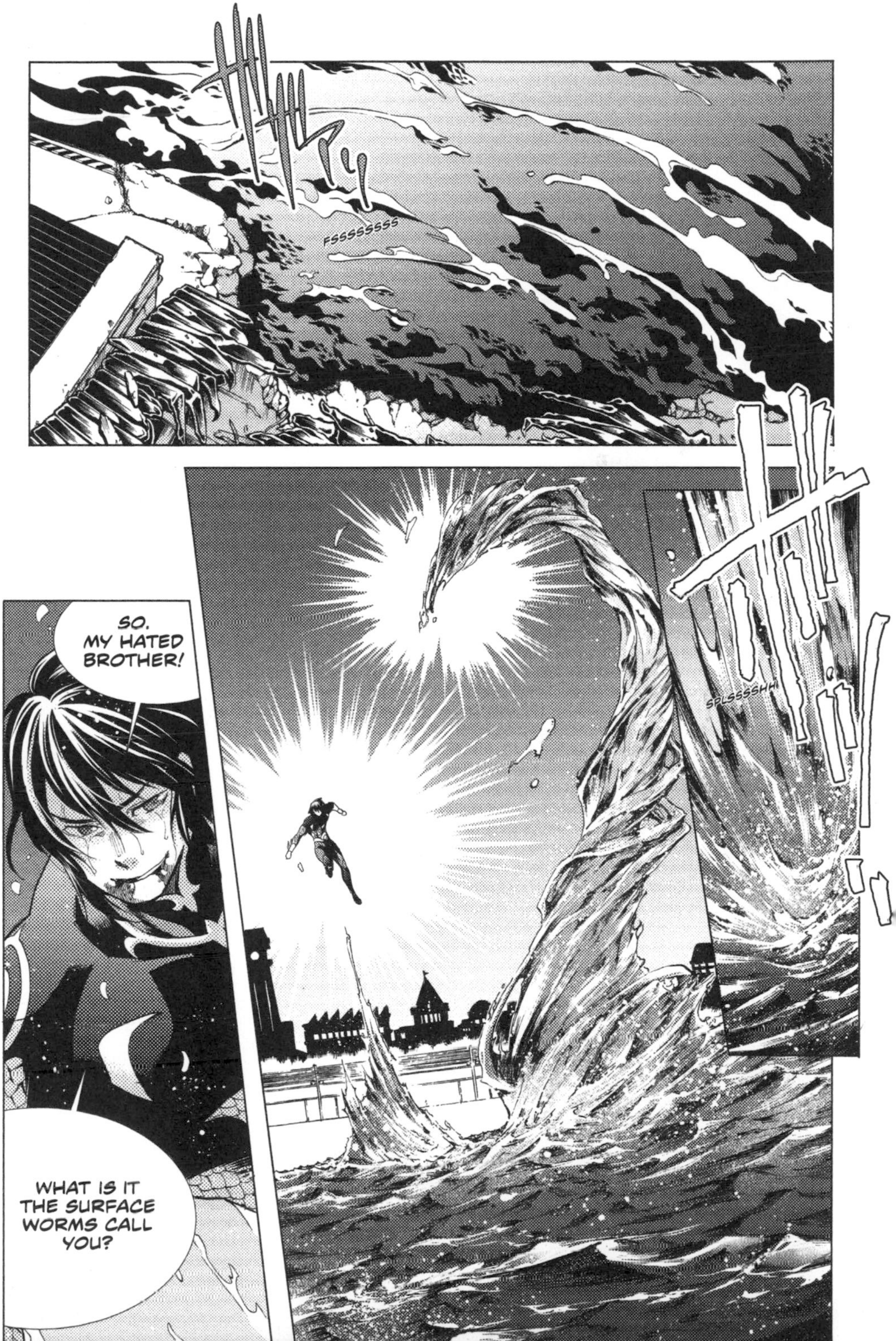
FSSSSSSSS
SPLSSSSSHH
SO. MY HATED BROTHER!
WHAT IS IT THE SURFACE WORMS CALL YOU?

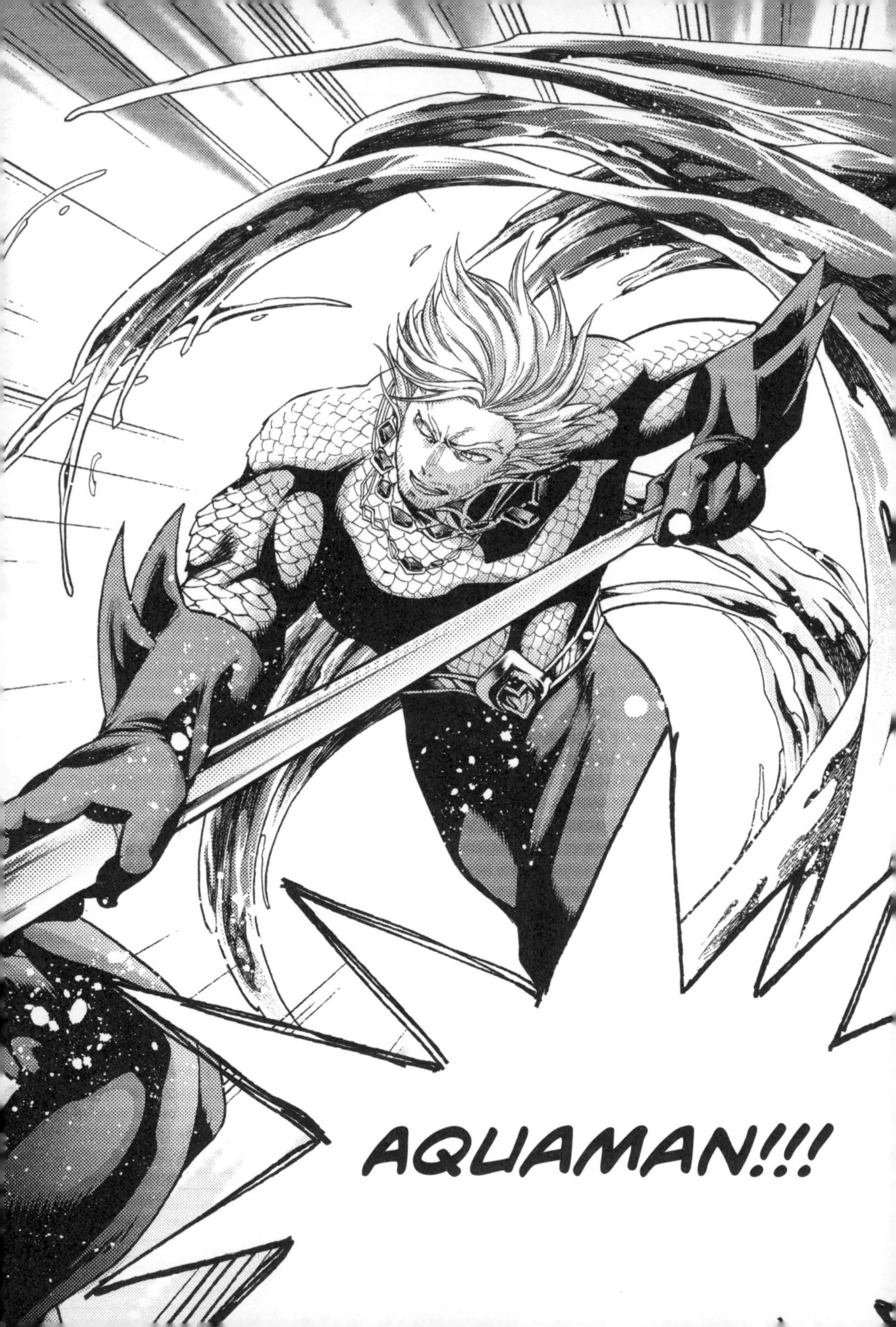
AQUAMAN!!!

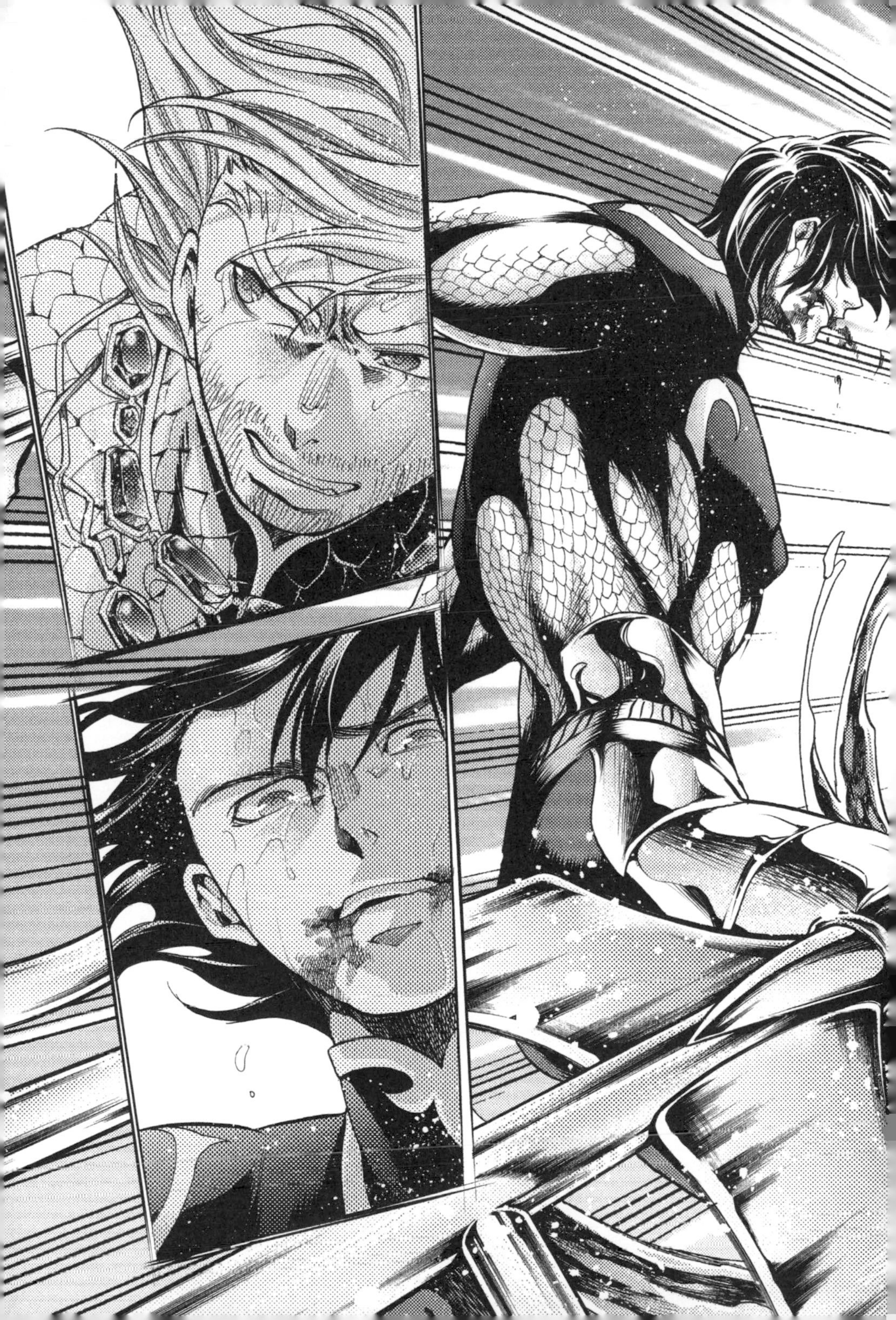

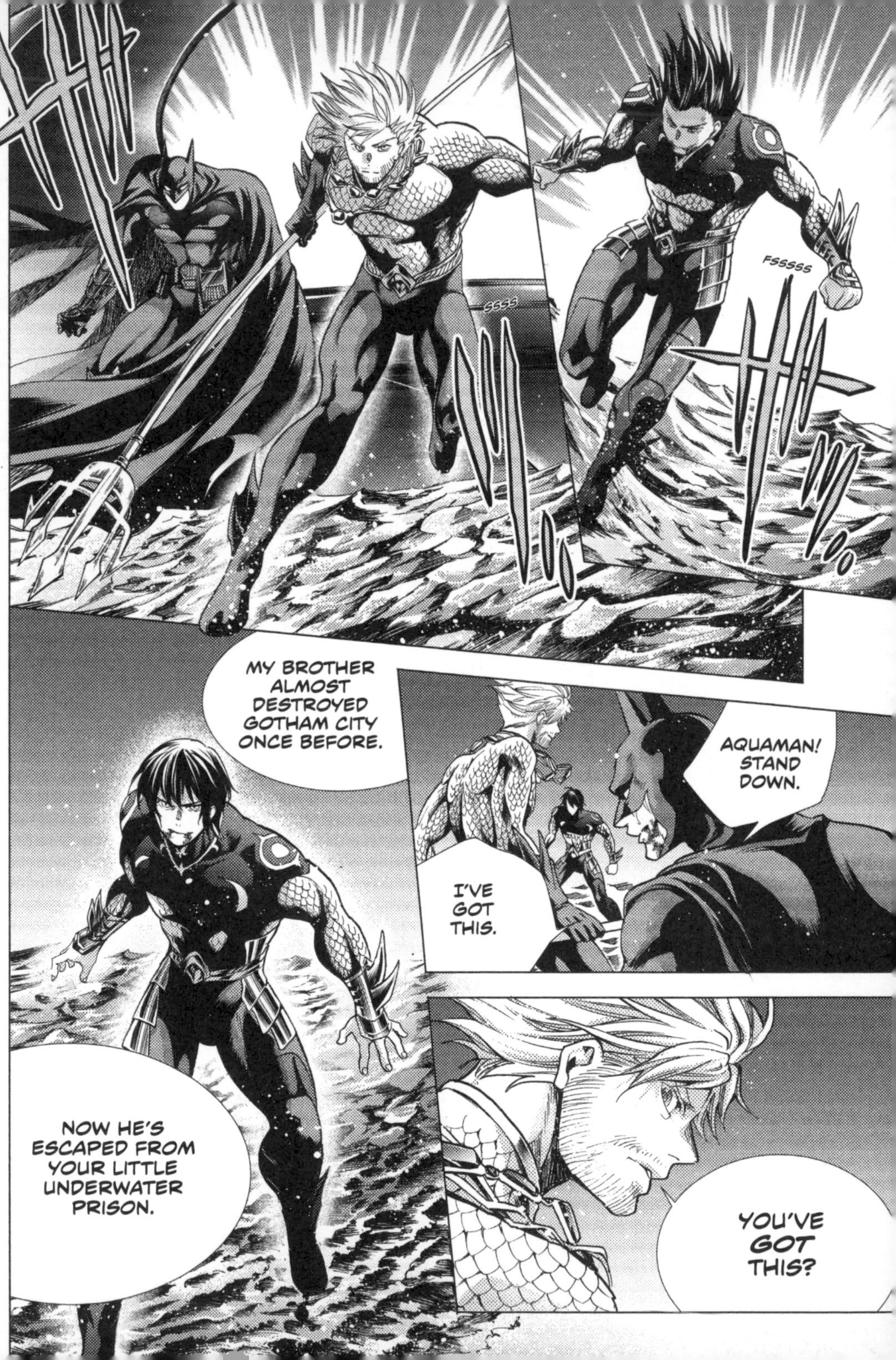
FSSSSS
SSSS
AQUAMAN! STAND DOWN.
I'VE GOT THIS.
YOU'VE GOT THIS?
MY BROTHER ALMOST DESTROYED GOTHAM CITY ONCE BEFORE.
NOW HE'S ESCAPED FROM YOUR LITTLE UNDERWATER PRISON.

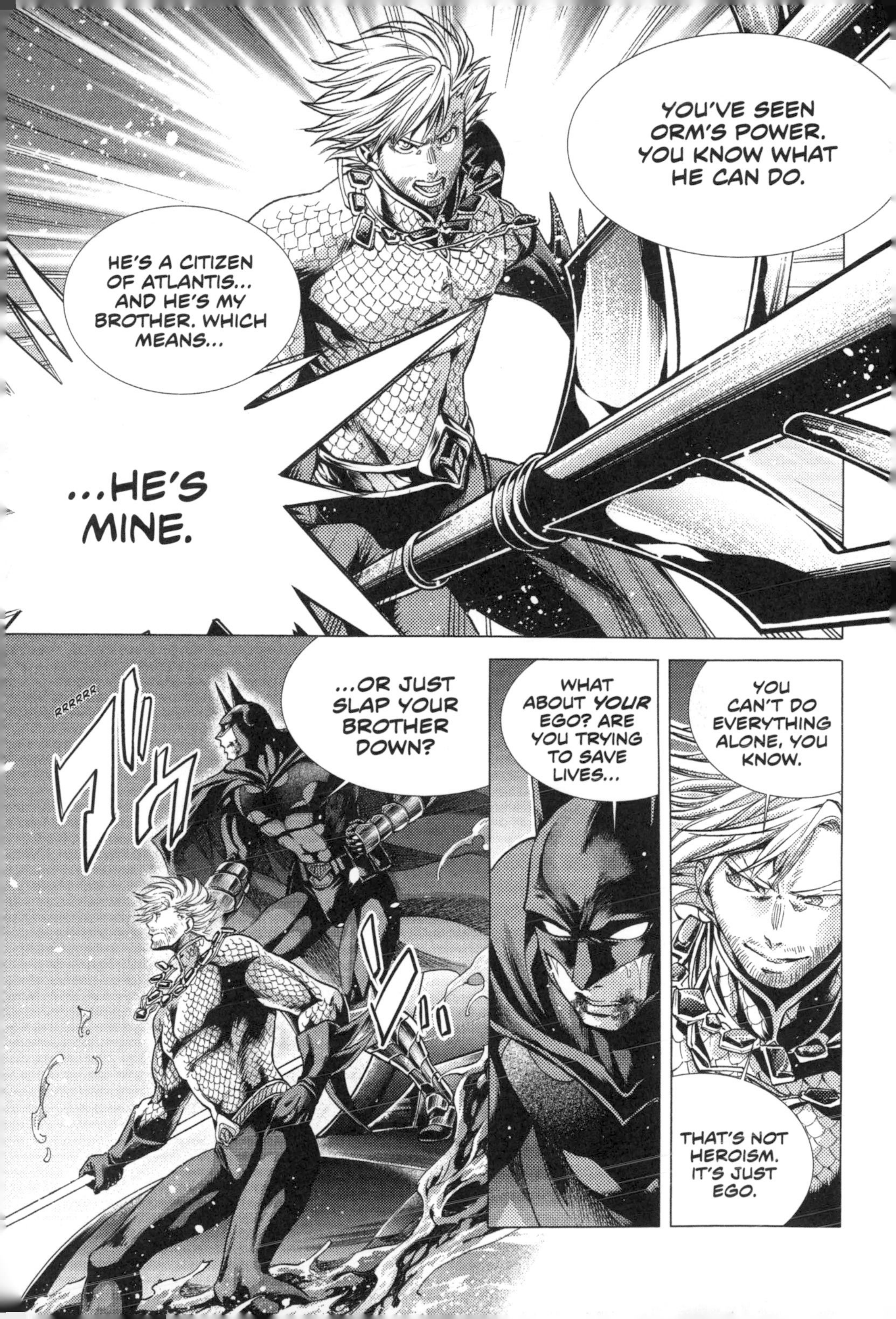
YOU'VE SEEN ORM'S POWER. YOU KNOW WHAT HE CAN DO.
HE'S A CITIZEN OF ATLANTIS... AND HE'S MY BROTHER. WHICH MEANS...
...HE'S MINE.
YOU CAN'T DO EVERYTHING ALONE, YOU KNOW.
THAT'S NOT HEROISM. IT'S JUST EGO.
WHAT ABOUT *YOUR* EGO? ARE YOU TRYING TO SAVE LIVES...
...OR JUST SLAP YOUR BROTHER DOWN?
RRRRRR

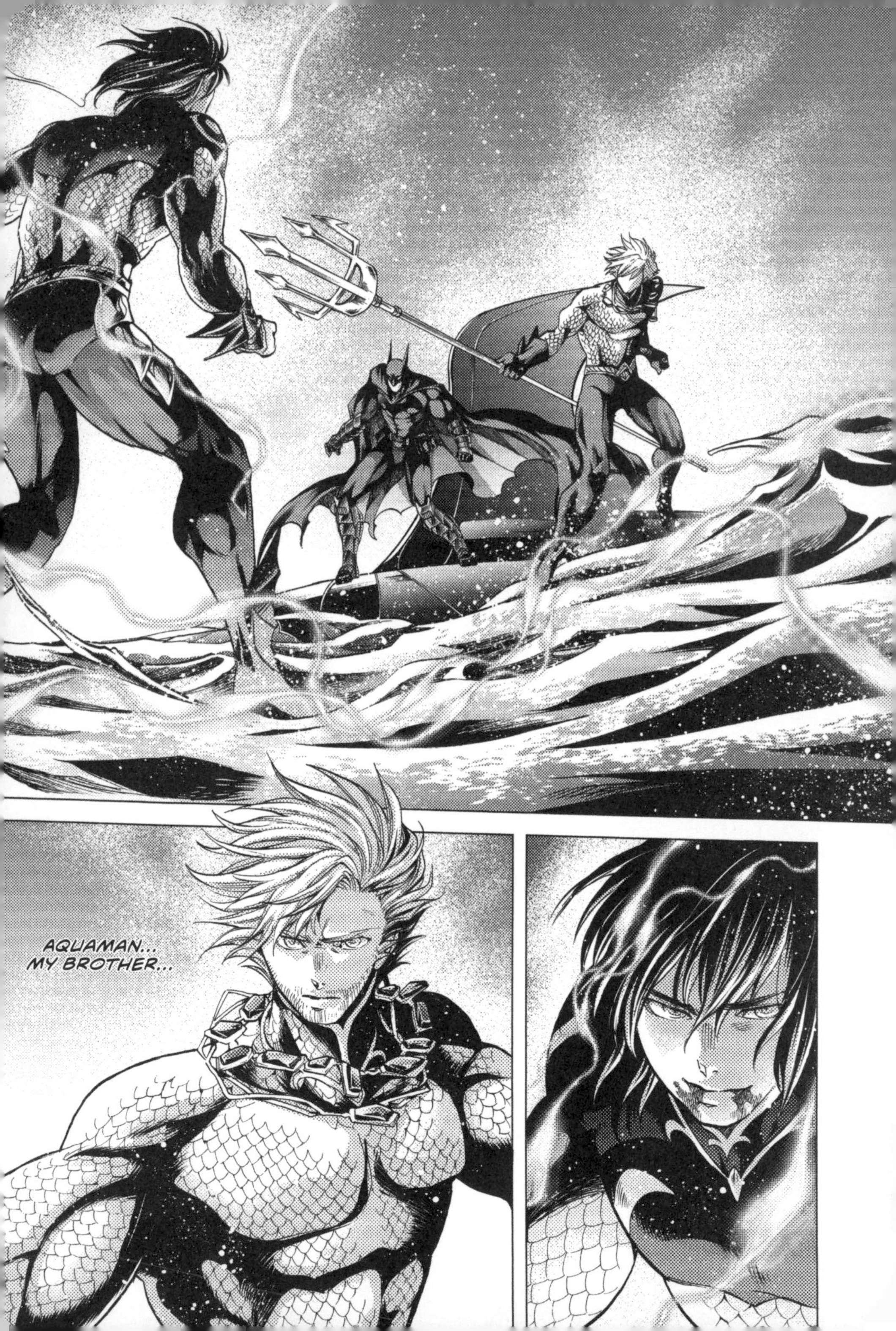
AQUAMAN...
MY BROTHER...

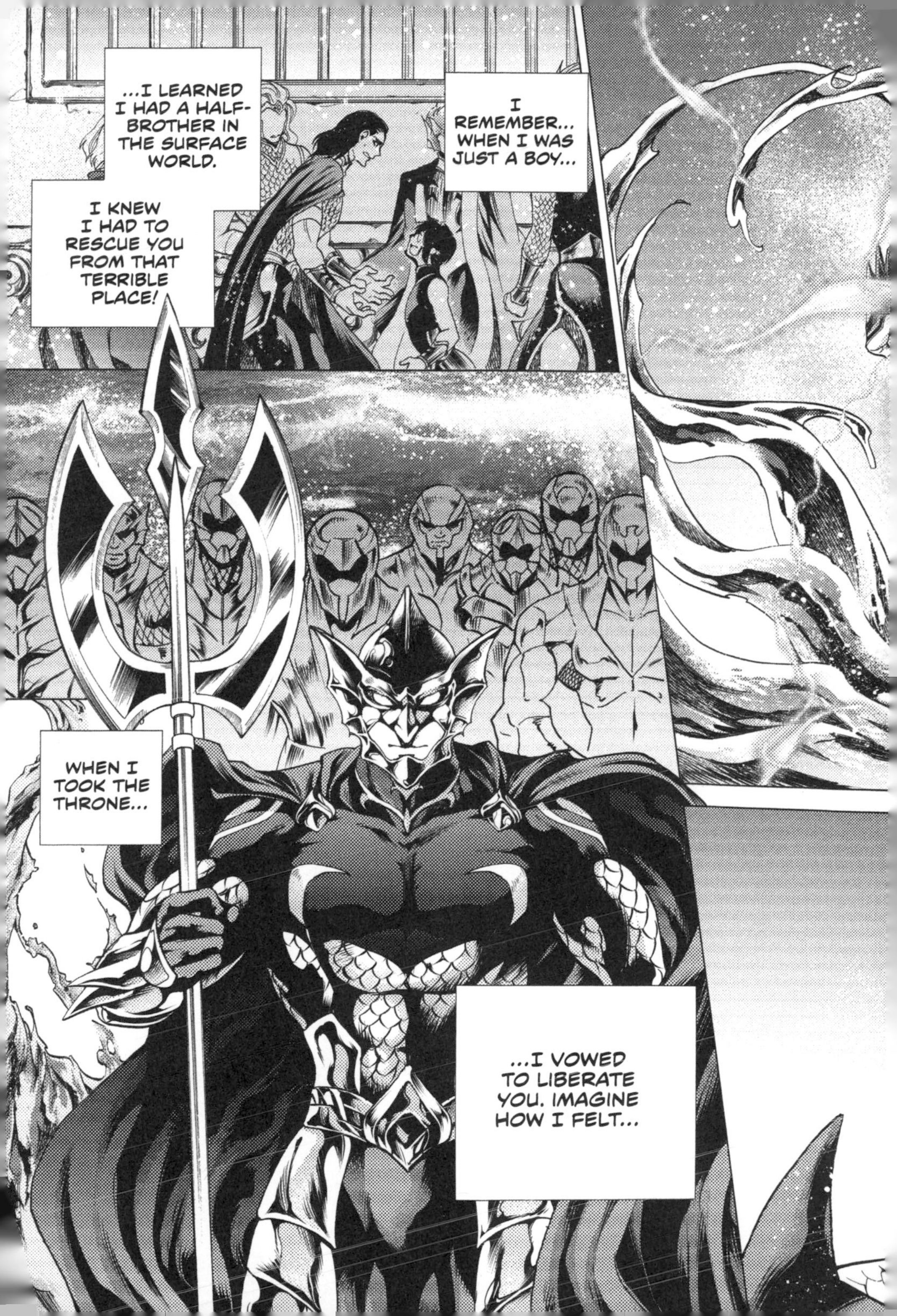
I REMEMBER... WHEN I WAS JUST A BOY...
...I LEARNED I HAD A HALF-BROTHER IN THE SURFACE WORLD.
I KNEW I HAD TO RESCUE YOU FROM THAT TERRIBLE PLACE!
WHEN I TOOK THE THRONE...
...I VOWED TO LIBERATE YOU. IMAGINE HOW I FELT...

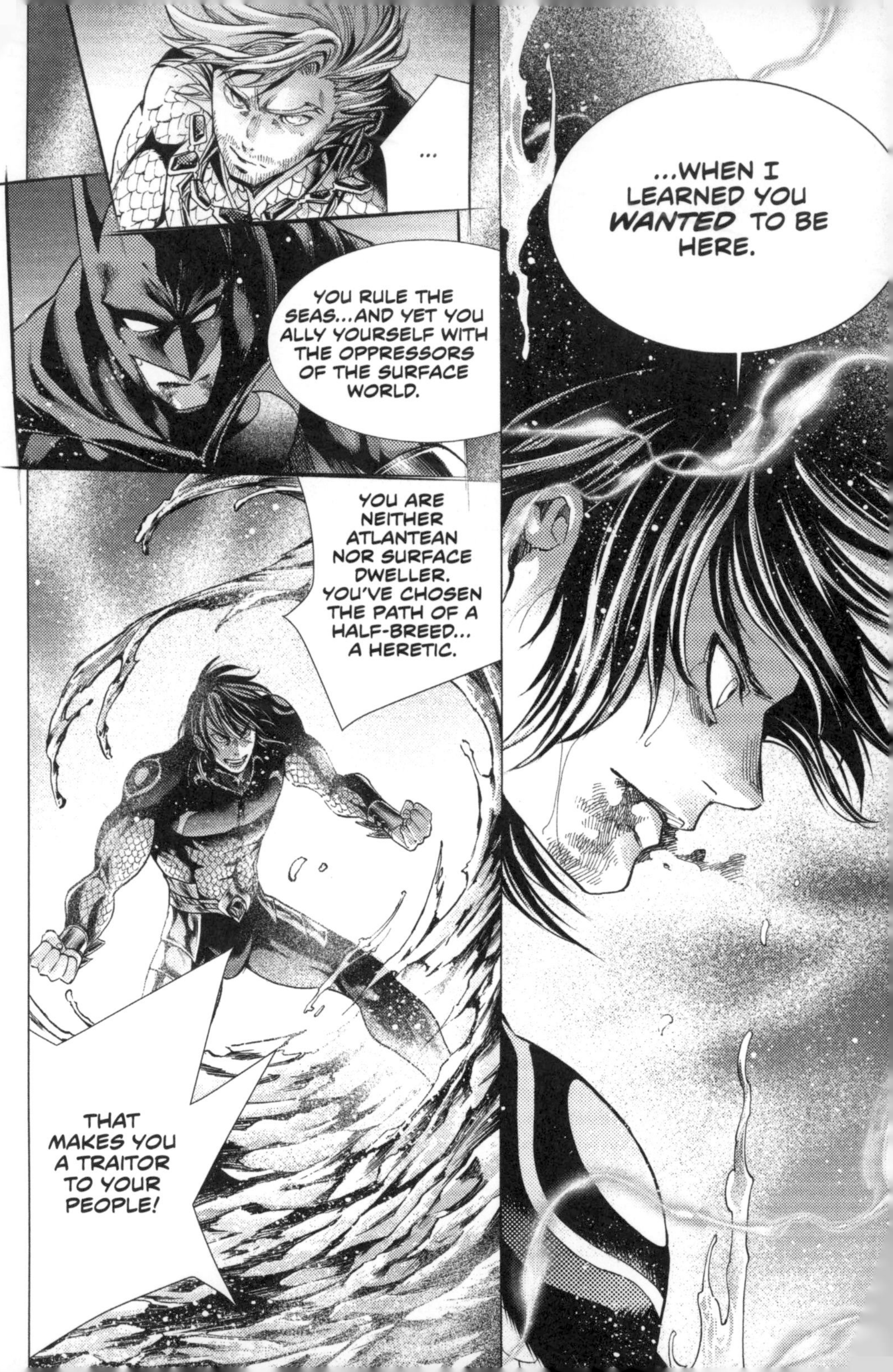
...WHEN I LEARNED YOU *WANTED* TO BE HERE.
...
YOU RULE THE SEAS...AND YET YOU ALLY YOURSELF WITH THE OPPRESSORS OF THE SURFACE WORLD.
YOU ARE NEITHER ATLANTEAN NOR SURFACE DWELLER. YOU'VE CHOSEN THE PATH OF A HALF-BREED... A HERETIC.
THAT MAKES YOU A TRAITOR TO YOUR PEOPLE!

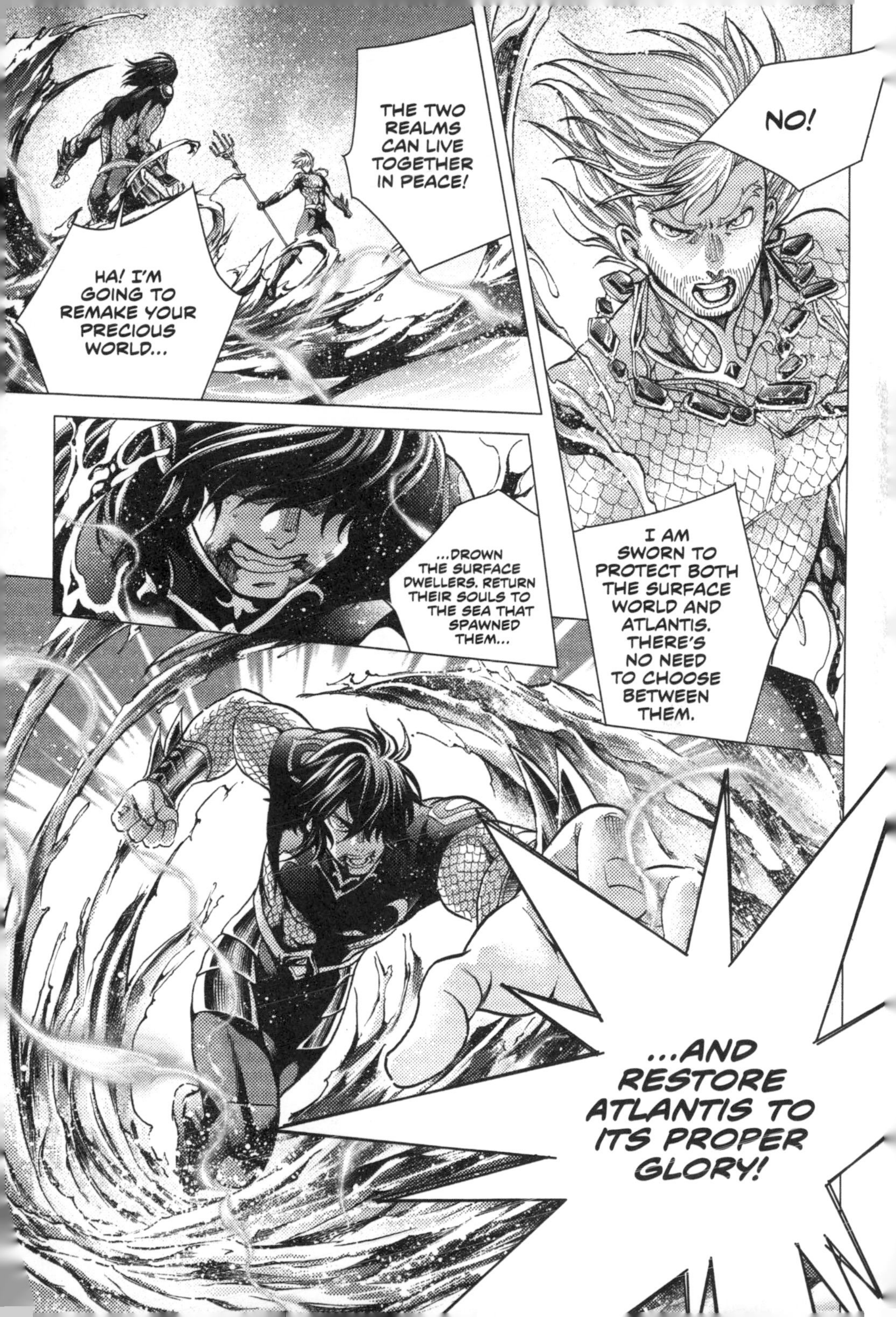
THE TWO REALMS CAN LIVE TOGETHER IN PEACE!
HA! I'M GOING TO REMAKE YOUR PRECIOUS WORLD...
...DROWN THE SURFACE DWELLERS. RETURN THEIR SOULS TO THE SEA THAT SPAWNED THEM...
NO!
I AM SWORN TO PROTECT BOTH THE SURFACE WORLD AND ATLANTIS. THERE'S NO NEED TO CHOOSE BETWEEN THEM.
...AND RESTORE ATLANTIS TO ITS PROPER GLORY!

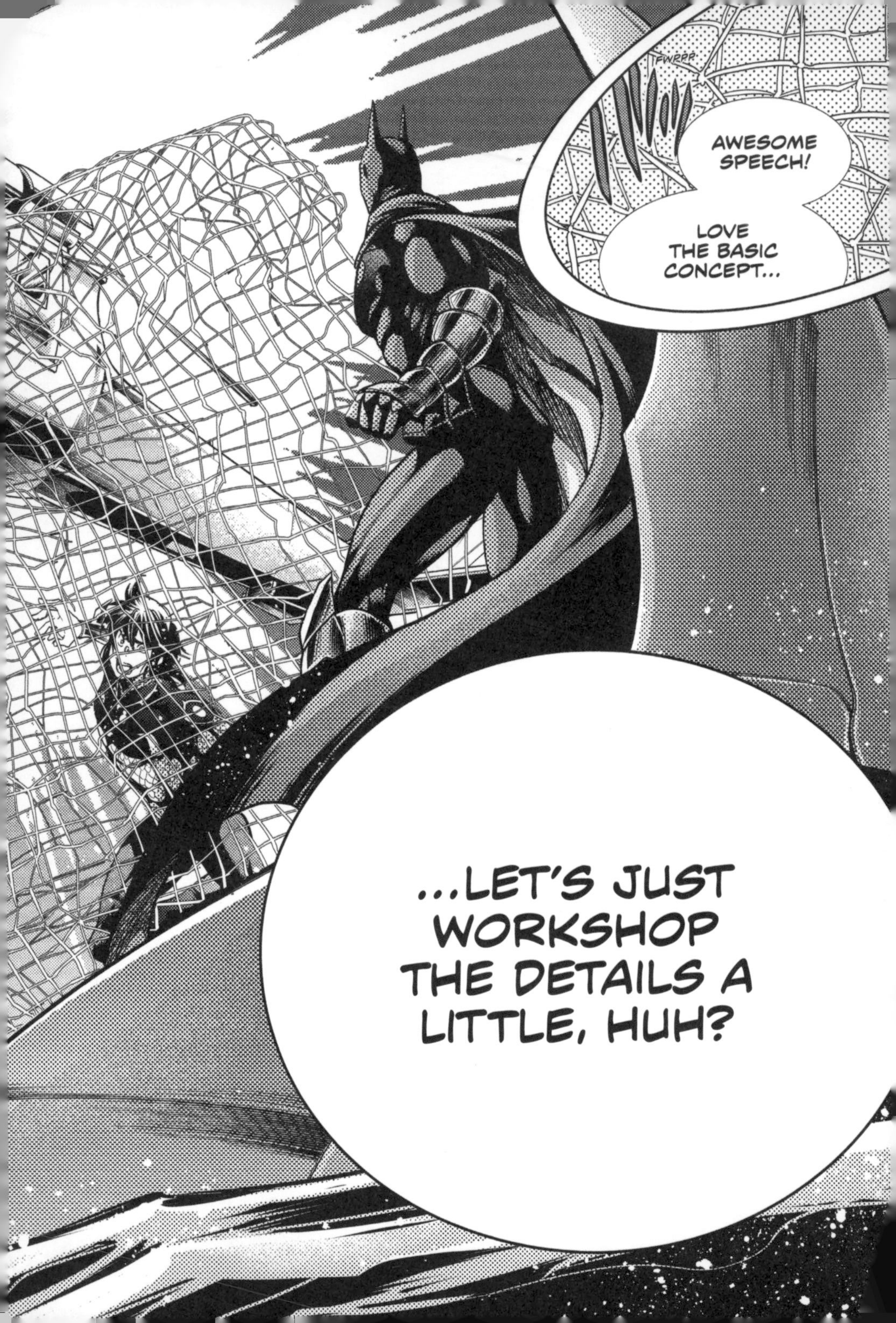
FWRPP
AWESOME SPEECH!
LOVE THE BASIC CONCEPT...
...LET'S JUST WORKSHOP THE DETAILS A LITTLE, HUH?

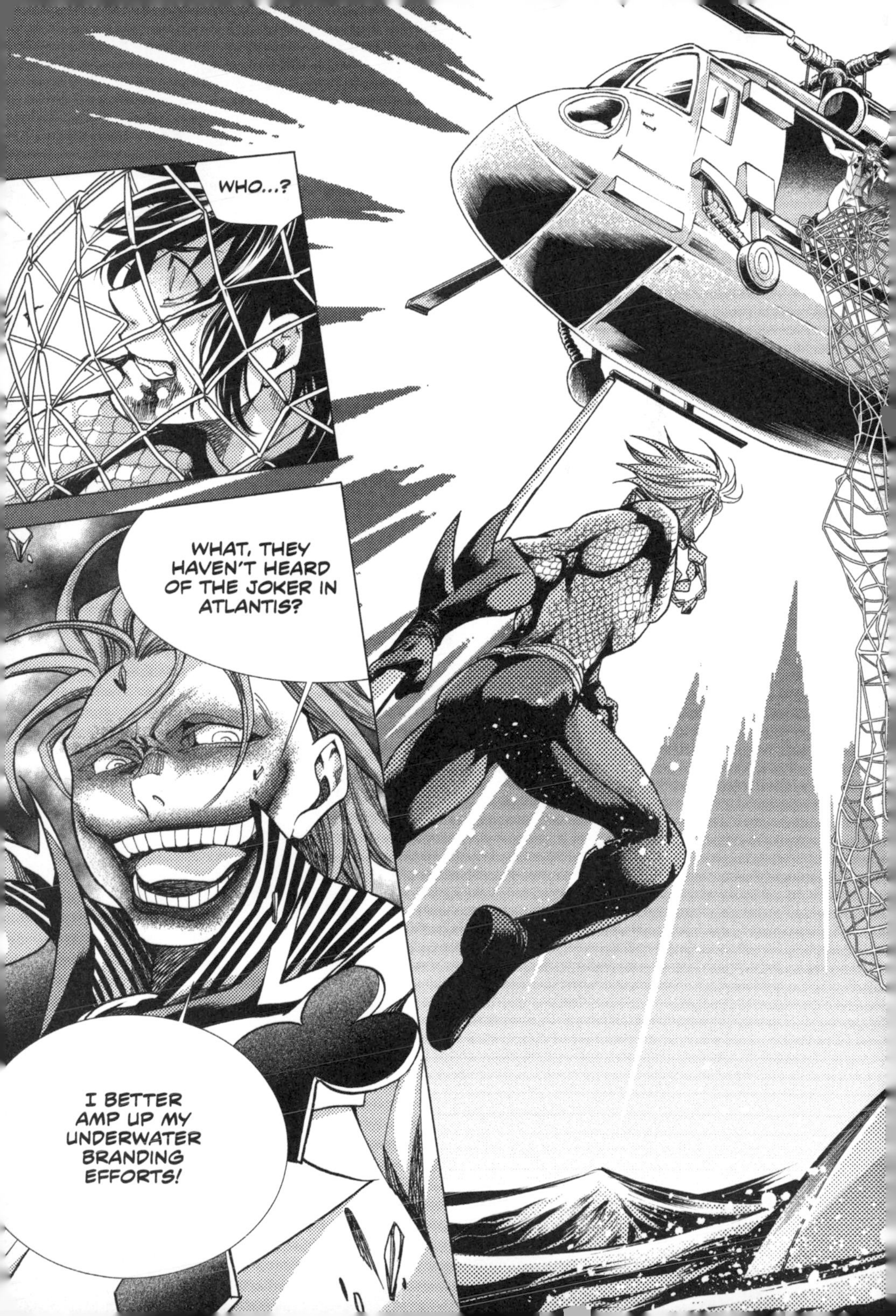
WHO...?
WHAT, THEY HAVEN'T HEARD OF THE JOKER IN ATLANTIS?
I BETTER AMP UP MY UNDERWATER BRANDING EFFORTS!

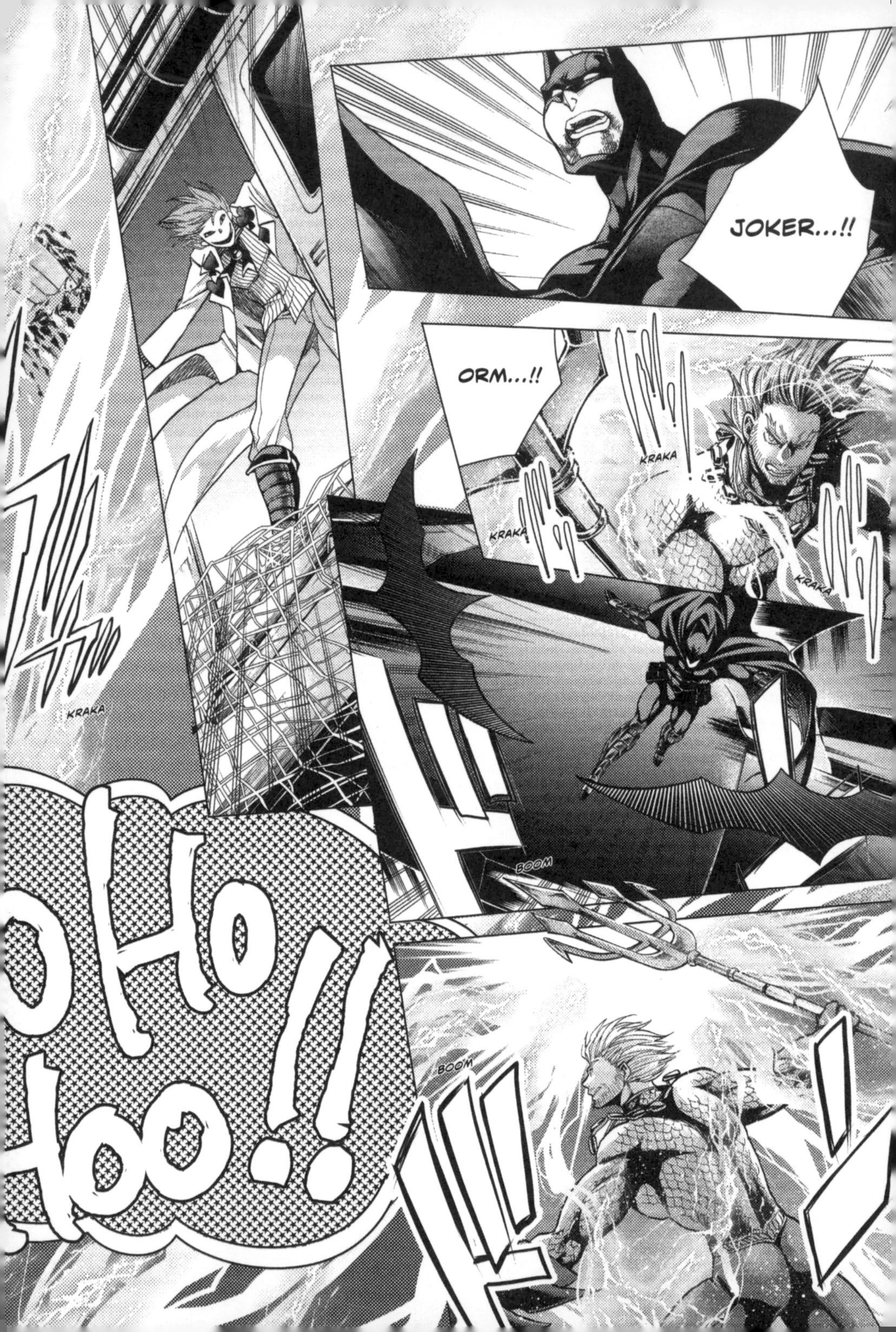
JOKER...!!
ORM...!!
KRAKA
KRAKA
KRAKA
BOOM
BOOM
KRAKA
HO HOO!!

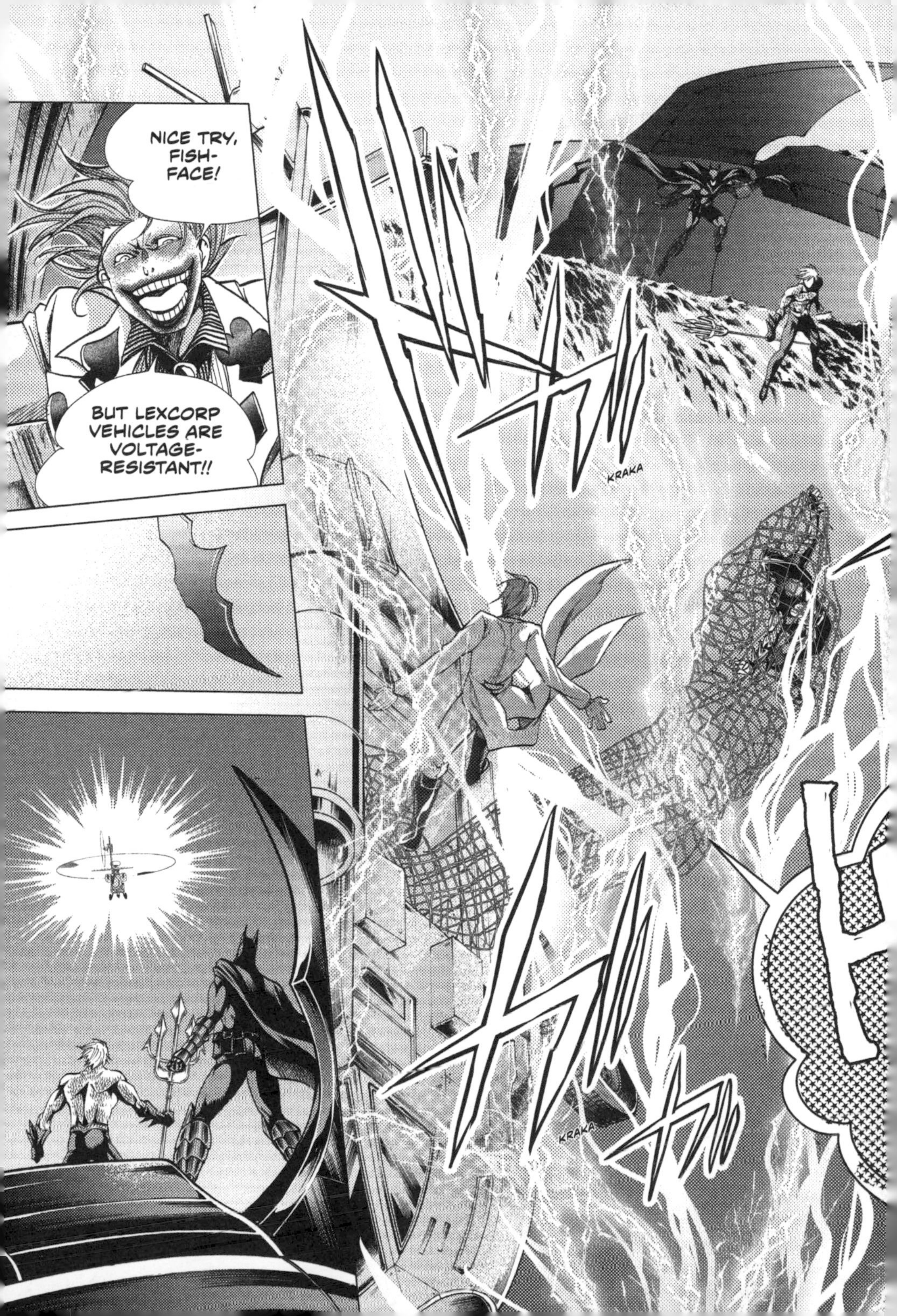
KRAKA
KRAKA
NICE TRY, FISH-FACE!
BUT LEXCORP VEHICLES ARE VOLTAGE-RESISTANT!!

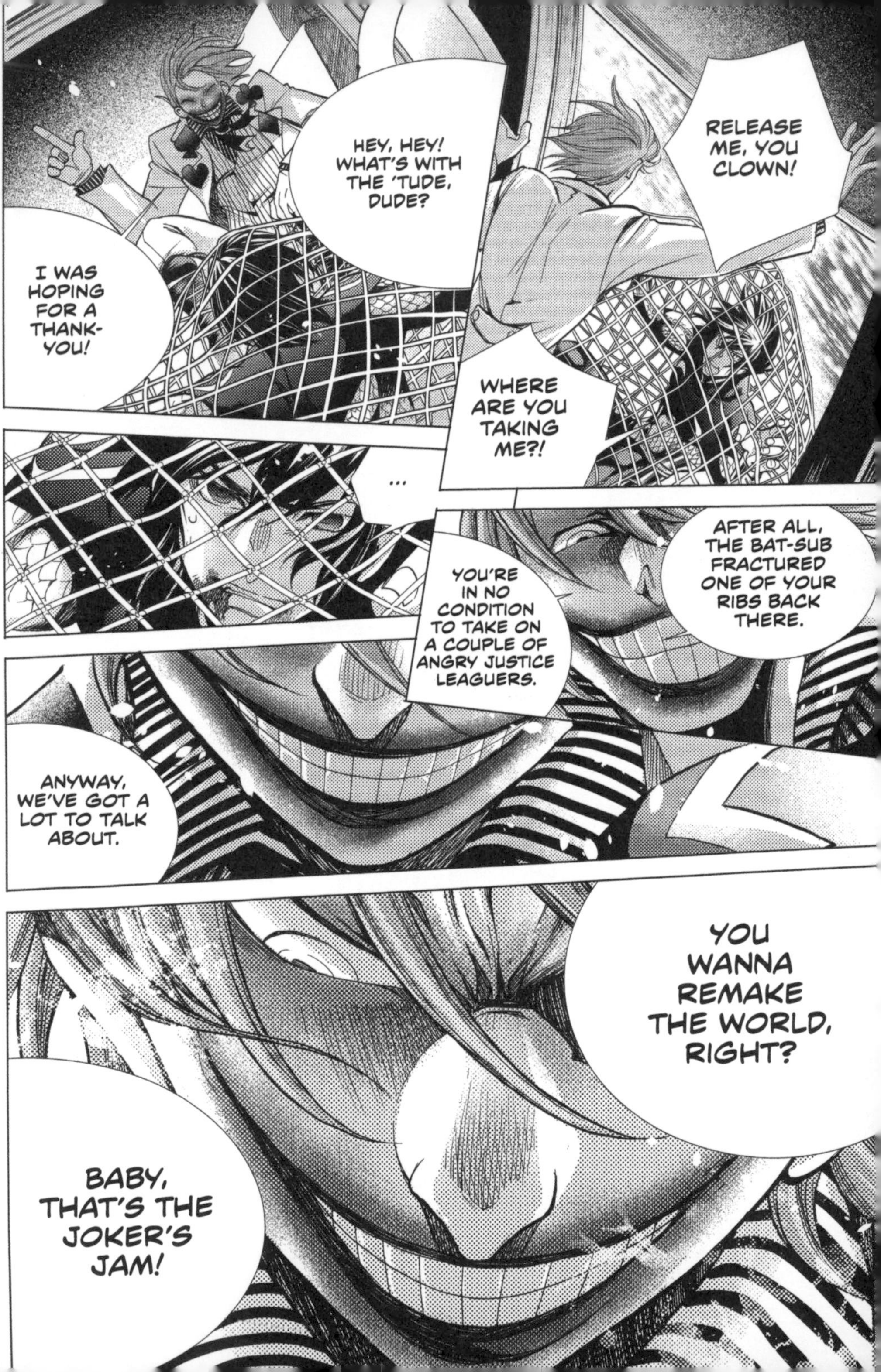
RELEASE ME, YOU CLOWN!
WHERE ARE YOU TAKING ME?!
HEY, HEY! WHAT'S WITH THE 'TUDE, DUDE?
I WAS HOPING FOR A THANK-YOU!
AFTER ALL, THE BAT-SUB FRACTURED ONE OF YOUR RIBS BACK THERE.
YOU'RE IN NO CONDITION TO TAKE ON A COUPLE OF ANGRY JUSTICE LEAGUERS.
...
ANYWAY, WE'VE GOT A LOT TO TALK ABOUT.
YOU WANNA REMAKE THE WORLD, RIGHT?
BABY, THAT'S THE JOKER'S JAM!

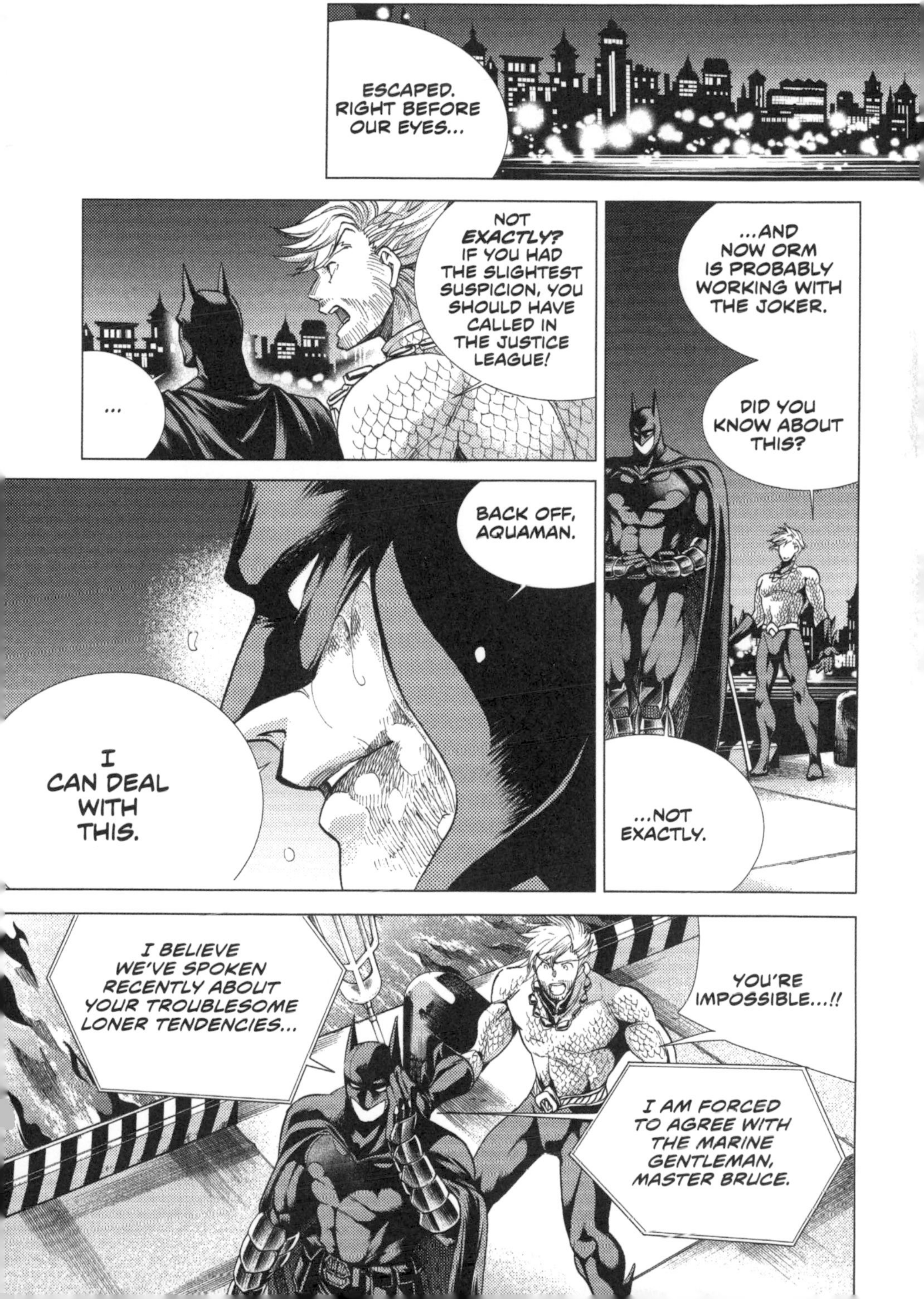
ESCAPED. RIGHT BEFORE OUR EYES...
...AND NOW ORM IS PROBABLY WORKING WITH THE JOKER.
DID YOU KNOW ABOUT THIS?
...NOT EXACTLY.
NOT *EXACTLY?* IF YOU HAD THE SLIGHTEST SUSPICION, YOU SHOULD HAVE CALLED IN THE JUSTICE LEAGUE!
...
BACK OFF, AQUAMAN.
I CAN DEAL WITH THIS.
YOU'RE IMPOSSIBLE...!!
I BELIEVE WE'VE SPOKEN RECENTLY ABOUT YOUR TROUBLESOME LONER TENDENCIES...
I AM FORCED TO AGREE WITH THE MARINE GENTLEMAN, MASTER BRUCE.

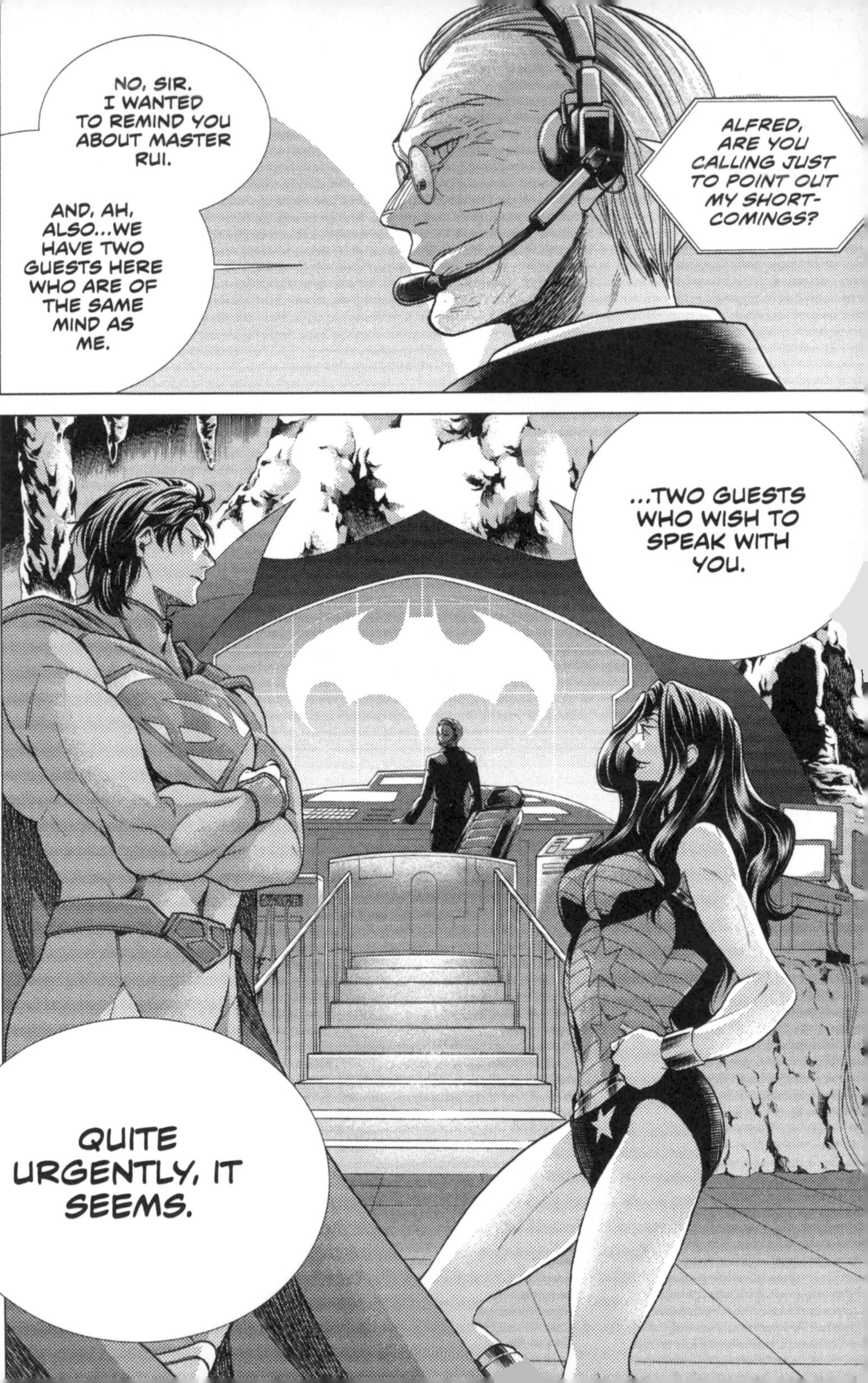
ALFRED, ARE YOU CALLING JUST TO POINT OUT MY SHORT-COMINGS?
NO, SIR. I WANTED TO REMIND YOU ABOUT MASTER RUI.
AND, AH, ALSO...WE HAVE TWO GUESTS HERE WHO ARE OF THE SAME MIND AS ME.
...TWO GUESTS WHO WISH TO SPEAK WITH YOU.
QUITE URGENTLY, IT SEEMS.

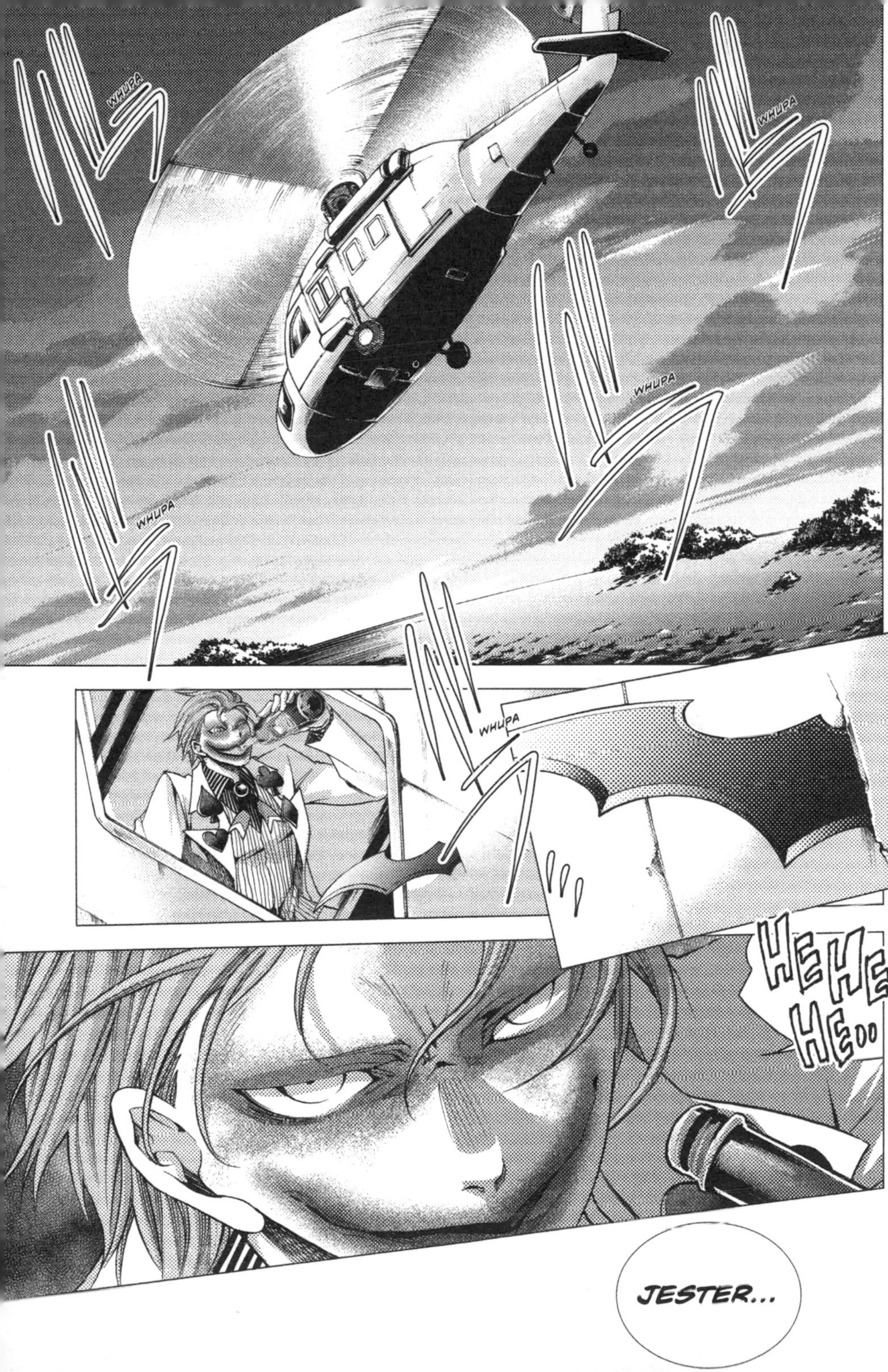
WHUPA
WHUPA
WHUPA
WHUPA
WHUPA
HEHEHE...
JESTER...

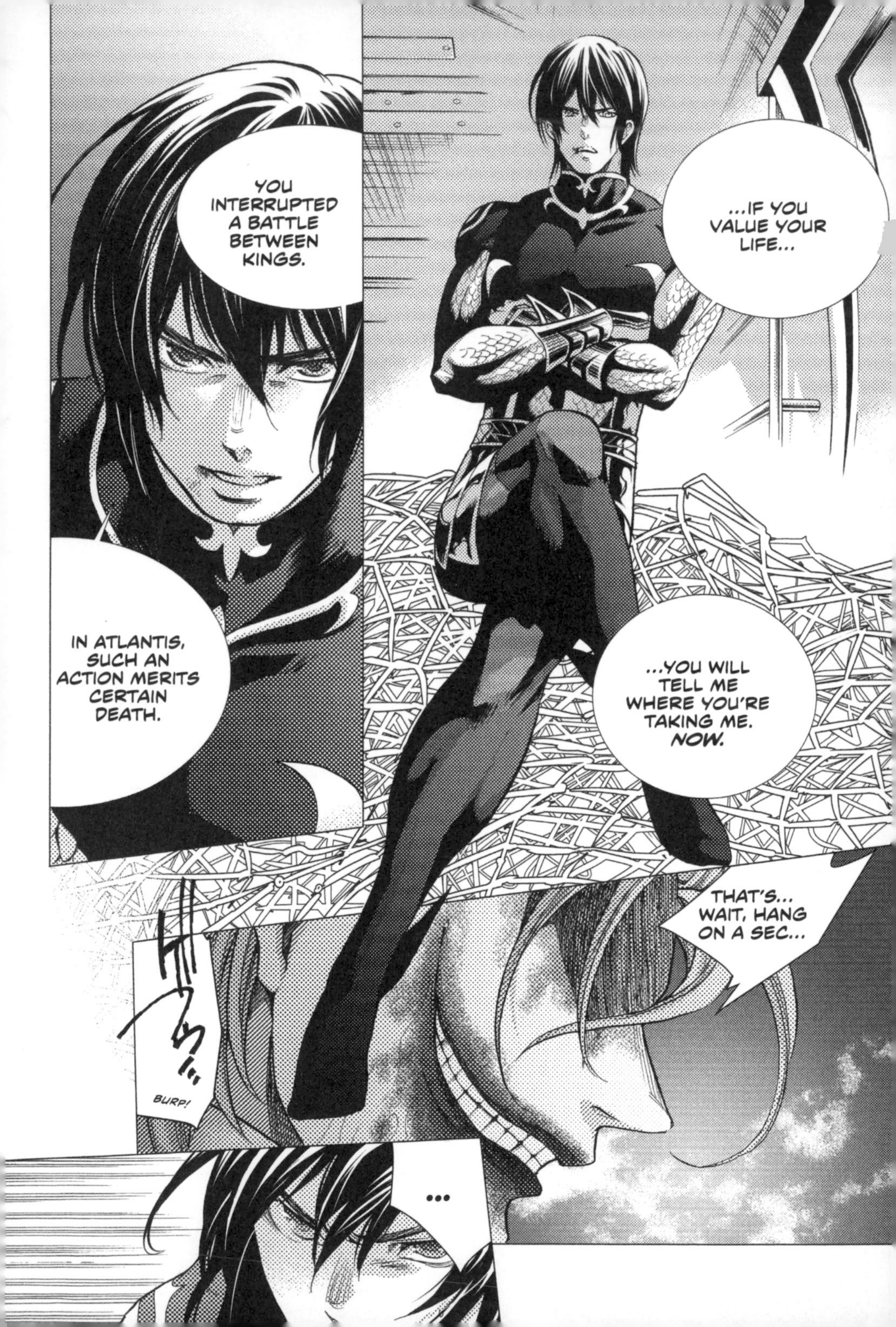
...IF YOU VALUE YOUR LIFE...
...YOU WILL TELL ME WHERE YOU'RE TAKING ME. NOW.
YOU INTERRUPTED A BATTLE BETWEEN KINGS.
IN ATLANTIS, SUCH AN ACTION MERITS CERTAIN DEATH.
THAT'S... WAIT, HANG ON A SEC...
BURP!
...

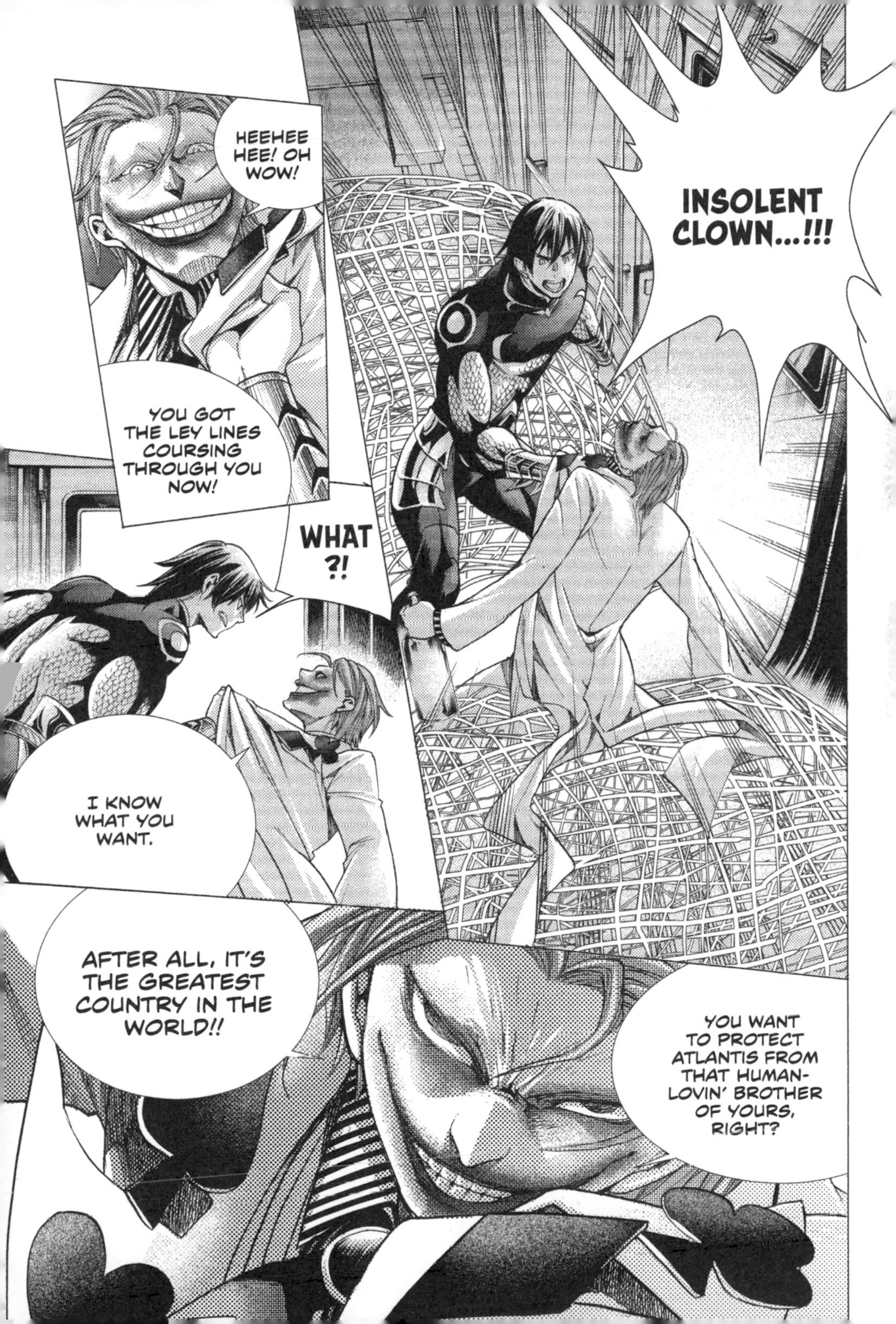
INSOLENT CLOWN...!!!
HEEHEE HEE! OH WOW!
YOU GOT THE LEY LINES COURSING THROUGH YOU NOW!
WHAT ?!
I KNOW WHAT YOU WANT.
YOU WANT TO PROTECT ATLANTIS FROM THAT HUMAN-LOVIN' BROTHER OF YOURS, RIGHT?
AFTER ALL, IT'S THE GREATEST COUNTRY IN THE WORLD!!

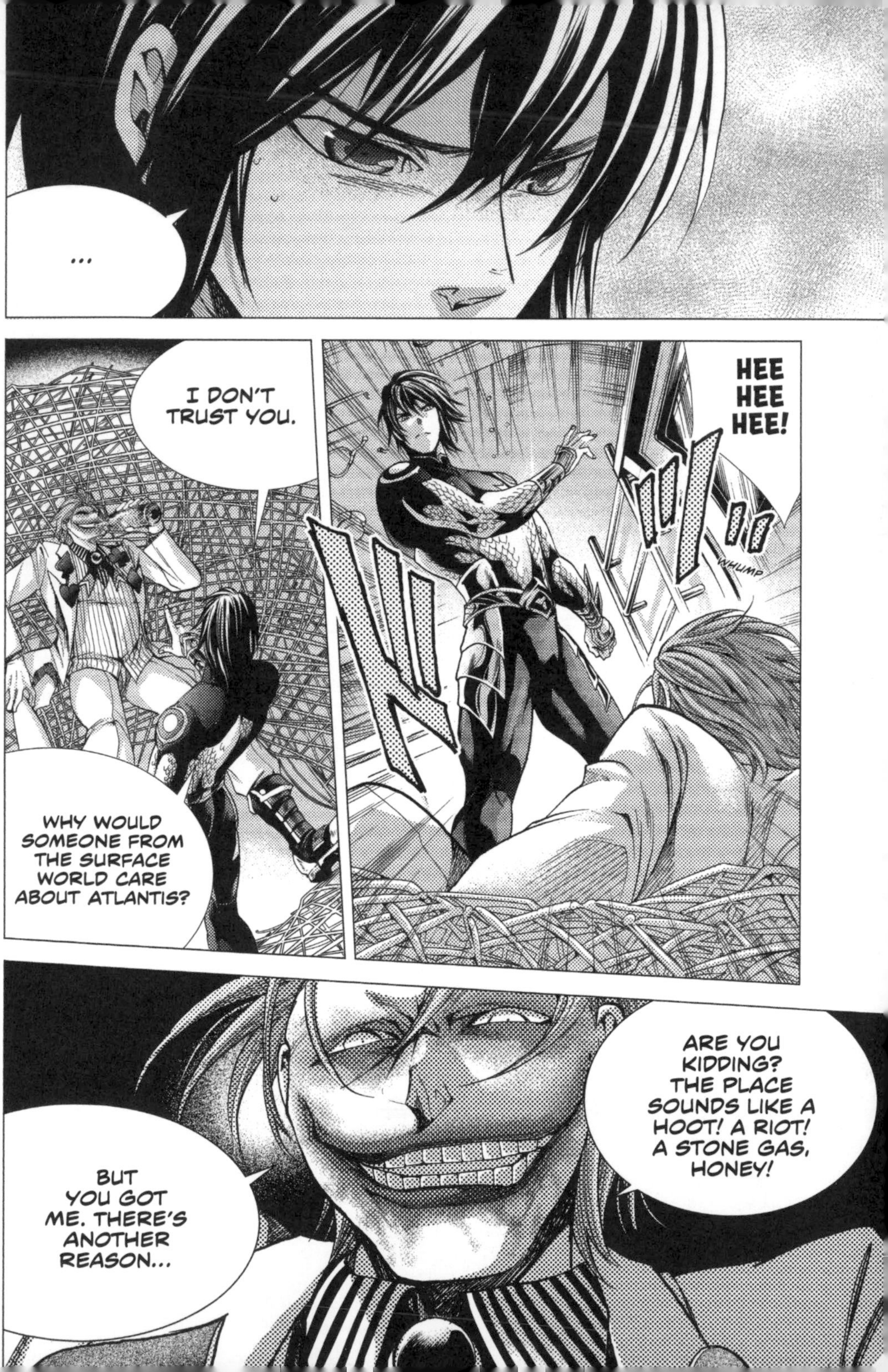
...
HEE HEE HEE!
WHUMP
I DON'T TRUST YOU.
WHY WOULD SOMEONE FROM THE SURFACE WORLD CARE ABOUT ATLANTIS?
ARE YOU KIDDING? THE PLACE SOUNDS LIKE A HOOT! A RIOT! A STONE GAS, HONEY!
BUT YOU GOT ME. THERE'S ANOTHER REASON...

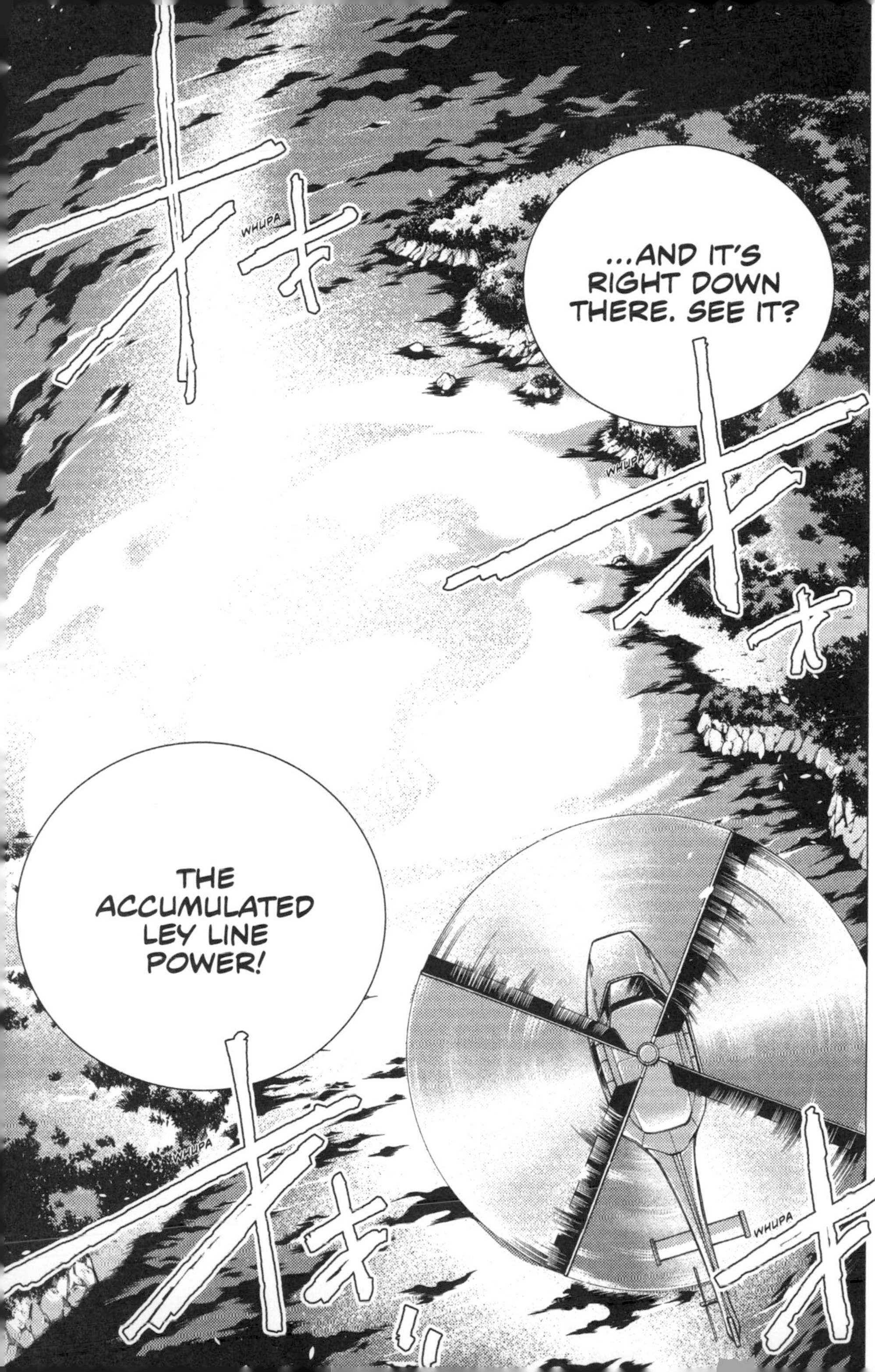
...AND IT'S RIGHT DOWN THERE. SEE IT?
WHUPA
WHUPA
WHUPA
THE ACCUMULATED LEY LINE POWER!
WHUPA

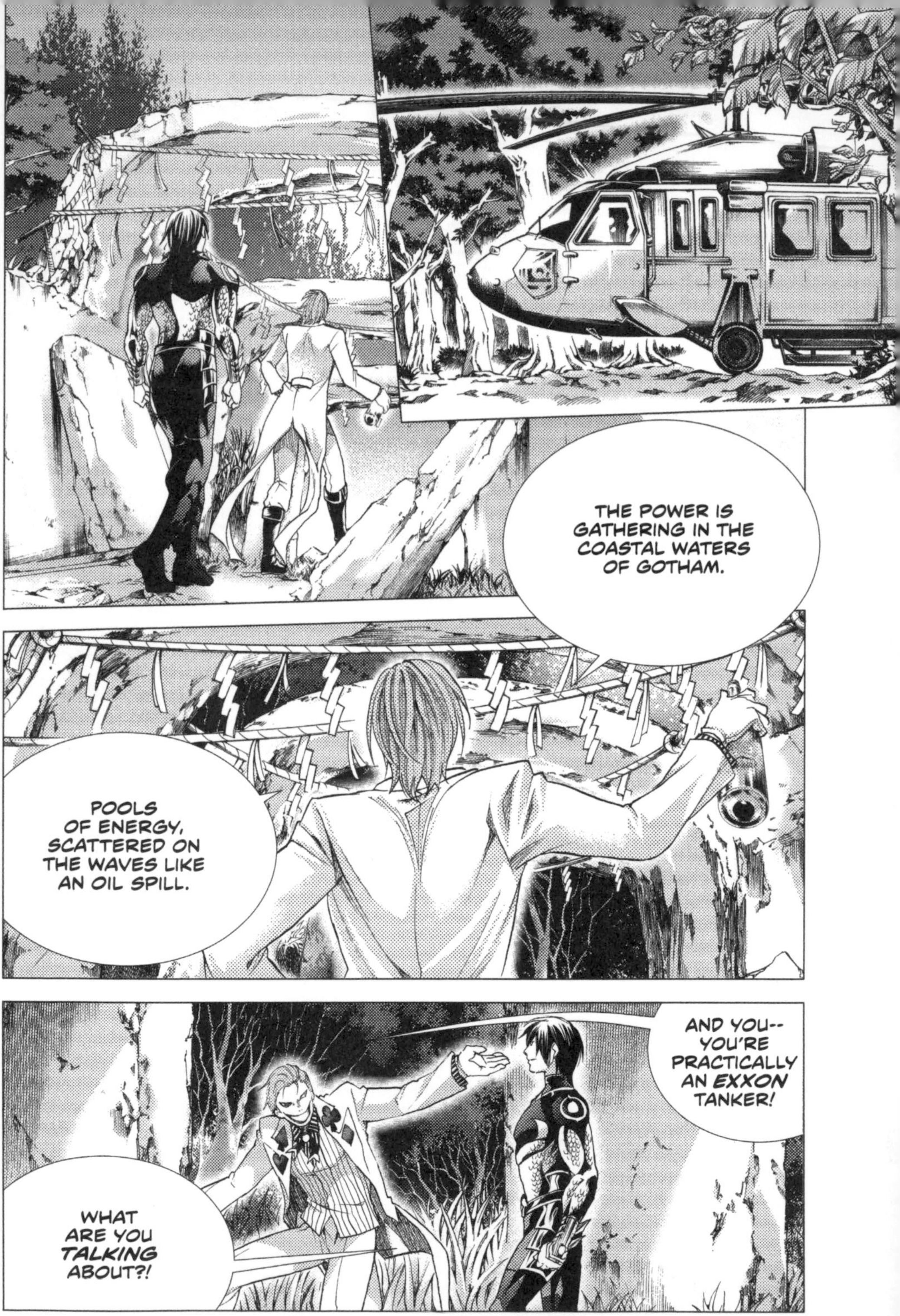
THE POWER IS GATHERING IN THE COASTAL WATERS OF GOTHAM.
POOLS OF ENERGY, SCATTERED ON THE WAVES LIKE AN OIL SPILL.
AND YOU-- YOU'RE PRACTICALLY AN *EXXON* TANKER!
WHAT ARE YOU *TALKING* ABOUT?!

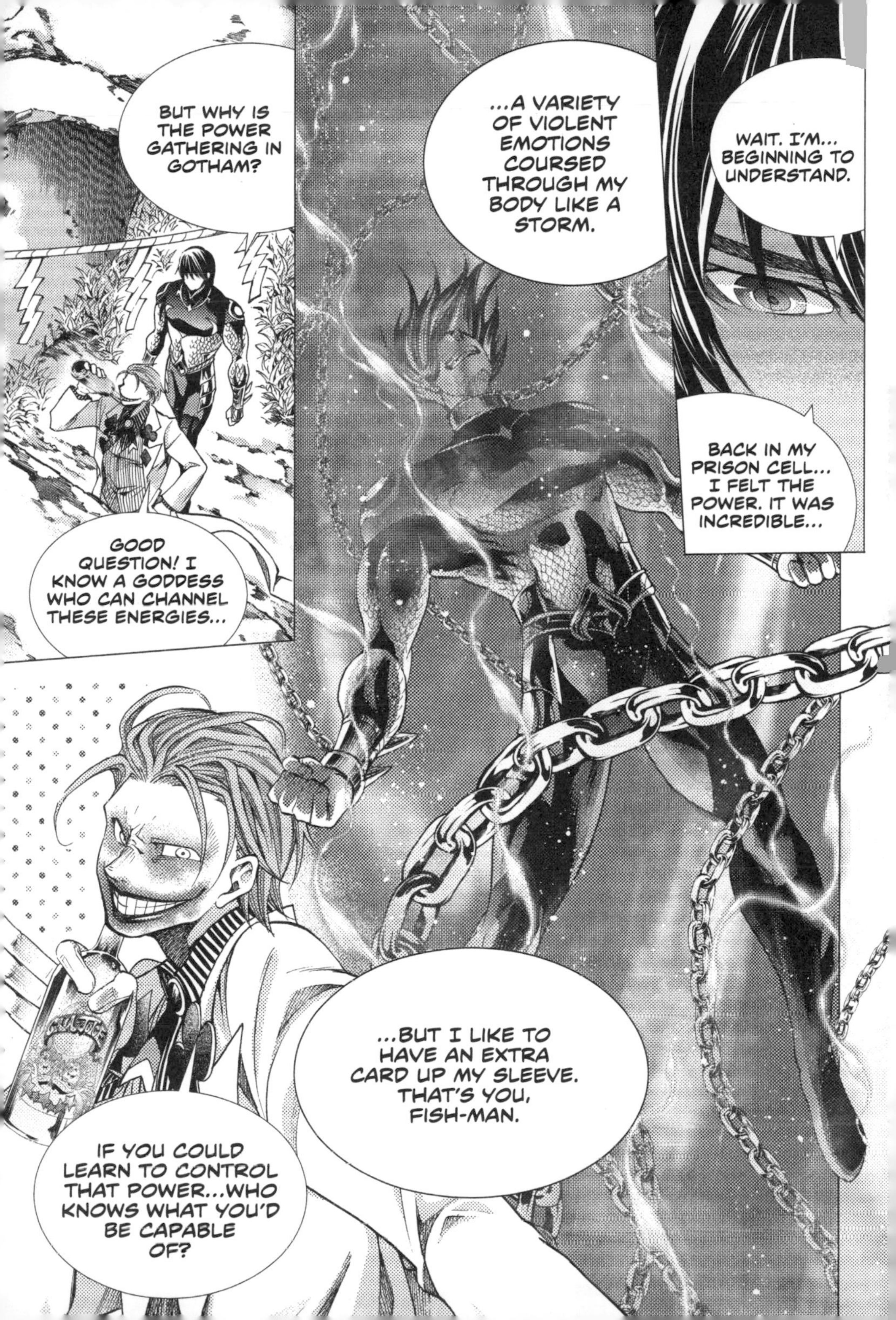
WAIT. I'M... BEGINNING TO UNDERSTAND.
BACK IN MY PRISON CELL... I FELT THE POWER. IT WAS INCREDIBLE...
...A VARIETY OF VIOLENT EMOTIONS COURSED THROUGH MY BODY LIKE A STORM.
BUT WHY IS THE POWER GATHERING IN GOTHAM?
GOOD QUESTION! I KNOW A GODDESS WHO CAN CHANNEL THESE ENERGIES...
...BUT I LIKE TO HAVE AN EXTRA CARD UP MY SLEEVE. THAT'S YOU, FISH-MAN.
IF YOU COULD LEARN TO CONTROL THAT POWER...WHO KNOWS WHAT YOU'D BE CAPABLE OF?

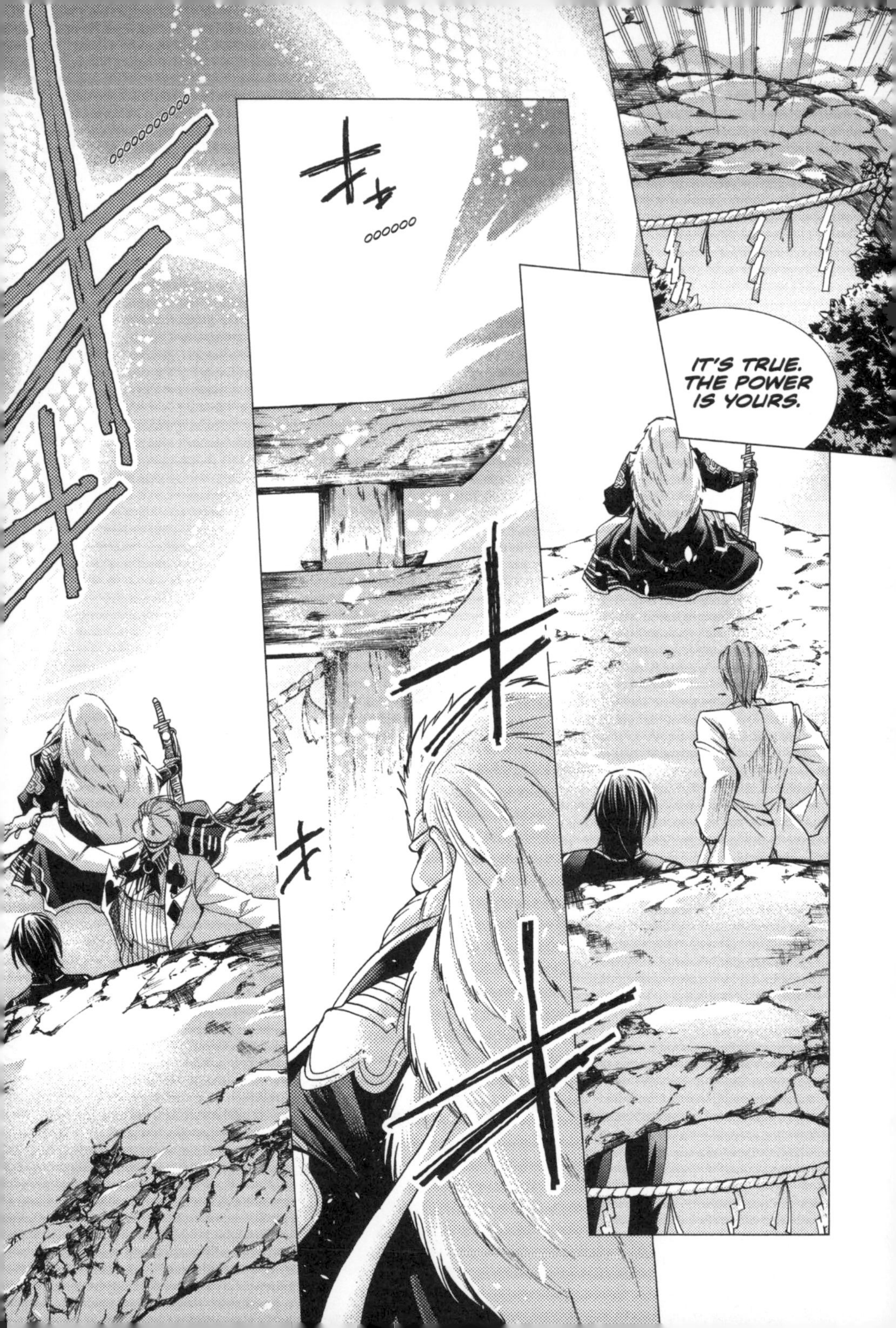
IT'S TRUE. THE POWER IS YOURS.
oooooo
ooooooooooo

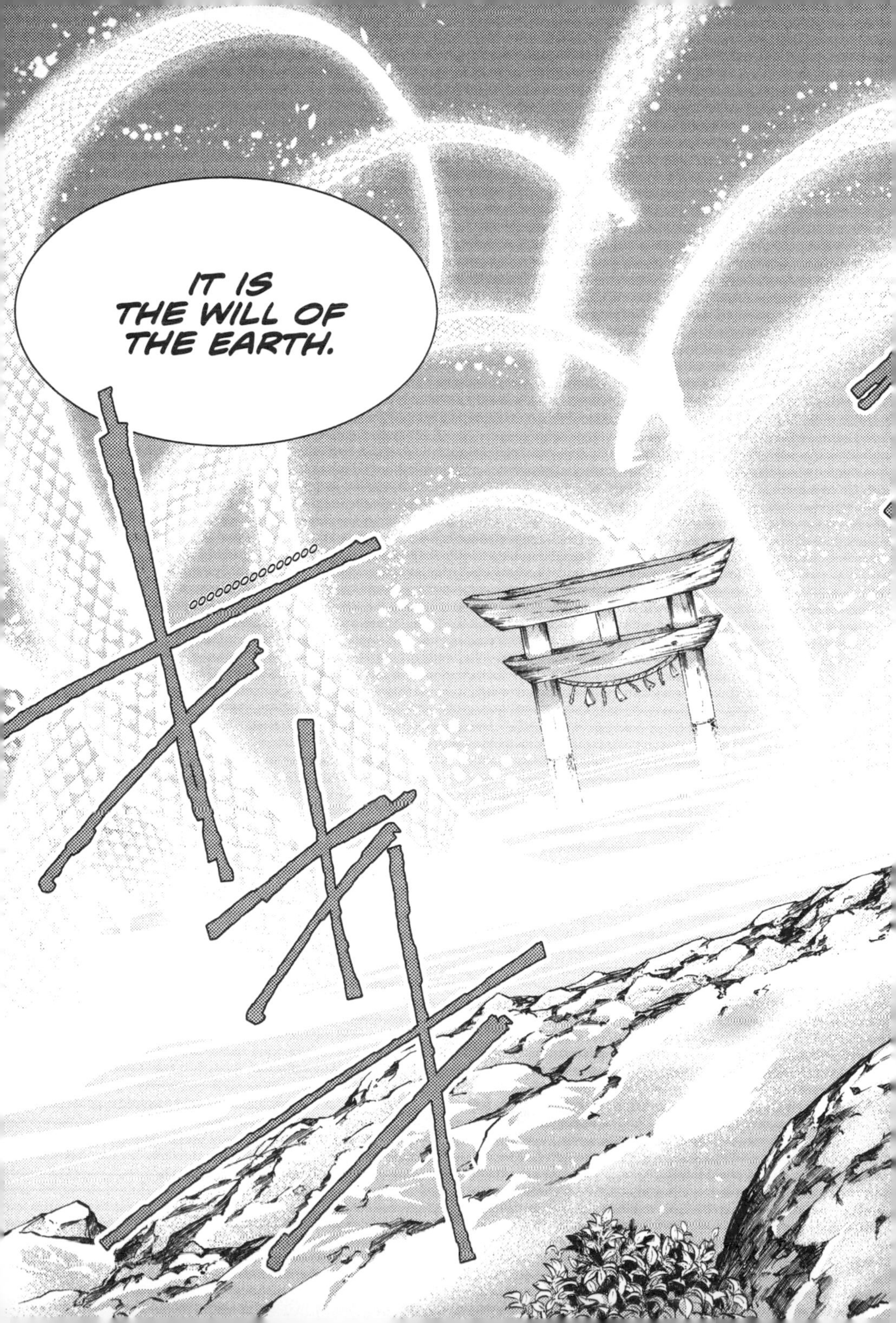

IT IS THE WILL OF THE EARTH.
OOOOOOOOOOOOOOO

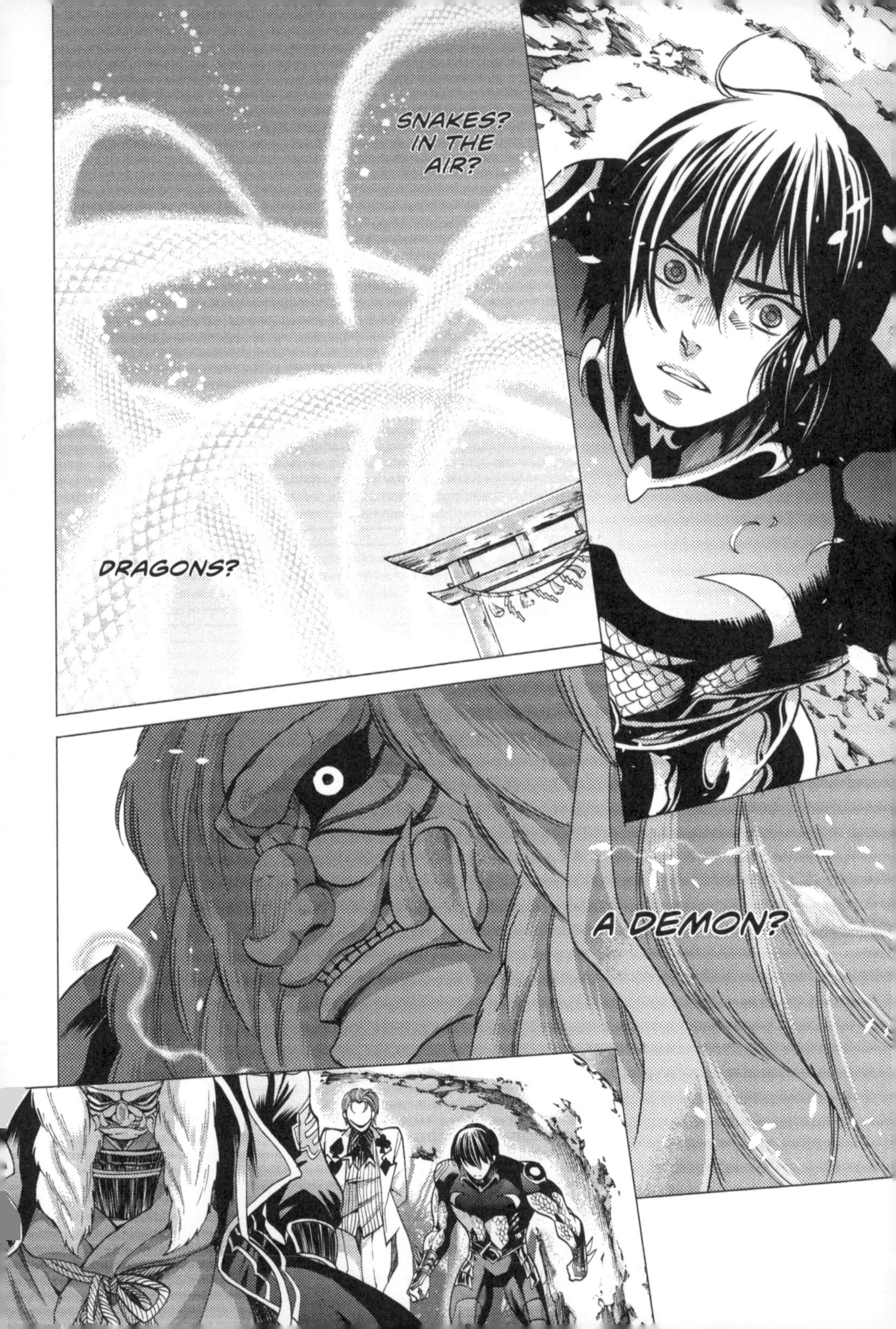
SNAKES? IN THE AIR?
DRAGONS?
A DEMON?

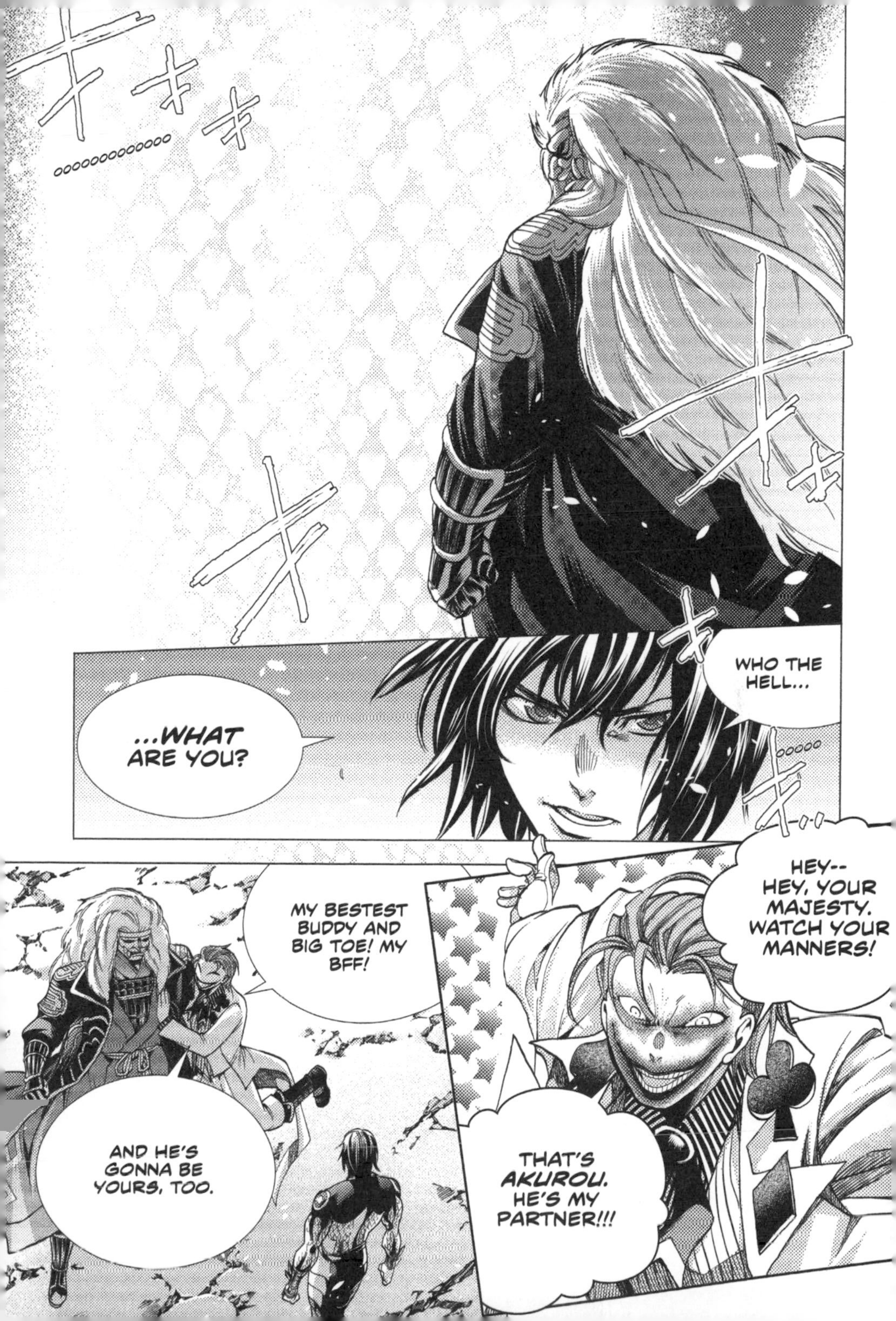
oooooooooooo
WHO THE HELL...
...WHAT ARE YOU?
ooooo
HEY-- HEY, YOUR MAJESTY. WATCH YOUR MANNERS!
THAT'S AKUROU. HE'S MY PARTNER!!!
MY BESTEST BUDDY AND BIG TOE! MY BFF!
AND HE'S GONNA BE YOURS, TOO.

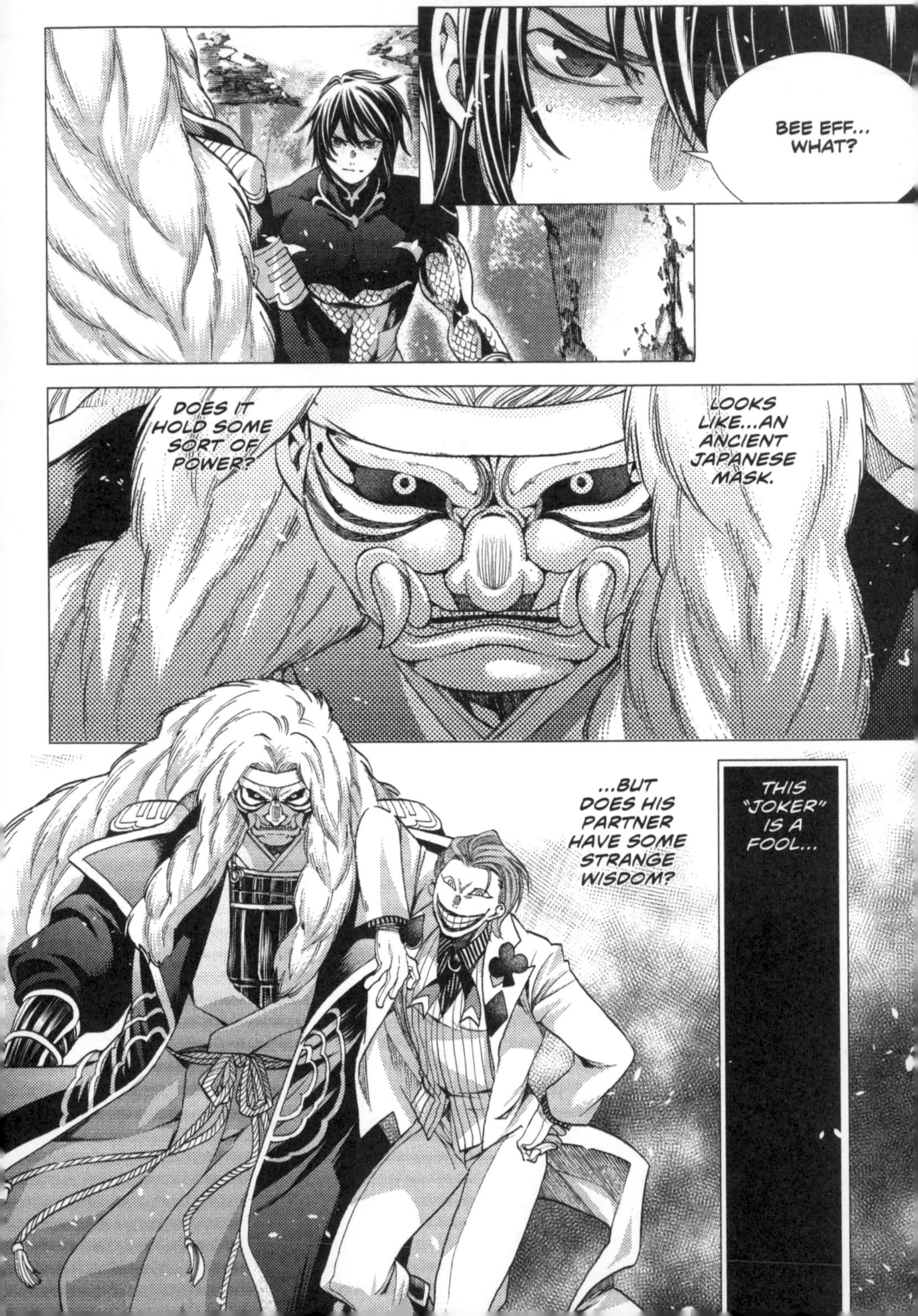
BEE EFF... WHAT?
LOOKS LIKE...AN ANCIENT JAPANESE MASK.
DOES IT HOLD SOME SORT OF POWER?
THIS "JOKER" IS A FOOL...
...BUT DOES HIS PARTNER HAVE SOME STRANGE WISDOM?

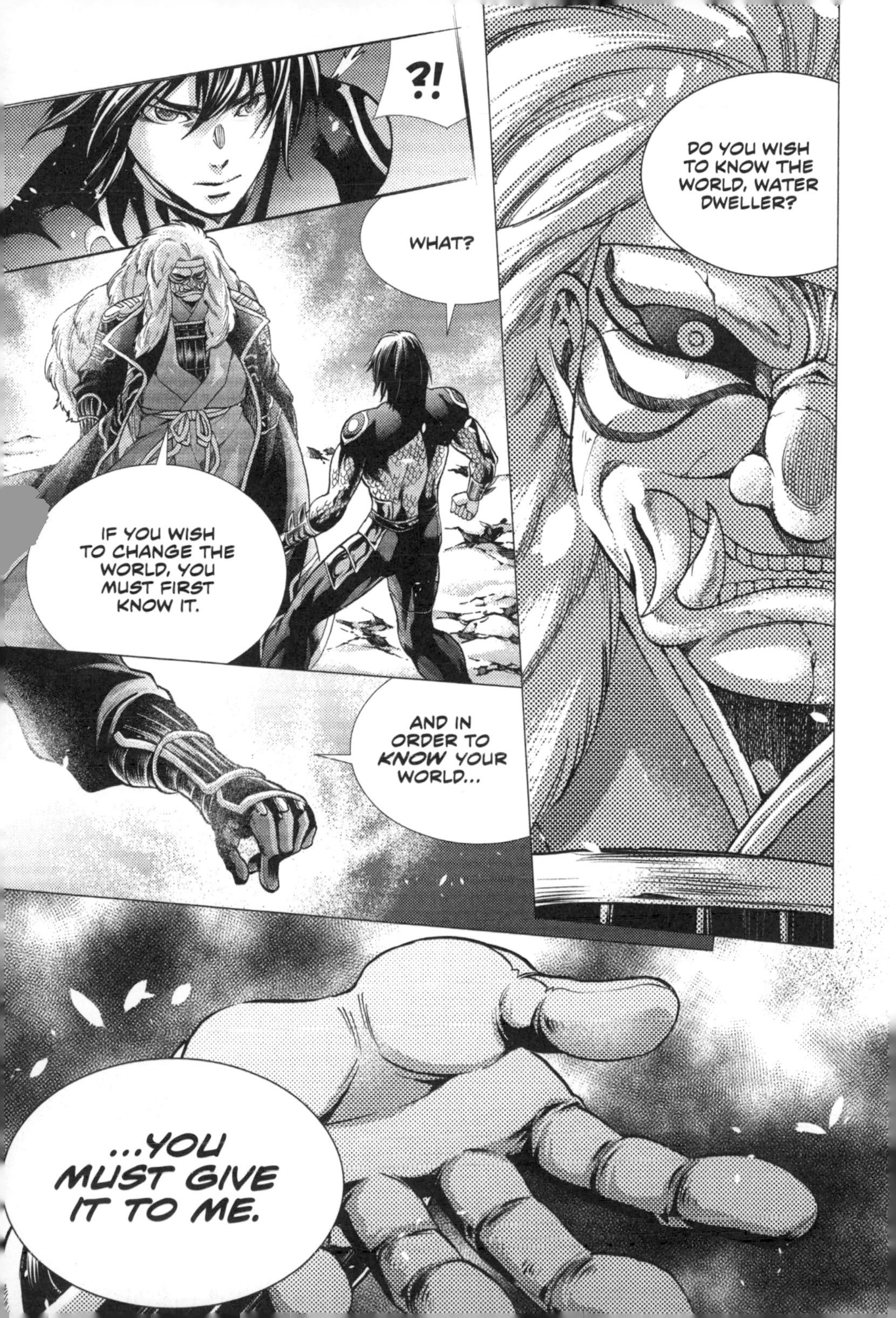
DO YOU WISH TO KNOW THE WORLD, WATER DWELLER?
?!
WHAT?
IF YOU WISH TO CHANGE THE WORLD, YOU MUST FIRST KNOW IT.
AND IN ORDER TO *KNOW* YOUR WORLD...
...YOU MUST GIVE IT TO ME.

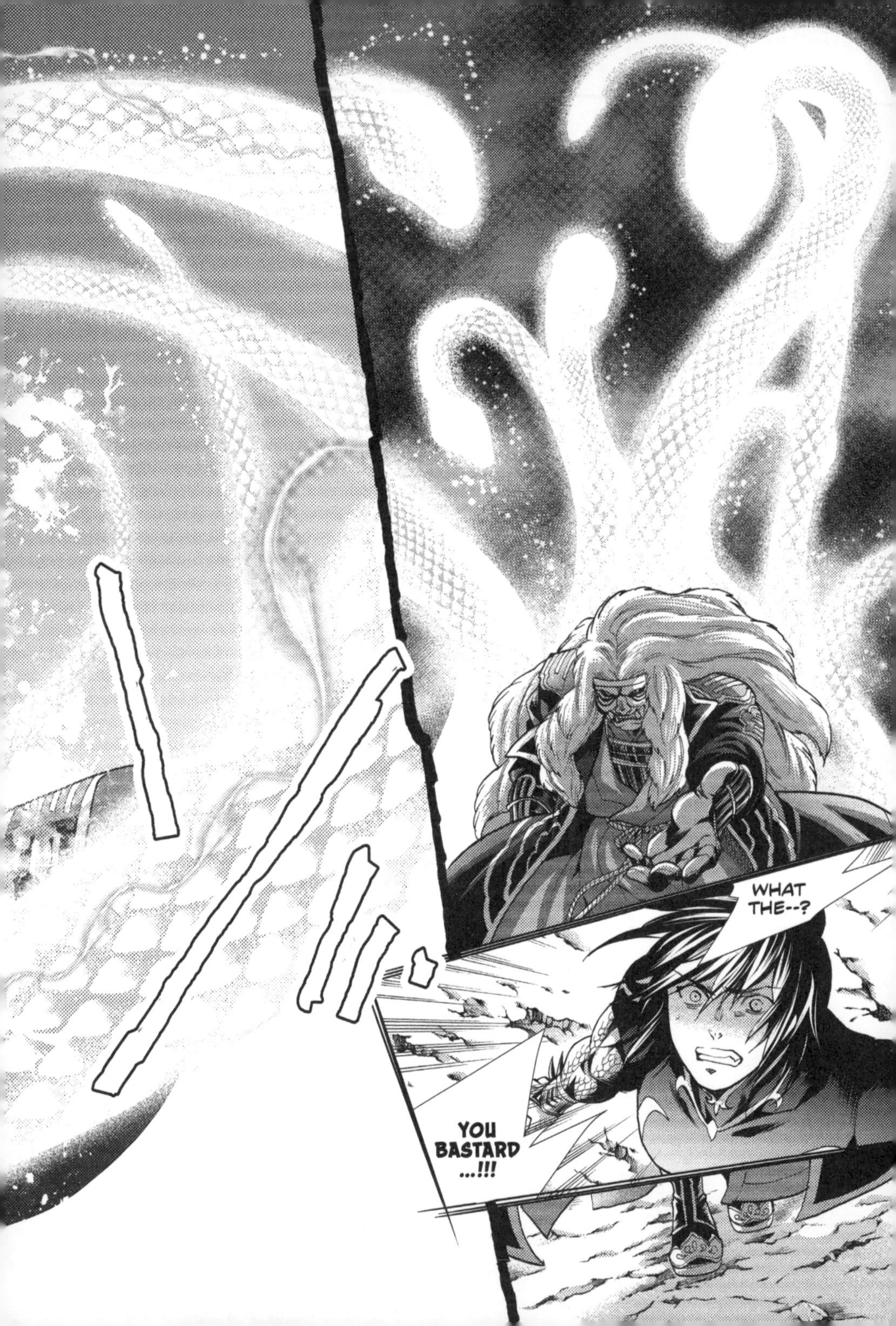
WHAT THE--?
YOU BASTARD ...!!!

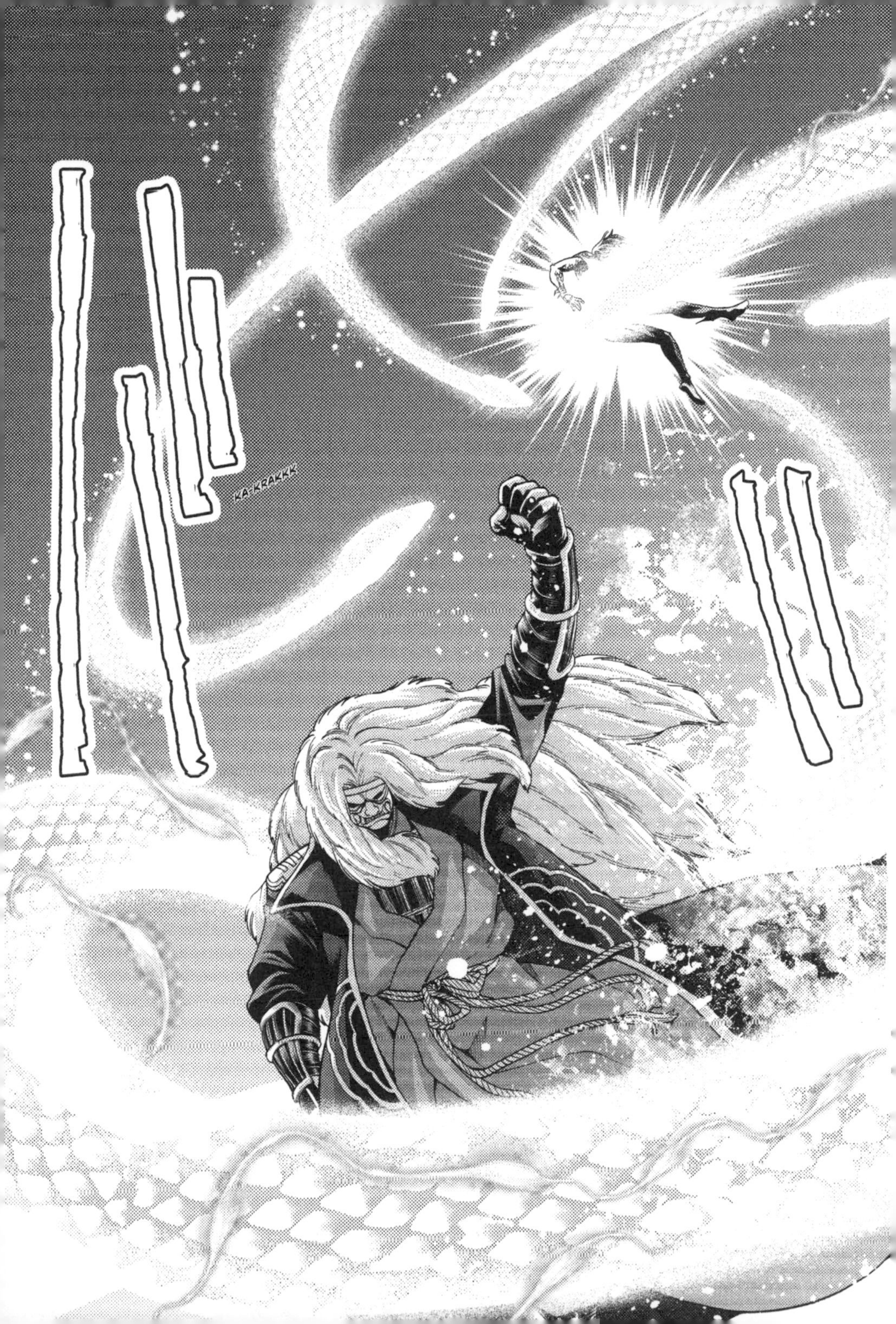
KA-KRAKKK

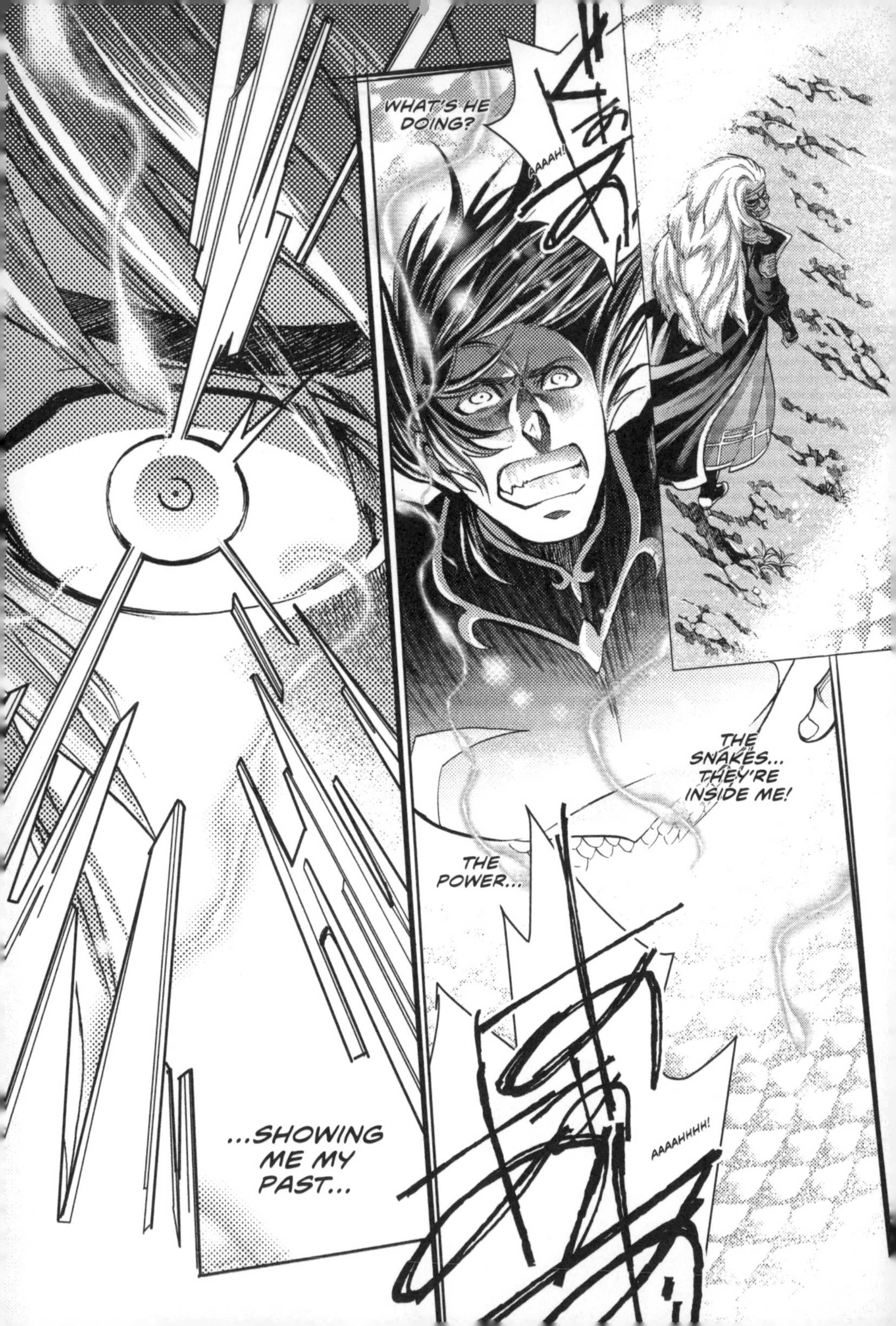
WHAT'S HE DOING?
AAAAH!
THE SNAKES... THEY'RE INSIDE ME!
THE POWER...
AAAAHHHH!
...SHOWING ME MY PAST...

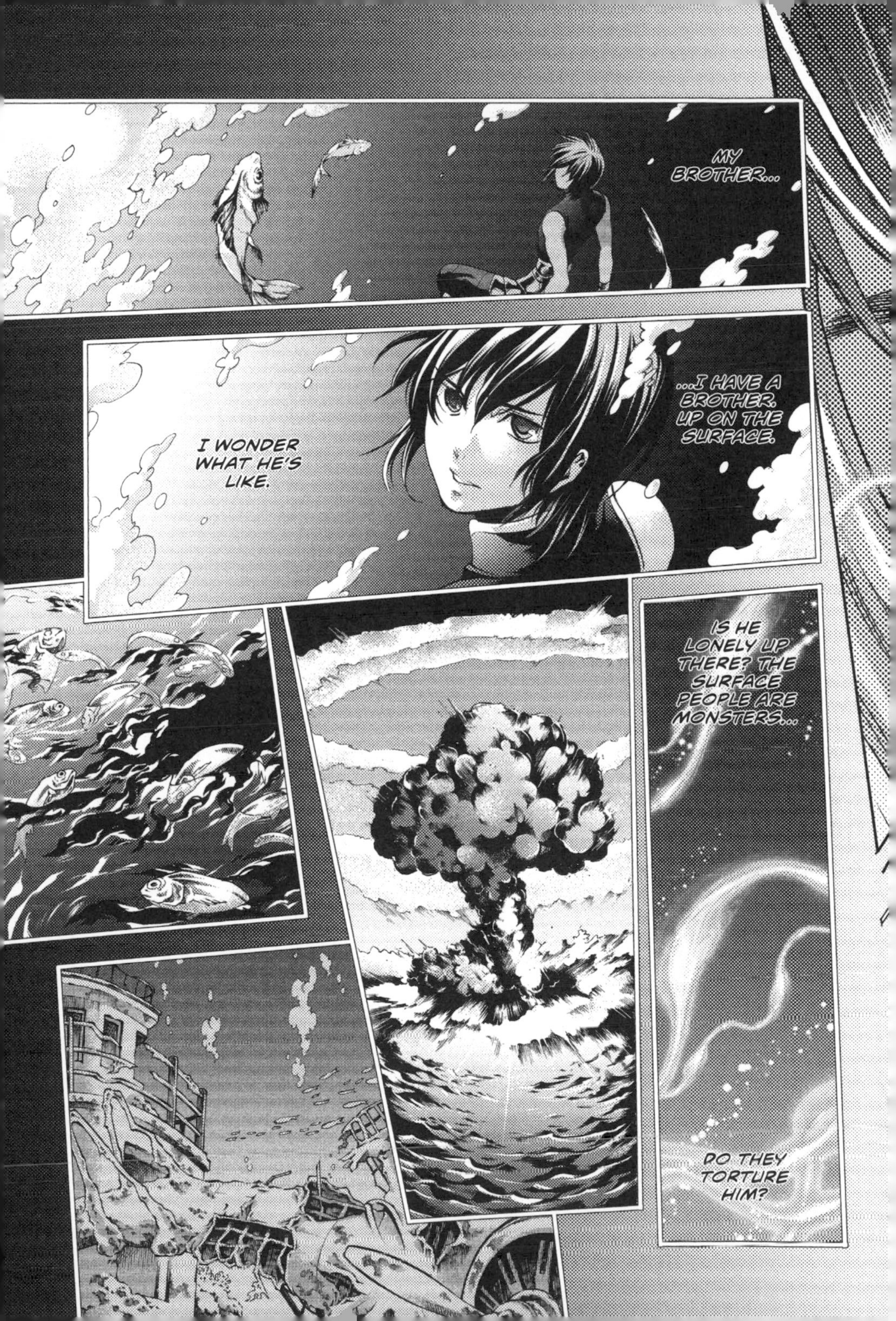
MY BROTHER...
...I HAVE A BROTHER. UP ON THE SURFACE.
I WONDER WHAT HE'S LIKE.
IS HE LONELY UP THERE? THE SURFACE PEOPLE ARE MONSTERS...
DO THEY TORTURE HIM?

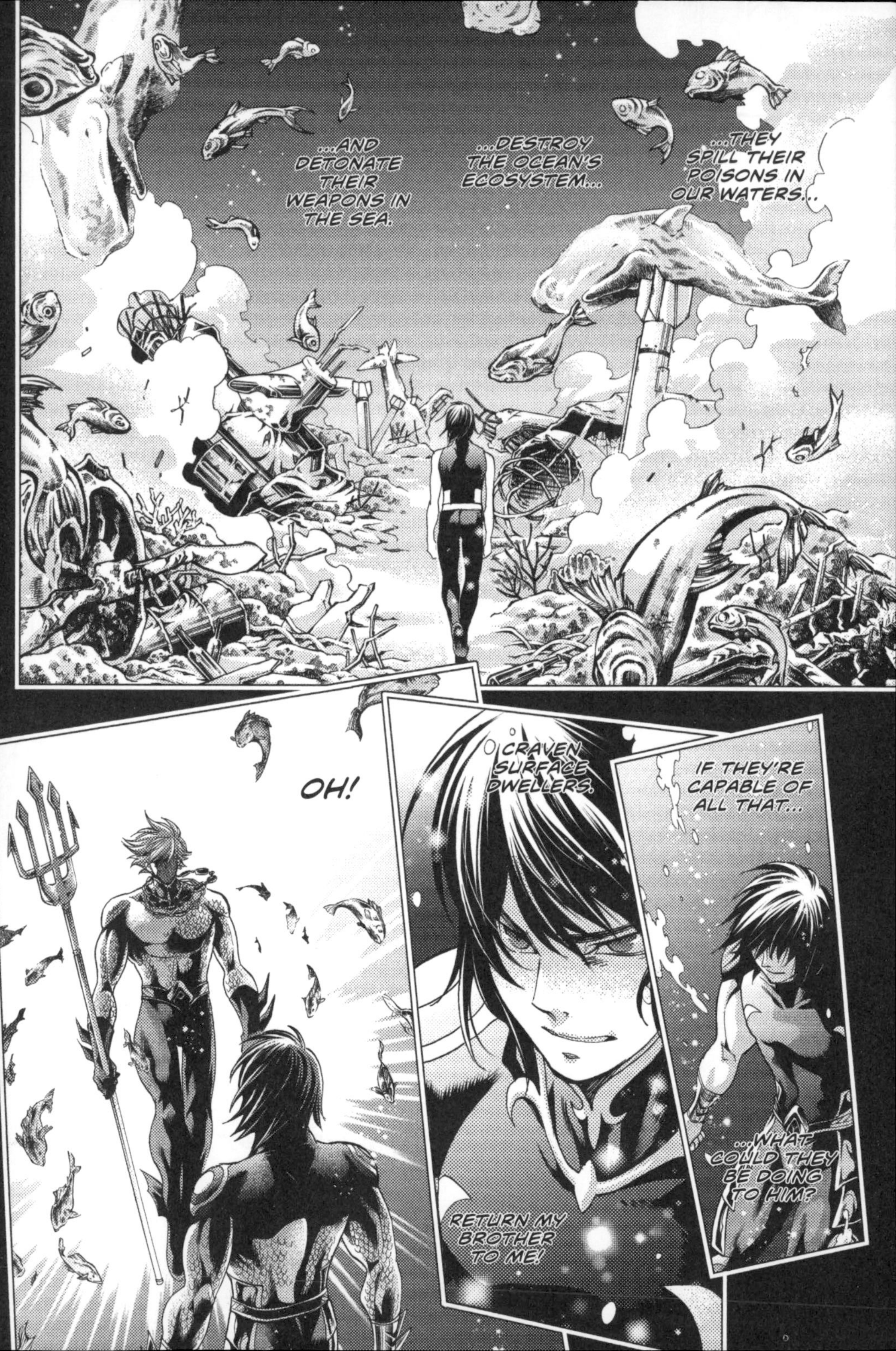
...THEY SPILL THEIR POISONS IN OUR WATERS...
...DESTROY THE OCEAN'S ECOSYSTEM...
...AND DETONATE THEIR WEAPONS IN THE SEA.
IF THEY'RE CAPABLE OF ALL THAT...
...WHAT COULD THEY BE DOING TO HIM?
CRAVEN SURFACE DWELLERS.
RETURN MY BROTHER TO ME!
OH!

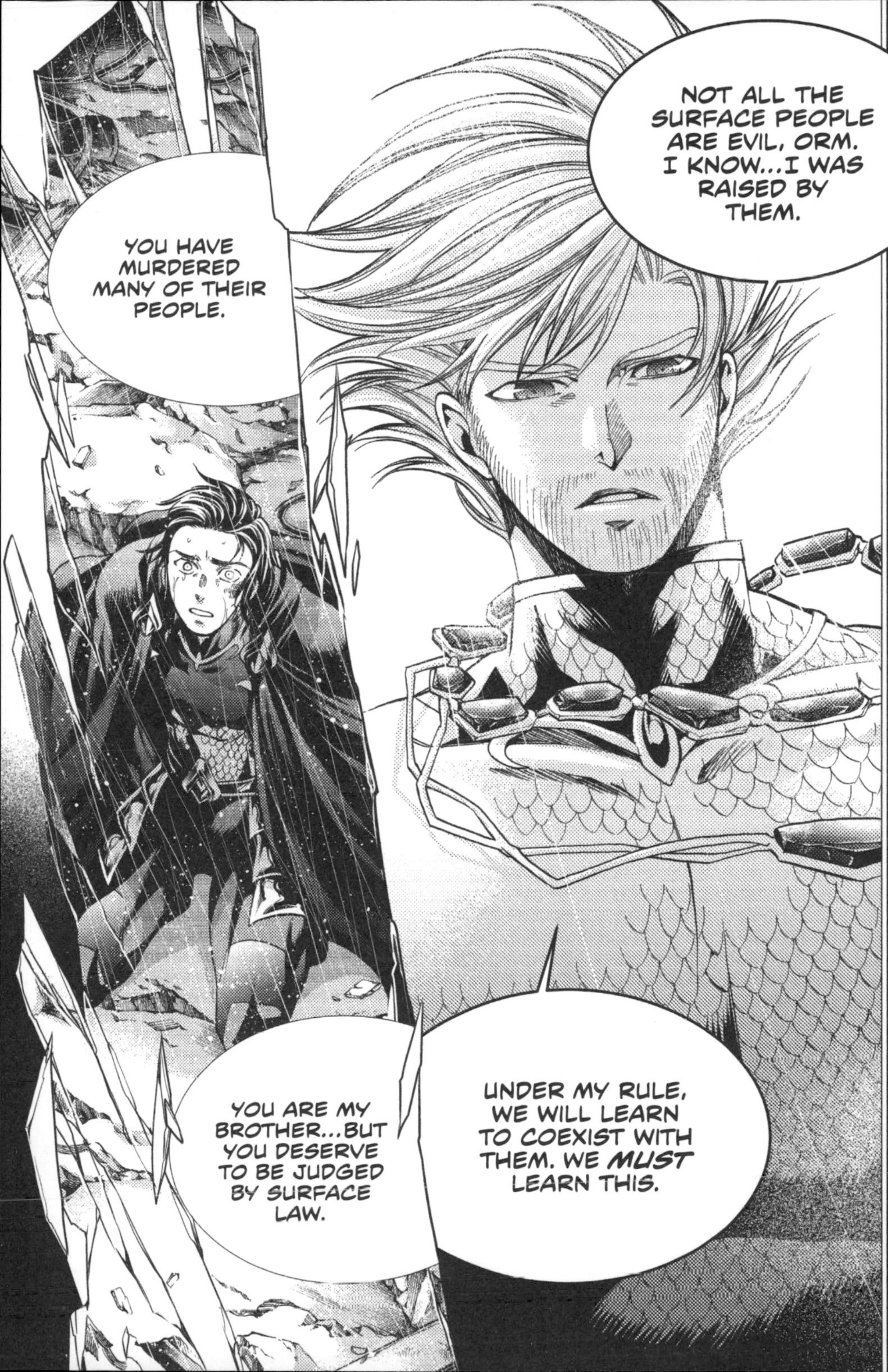
NOT ALL THE SURFACE PEOPLE ARE EVIL, ORM. I KNOW...I WAS RAISED BY THEM.
UNDER MY RULE, WE WILL LEARN TO COEXIST WITH THEM. WE *MUST* LEARN THIS.
YOU HAVE MURDERED MANY OF THEIR PEOPLE.
YOU ARE MY BROTHER...BUT YOU DESERVE TO BE JUDGED BY SURFACE LAW.

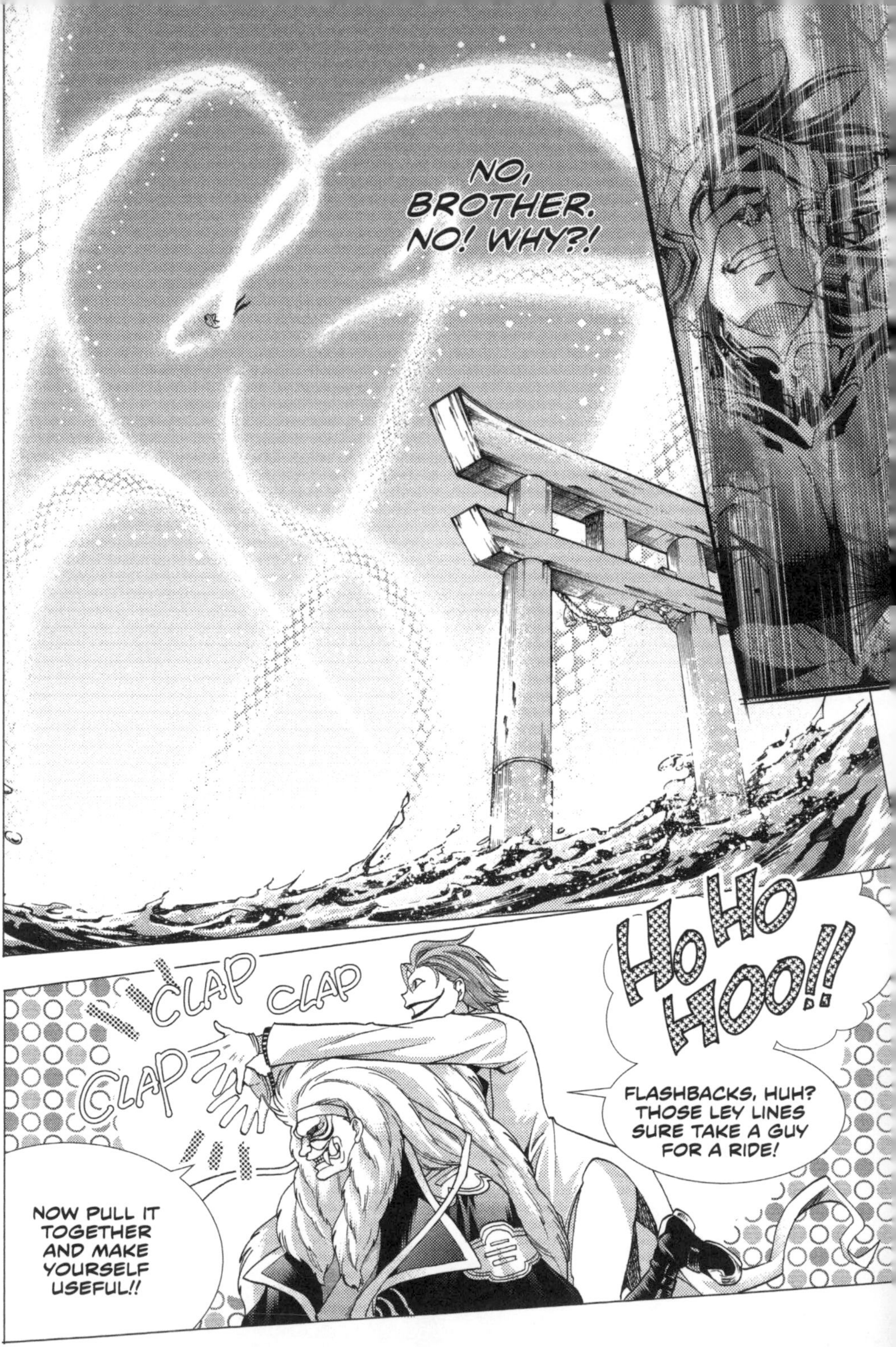
NO, BROTHER. NO! WHY?!
HO HO HOO!!
FLASHBACKS, HUH? THOSE LEY LINES SURE TAKE A GUY FOR A RIDE!
CLAP CLAP
CLAP
NOW PULL IT TOGETHER AND MAKE YOURSELF USEFUL!!

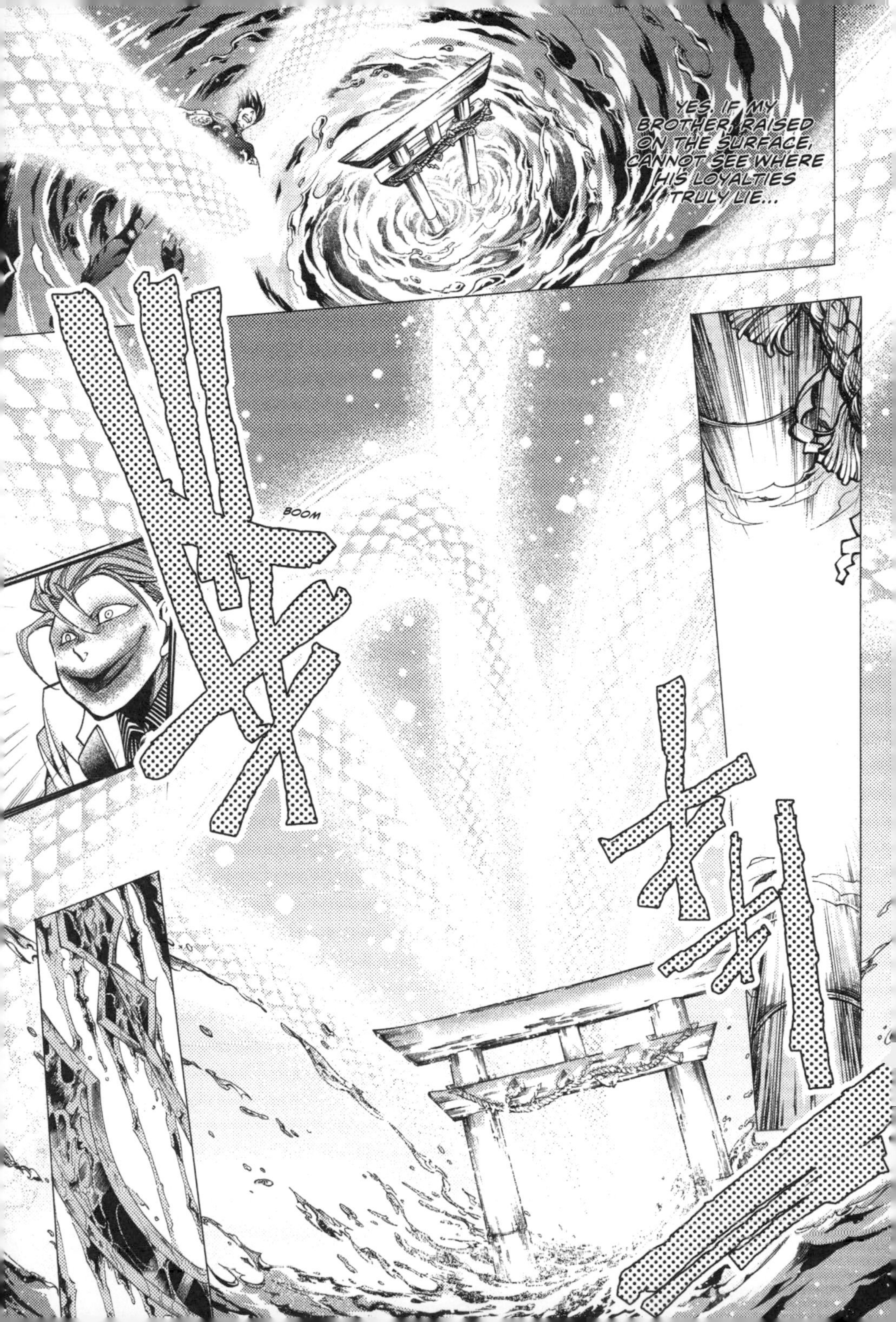
YES. IF MY BROTHER, RAISED ON THE SURFACE, CANNOT SEE WHERE HIS LOYALTIES TRULY LIE...
BOOM

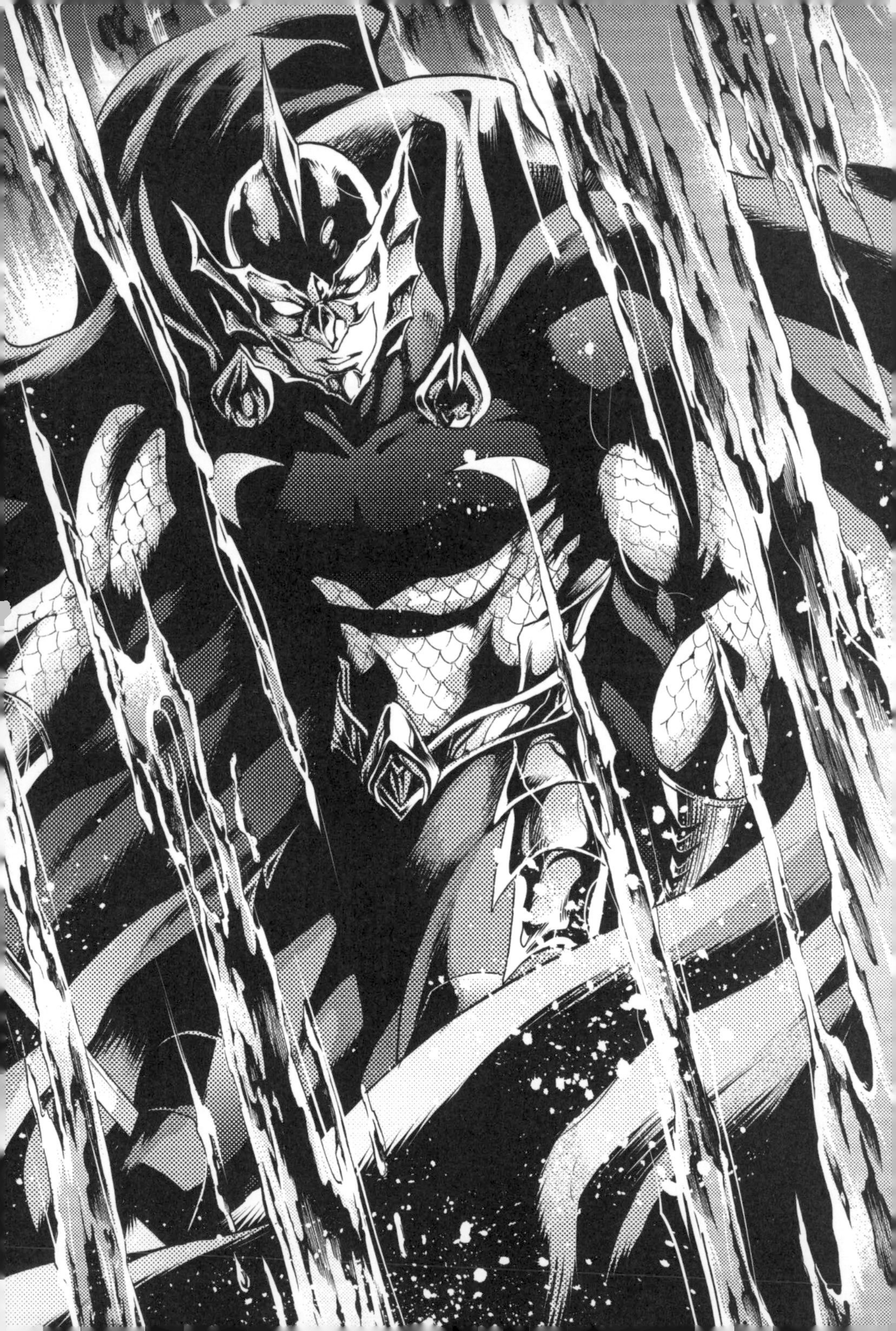

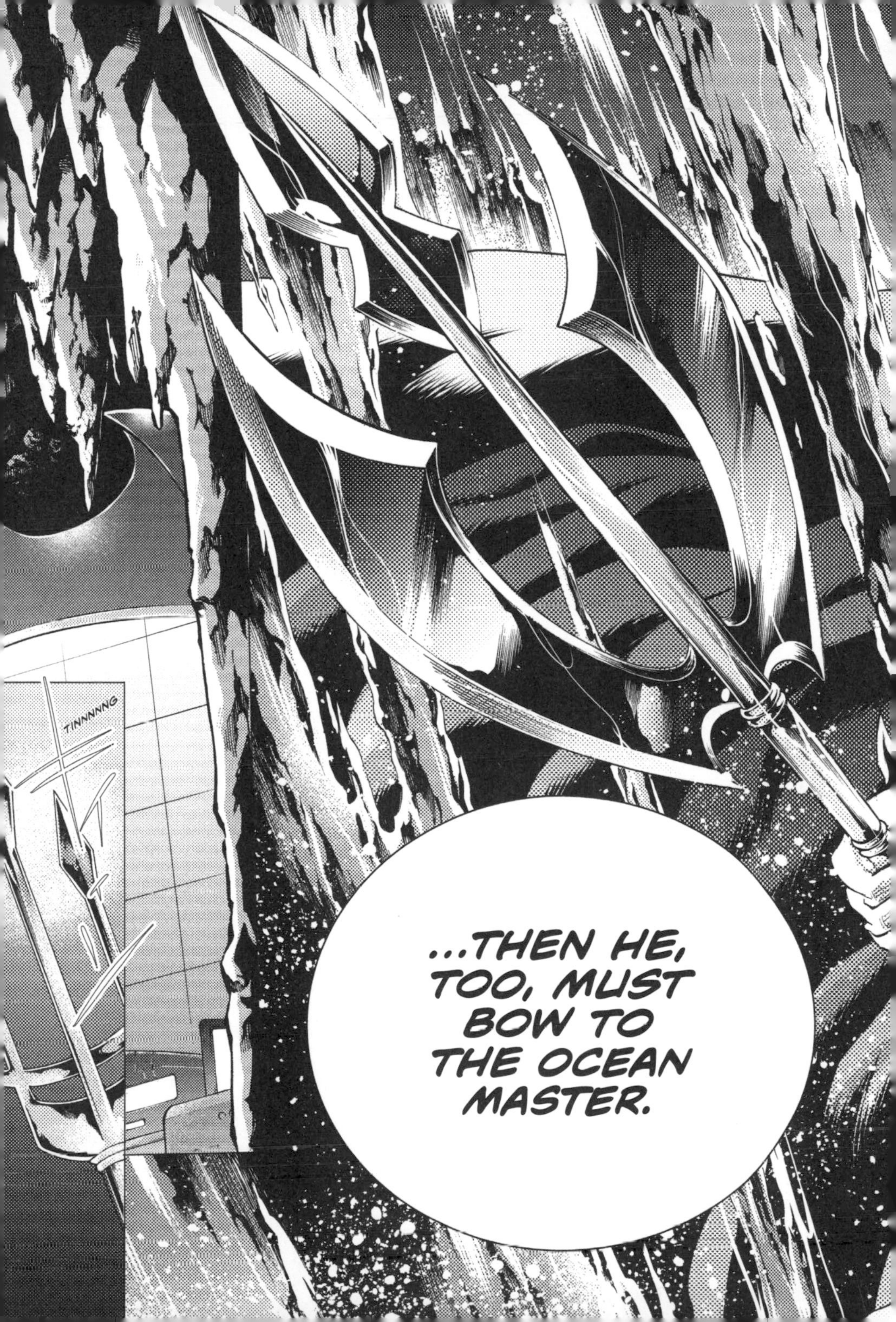
...THEN HE, TOO, MUST BOW TO THE OCEAN MASTER.
TINNNNNG

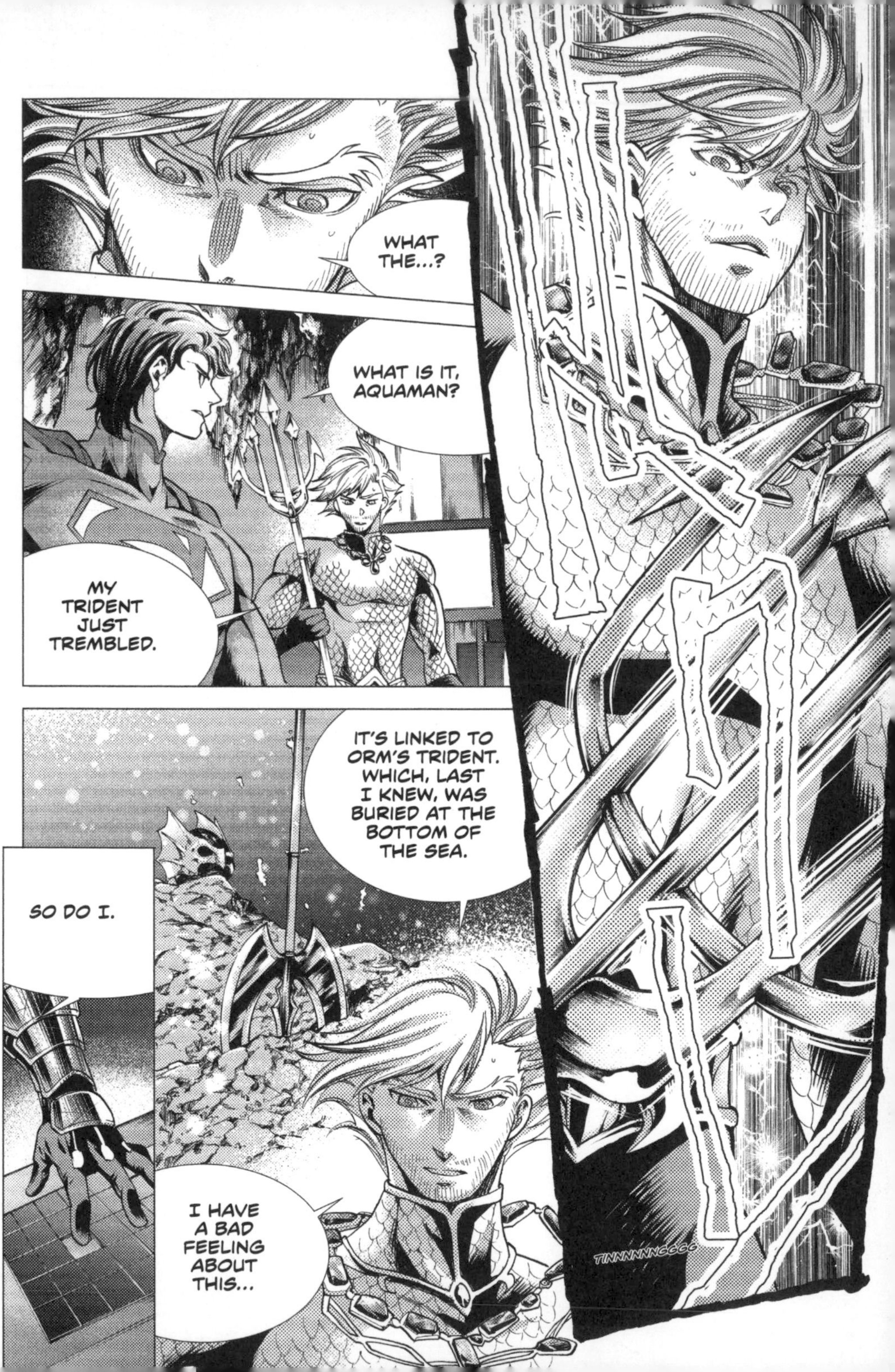
TINNNNNNNGGGG
WHAT THE...?
WHAT IS IT, AQUAMAN?
MY TRIDENT JUST TREMBLED.
IT'S LINKED TO ORM'S TRIDENT. WHICH, LAST I KNEW, WAS BURIED AT THE BOTTOM OF THE SEA.
SO DO I.
I HAVE A BAD FEELING ABOUT THIS...

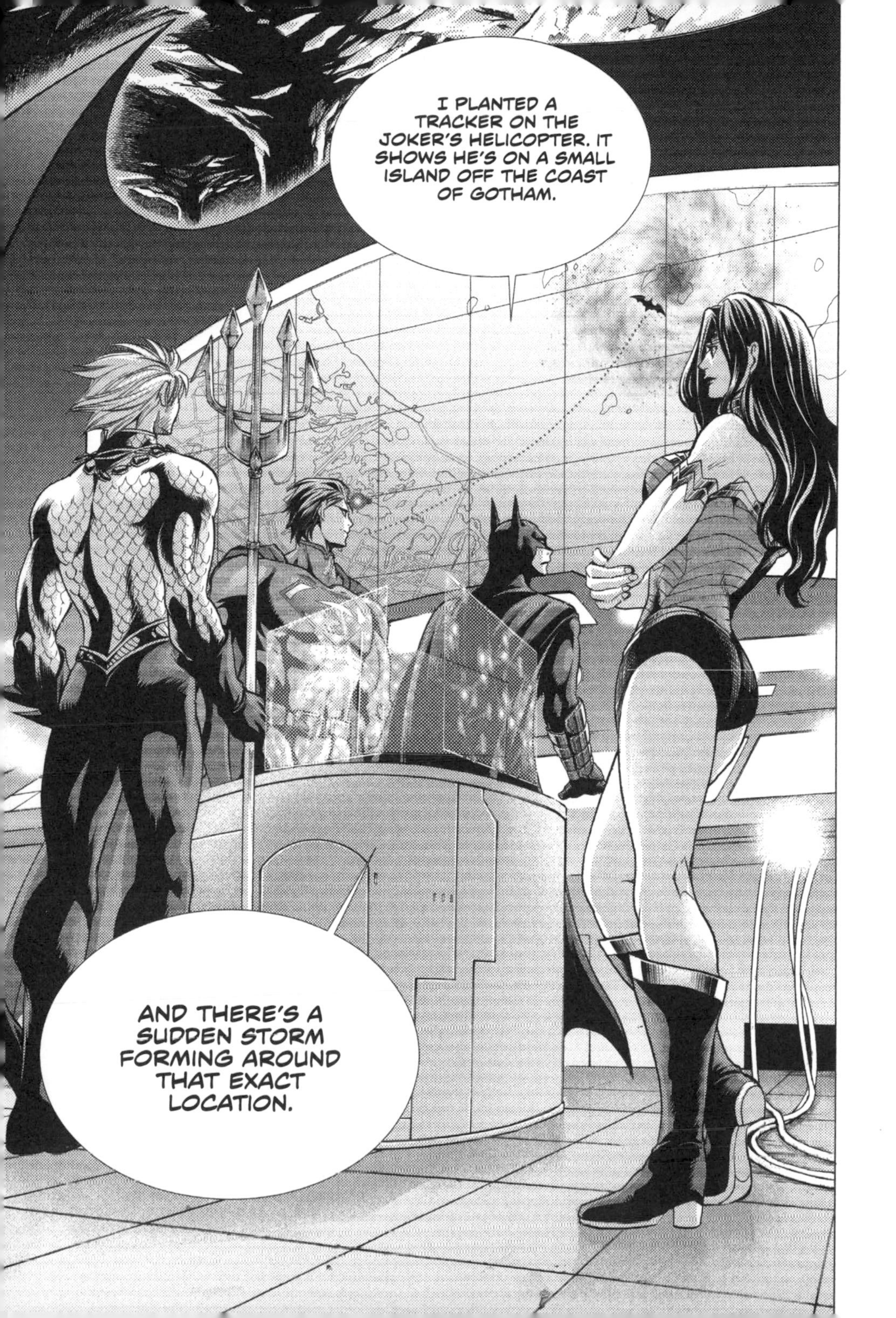
I PLANTED A TRACKER ON THE JOKER'S HELICOPTER. IT SHOWS HE'S ON A SMALL ISLAND OFF THE COAST OF GOTHAM.
AND THERE'S A SUDDEN STORM FORMING AROUND THAT EXACT LOCATION.

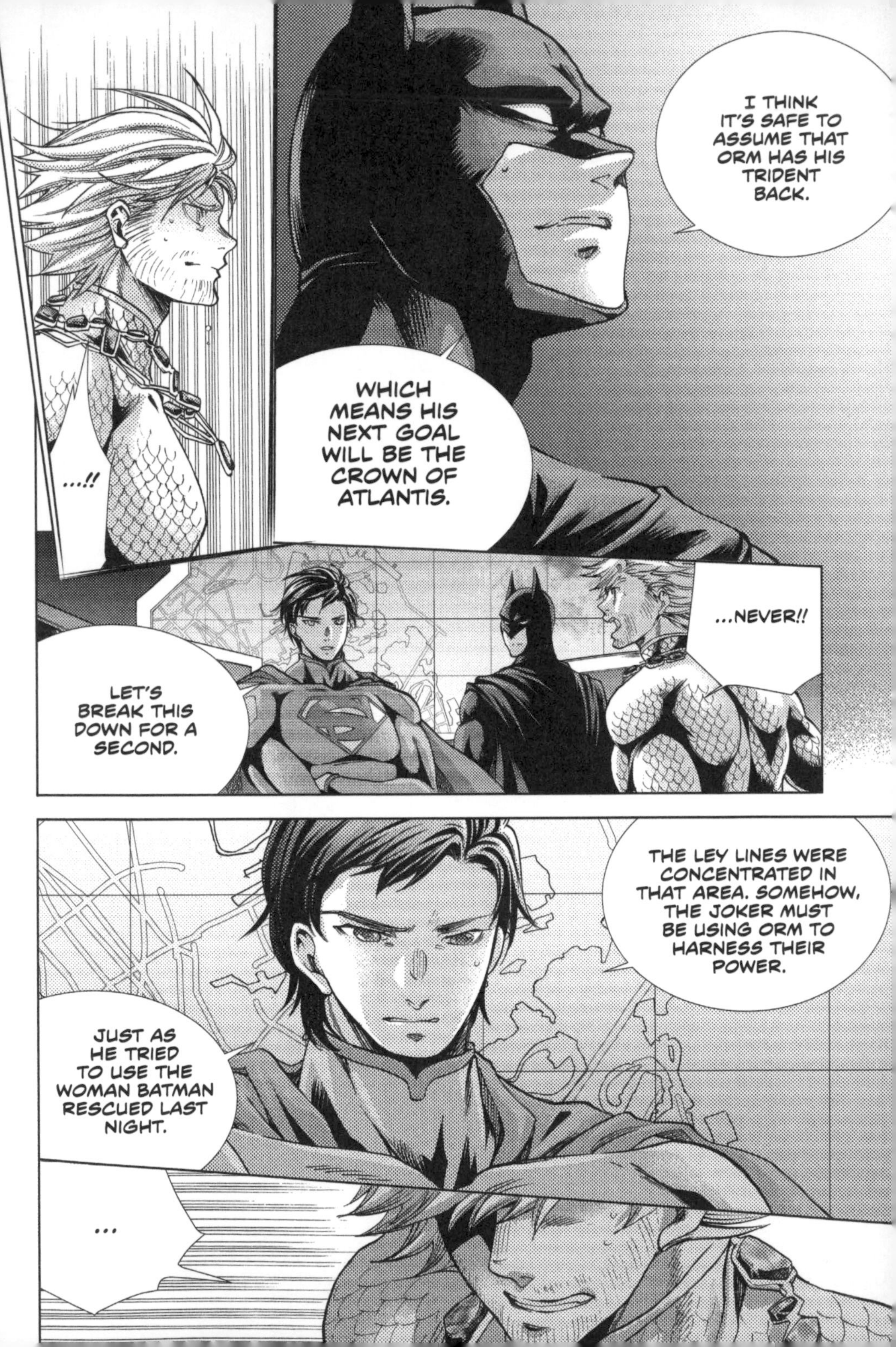
I THINK IT'S SAFE TO ASSUME THAT ORM HAS HIS TRIDENT BACK.
WHICH MEANS HIS NEXT GOAL WILL BE THE CROWN OF ATLANTIS.
...!!
...NEVER!!
LET'S BREAK THIS DOWN FOR A SECOND.
THE LEY LINES WERE CONCENTRATED IN THAT AREA. SOMEHOW, THE JOKER MUST BE USING ORM TO HARNESS THEIR POWER.
JUST AS HE TRIED TO USE THE WOMAN BATMAN RESCUED LAST NIGHT.
...

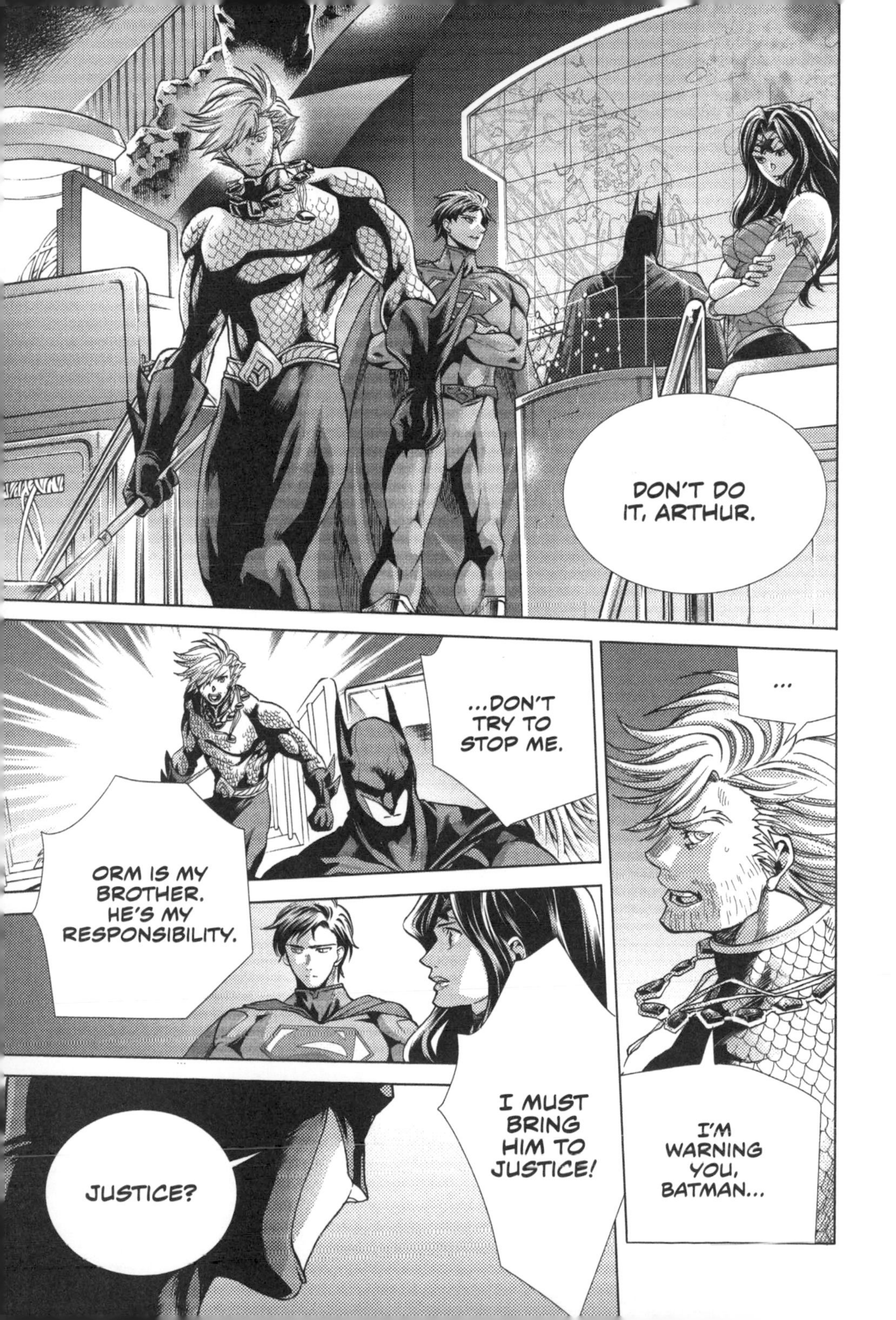
DON'T DO IT, ARTHUR.
...
I'M WARNING YOU, BATMAN...
...DON'T TRY TO STOP ME.
ORM IS MY BROTHER. HE'S MY RESPONSIBILITY.
I MUST BRING HIM TO JUSTICE!
JUSTICE?

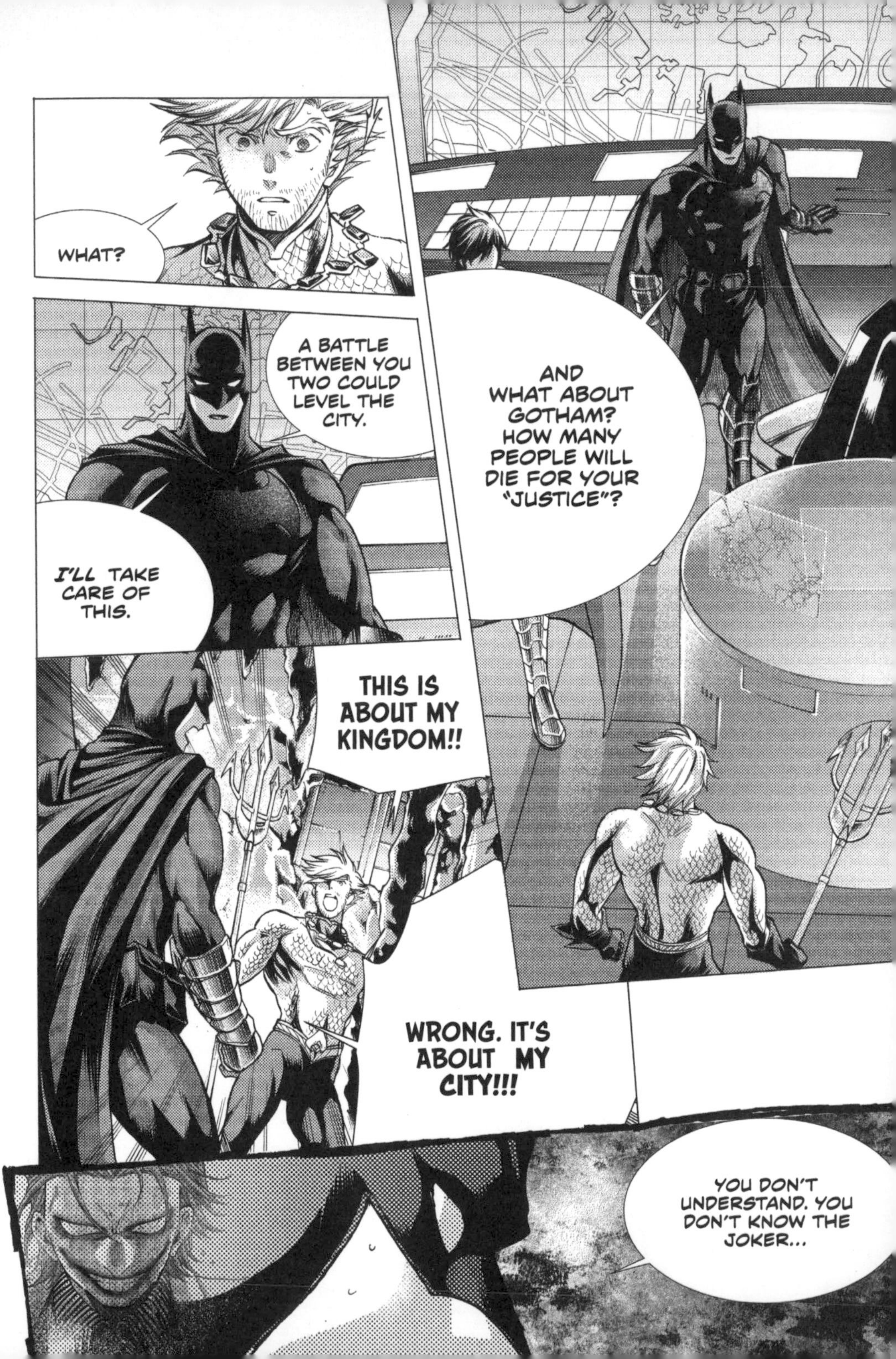
AND WHAT ABOUT GOTHAM? HOW MANY PEOPLE WILL DIE FOR YOUR "JUSTICE"?
WHAT?
A BATTLE BETWEEN YOU TWO COULD LEVEL THE CITY.
I'LL TAKE CARE OF THIS.
THIS IS ABOUT MY KINGDOM!!
WRONG. IT'S ABOUT MY CITY!!!
YOU DON'T UNDERSTAND. YOU DON'T KNOW THE JOKER...

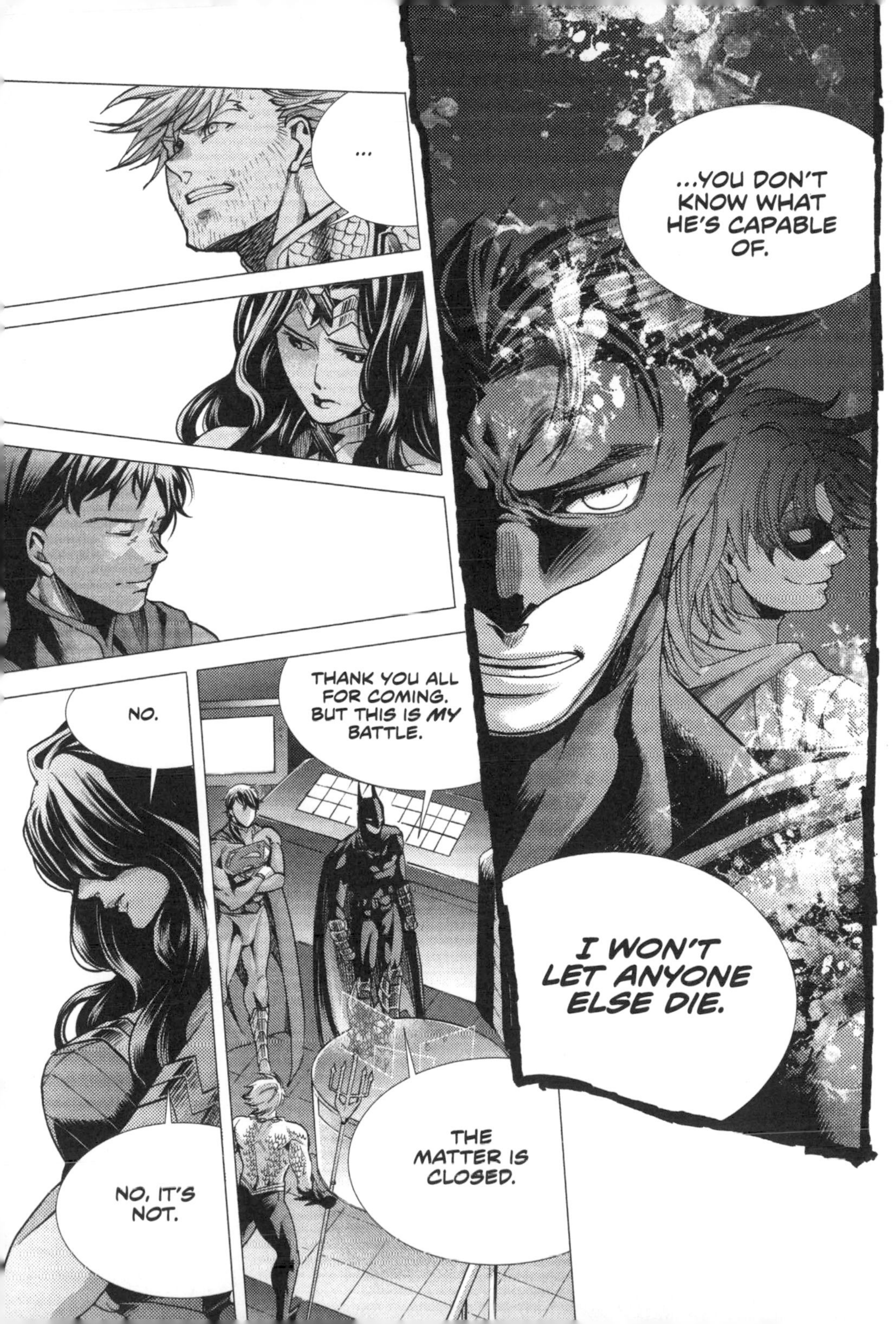
...YOU DON'T KNOW WHAT HE'S CAPABLE OF.
I WON'T LET ANYONE ELSE DIE.
...
THANK YOU ALL FOR COMING. BUT THIS IS *MY* BATTLE.
THE MATTER IS CLOSED.
NO.
NO, IT'S NOT.

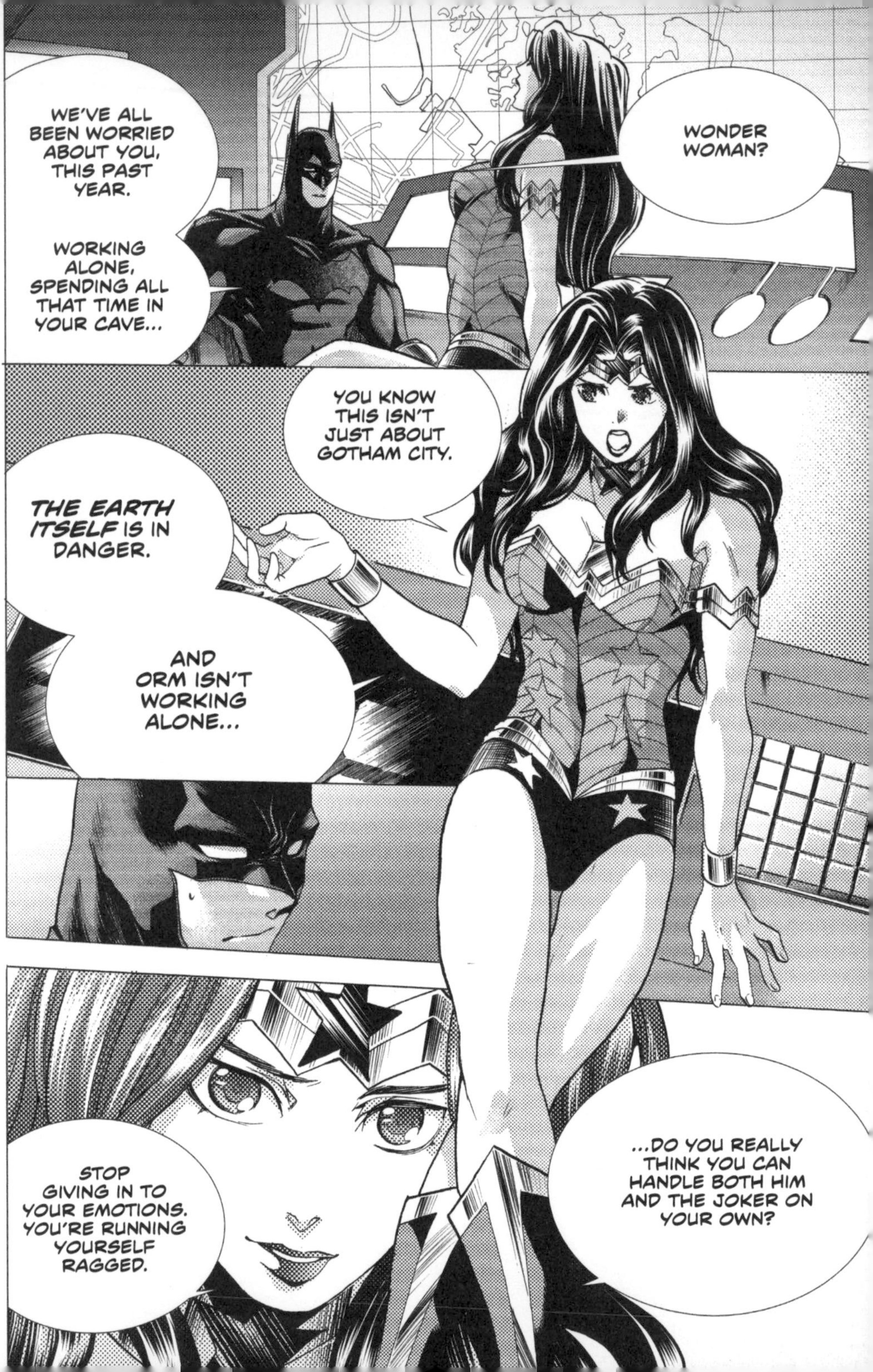
WONDER WOMAN?
WE'VE ALL BEEN WORRIED ABOUT YOU, THIS PAST YEAR.
WORKING ALONE, SPENDING ALL THAT TIME IN YOUR CAVE...
YOU KNOW THIS ISN'T JUST ABOUT GOTHAM CITY.
THE EARTH ITSELF IS IN DANGER.
AND ORM ISN'T WORKING ALONE...
...DO YOU REALLY THINK YOU CAN HANDLE BOTH HIM AND THE JOKER ON YOUR OWN?
STOP GIVING IN TO YOUR EMOTIONS. YOU'RE RUNNING YOURSELF RAGGED.

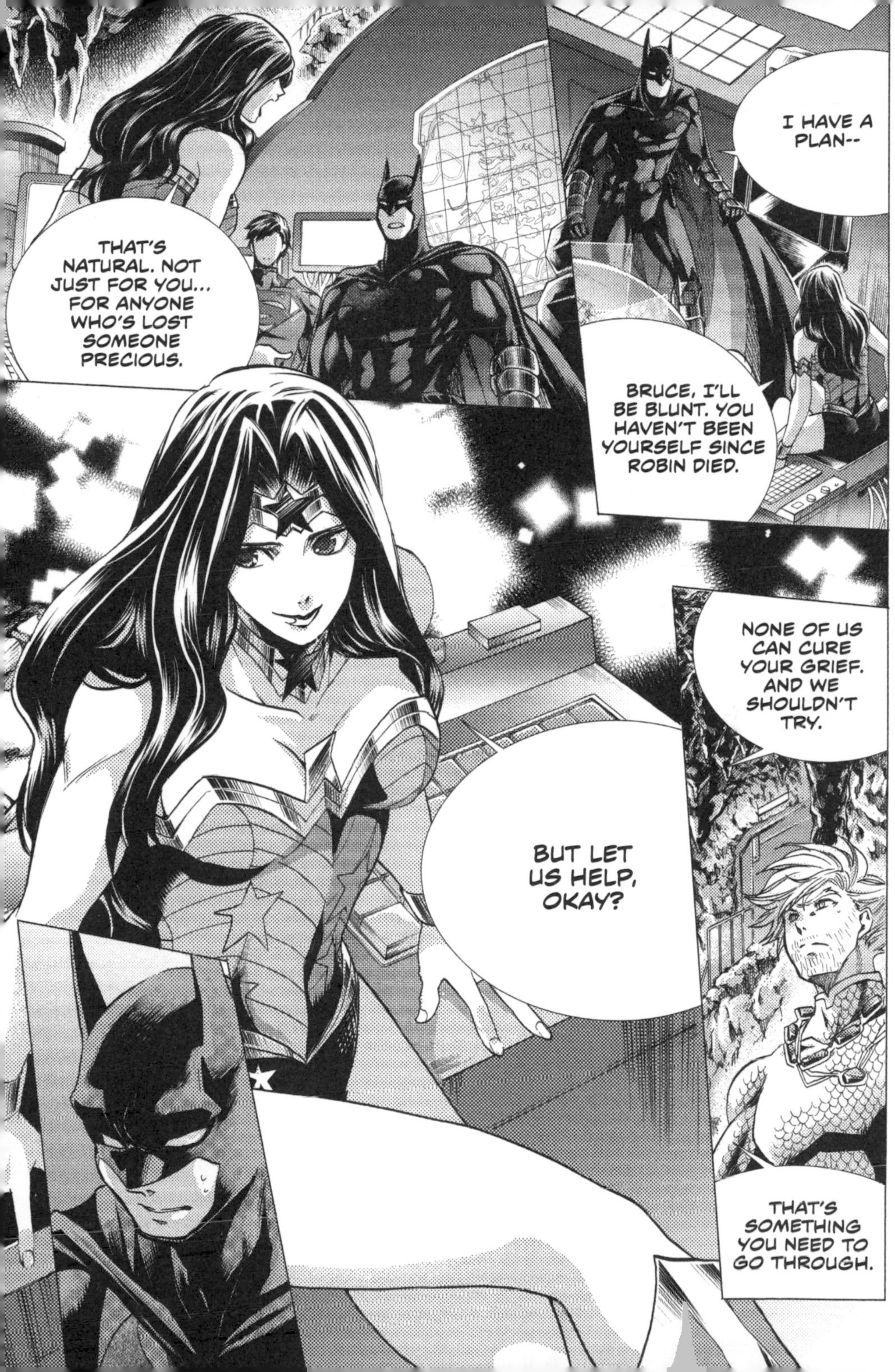
I HAVE A PLAN--
BRUCE, I'LL BE BLUNT. YOU HAVEN'T BEEN YOURSELF SINCE ROBIN DIED.
THAT'S NATURAL. NOT JUST FOR YOU... FOR ANYONE WHO'S LOST SOMEONE PRECIOUS.
NONE OF US CAN CURE YOUR GRIEF. AND WE SHOULDN'T TRY.
THAT'S SOMETHING YOU NEED TO GO THROUGH.
BUT LET US HELP, OKAY?

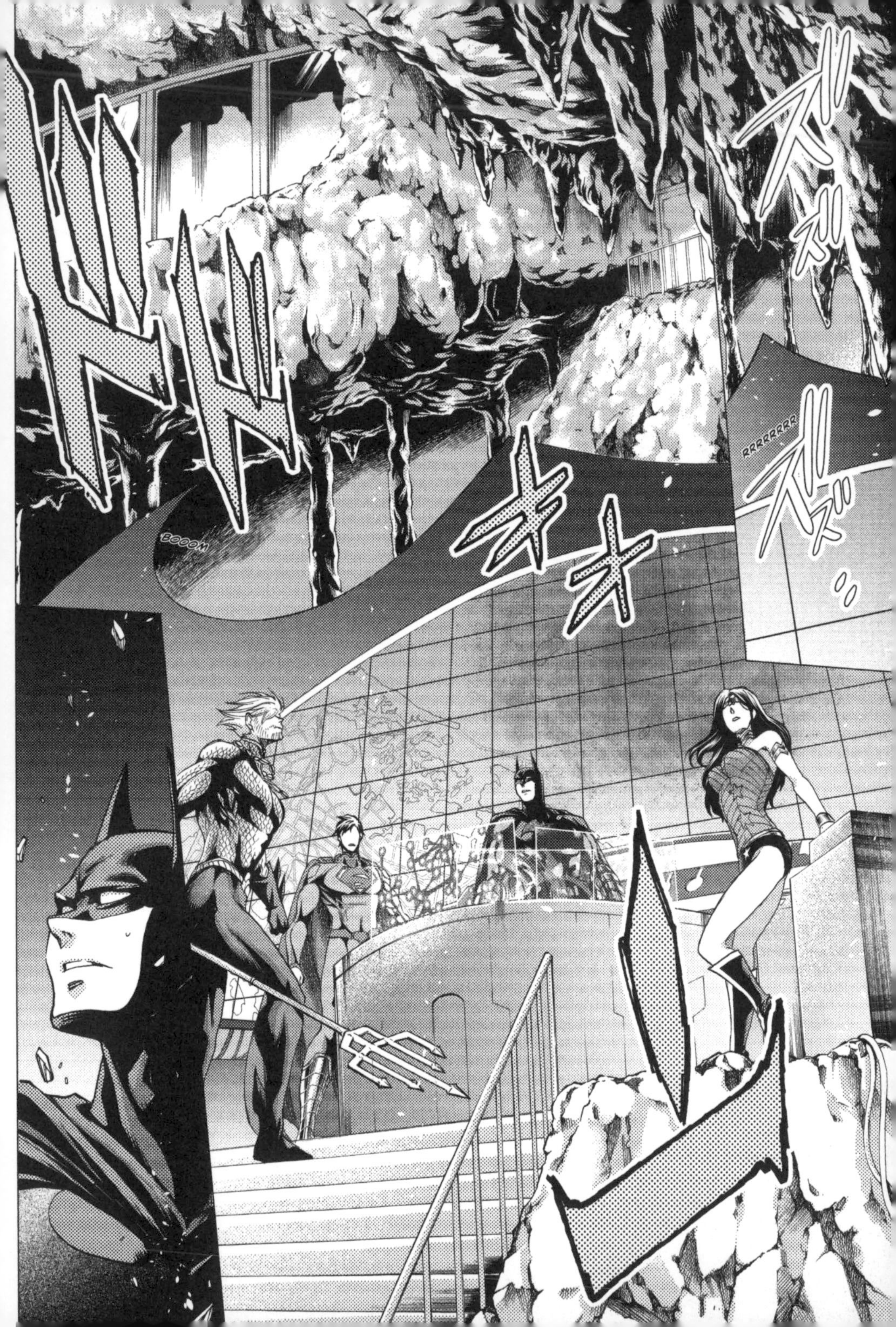
RRRRRRRR
BOOOM

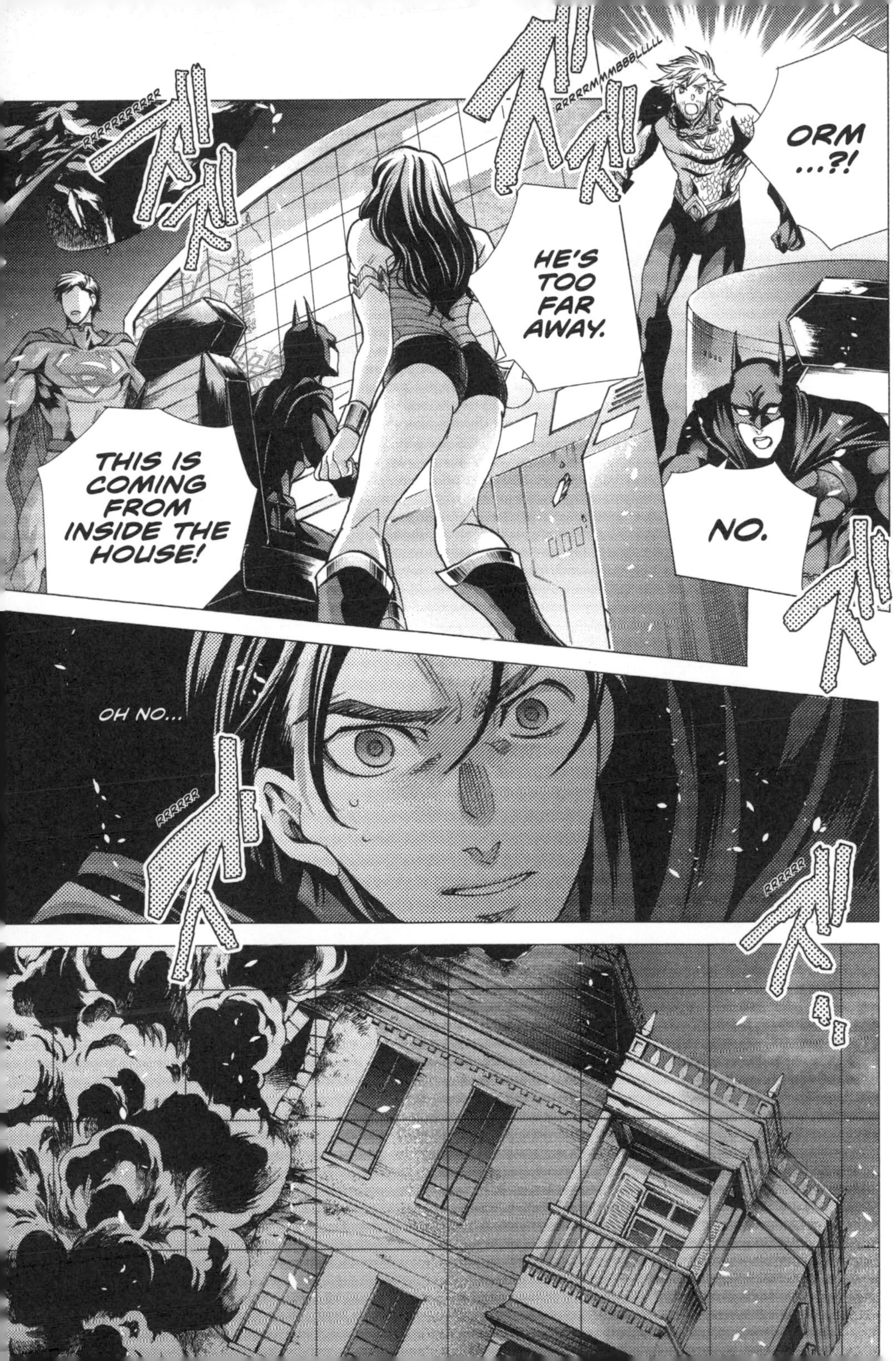
RRRRRMMMMBBBLLLLL
RRRRRRRRRRR
ORM ...?!
HE'S TOO FAR AWAY.
NO.
THIS IS COMING FROM INSIDE THE HOUSE!
RRRRRR
OH NO...
RRRRRR

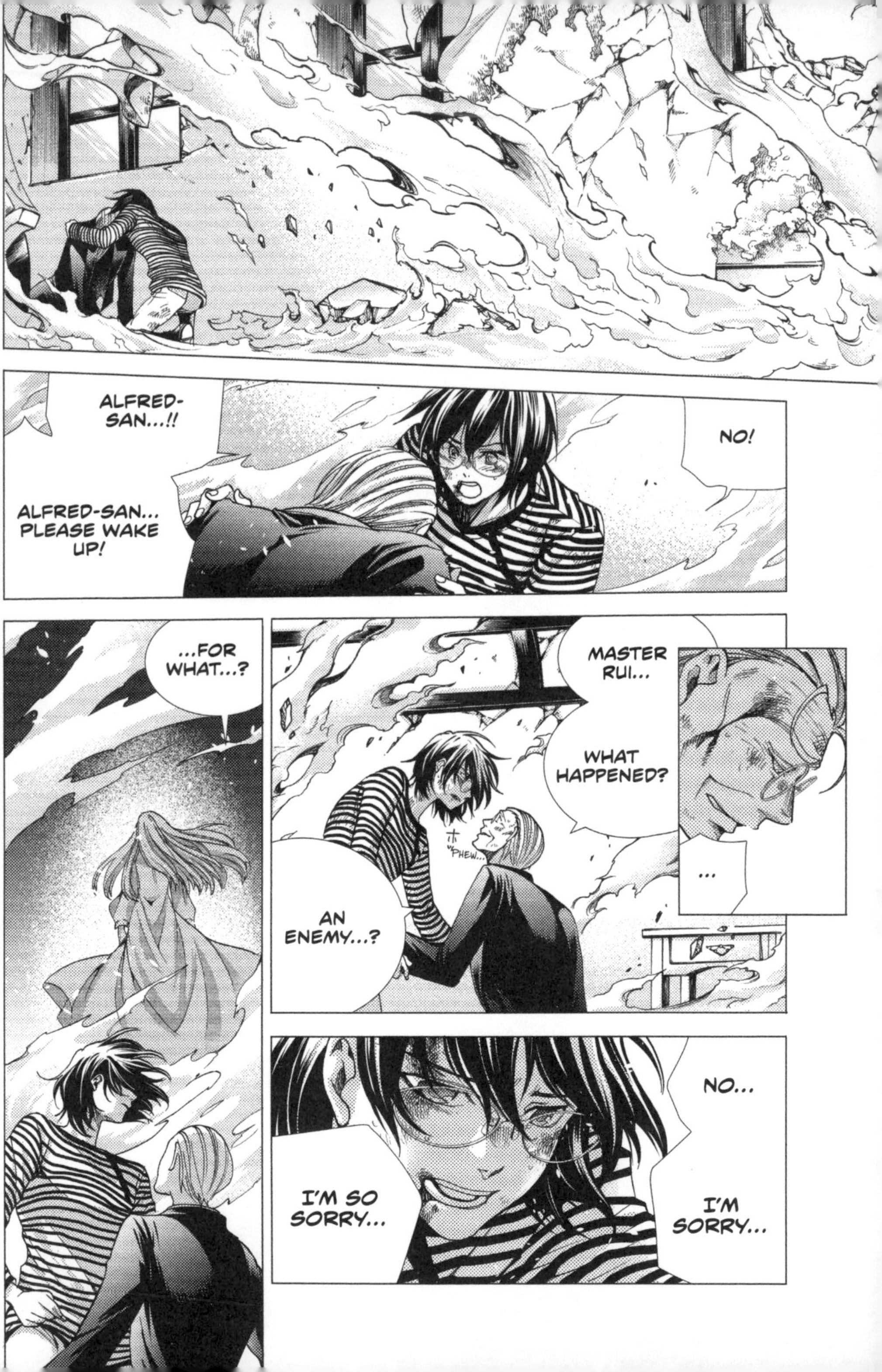
ALFRED-SAN...!!
NO!
ALFRED-SAN... PLEASE WAKE UP!
MASTER RUI...
WHAT HAPPENED?
PHEW...
AN ENEMY...?
...
NO...
I'M SORRY...
I'M SO SORRY...
...FOR WHAT...?

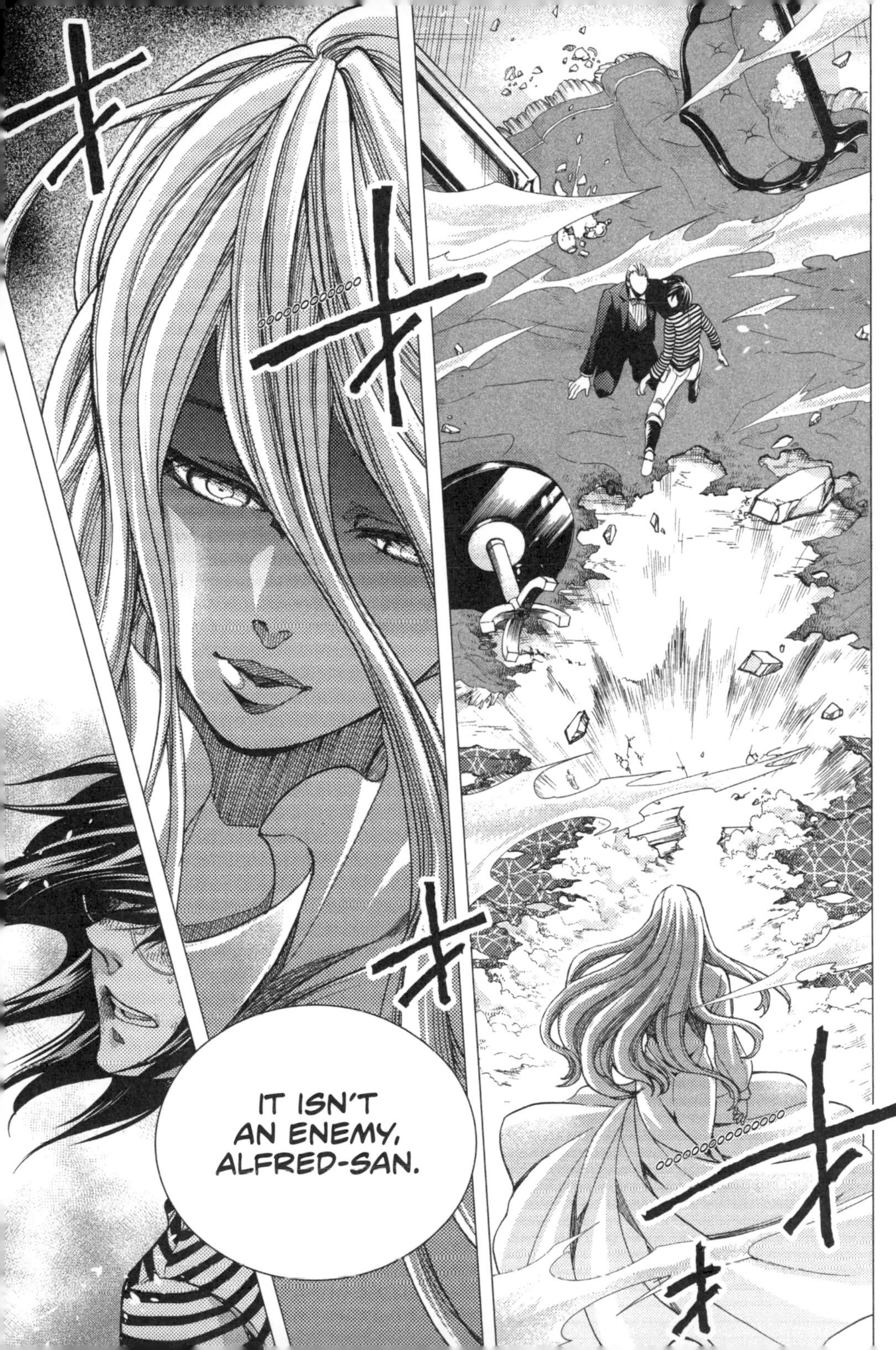
IT ISN'T AN ENEMY, ALFRED-SAN.

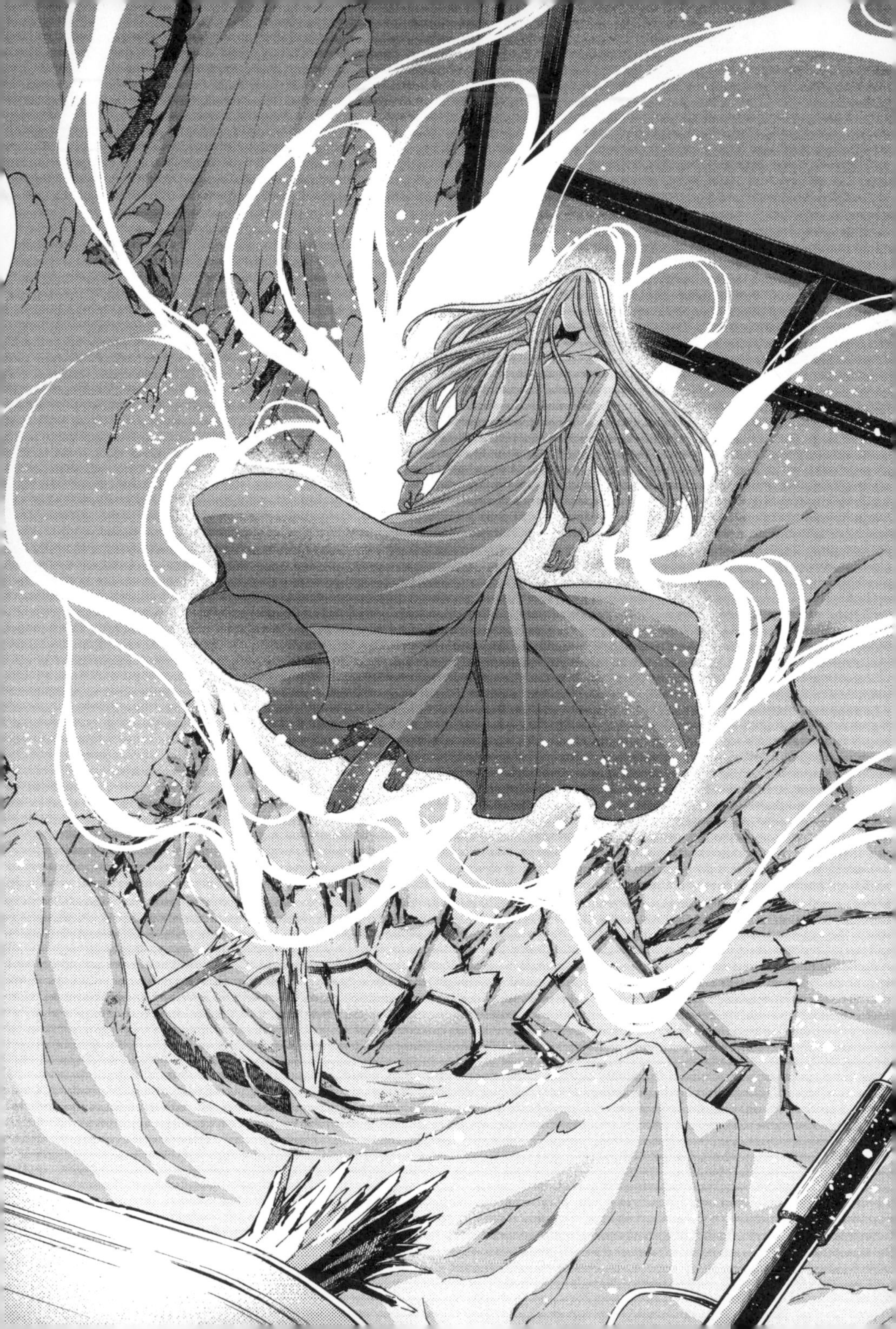

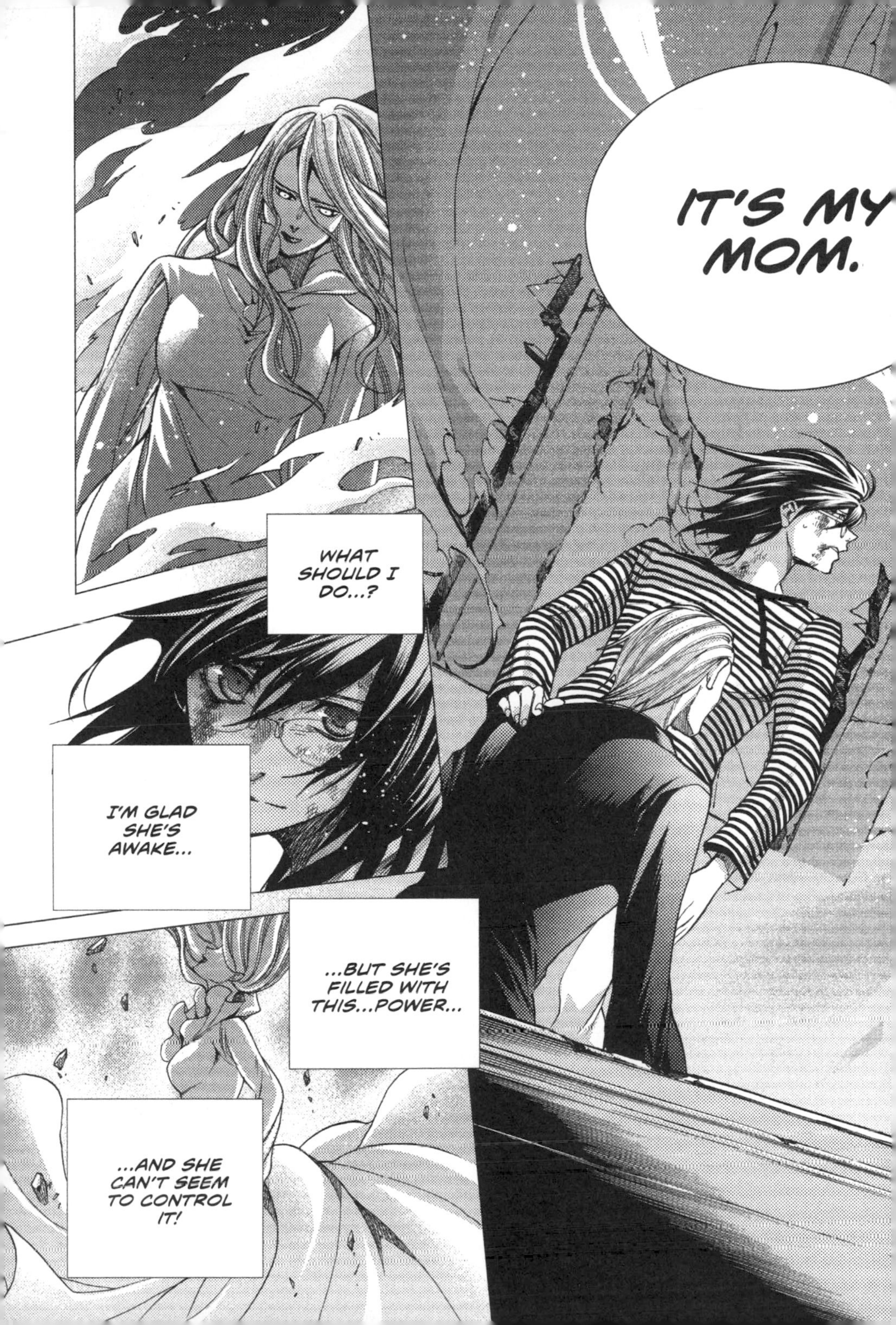
IT'S MY MOM.
WHAT SHOULD I DO...?
I'M GLAD SHE'S AWAKE...
...BUT SHE'S FILLED WITH THIS...POWER...
...AND SHE CAN'T SEEM TO CONTROL IT!

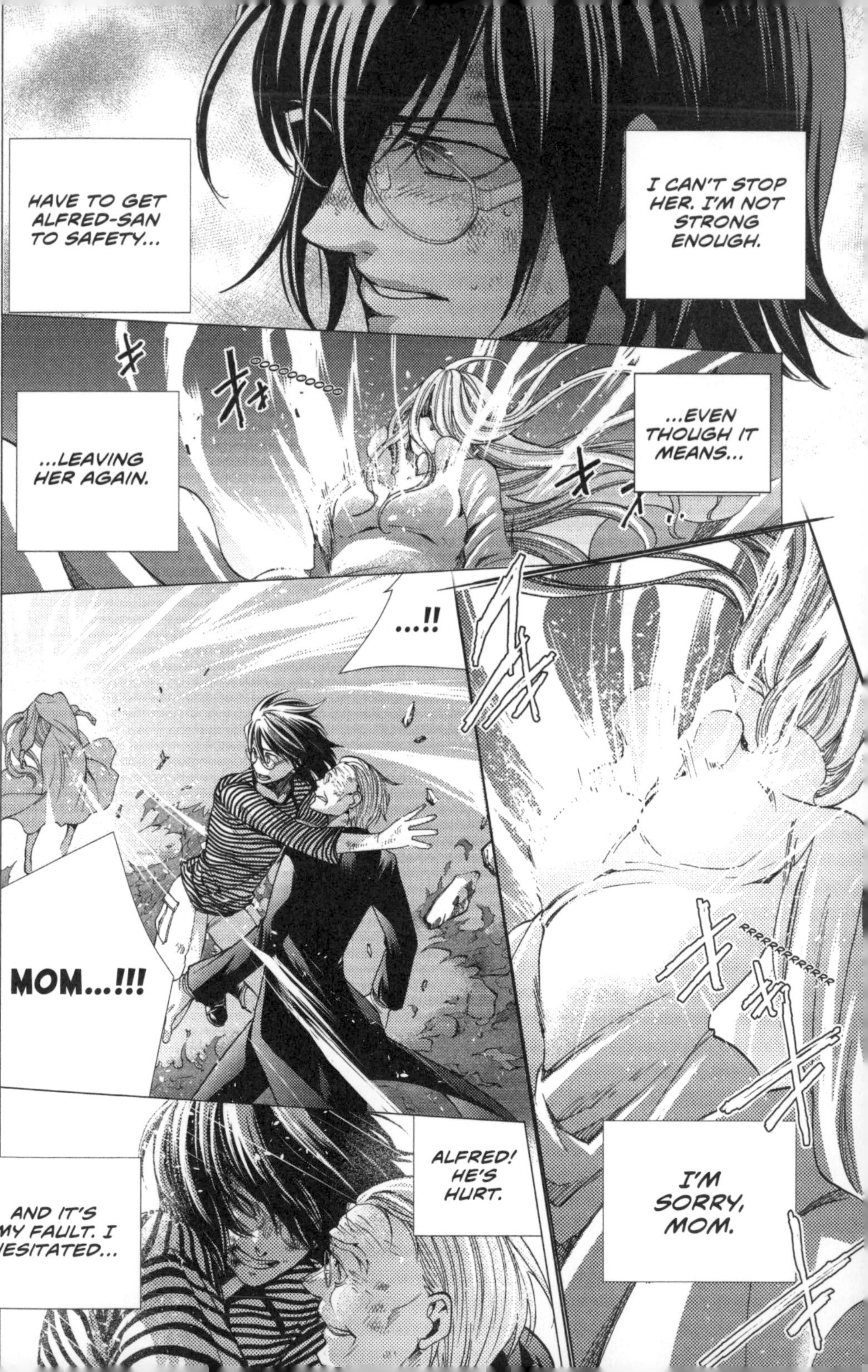
I CAN'T STOP HER. I'M NOT STRONG ENOUGH.
HAVE TO GET ALFRED-SAN TO SAFETY...
...EVEN THOUGH IT MEANS...
...LEAVING HER AGAIN.
I'M SORRY, MOM.
...!!
MOM...!!!
ALFRED! HE'S HURT.
AND IT'S MY FAULT. I HESITATED...

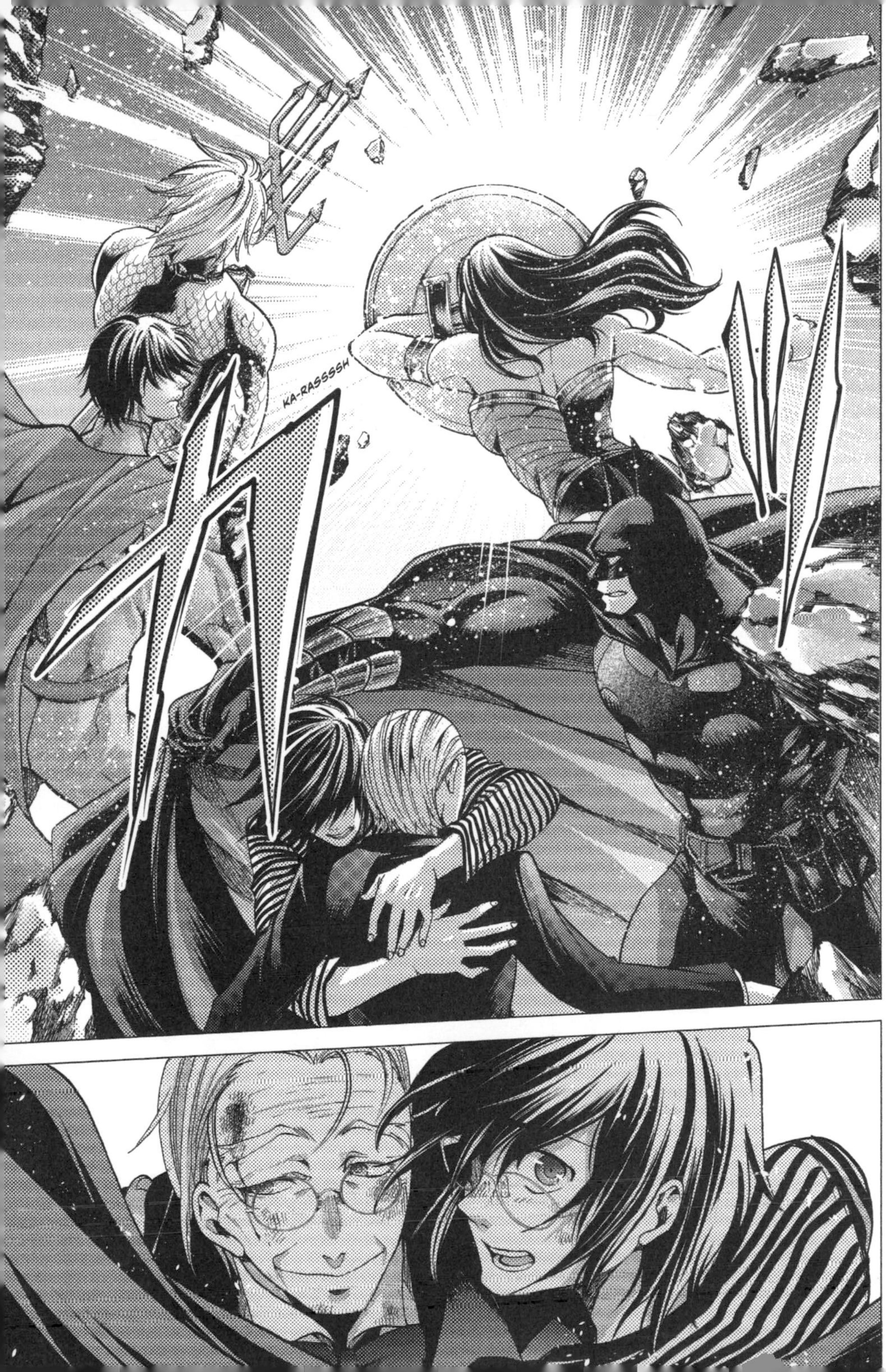
KA-RASSSSH

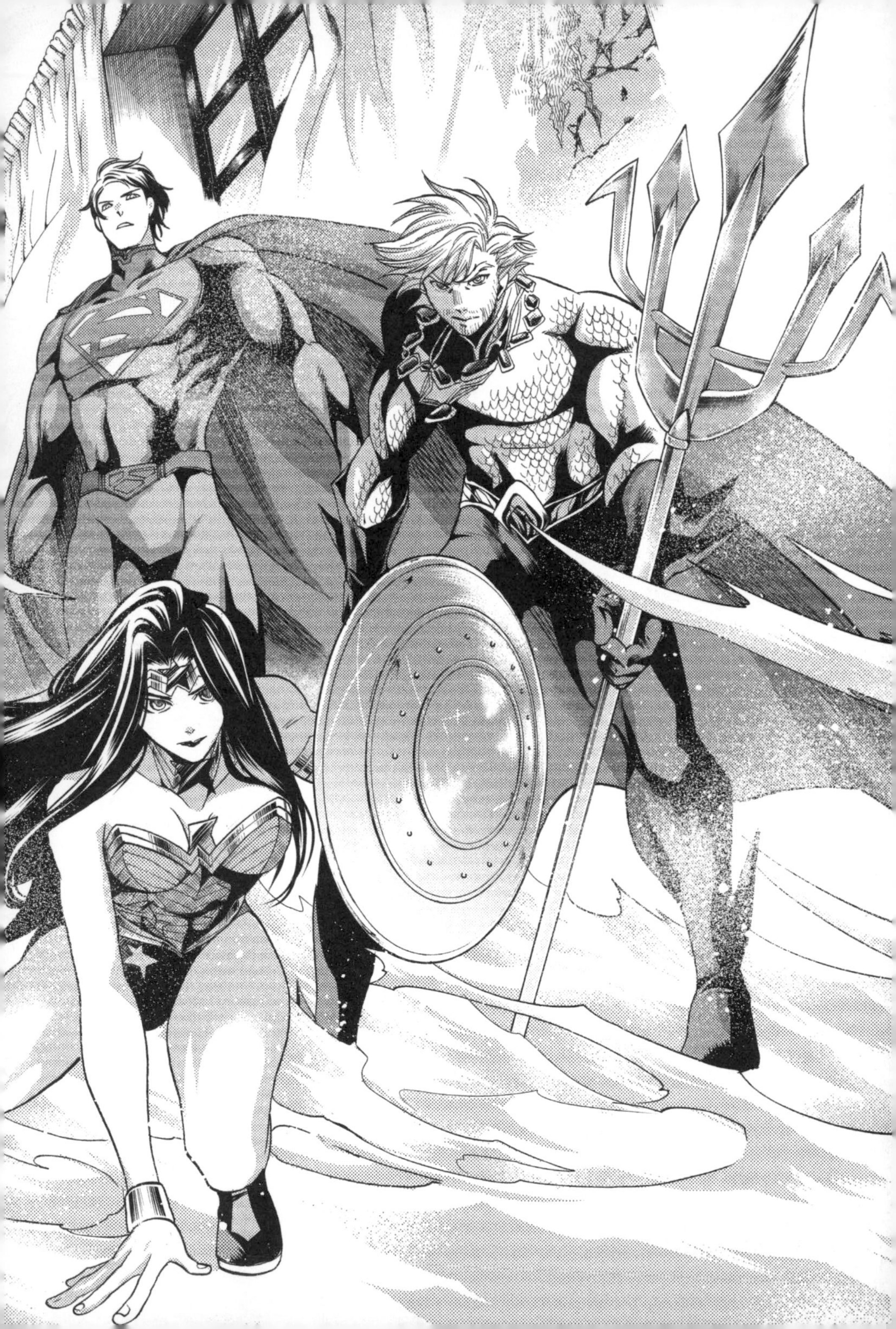

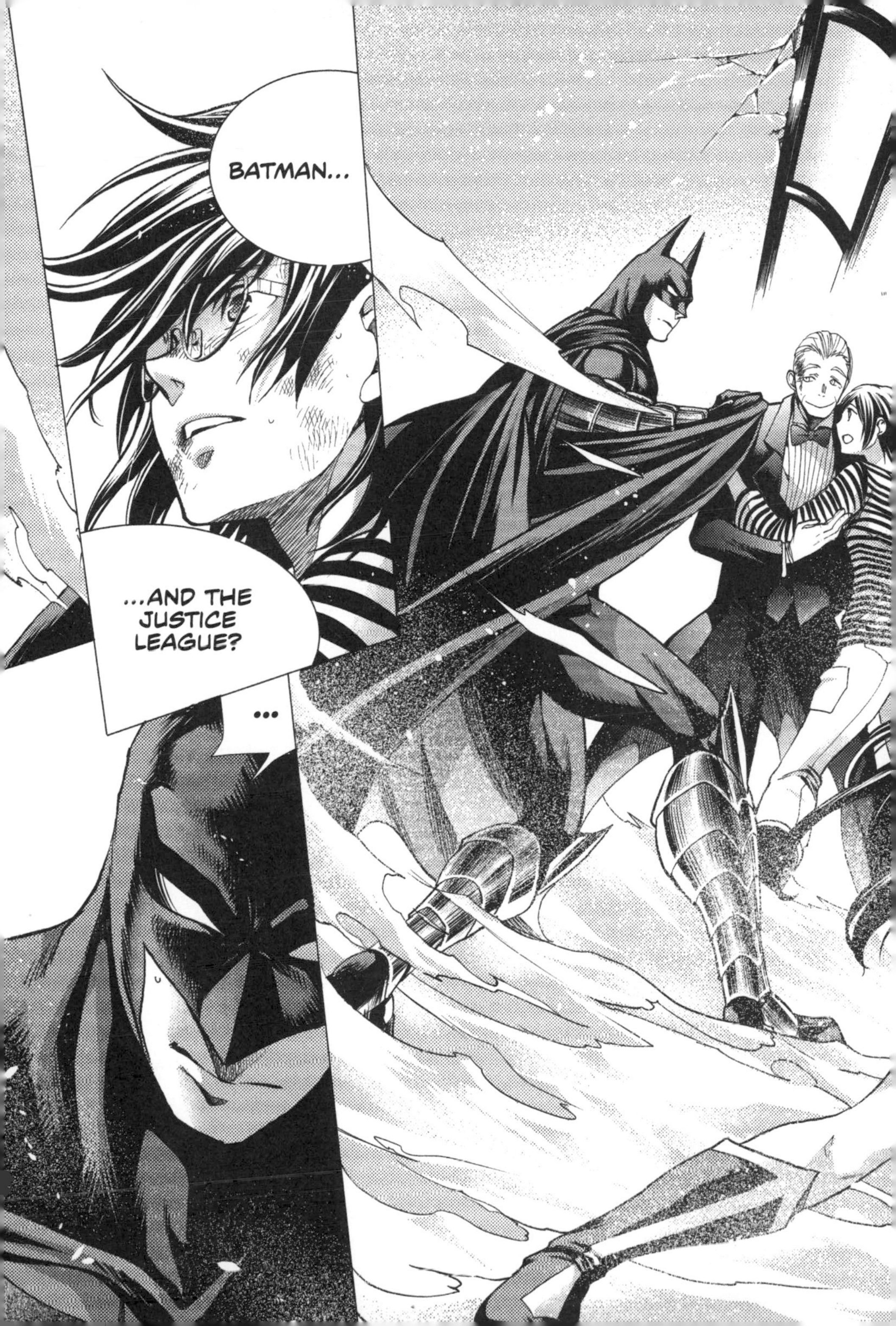
BATMAN...
...AND THE JUSTICE LEAGUE?
...

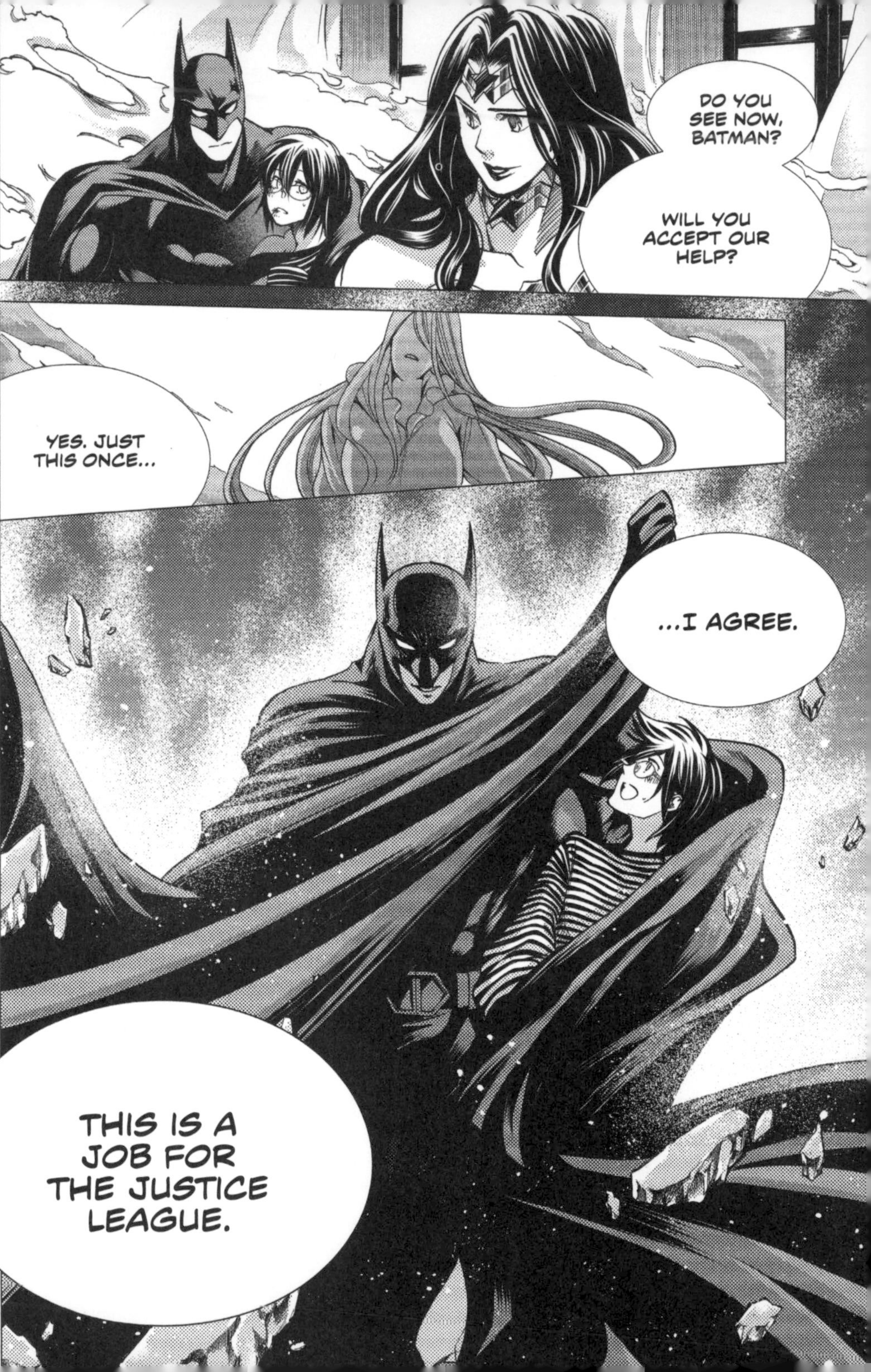
DO YOU SEE NOW, BATMAN?
WILL YOU ACCEPT OUR HELP?
YES. JUST THIS ONCE...
...I AGREE.
THIS IS A JOB FOR THE JUSTICE LEAGUE.

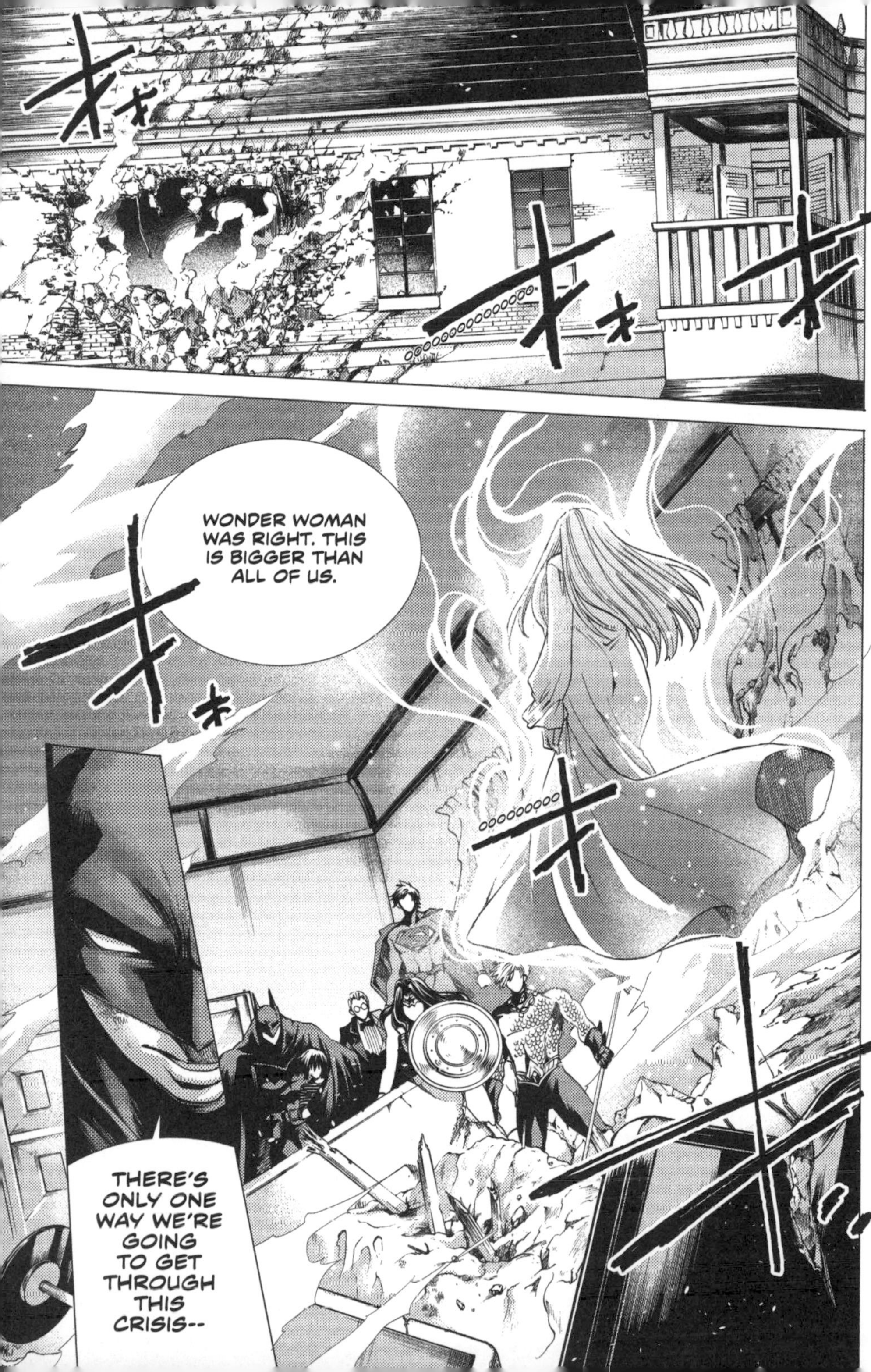
WONDER WOMAN WAS RIGHT. THIS IS BIGGER THAN ALL OF US.
THERE'S ONLY ONE WAY WE'RE GOING TO GET THROUGH THIS CRISIS--

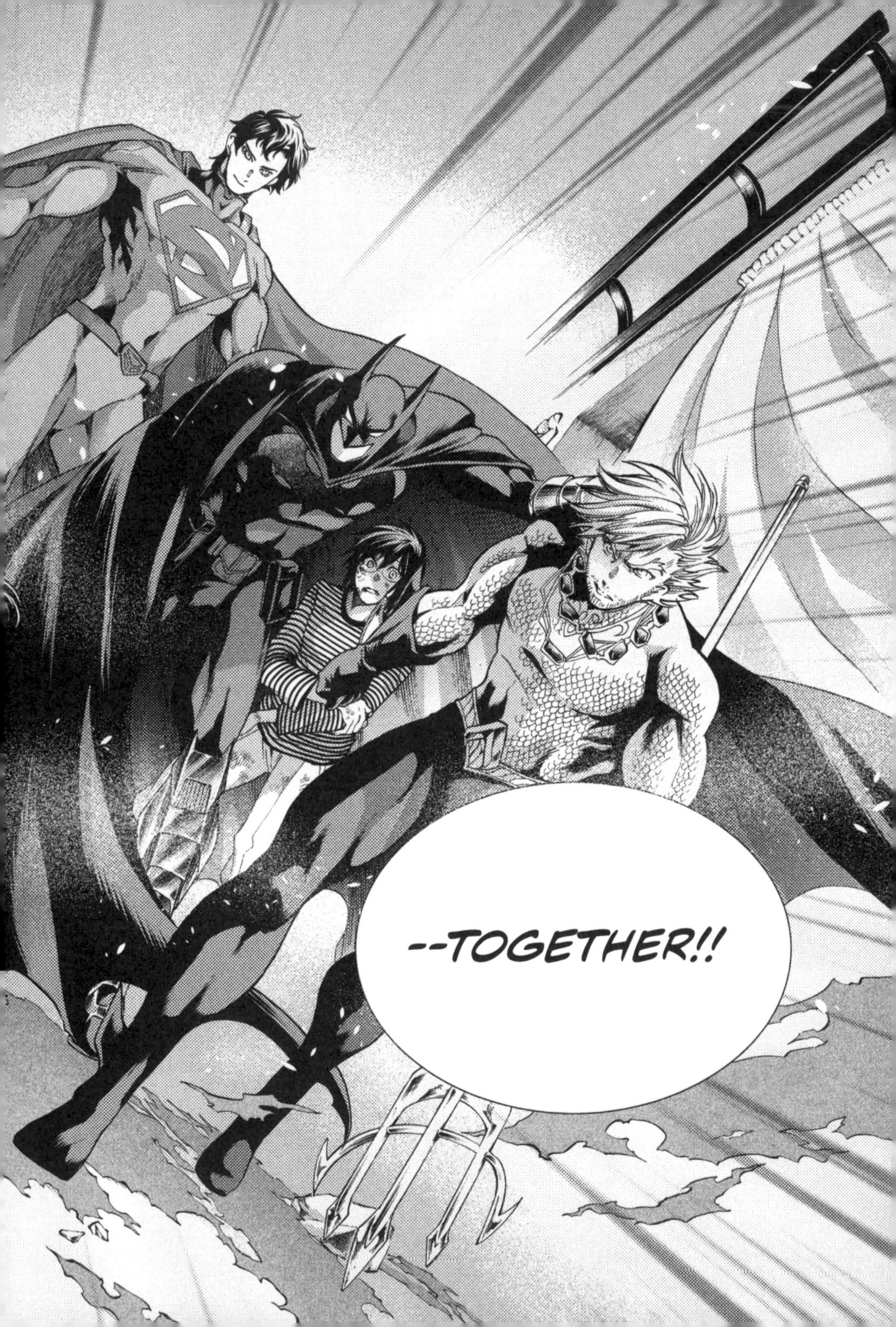
--TOGETHER!!

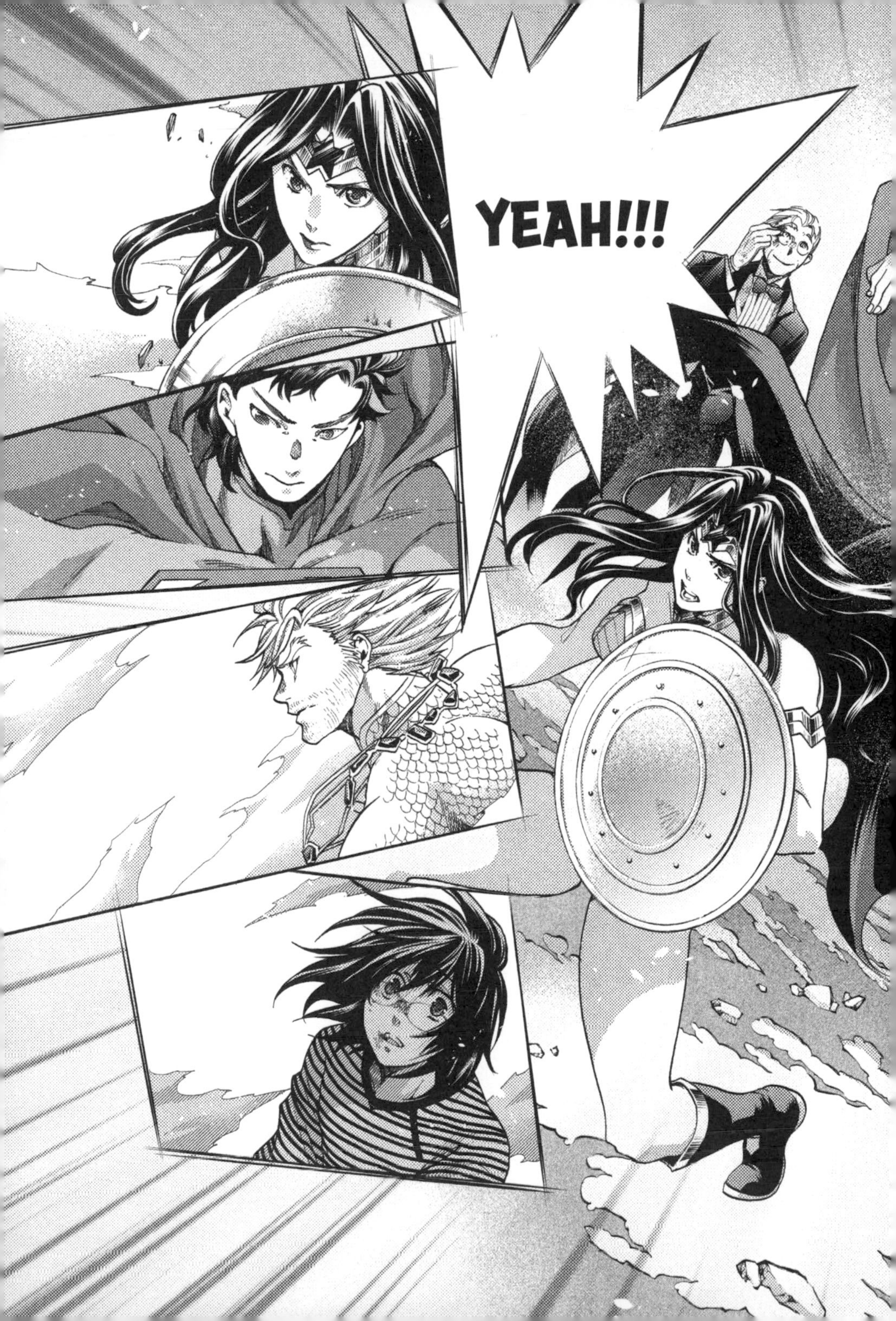
YEAH!!!

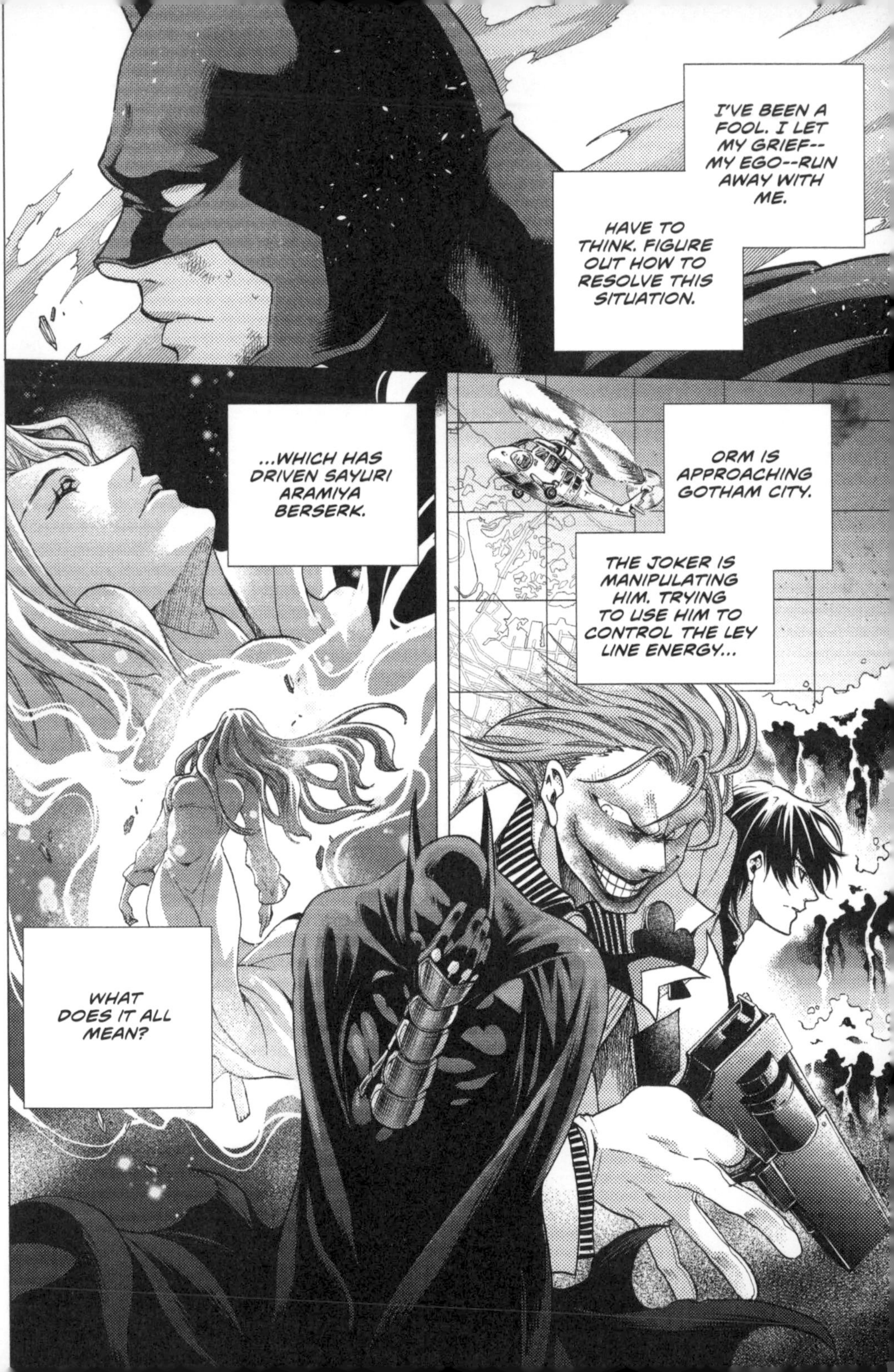
I'VE BEEN A FOOL. I LET MY GRIEF-- MY EGO--RUN AWAY WITH ME.
HAVE TO THINK. FIGURE OUT HOW TO RESOLVE THIS SITUATION.
ORM IS APPROACHING GOTHAM CITY.
THE JOKER IS MANIPULATING HIM. TRYING TO USE HIM TO CONTROL THE LEY LINE ENERGY...
...WHICH HAS DRIVEN SAYURI ARAMIYA BERSERK.
WHAT DOES IT ALL MEAN?

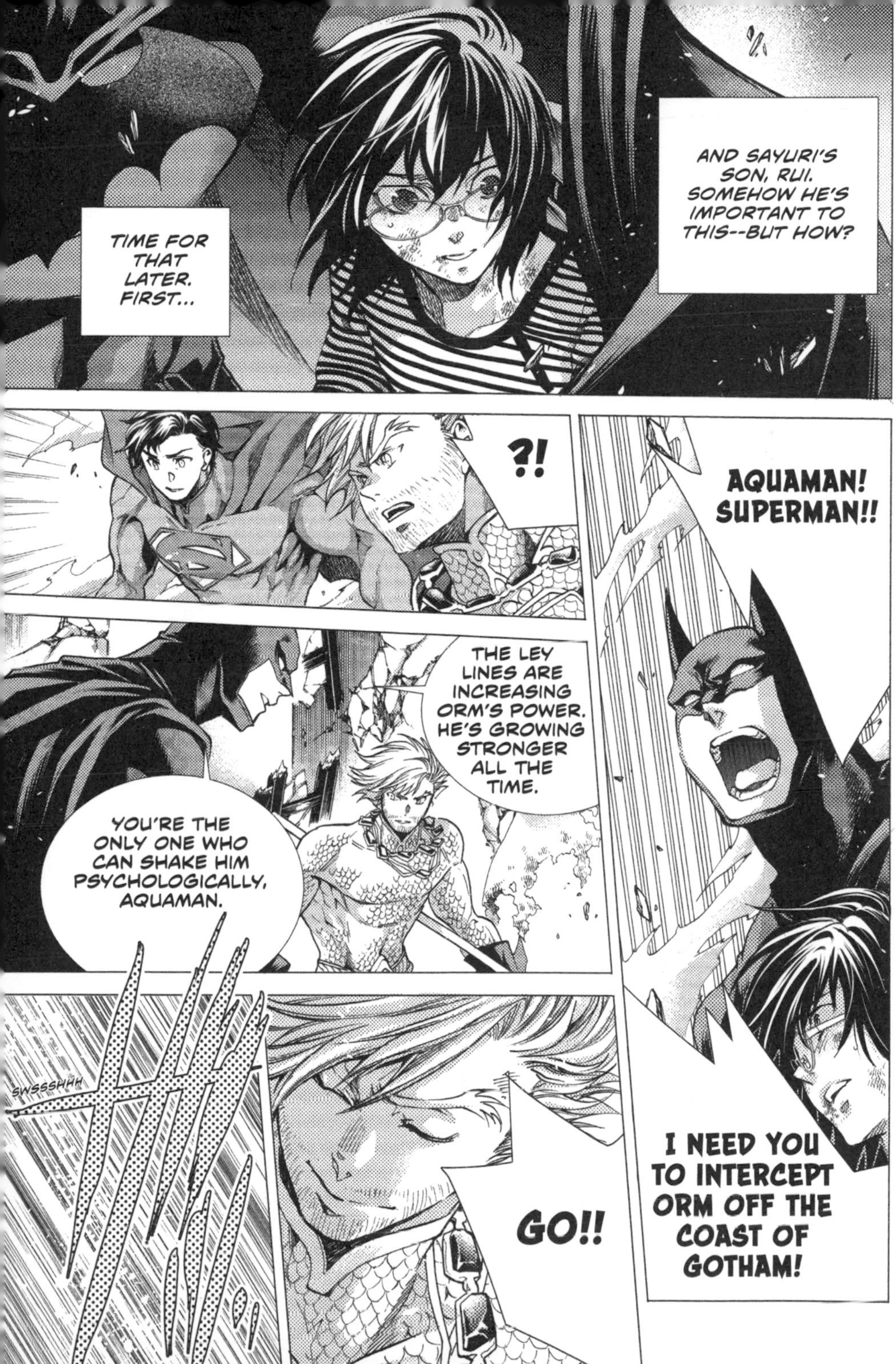
AND SAYURI'S SON, RUI. SOMEHOW HE'S IMPORTANT TO THIS--BUT HOW?
TIME FOR THAT LATER. FIRST...
AQUAMAN! SUPERMAN!!
I NEED YOU TO INTERCEPT ORM OFF THE COAST OF GOTHAM!
?!
THE LEY LINES ARE INCREASING ORM'S POWER. HE'S GROWING STRONGER ALL THE TIME.
YOU'RE THE ONLY ONE WHO CAN SHAKE HIM PSYCHOLOGICALLY, AQUAMAN.
GO!!
SWSSSHHH

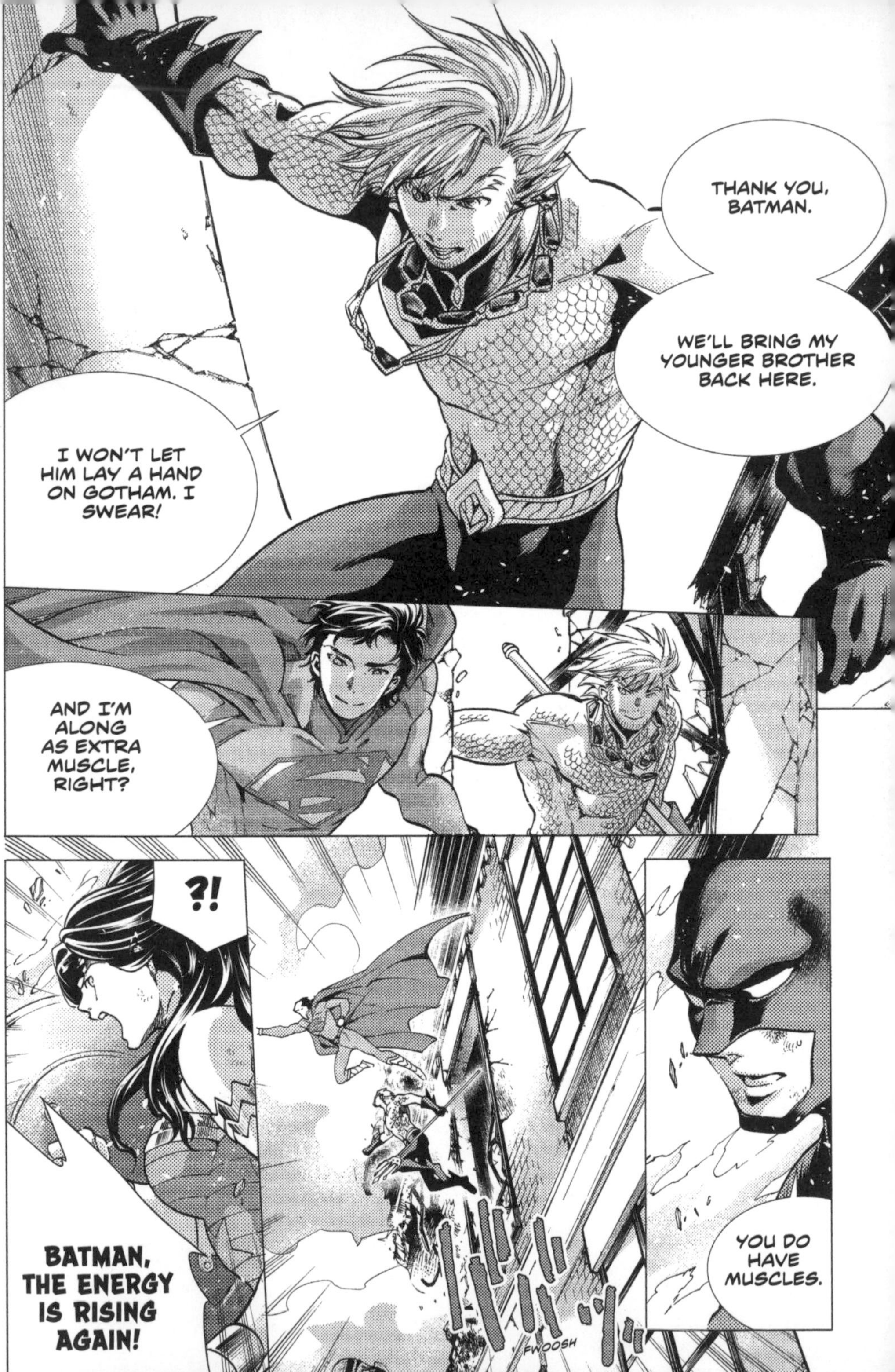
THANK YOU, BATMAN.
WE'LL BRING MY YOUNGER BROTHER BACK HERE.
I WON'T LET HIM LAY A HAND ON GOTHAM. I SWEAR!
AND I'M ALONG AS EXTRA MUSCLE, RIGHT?
YOU DO HAVE MUSCLES.
FWOOSH
?!
BATMAN, THE ENERGY IS RISING AGAIN!

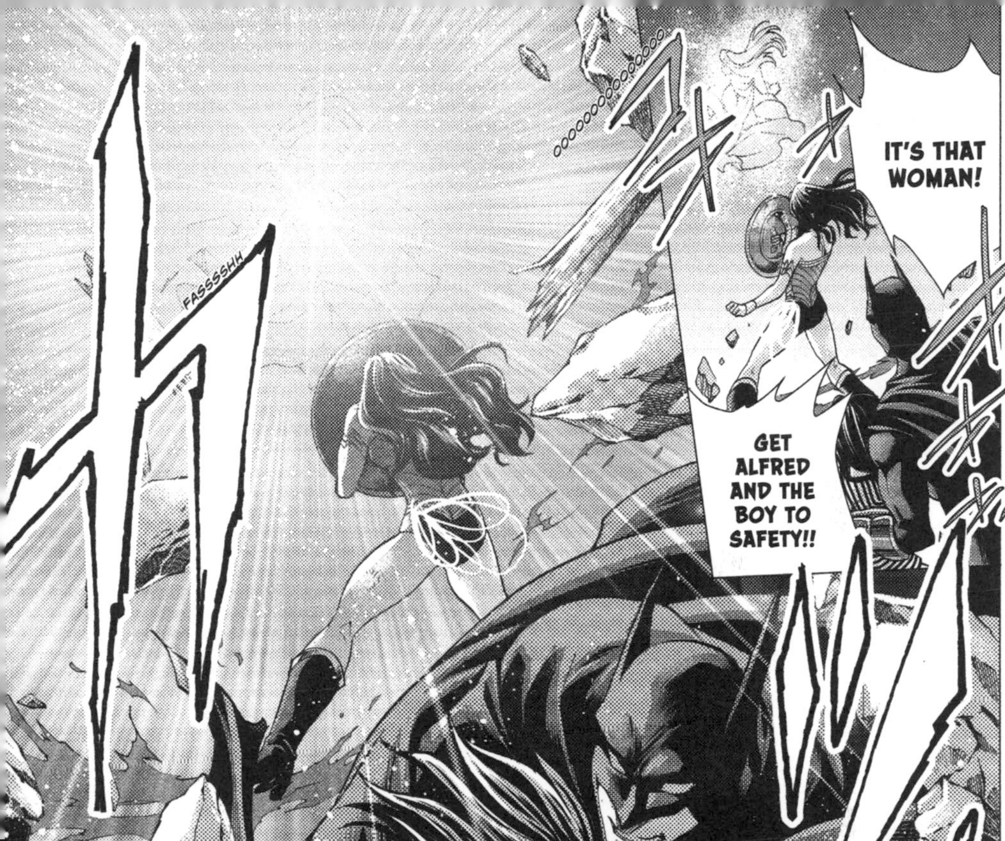
IT'S THAT WOMAN!
GET ALFRED AND THE BOY TO SAFETY!!
FASSSSHH

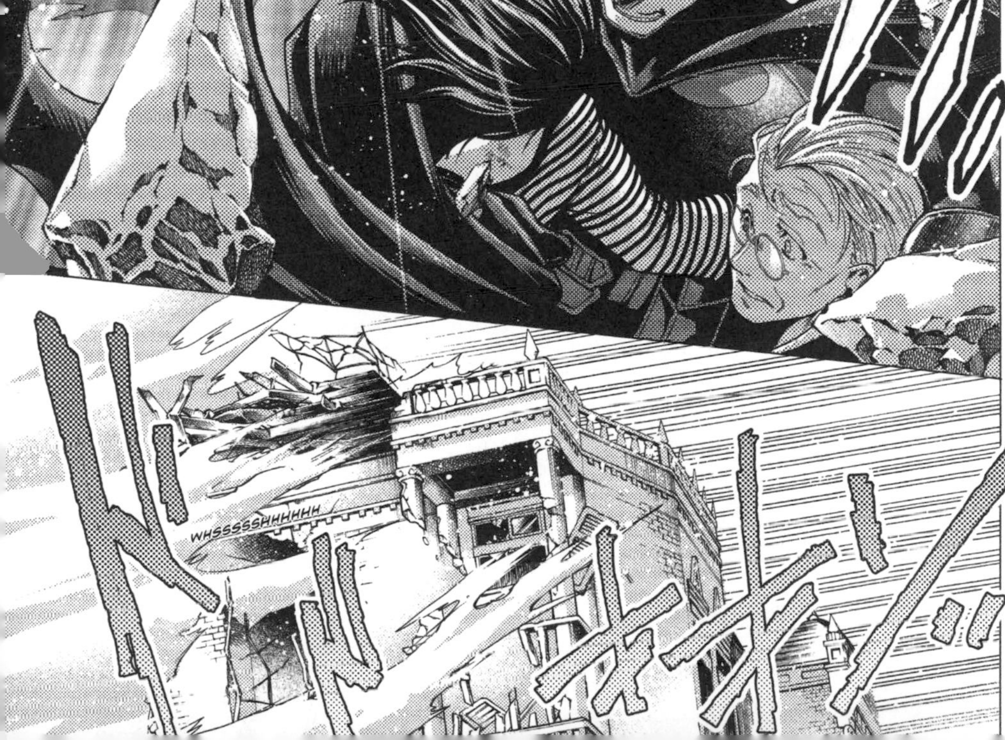
WHSSSSSHHHHHH

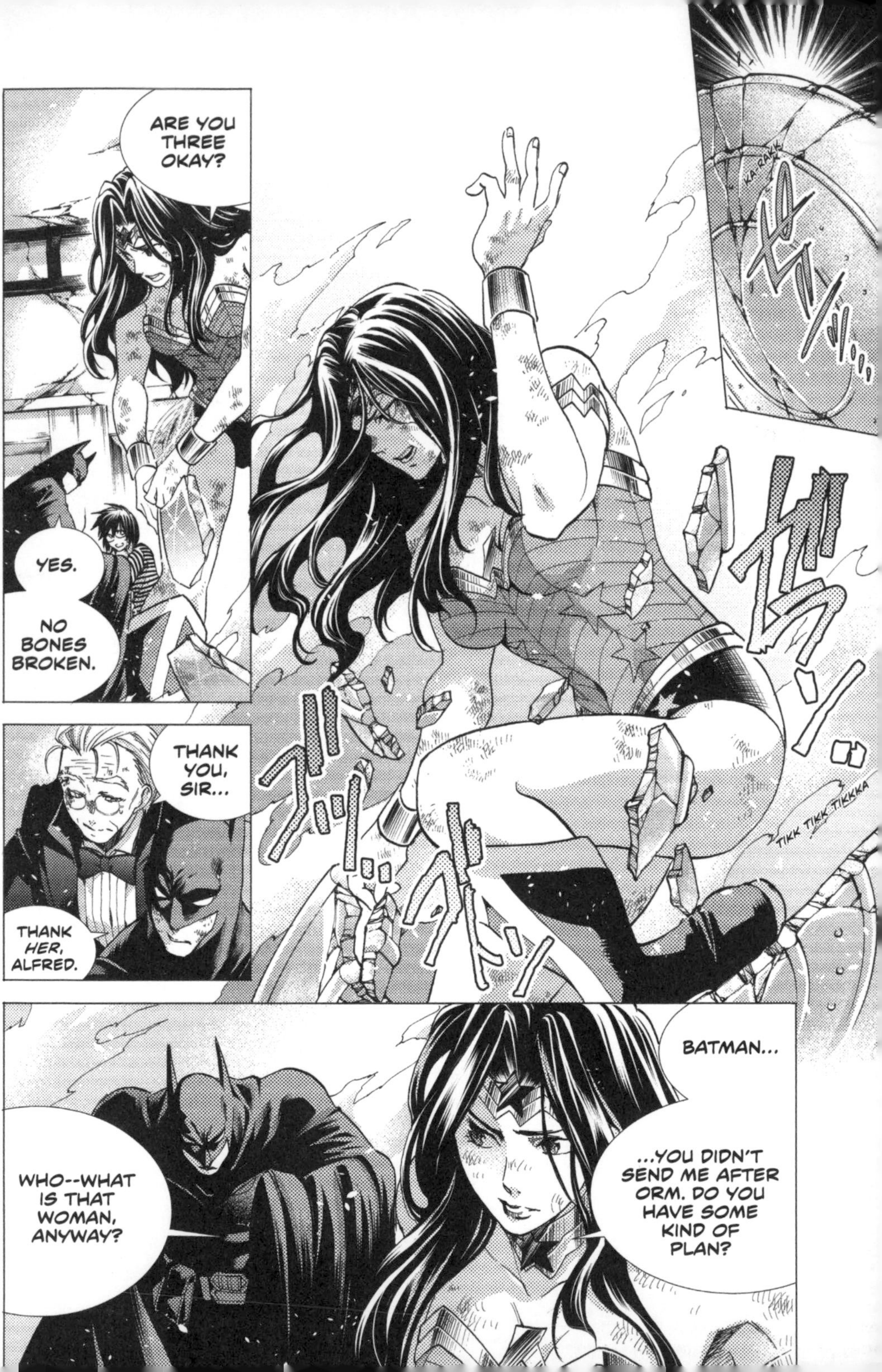
KA-RAKK
TIKK TIKK TIKKA
ARE YOU THREE OKAY?
YES.
NO BONES BROKEN.
THANK YOU, SIR...
THANK HER, ALFRED.
BATMAN...
...YOU DIDN'T SEND ME AFTER ORM. DO YOU HAVE SOME KIND OF PLAN?
WHO--WHAT IS THAT WOMAN, ANYWAY?

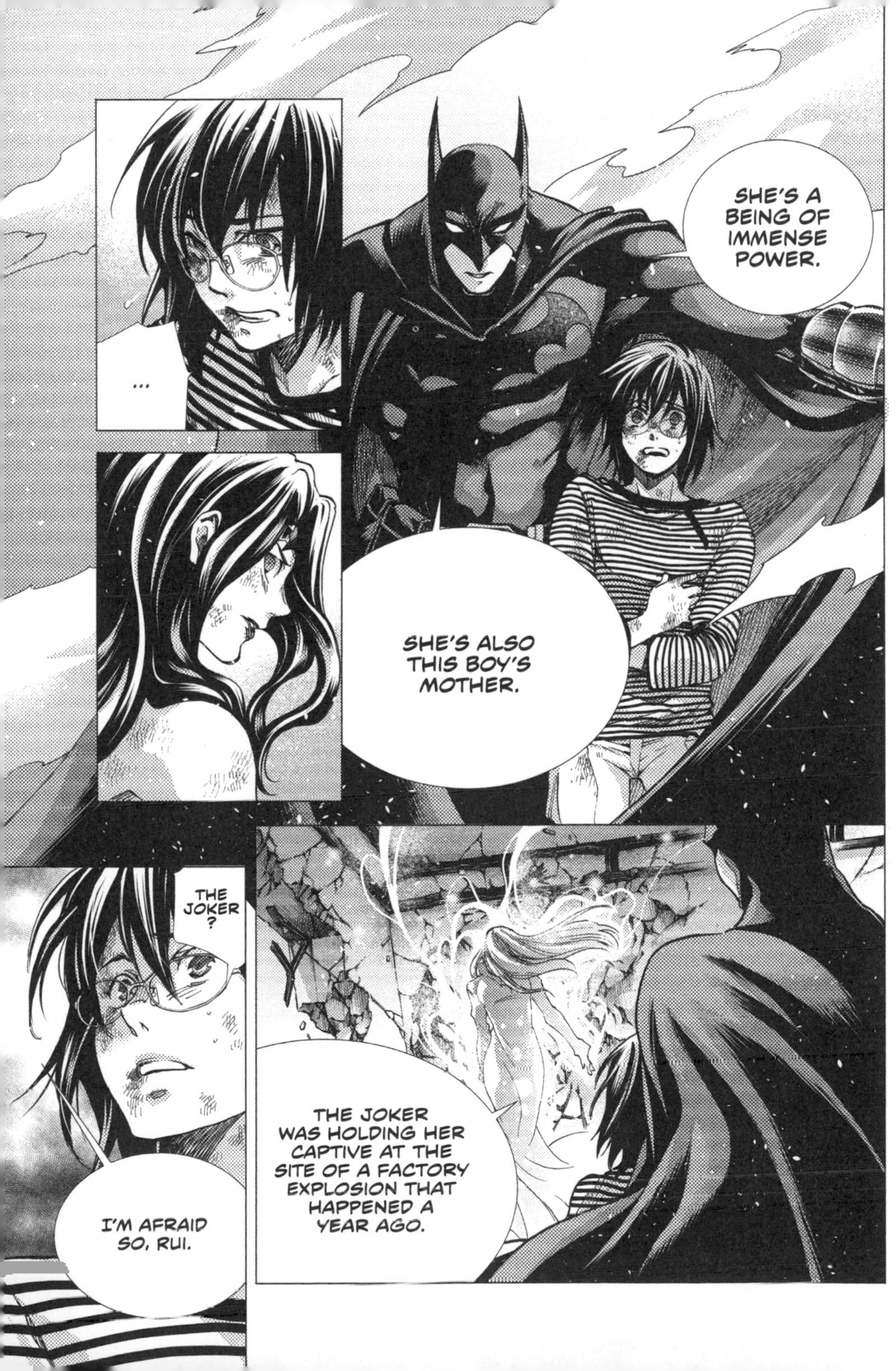
SHE'S A BEING OF IMMENSE POWER.
SHE'S ALSO THIS BOY'S MOTHER.
...
THE JOKER WAS HOLDING HER CAPTIVE AT THE SITE OF A FACTORY EXPLOSION THAT HAPPENED A YEAR AGO.
THE JOKER?
I'M AFRAID SO, RUI.

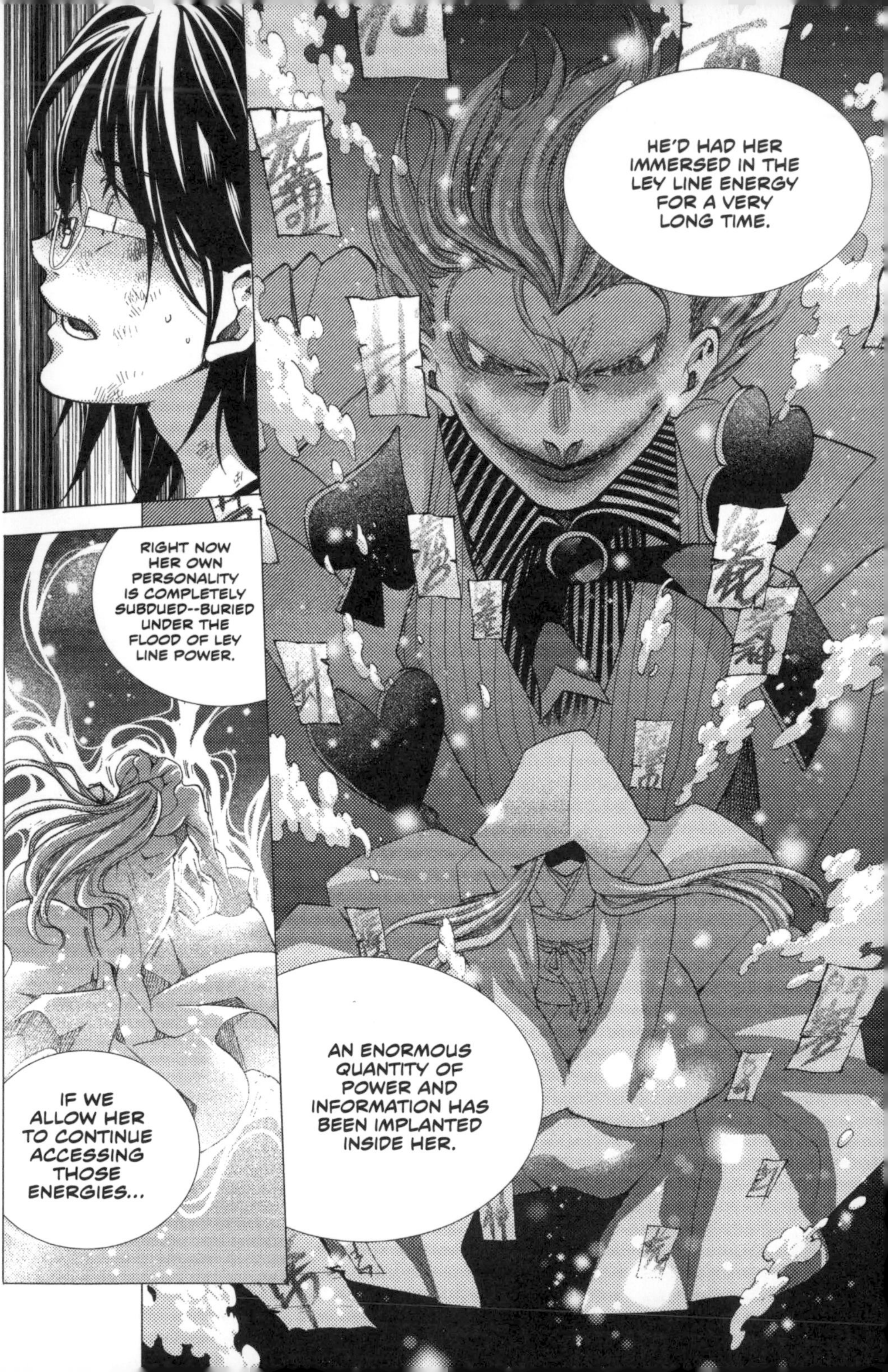
HE'D HAD HER IMMERSED IN THE LEY LINE ENERGY FOR A VERY LONG TIME.
AN ENORMOUS QUANTITY OF POWER AND INFORMATION HAS BEEN IMPLANTED INSIDE HER.
RIGHT NOW HER OWN PERSONALITY IS COMPLETELY SUBDUED--BURIED UNDER THE FLOOD OF LEY LINE POWER.
IF WE ALLOW HER TO CONTINUE ACCESSING THOSE ENERGIES...

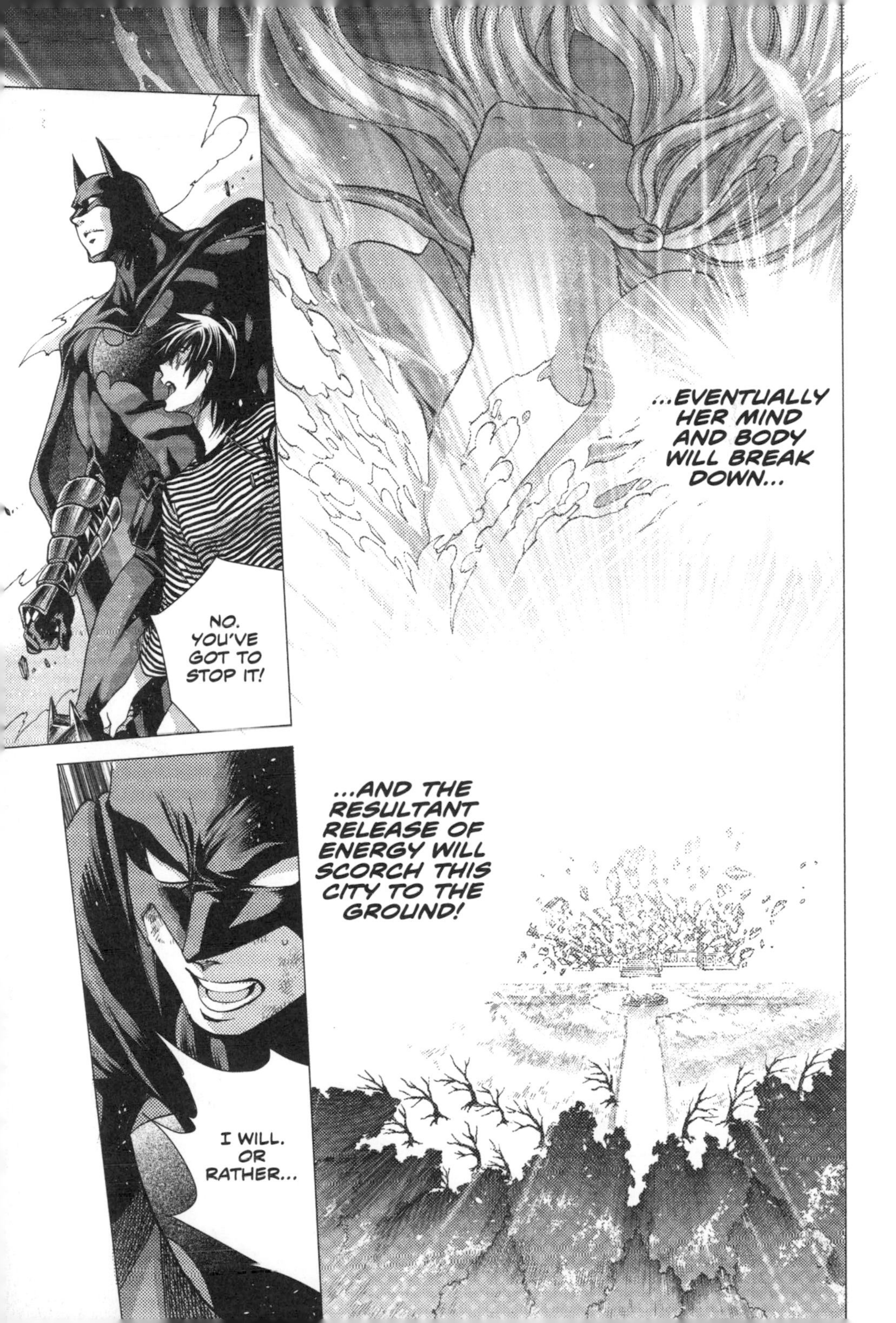
...EVENTUALLY HER MIND AND BODY WILL BREAK DOWN...
...AND THE RESULTANT RELEASE OF ENERGY WILL SCORCH THIS CITY TO THE GROUND!
NO. YOU'VE GOT TO STOP IT!
I WILL. OR RATHER...

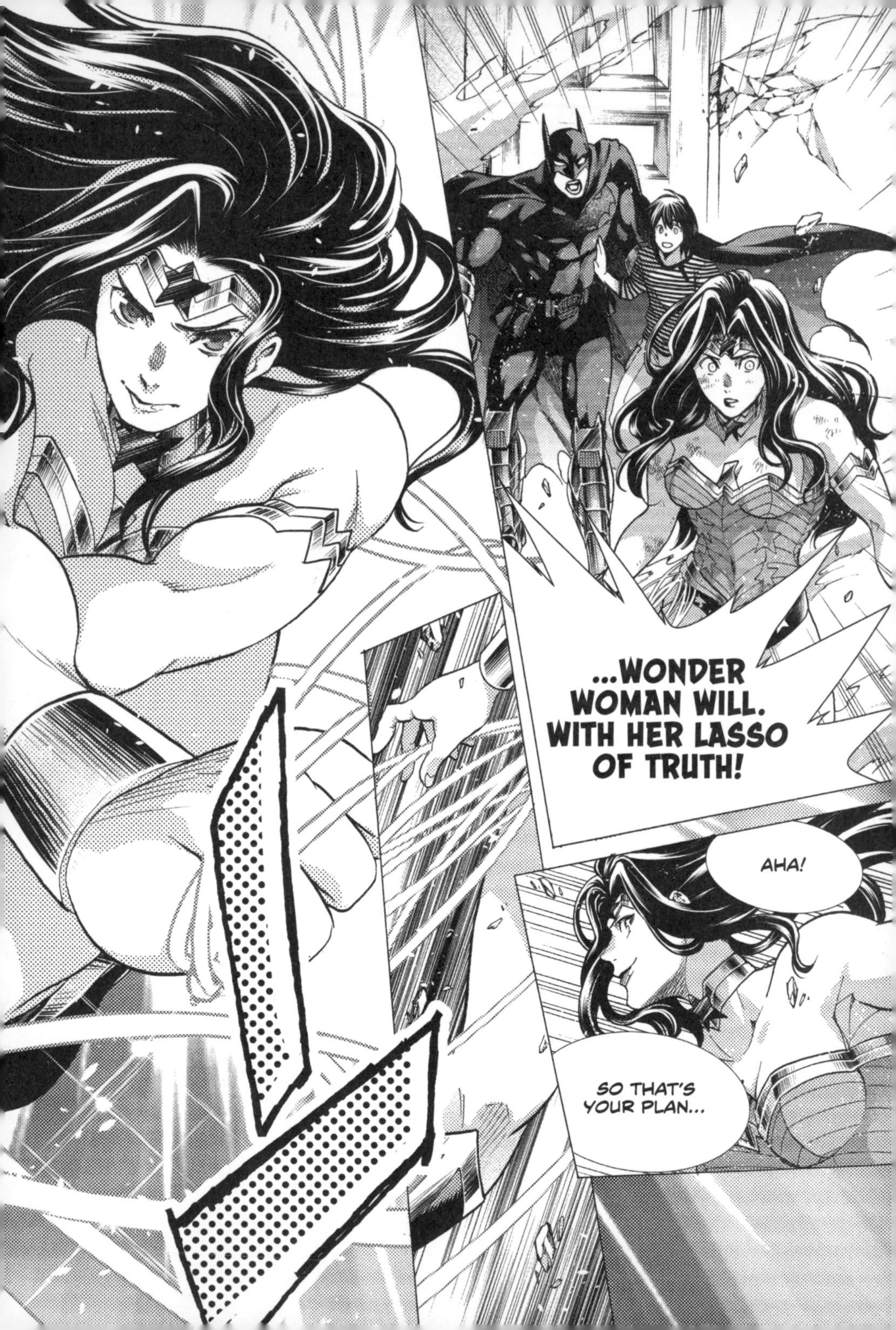
...WONDER WOMAN WILL. WITH HER LASSO OF TRUTH!
AHA!
SO THAT'S YOUR PLAN...

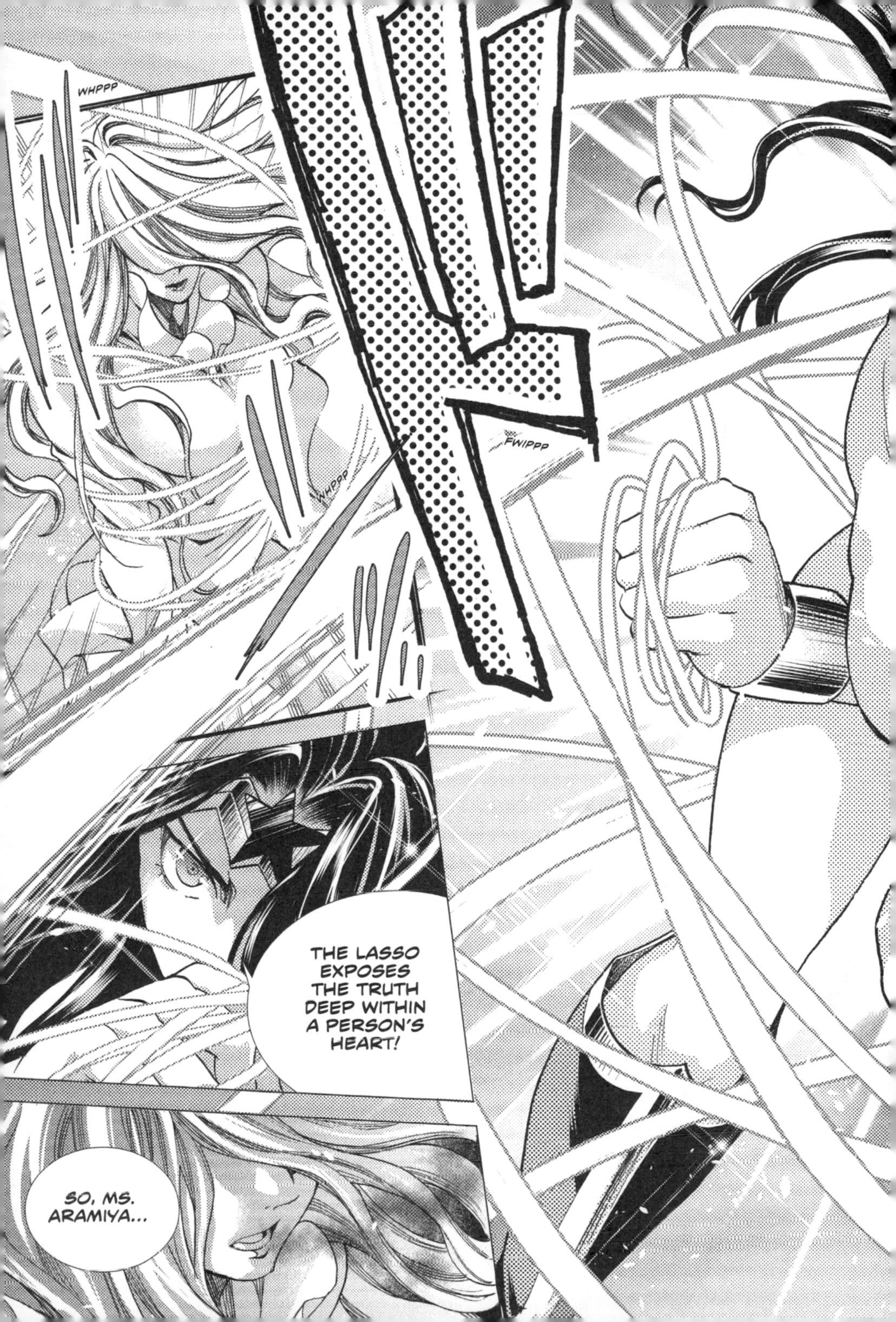
WHPPP
FWIPPP
WHPPP
THE LASSO EXPOSES THE TRUTH DEEP WITHIN A PERSON'S HEART!
SO, MS. ARAMIYA...

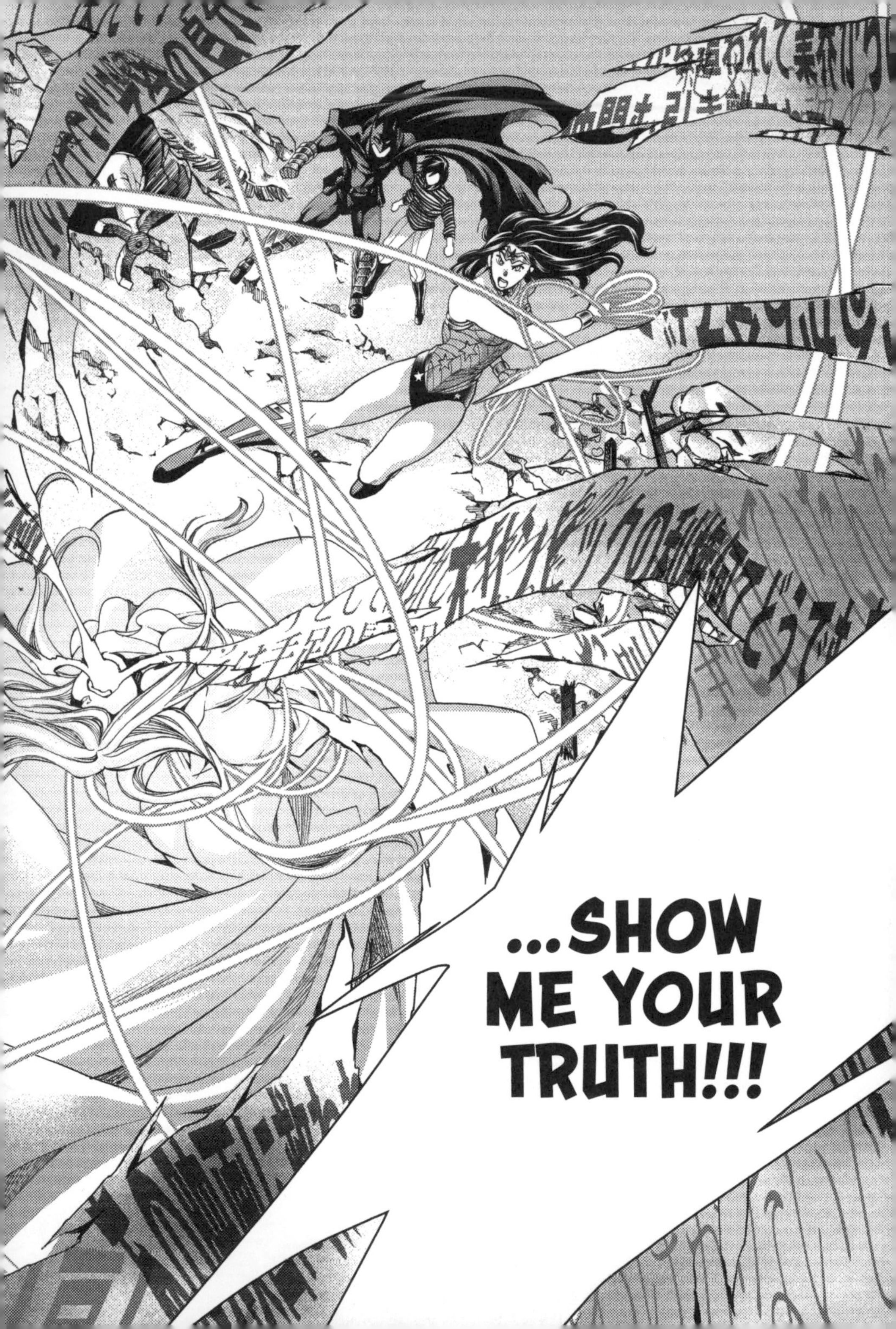
...SHOW ME YOUR TRUTH!!!

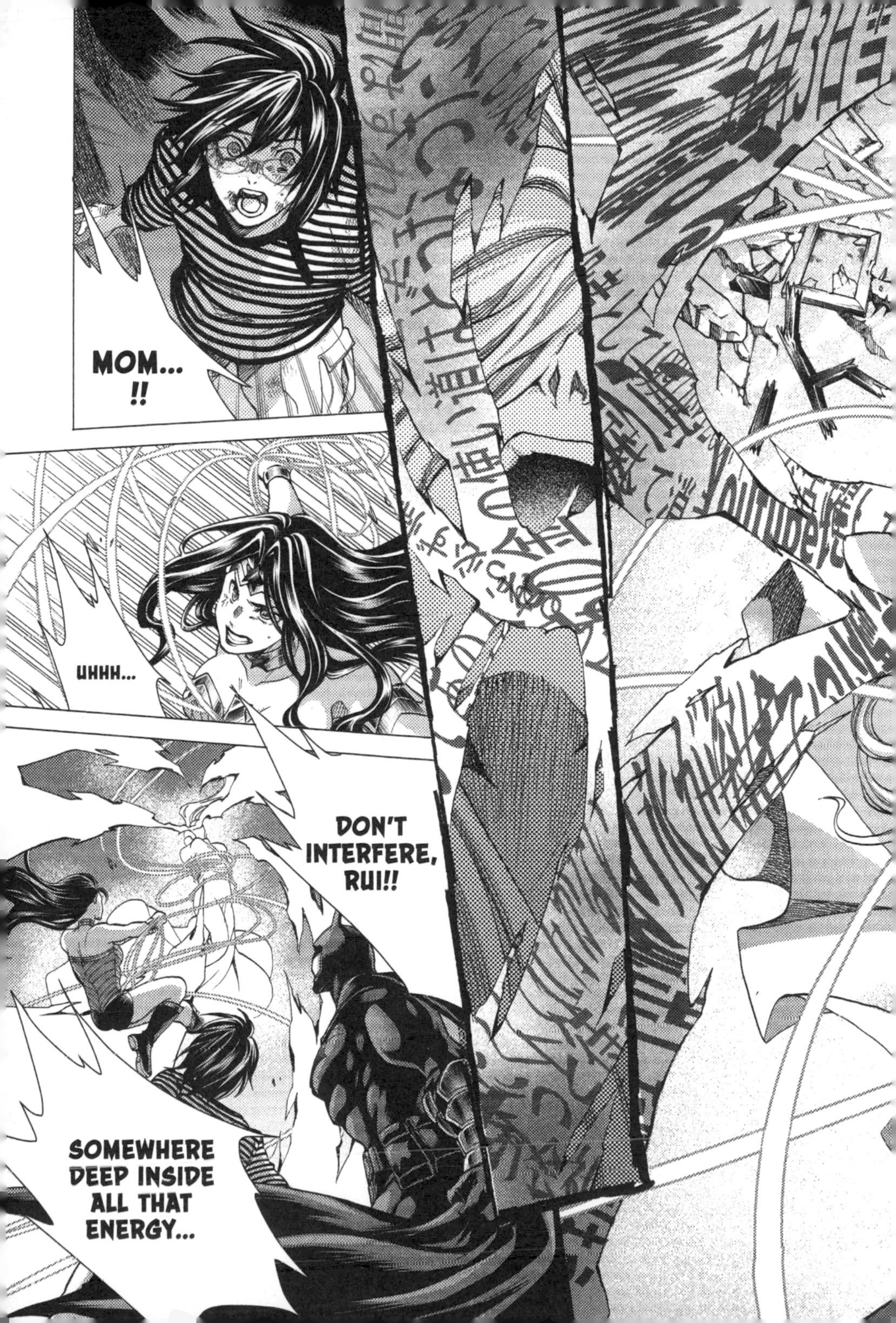
MOM... !!
UHHH...
DON'T INTERFERE, RUI!!
SOMEWHERE DEEP INSIDE ALL THAT ENERGY...

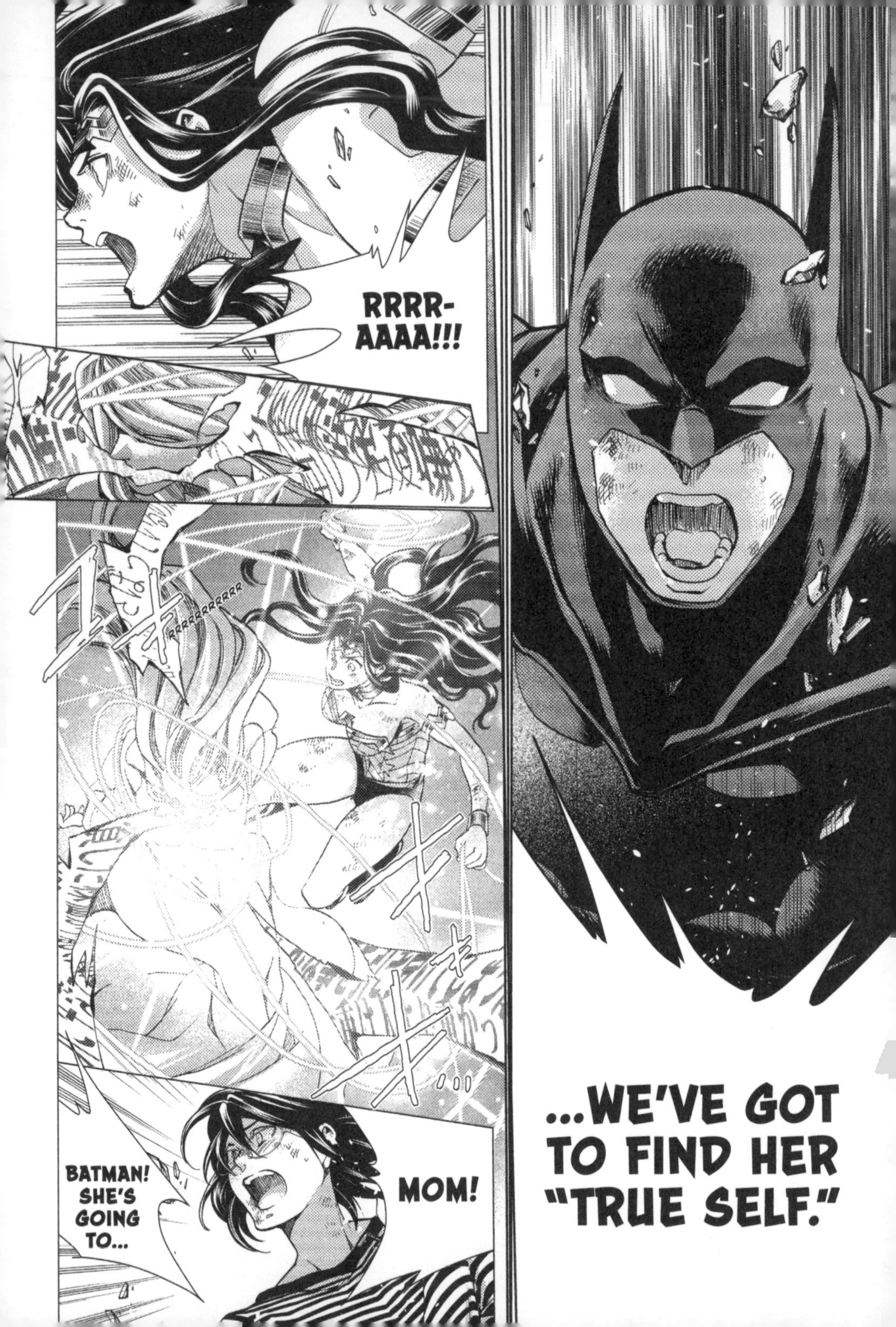
...WE'VE GOT TO FIND HER "TRUE SELF."
RRRR-AAAA!!!
RRRRRRRRRRR
MOM!
BATMAN! SHE'S GOING TO...

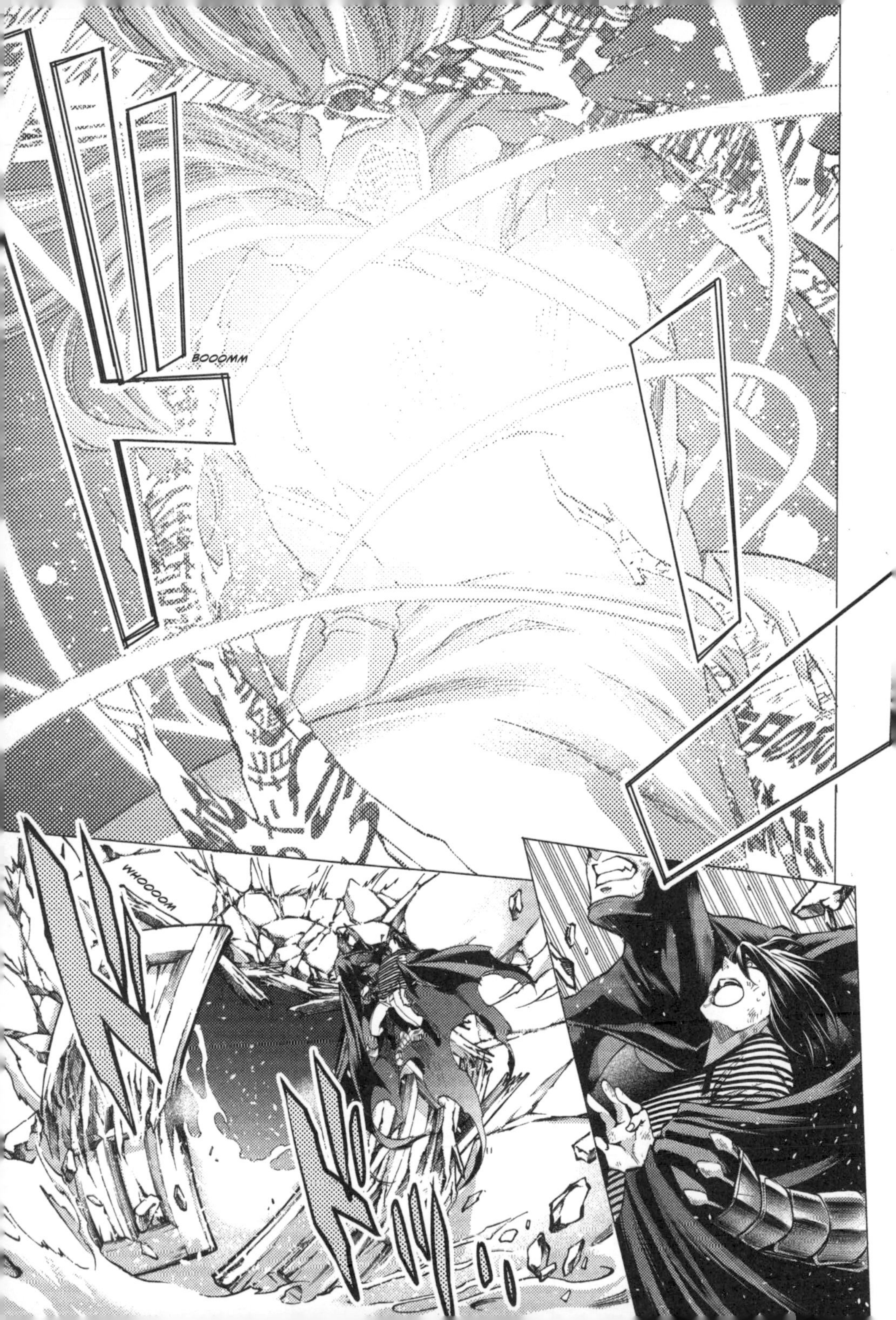
BOOOMM
WHOOOOOM

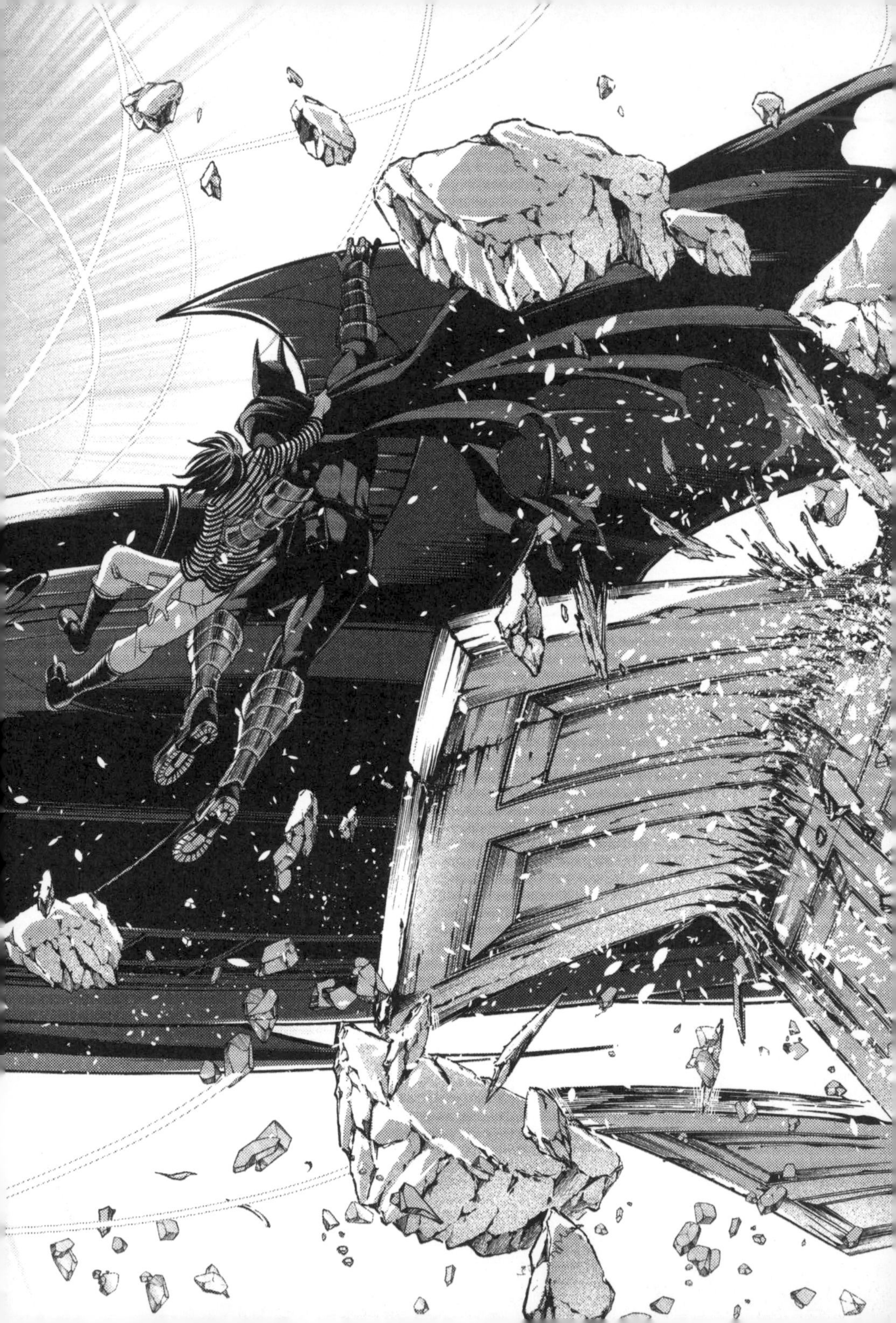

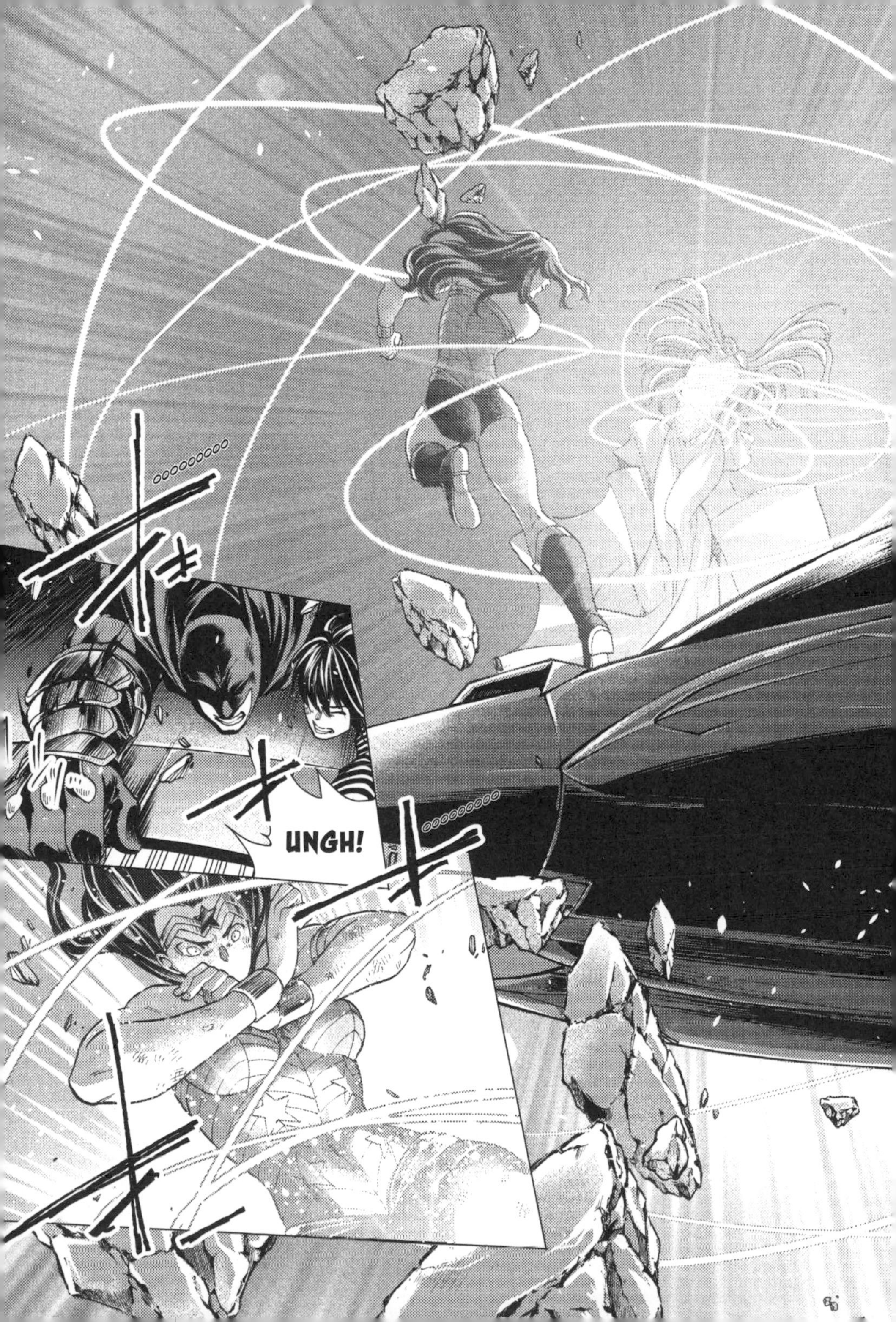
ooooooooo
ooooooooo
UNGH!

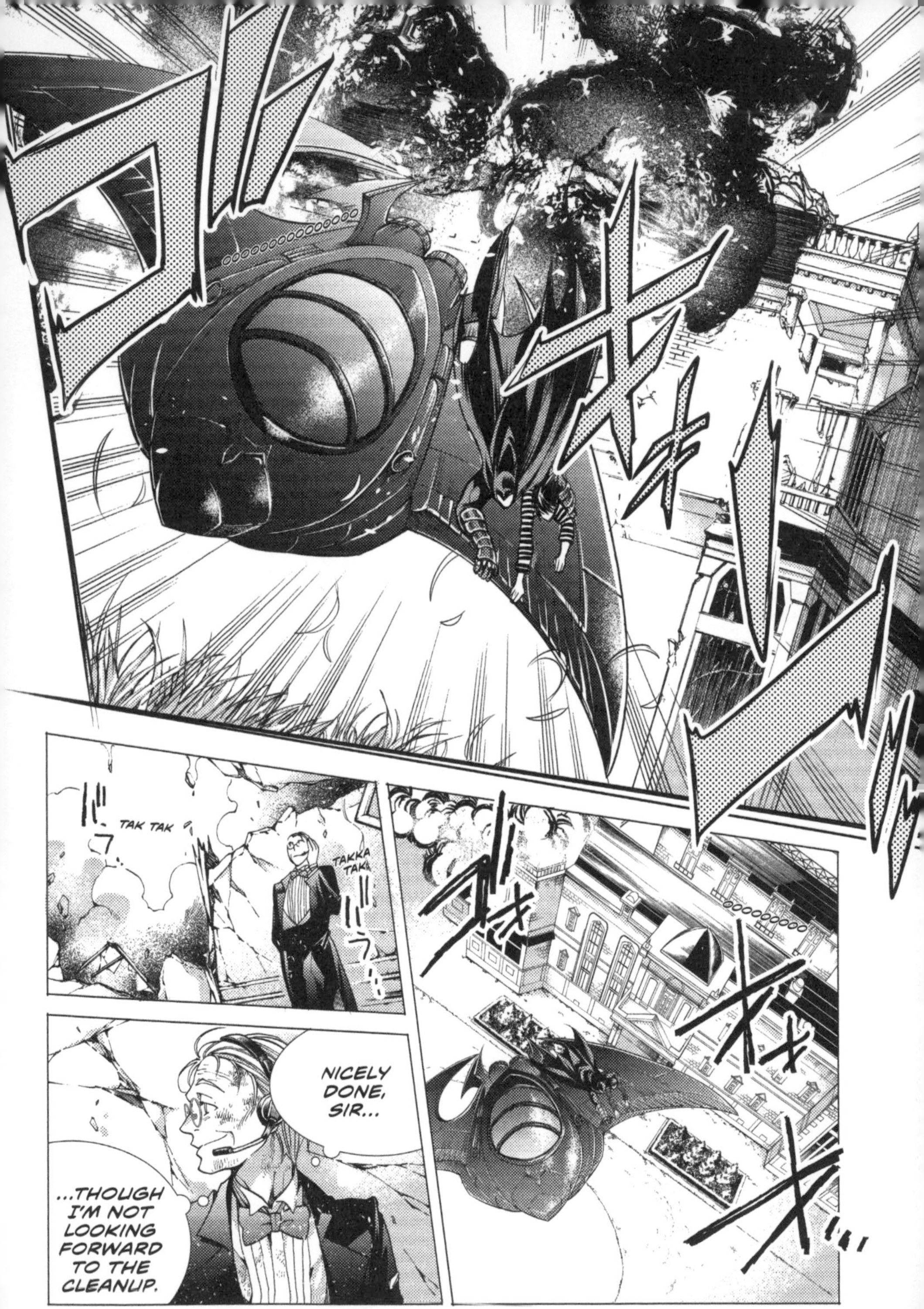
TAK TAK
TAKKA TAK
NICELY DONE, SIR...
...THOUGH I'M NOT LOOKING FORWARD TO THE CLEANUP.

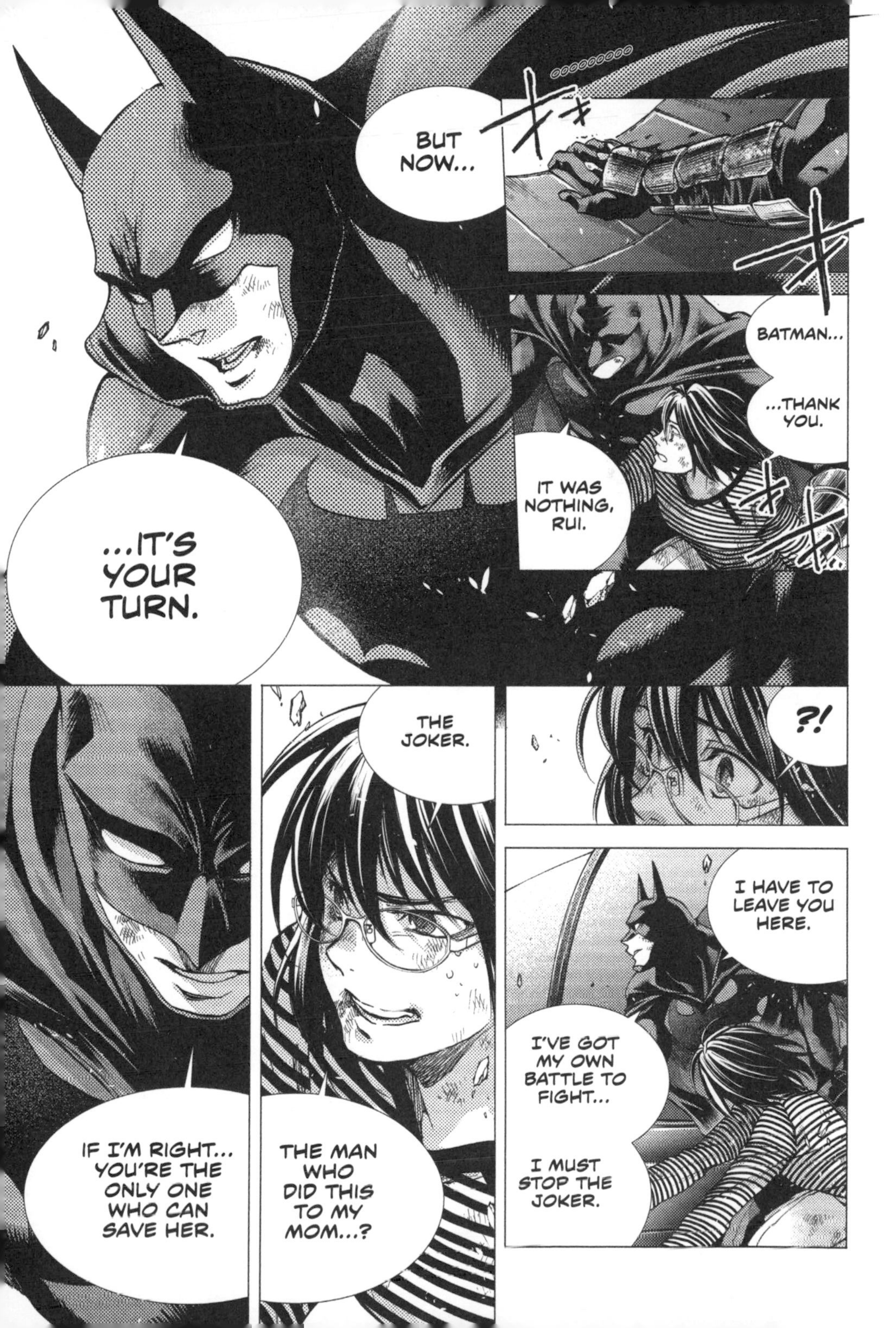
BATMAN...
...THANK YOU.
IT WAS NOTHING, RUI.
BUT NOW...
...IT'S YOUR TURN.
?!
I HAVE TO LEAVE YOU HERE.
I'VE GOT MY OWN BATTLE TO FIGHT...
I MUST STOP THE JOKER.
THE JOKER.
THE MAN WHO DID THIS TO MY MOM...?
IF I'M RIGHT... YOU'RE THE ONLY ONE WHO CAN SAVE HER.

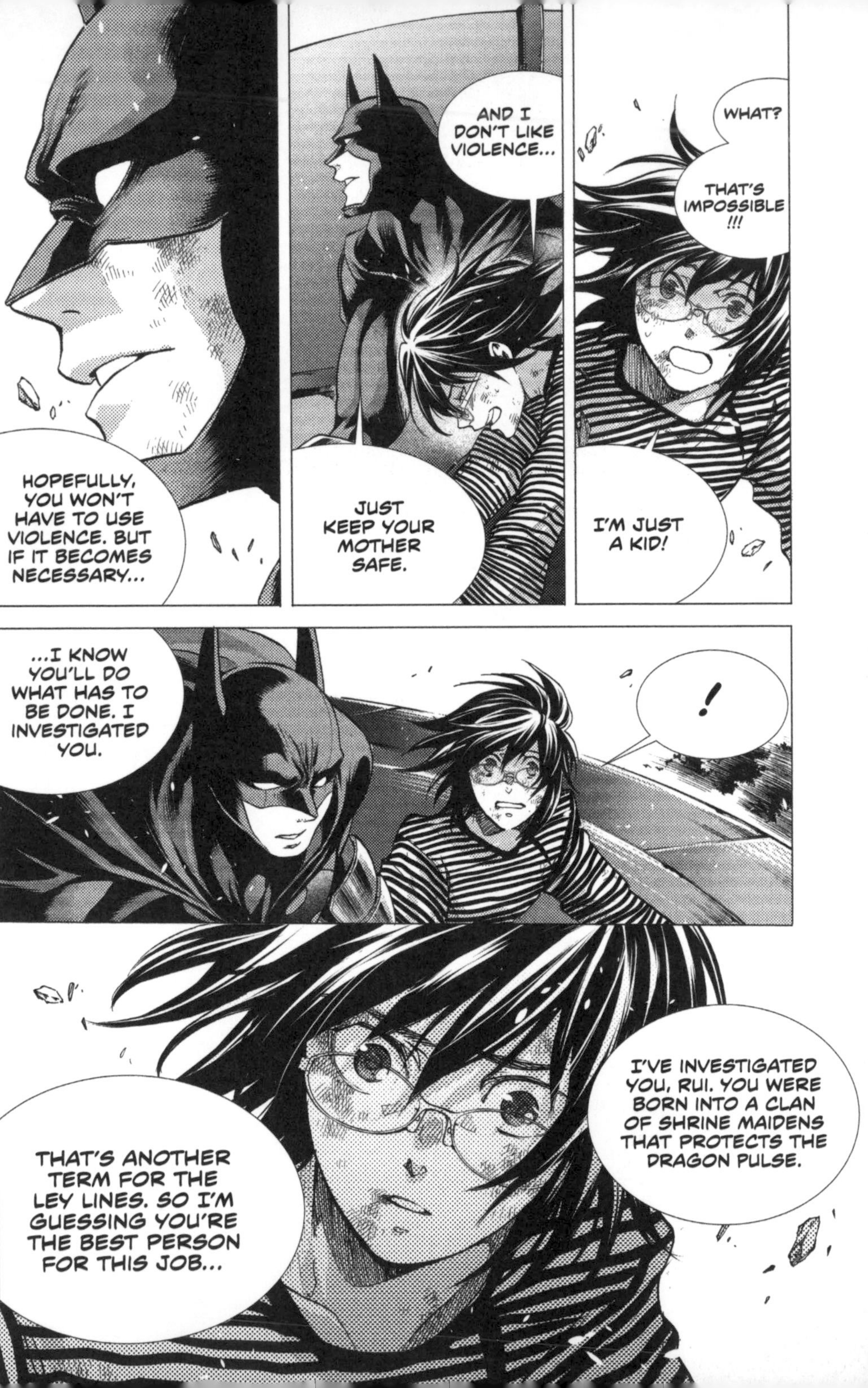
WHAT?
THAT'S IMPOSSIBLE!!!
I'M JUST A KID!
AND I DON'T LIKE VIOLENCE...
JUST KEEP YOUR MOTHER SAFE.
HOPEFULLY, YOU WON'T HAVE TO USE VIOLENCE. BUT IF IT BECOMES NECESSARY...
...I KNOW YOU'LL DO WHAT HAS TO BE DONE. I INVESTIGATED YOU.
!
I'VE INVESTIGATED YOU, RUI. YOU WERE BORN INTO A CLAN OF SHRINE MAIDENS THAT PROTECTS THE DRAGON PULSE.
THAT'S ANOTHER TERM FOR THE LEY LINES. SO I'M GUESSING YOU'RE THE BEST PERSON FOR THIS JOB...

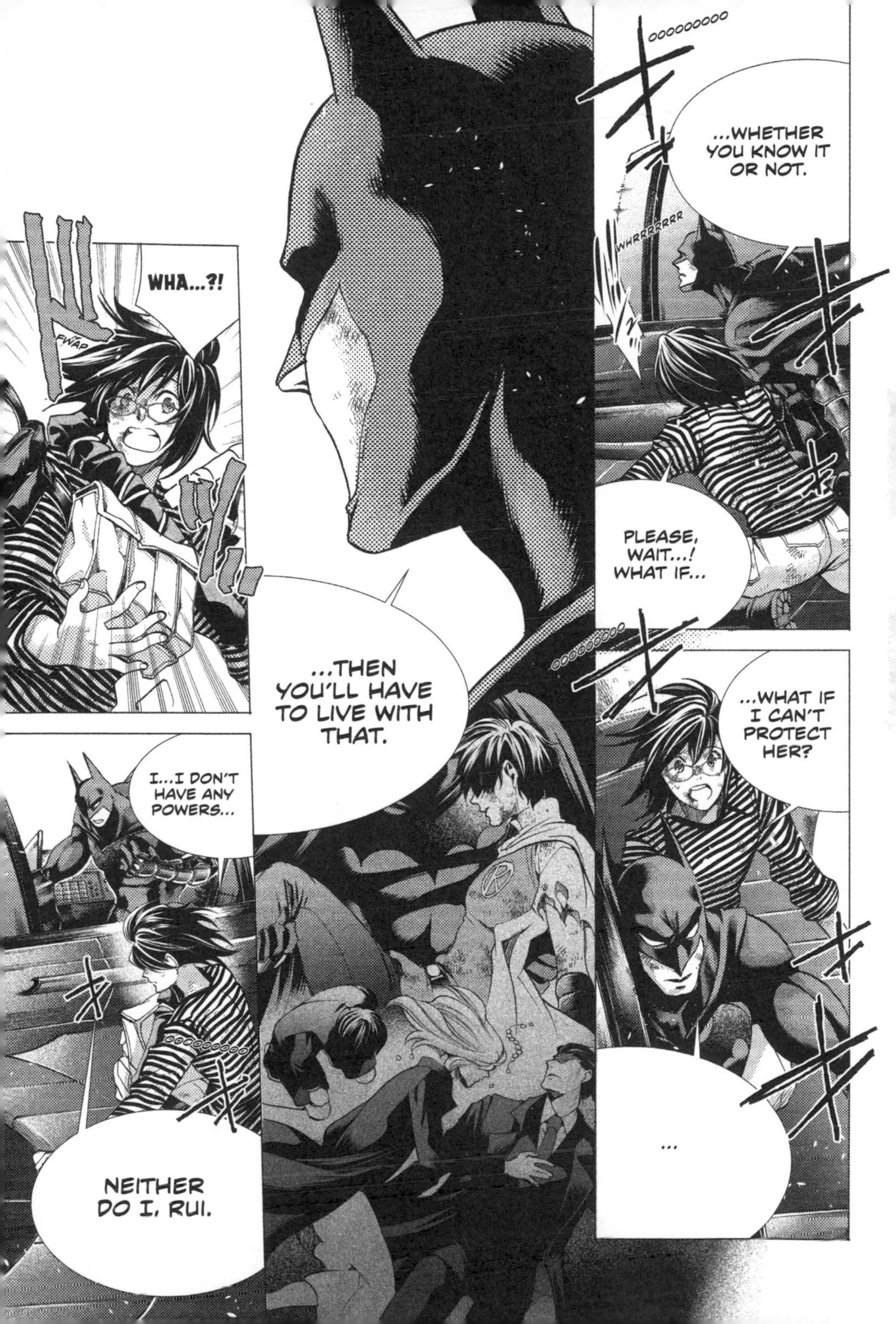
OOOOOOOOO
...WHETHER YOU KNOW IT OR NOT.
WHRRRRRRR
PLEASE, WAIT...! WHAT IF...
OOOOOOOOO
...WHAT IF I CAN'T PROTECT HER?
...
...THEN YOU'LL HAVE TO LIVE WITH THAT.
WHA...?!
FWAP
I...I DON'T HAVE ANY POWERS...
OOOOOOOOO
NEITHER DO I, RUI.

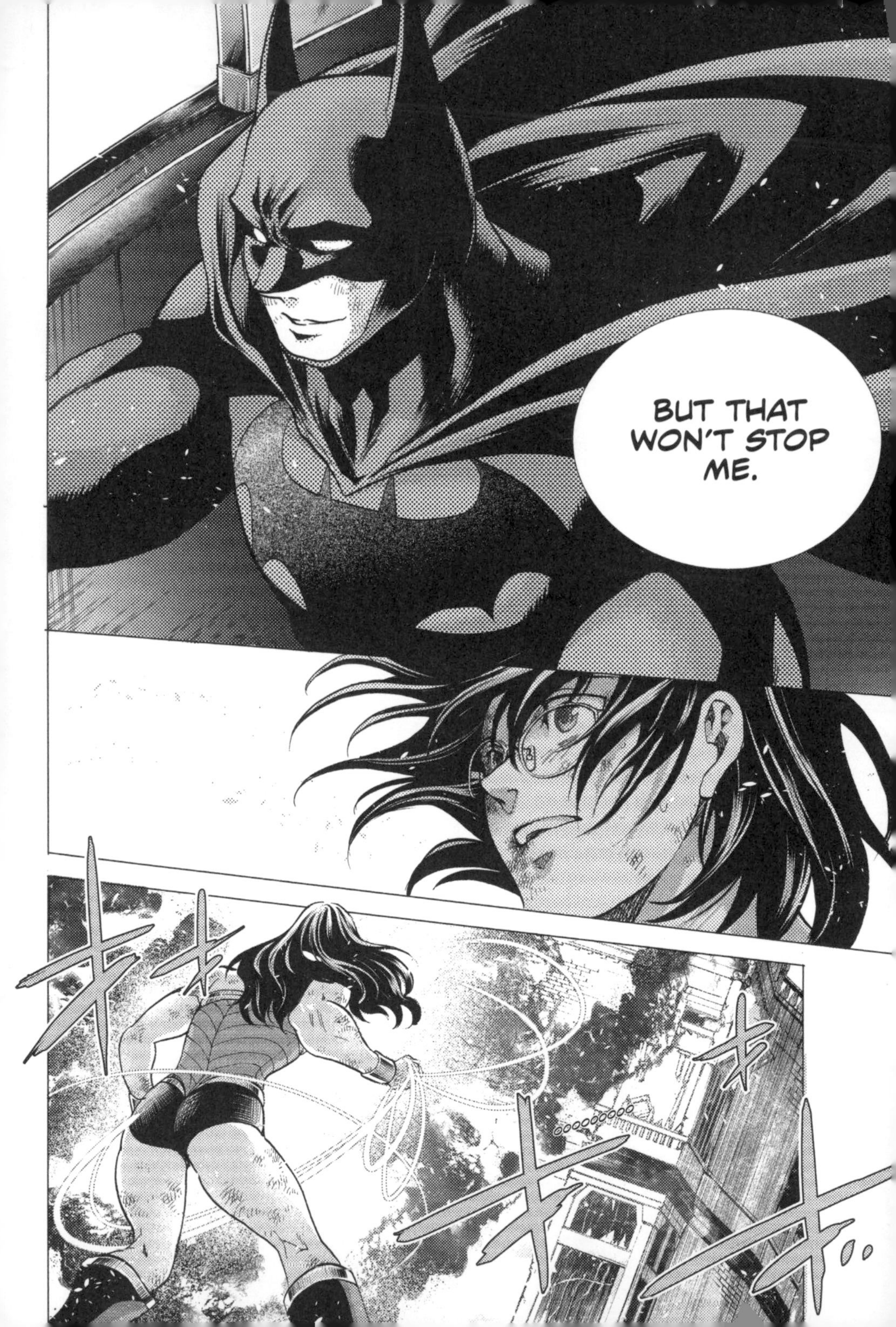
BUT THAT WON'T STOP ME.

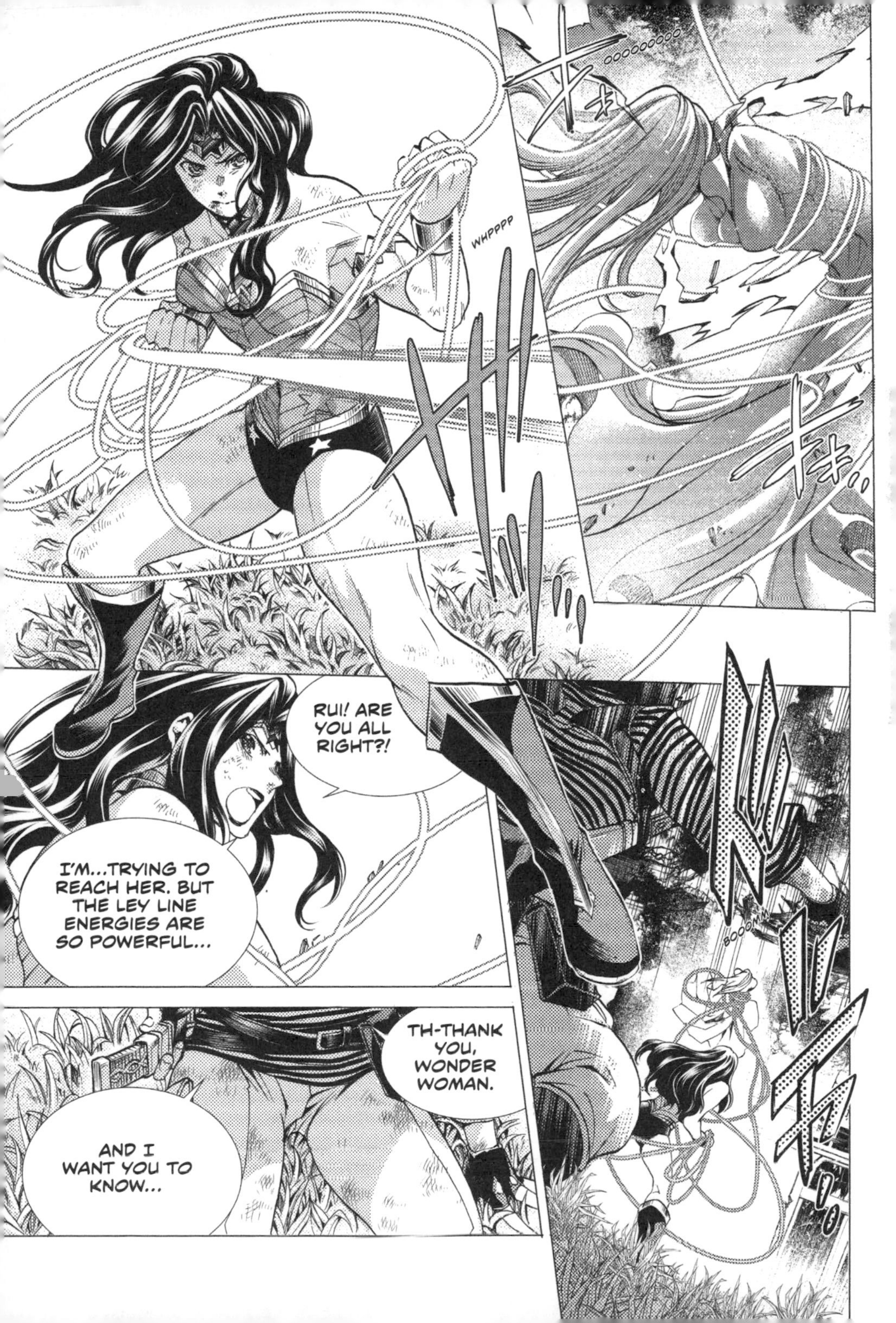
OOOOOOOOO
WHPPPP
BOOOMM
RUI! ARE YOU ALL RIGHT?!
I'M...TRYING TO REACH HER. BUT THE LEY LINE ENERGIES ARE SO POWERFUL...
TH-THANK YOU, WONDER WOMAN.
AND I WANT YOU TO KNOW...

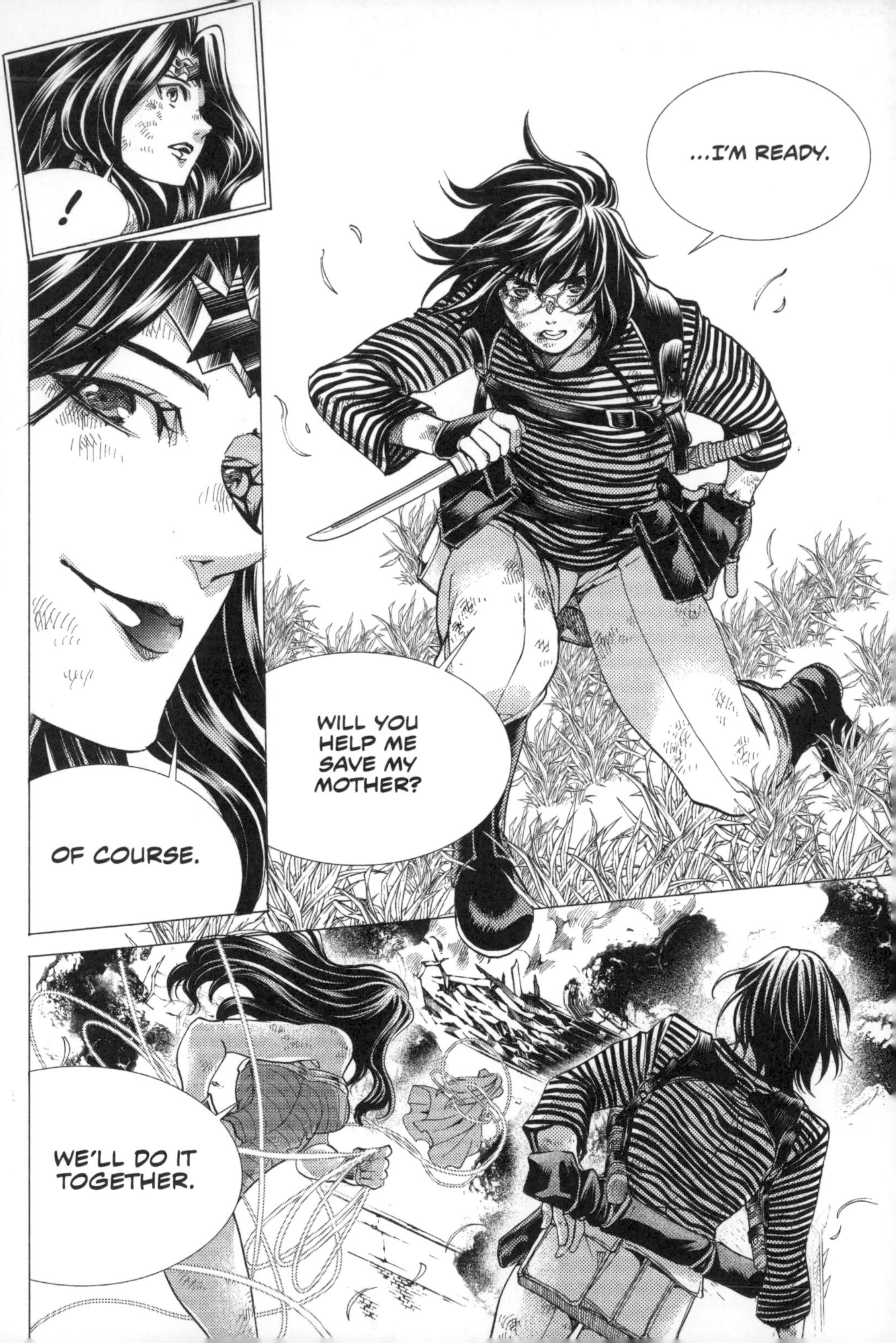
...I'M READY.
WILL YOU HELP ME SAVE MY MOTHER?
!
OF COURSE.
WE'LL DO IT TOGETHER.

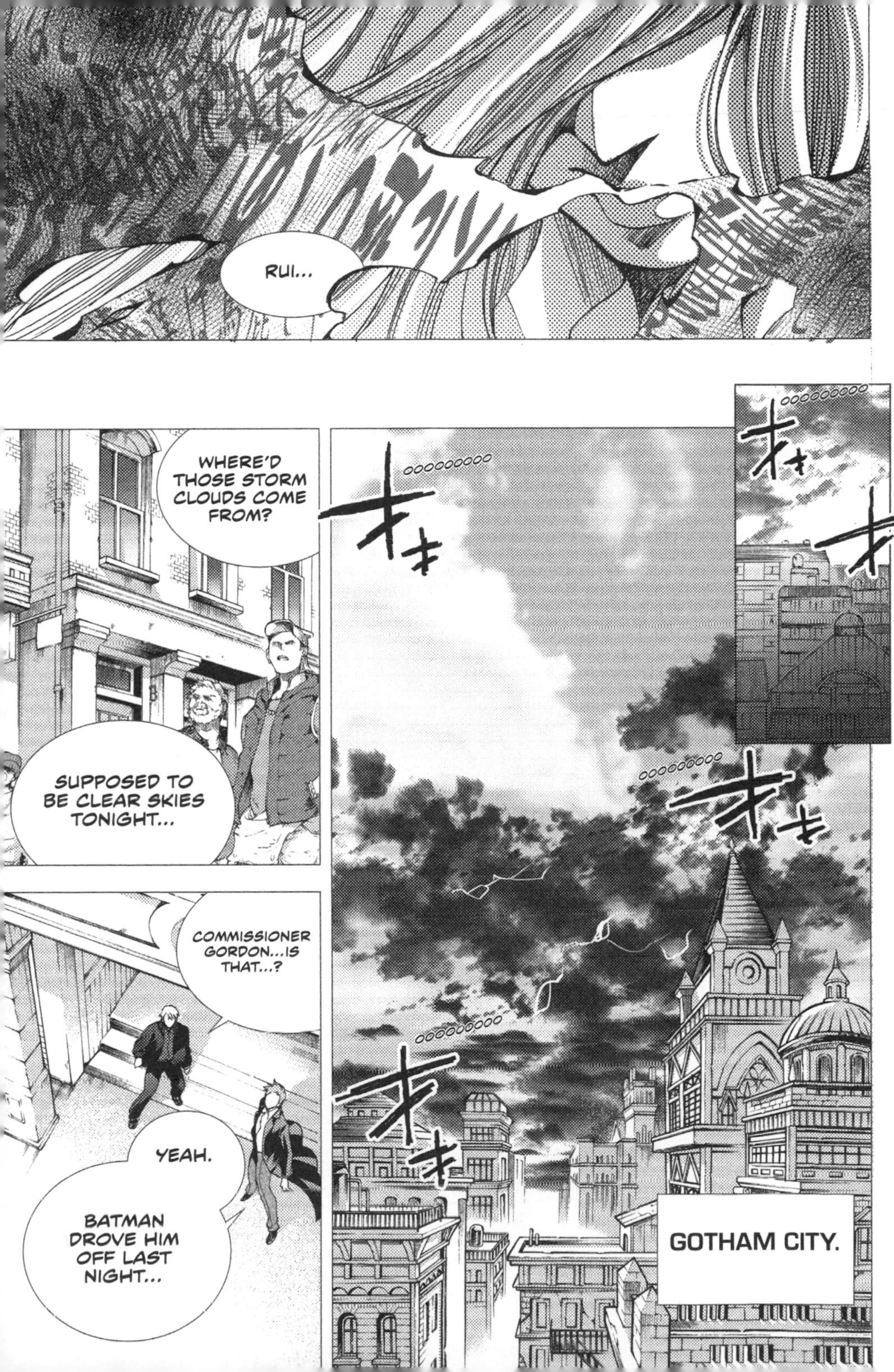
RUI...
GOTHAM CITY.
WHERE'D THOSE STORM CLOUDS COME FROM?
SUPPOSED TO BE CLEAR SKIES TONIGHT...
COMMISSIONER GORDON...IS THAT...?
YEAH.
BATMAN DROVE HIM OFF LAST NIGHT...

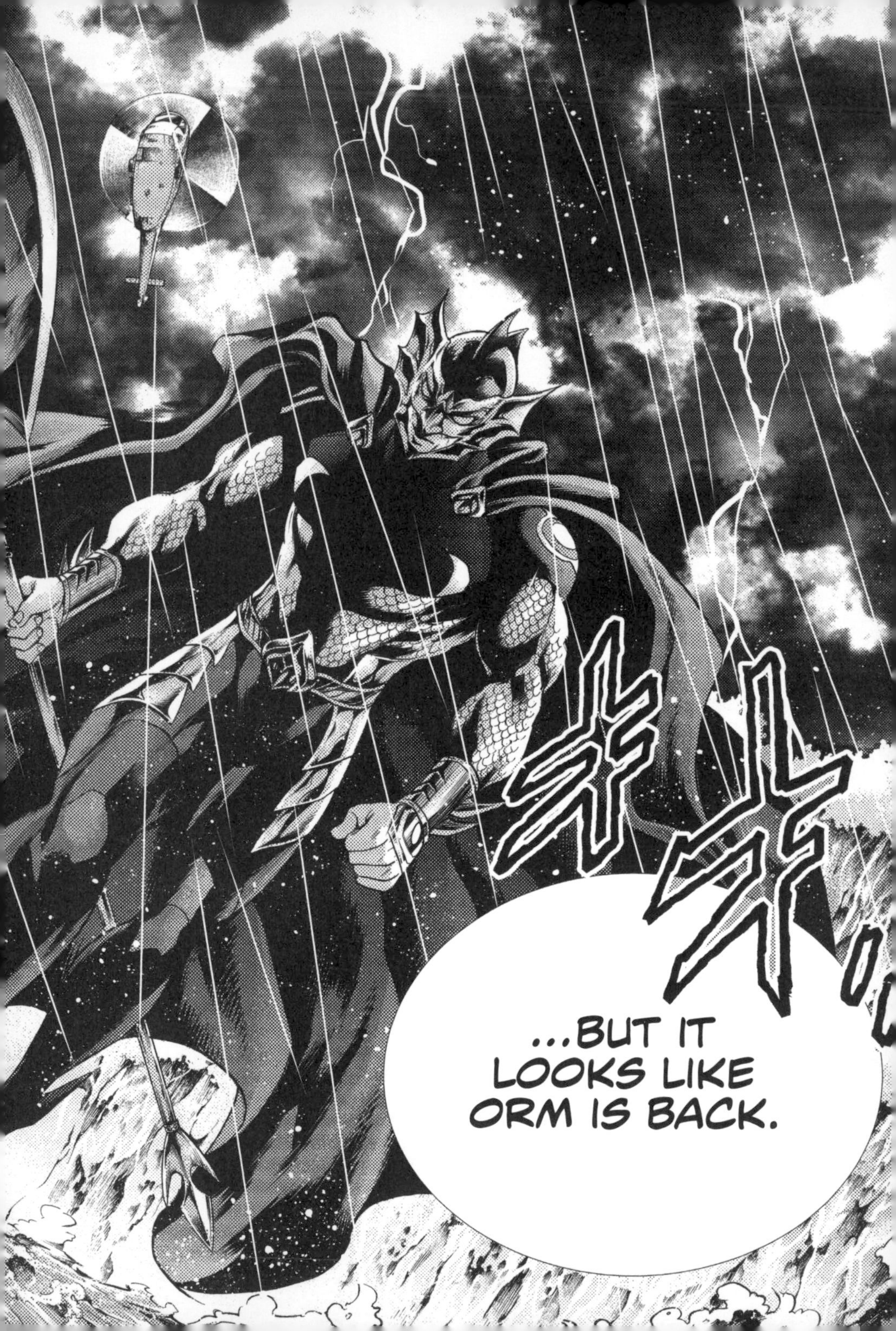
...BUT IT LOOKS LIKE ORM IS BACK.

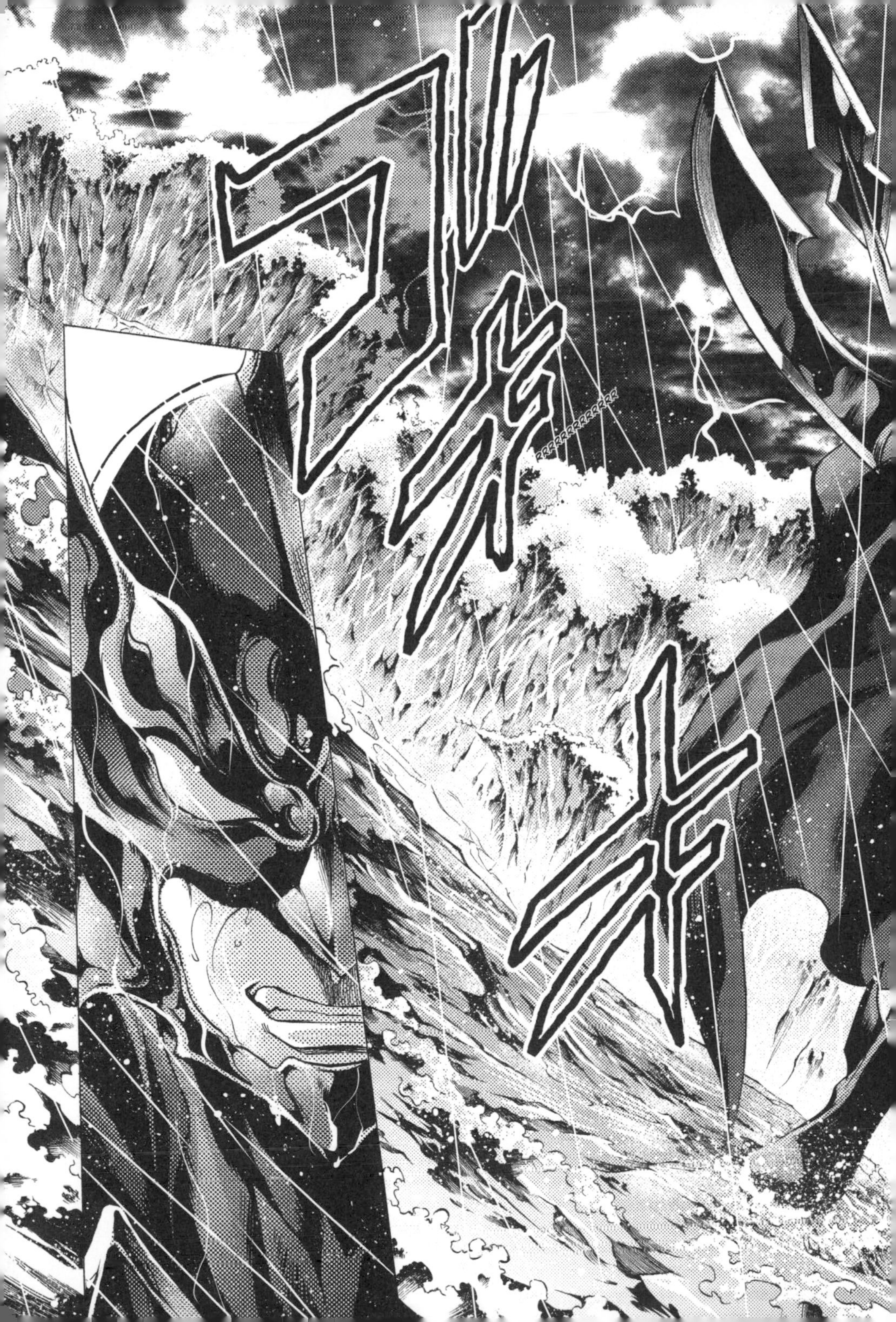
RRRRRRRRRRRRR

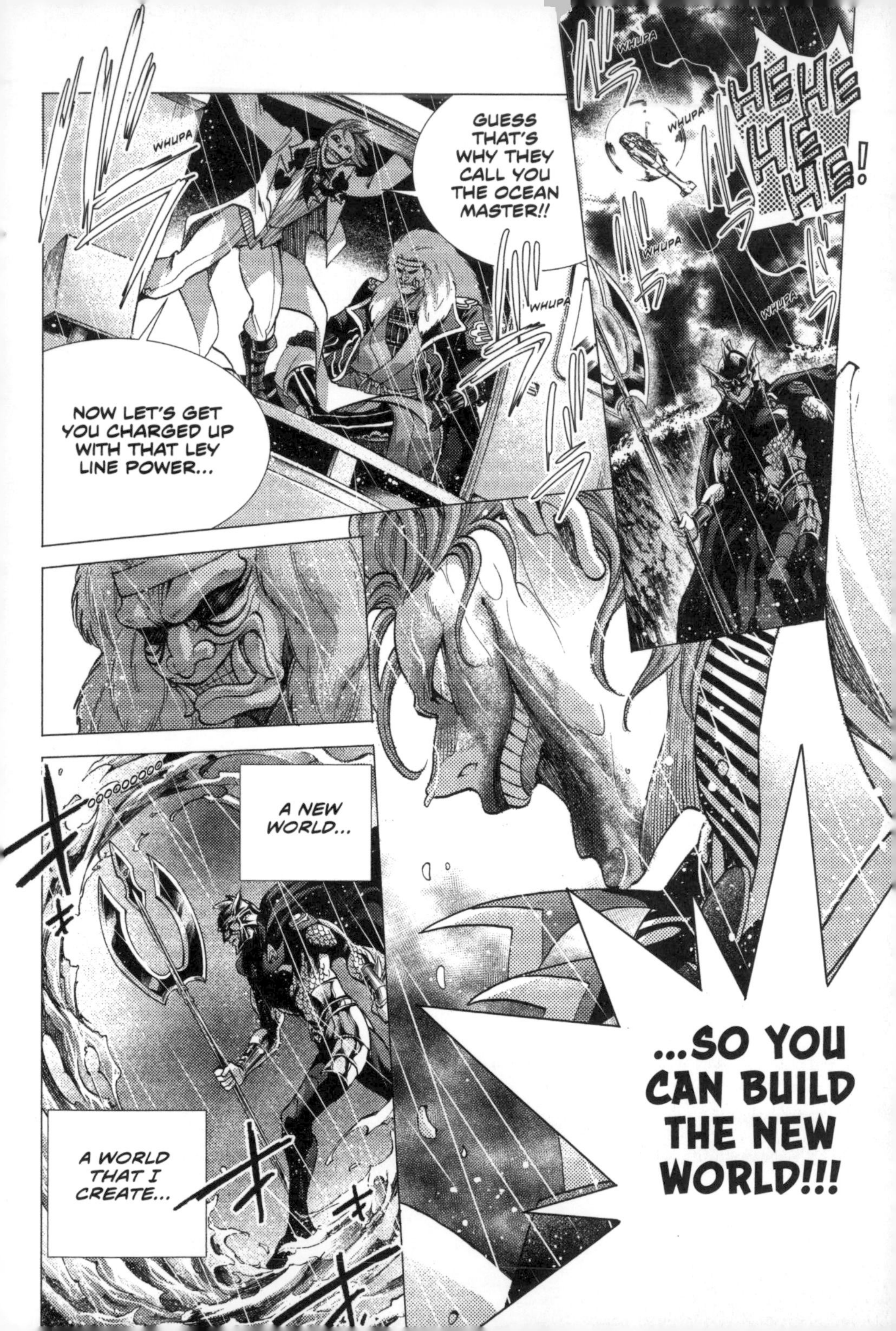
WHUPA
HEHE HE HE!
WHUPA
WHUPA
WHUPA
GUESS THAT'S WHY THEY CALL YOU THE OCEAN MASTER!!
WHUPA
WHUPA
NOW LET'S GET YOU CHARGED UP WITH THAT LEY LINE POWER...
...SO YOU CAN BUILD THE NEW WORLD!!!
OOOOOOOOO
A NEW WORLD...
A WORLD THAT I CREATE...

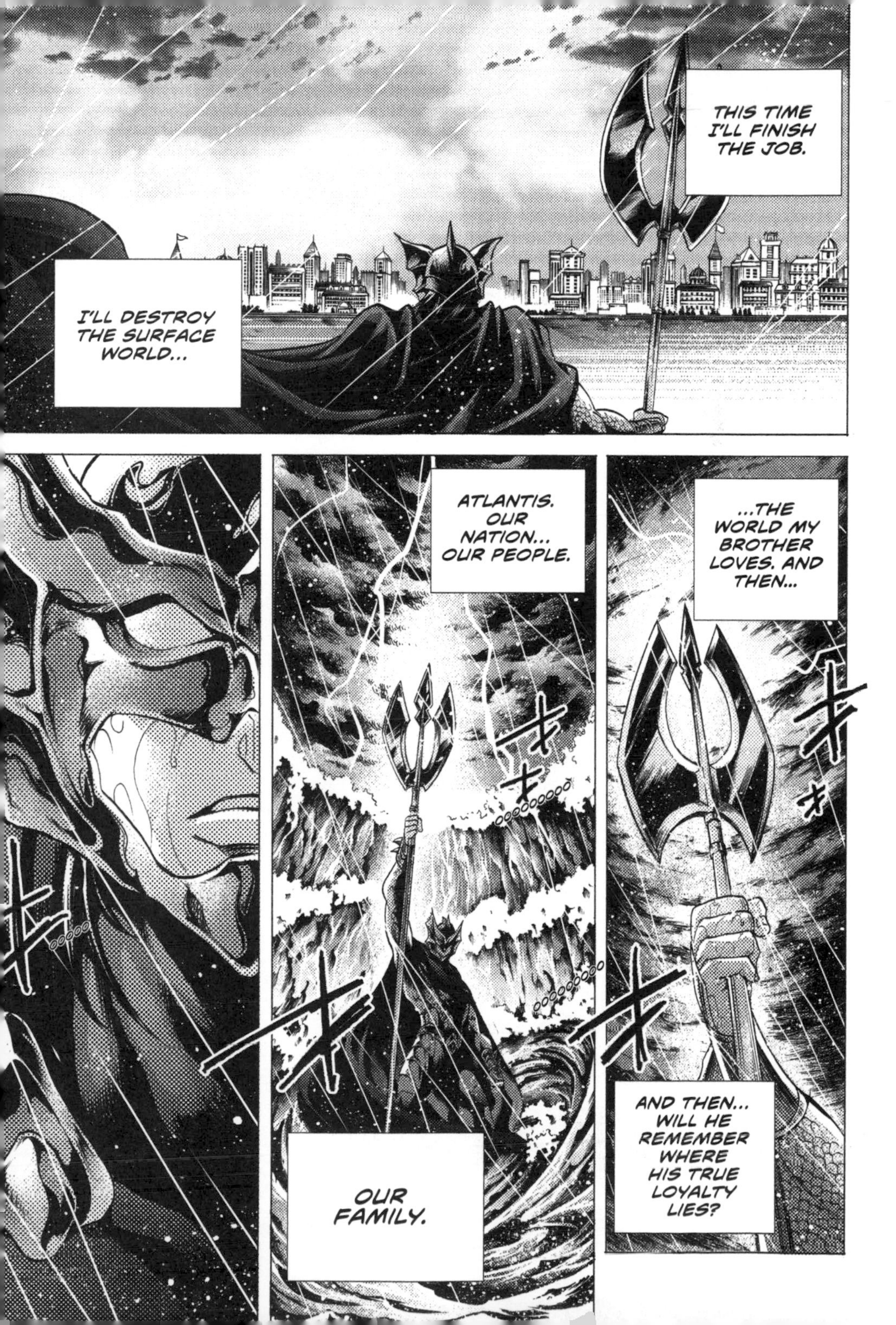
THIS TIME I'LL FINISH THE JOB.
I'LL DESTROY THE SURFACE WORLD...
...THE WORLD MY BROTHER LOVES. AND THEN...
AND THEN... WILL HE REMEMBER WHERE HIS TRUE LOYALTY LIES?
ATLANTIS. OUR NATION... OUR PEOPLE.
OUR FAMILY.

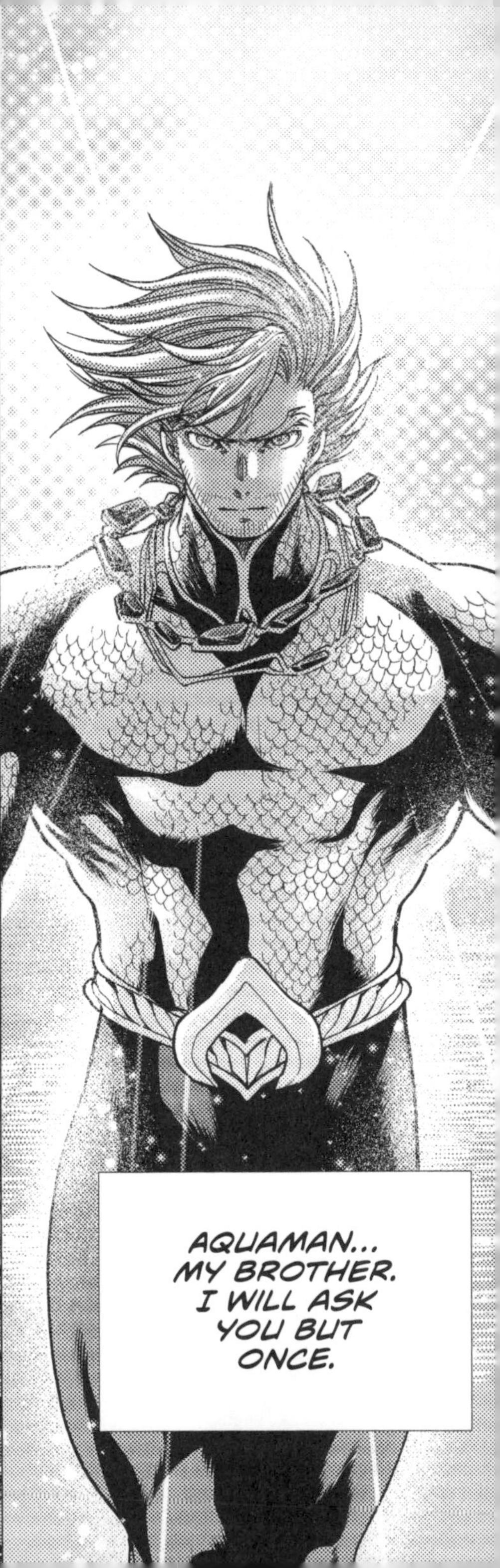
AQUAMAN... MY BROTHER. I WILL ASK YOU BUT ONCE.
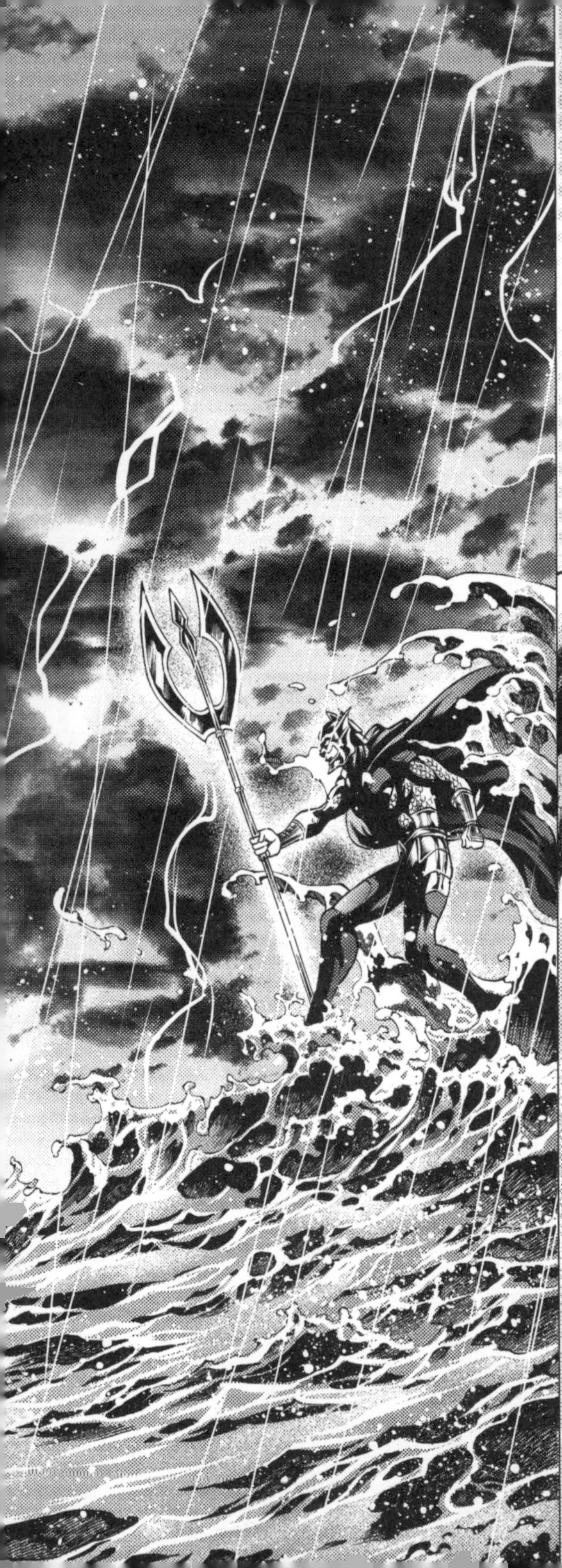

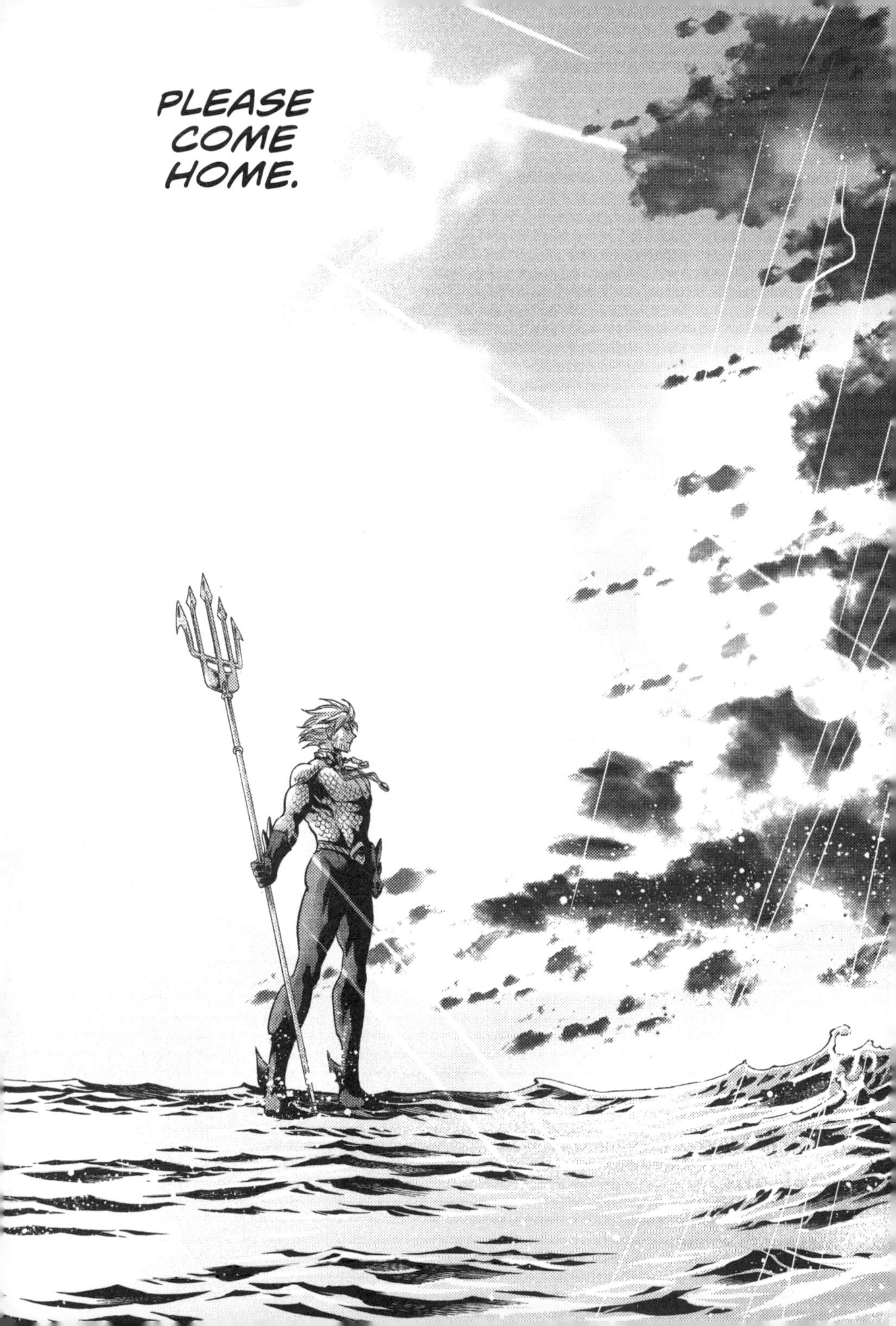
PLEASE COME HOME.

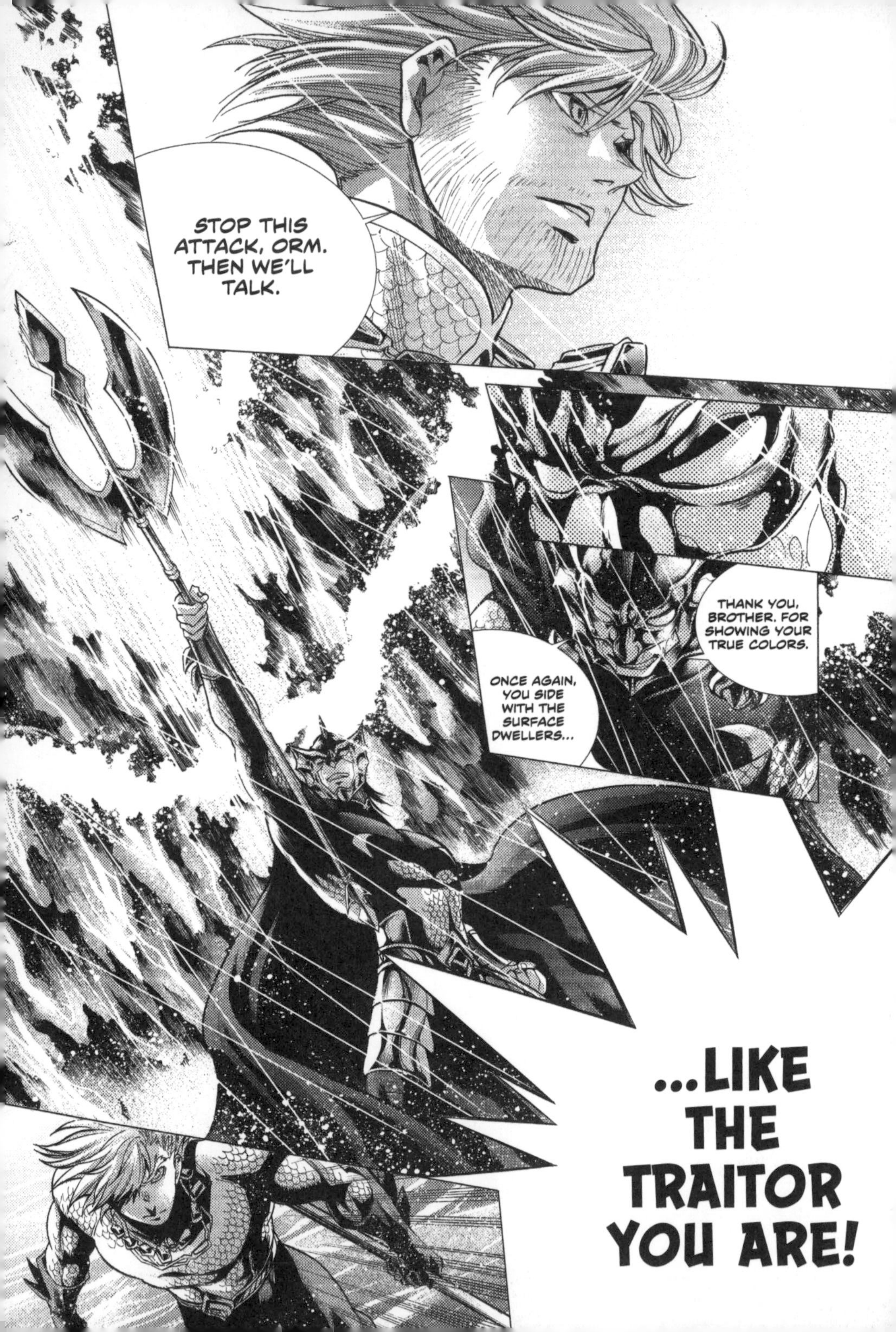
STOP THIS ATTACK, ORM. THEN WE'LL TALK.
THANK YOU, BROTHER. FOR SHOWING YOUR TRUE COLORS.
ONCE AGAIN, YOU SIDE WITH THE SURFACE DWELLERS...
...LIKE THE TRAITOR YOU ARE!

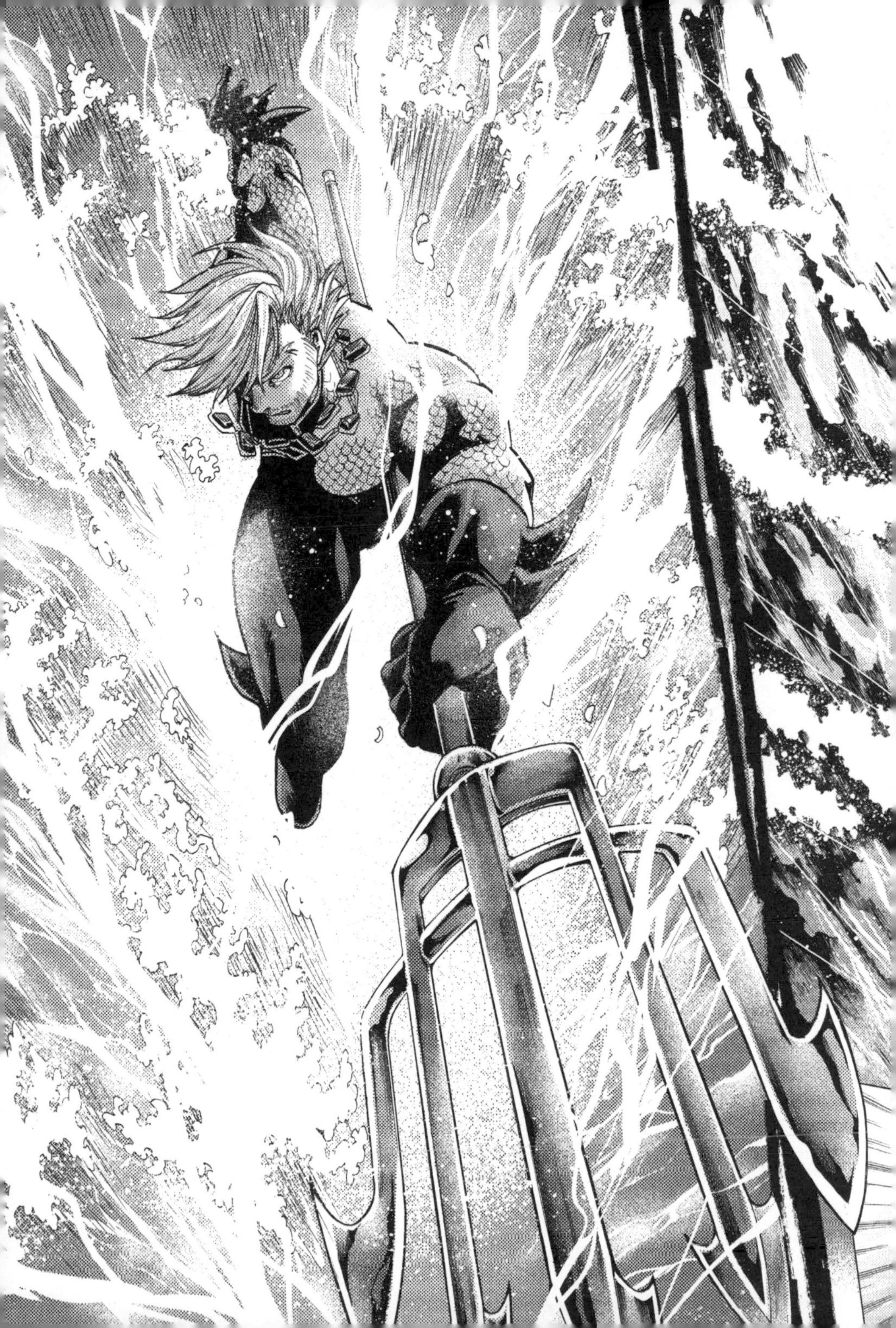

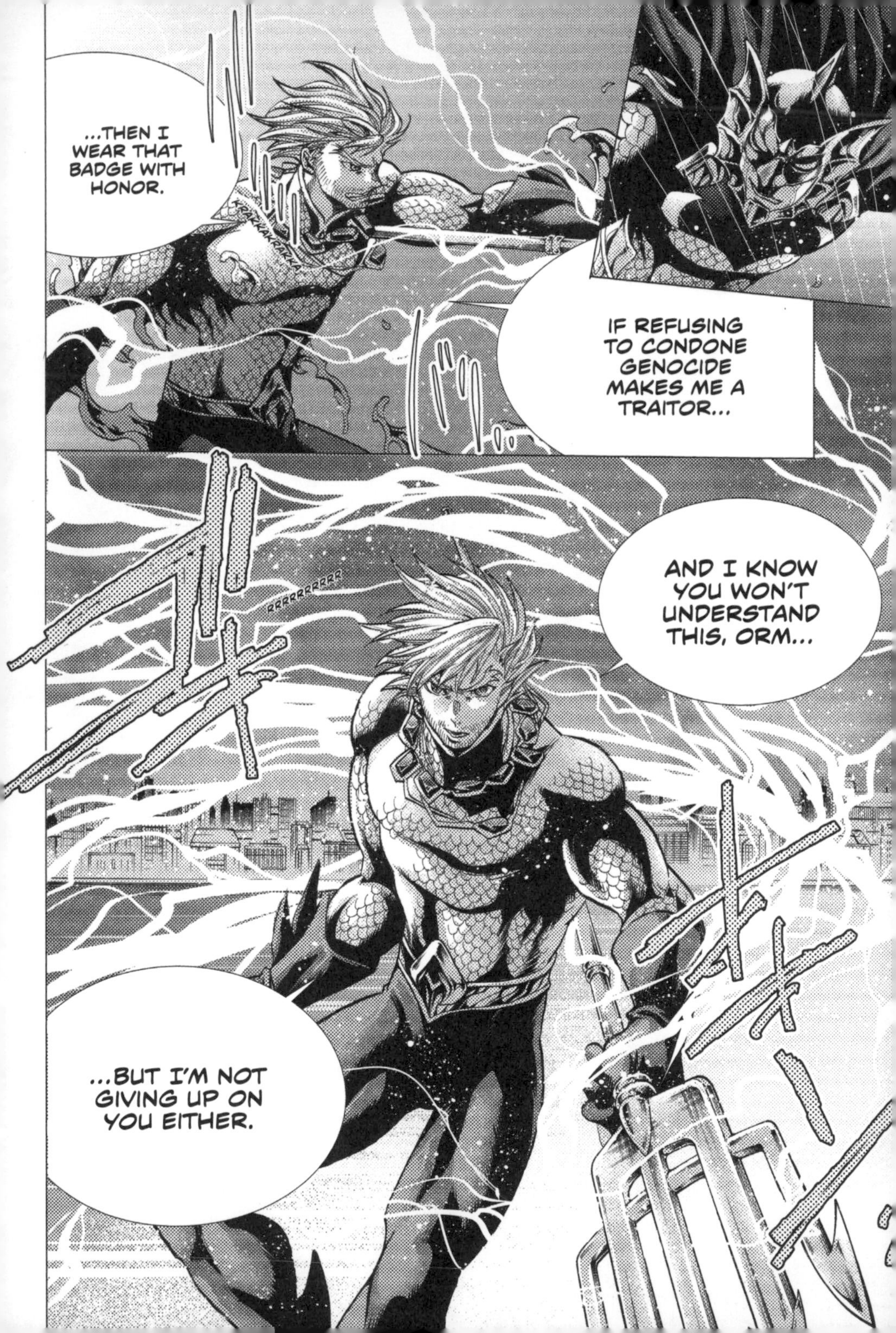
IF REFUSING TO CONDONE GENOCIDE MAKES ME A TRAITOR...
...THEN I WEAR THAT BADGE WITH HONOR.
KRAKKAKRAKKA
AND I KNOW YOU WON'T UNDERSTAND THIS, ORM...
RRRRRRRRRR
...BUT I'M NOT GIVING UP ON YOU EITHER.

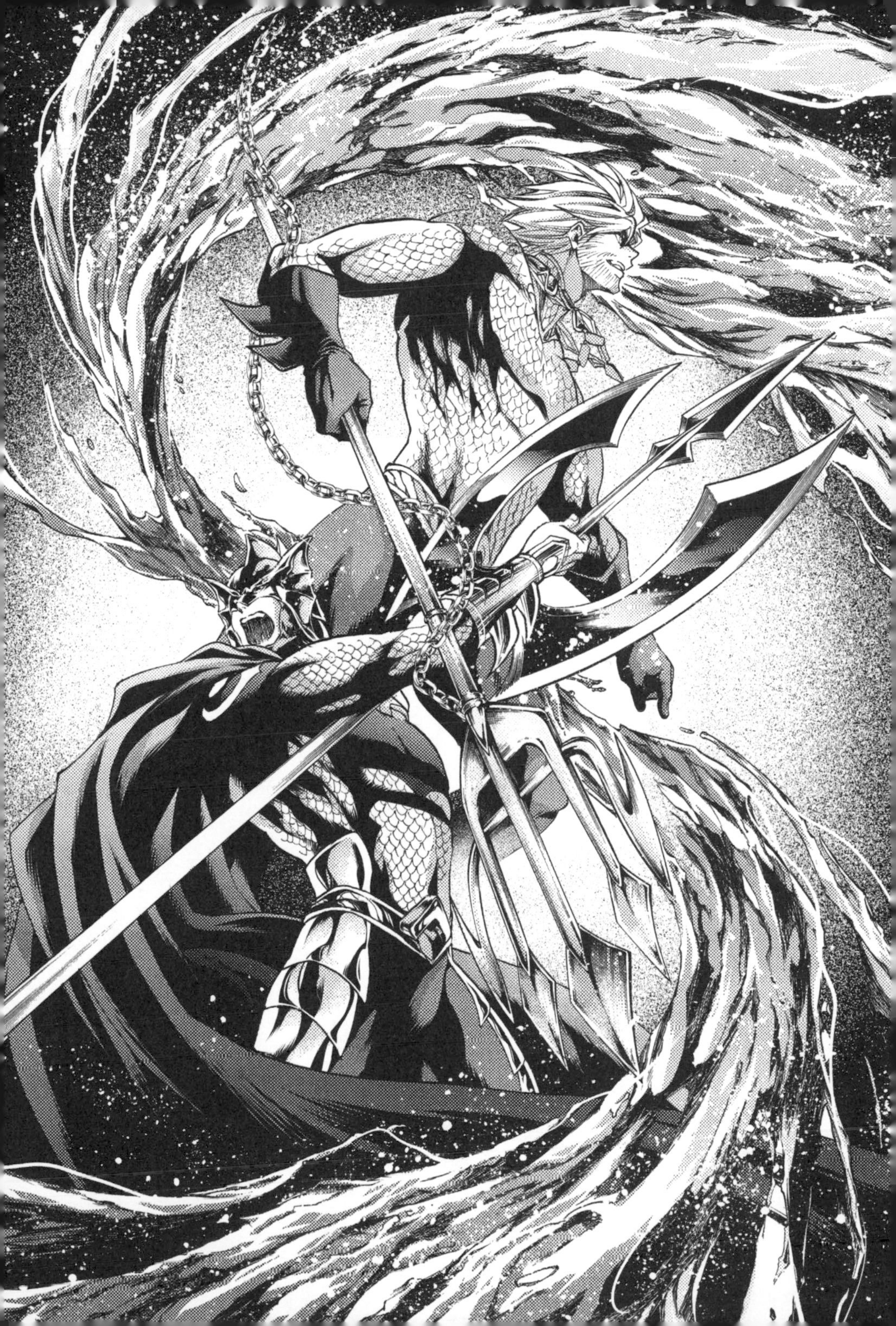

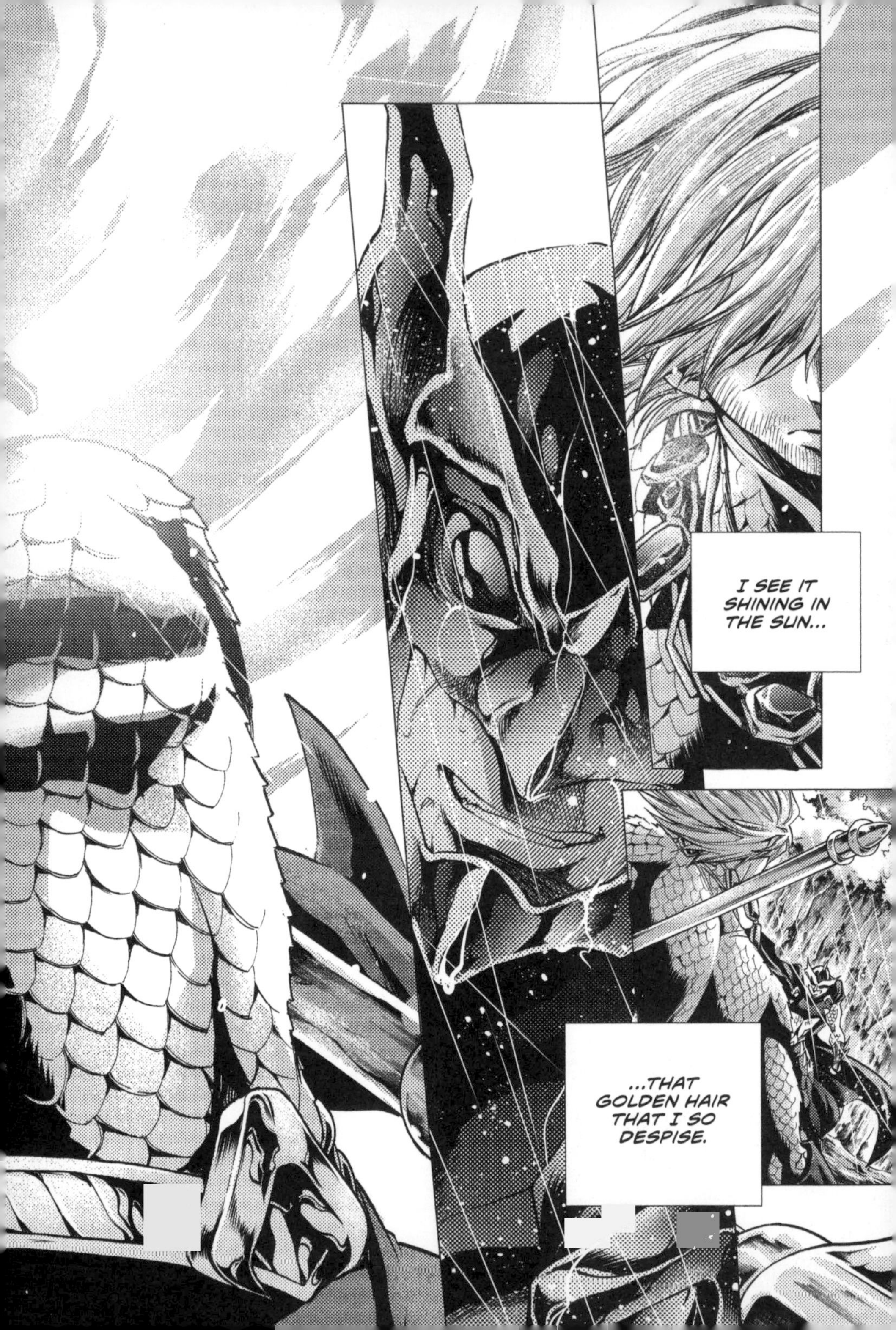
I SEE IT SHINING IN THE SUN...
...THAT GOLDEN HAIR THAT I SO DESPISE.

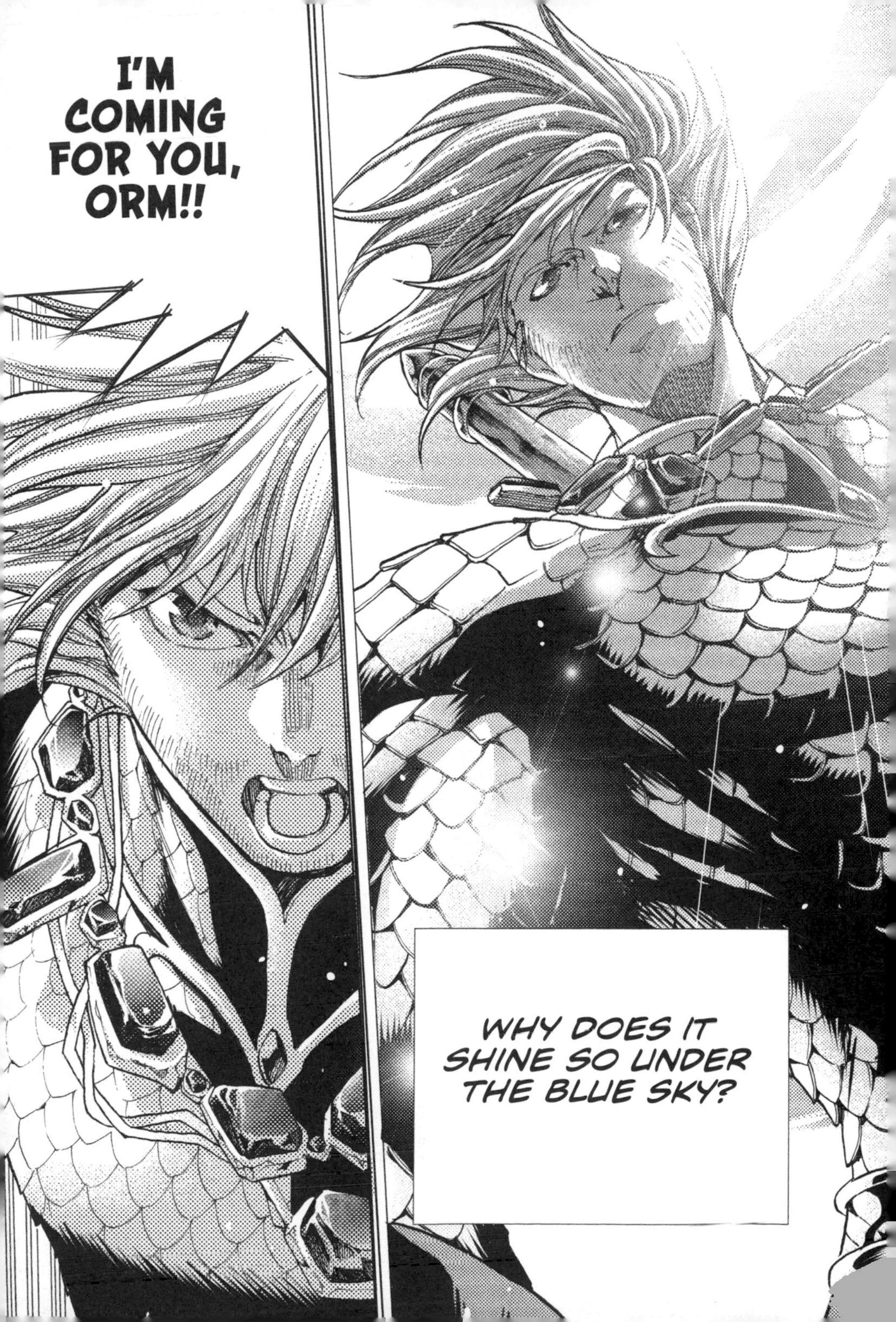
WHY DOES IT SHINE SO UNDER THE BLUE SKY?
I'M COMING FOR YOU, ORM!!

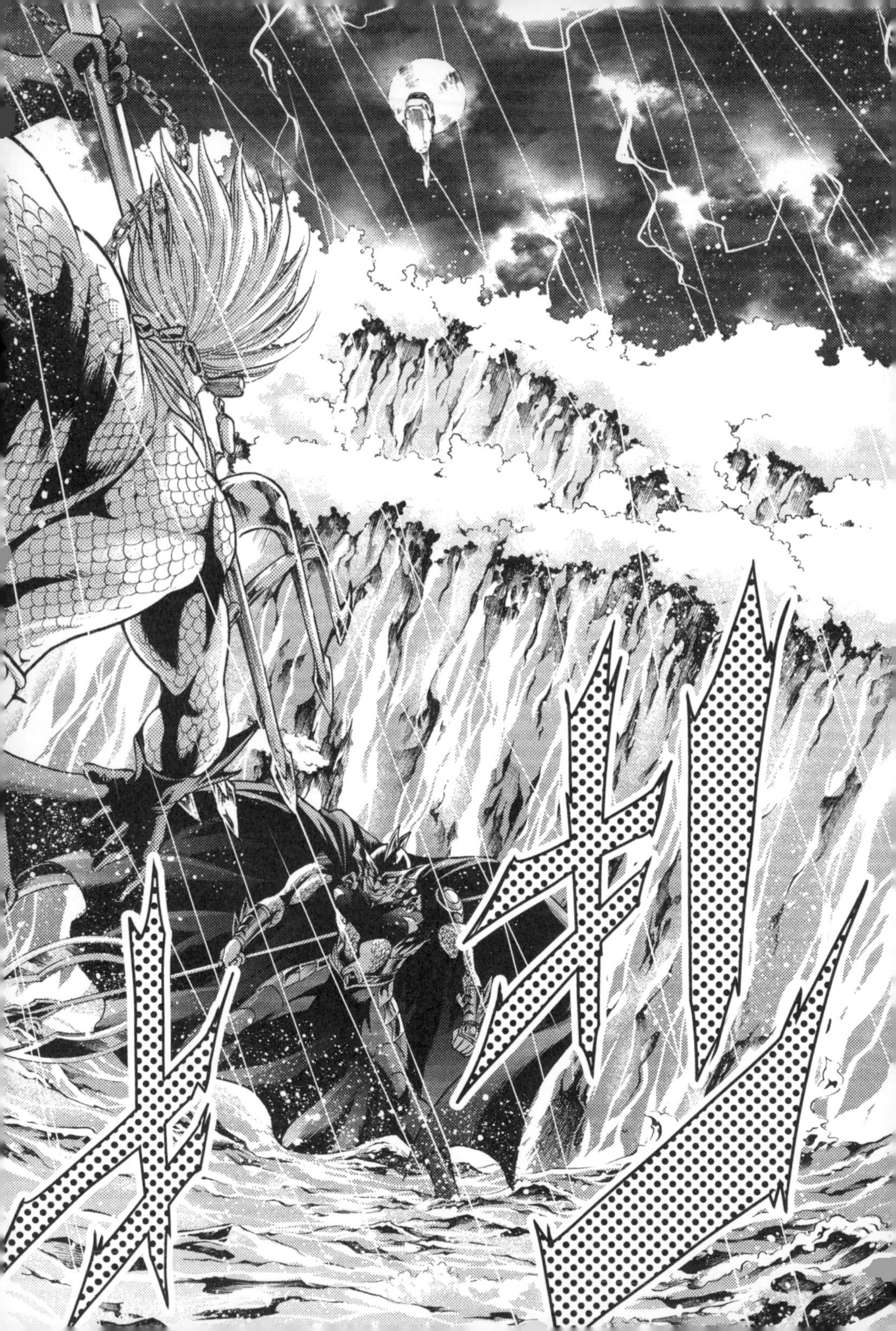

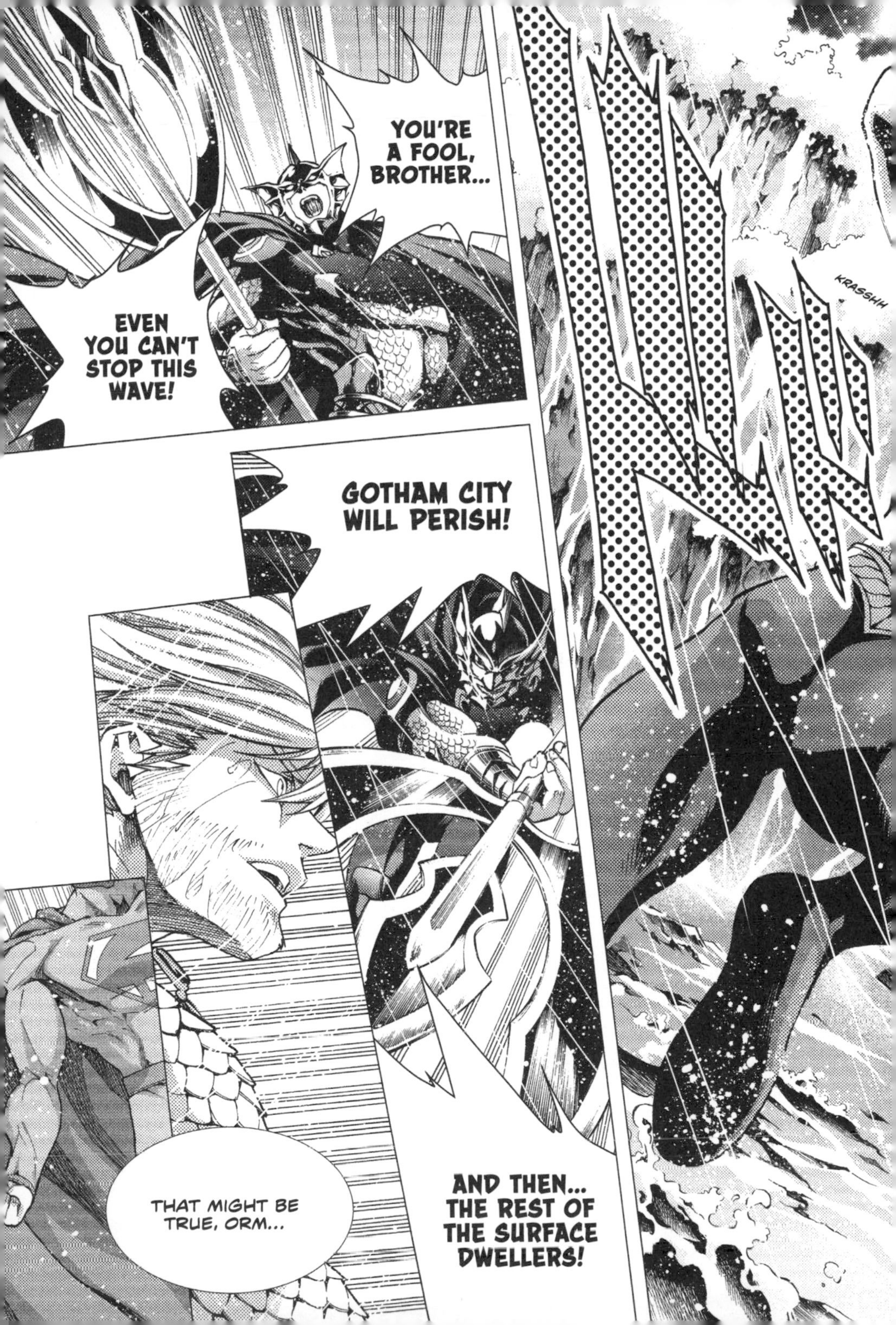
KRASSHH
YOU'RE A FOOL, BROTHER...
EVEN YOU CAN'T STOP THIS WAVE!
GOTHAM CITY WILL PERISH!
AND THEN... THE REST OF THE SURFACE DWELLERS!
THAT MIGHT BE TRUE, ORM...

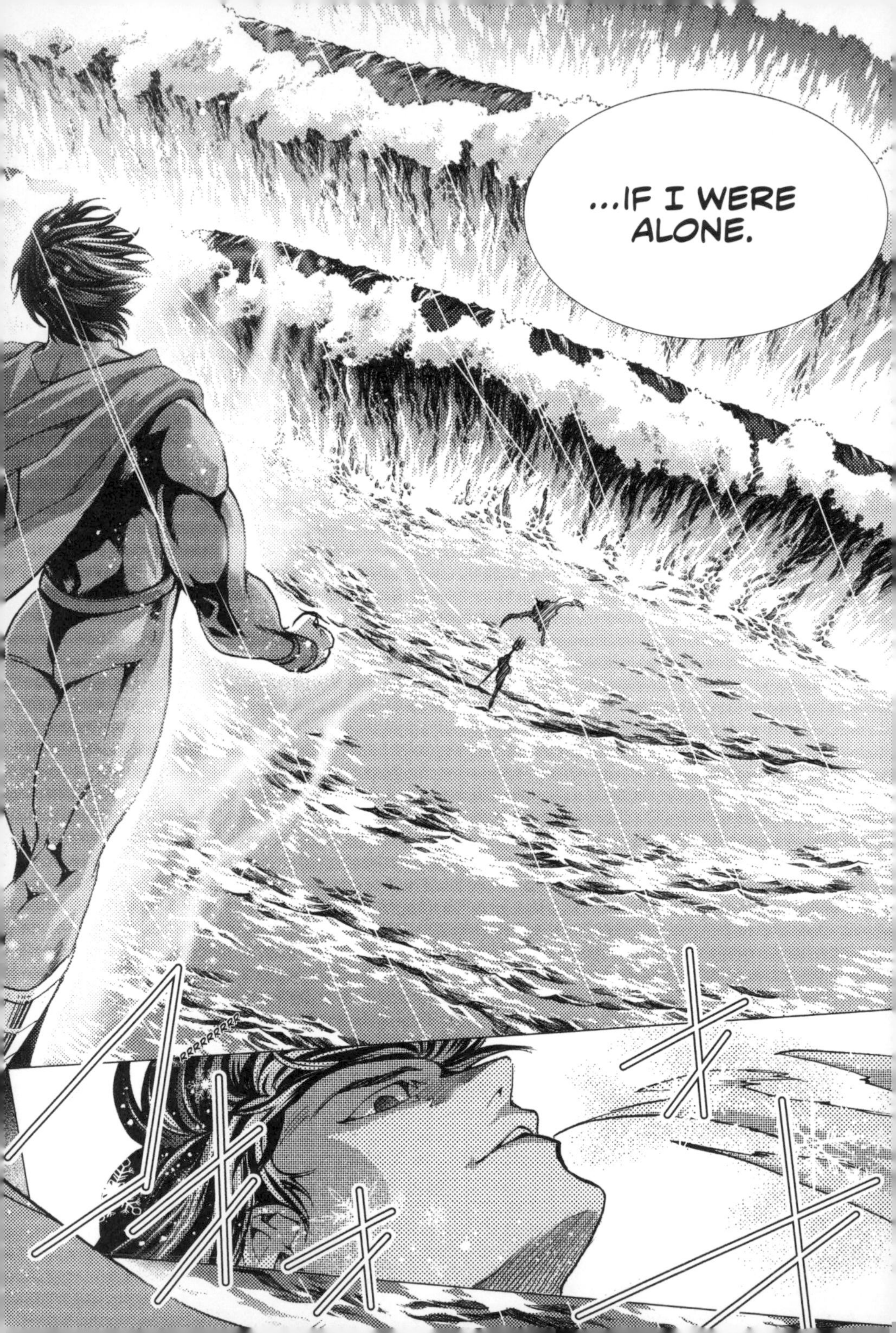
...IF I WERE ALONE.

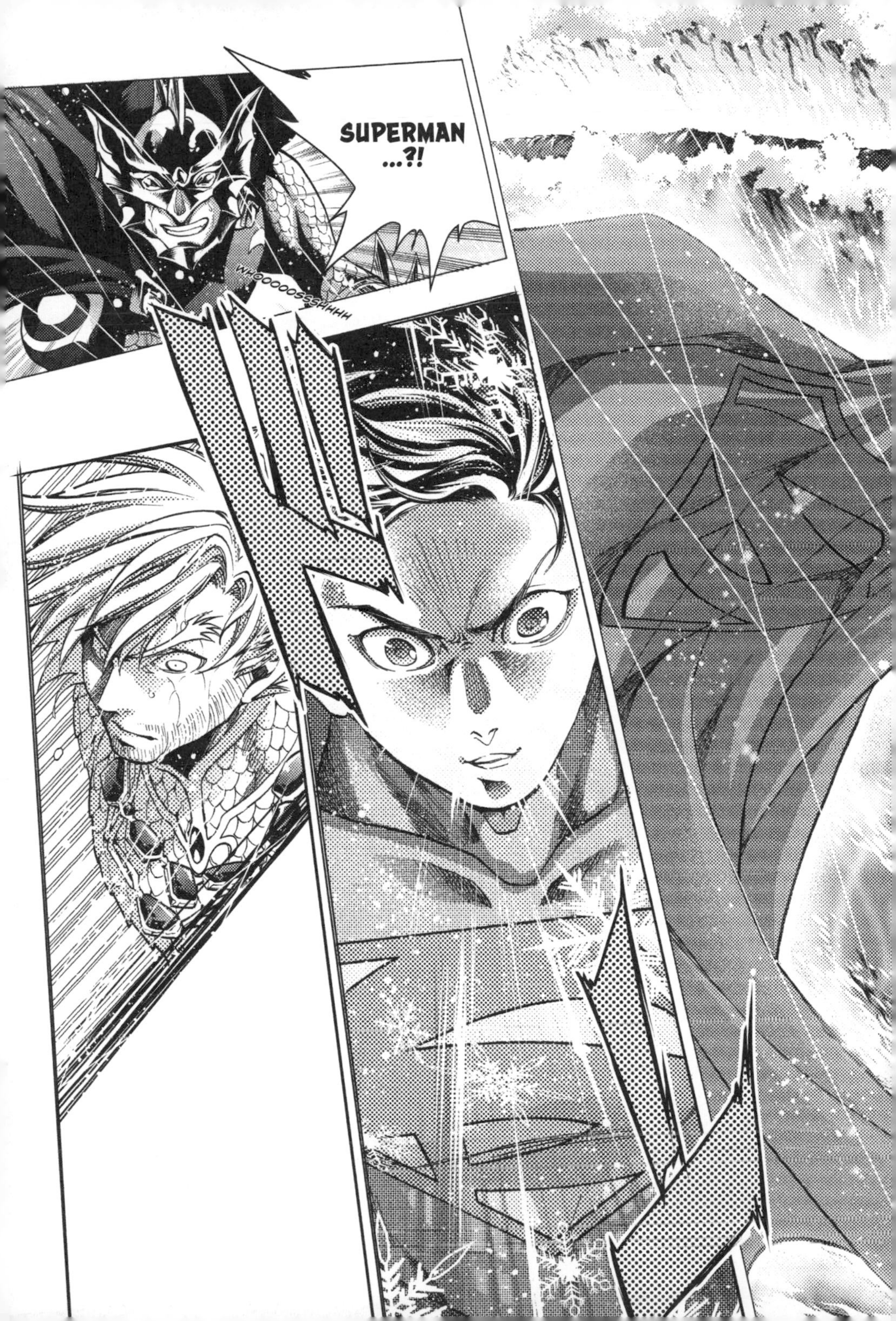
SUPERMAN ...?!
WHOOOOOOSSSSHHHH

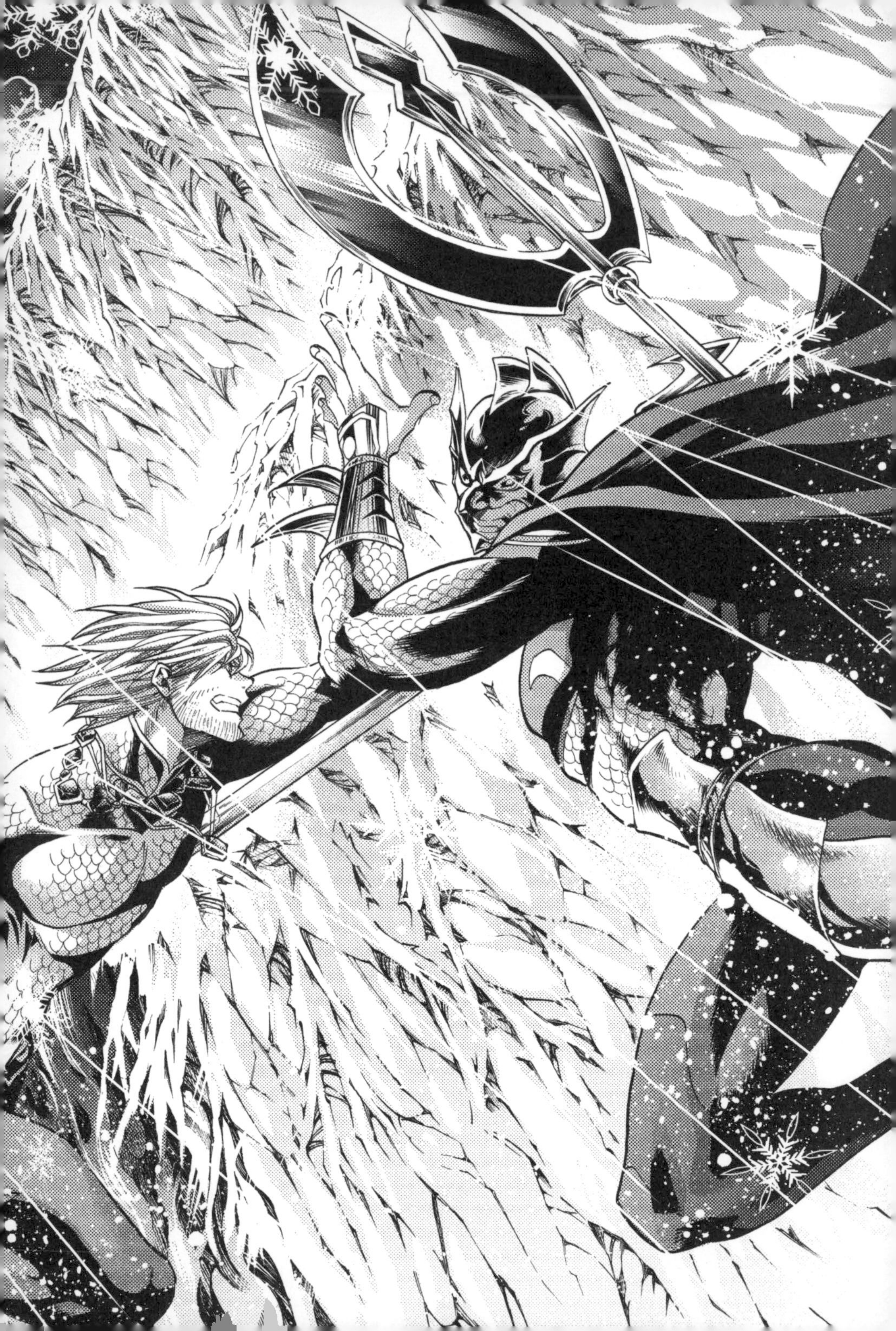

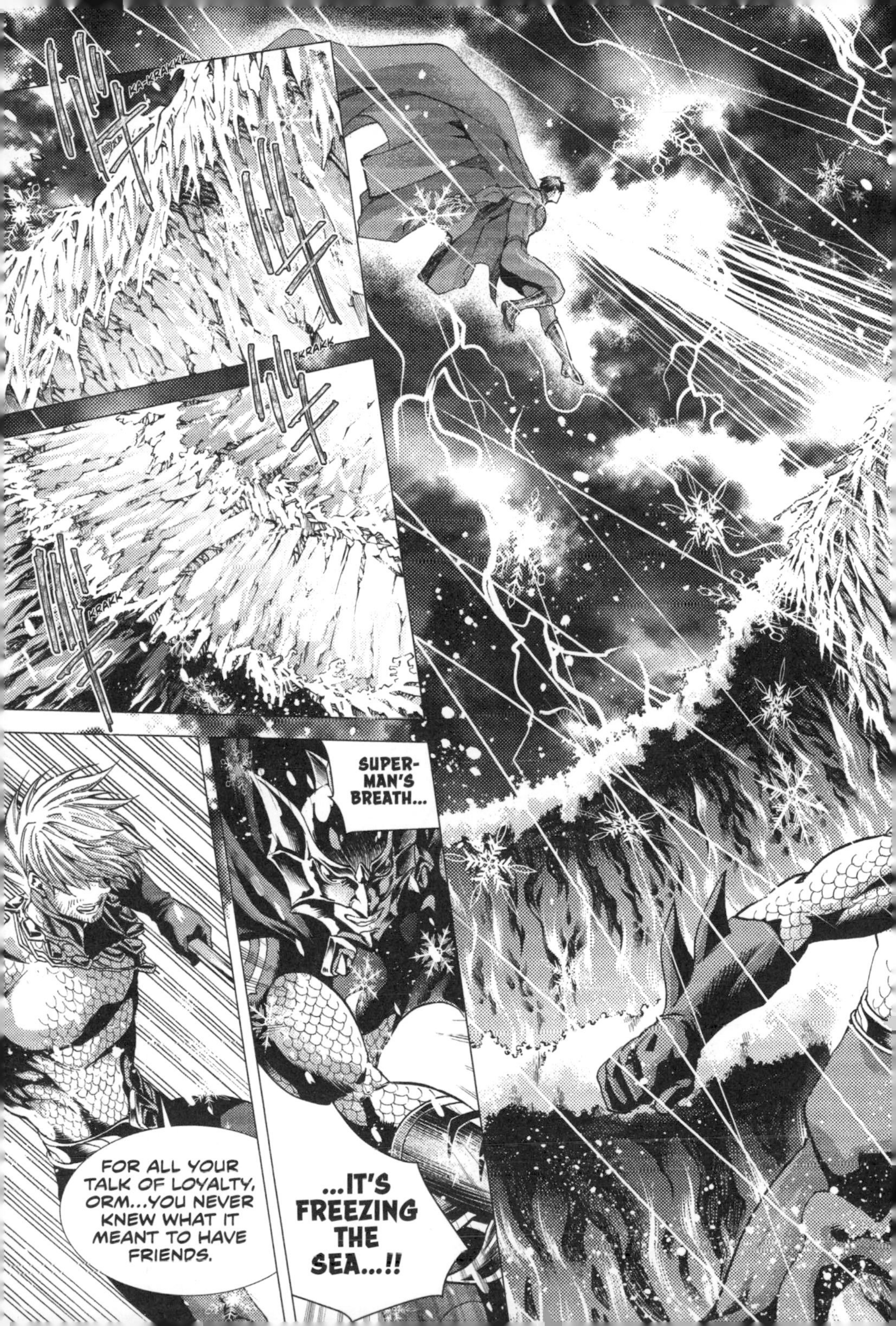

KA-KRAKKK
KRAKK
KRAKK
SUPER-MAN'S BREATH...
...IT'S FREEZING THE SEA...!!
FOR ALL YOUR TALK OF LOYALTY, ORM...YOU NEVER KNEW WHAT IT MEANT TO HAVE FRIENDS.

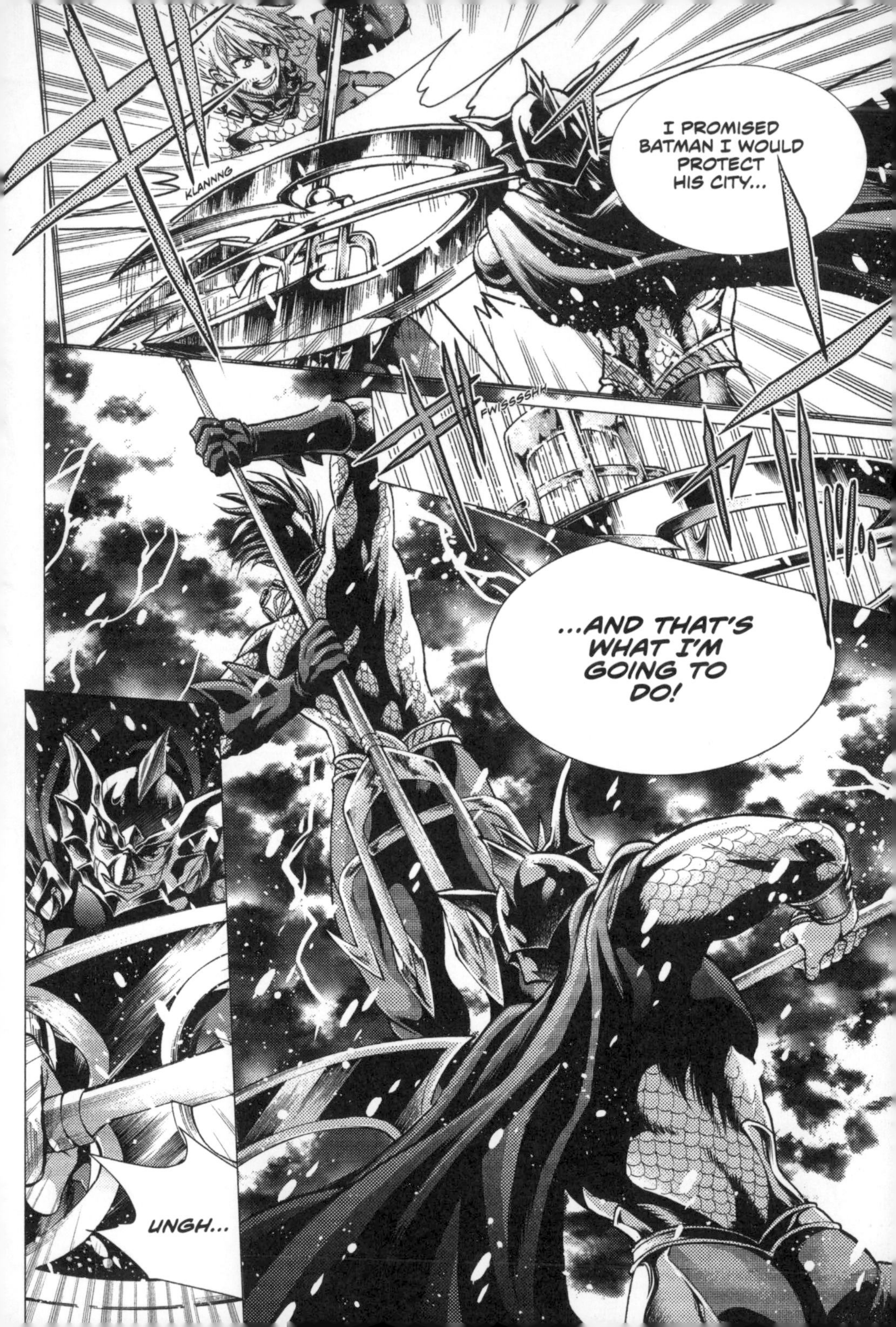
I PROMISED BATMAN I WOULD PROTECT HIS CITY...
KLANNNG
FWISSSSHH
...AND THAT'S WHAT I'M GOING TO DO!
UNGH...

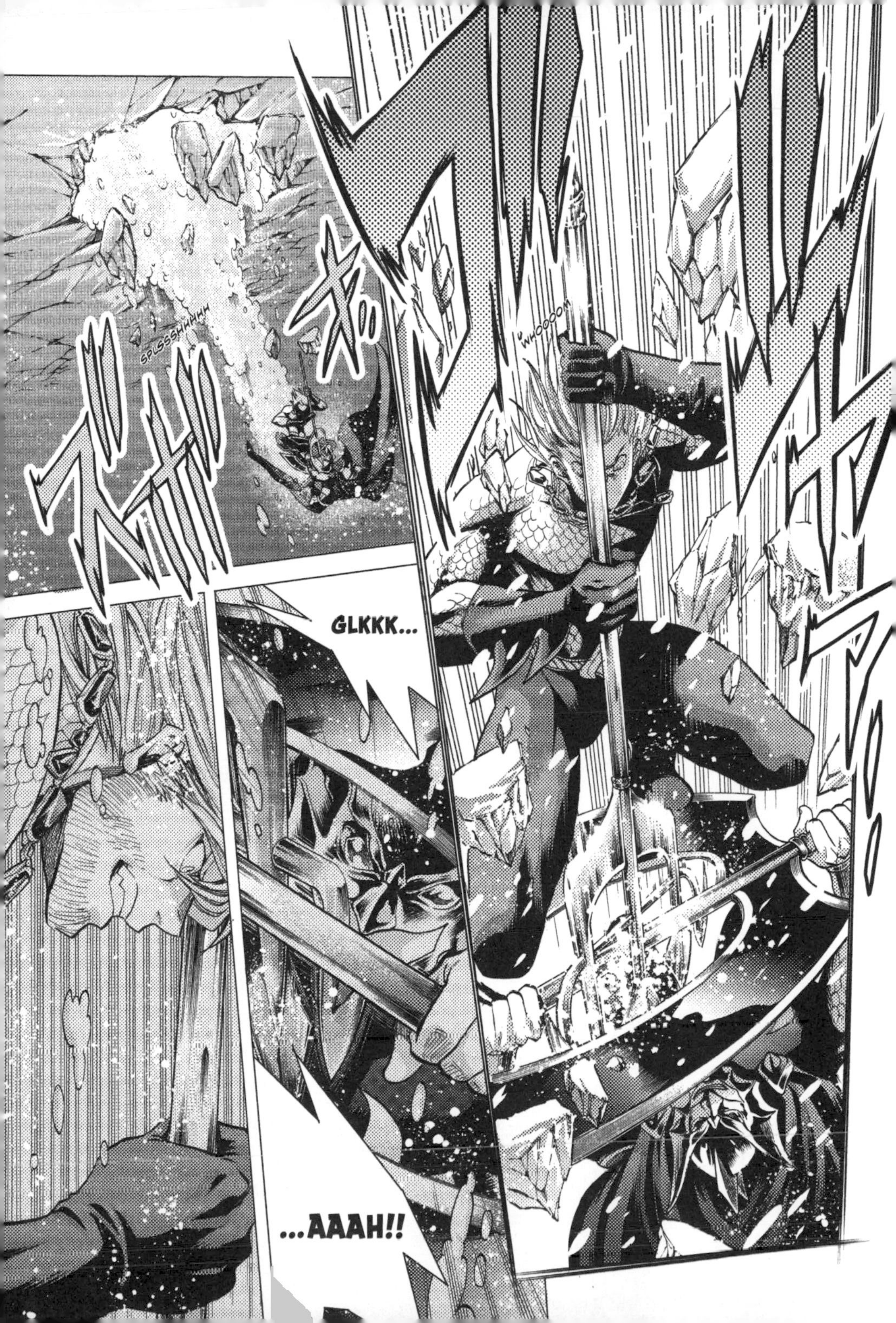
WHOOOOM
SPLSSSHHHHH
GLKKK...
...AAAH!!

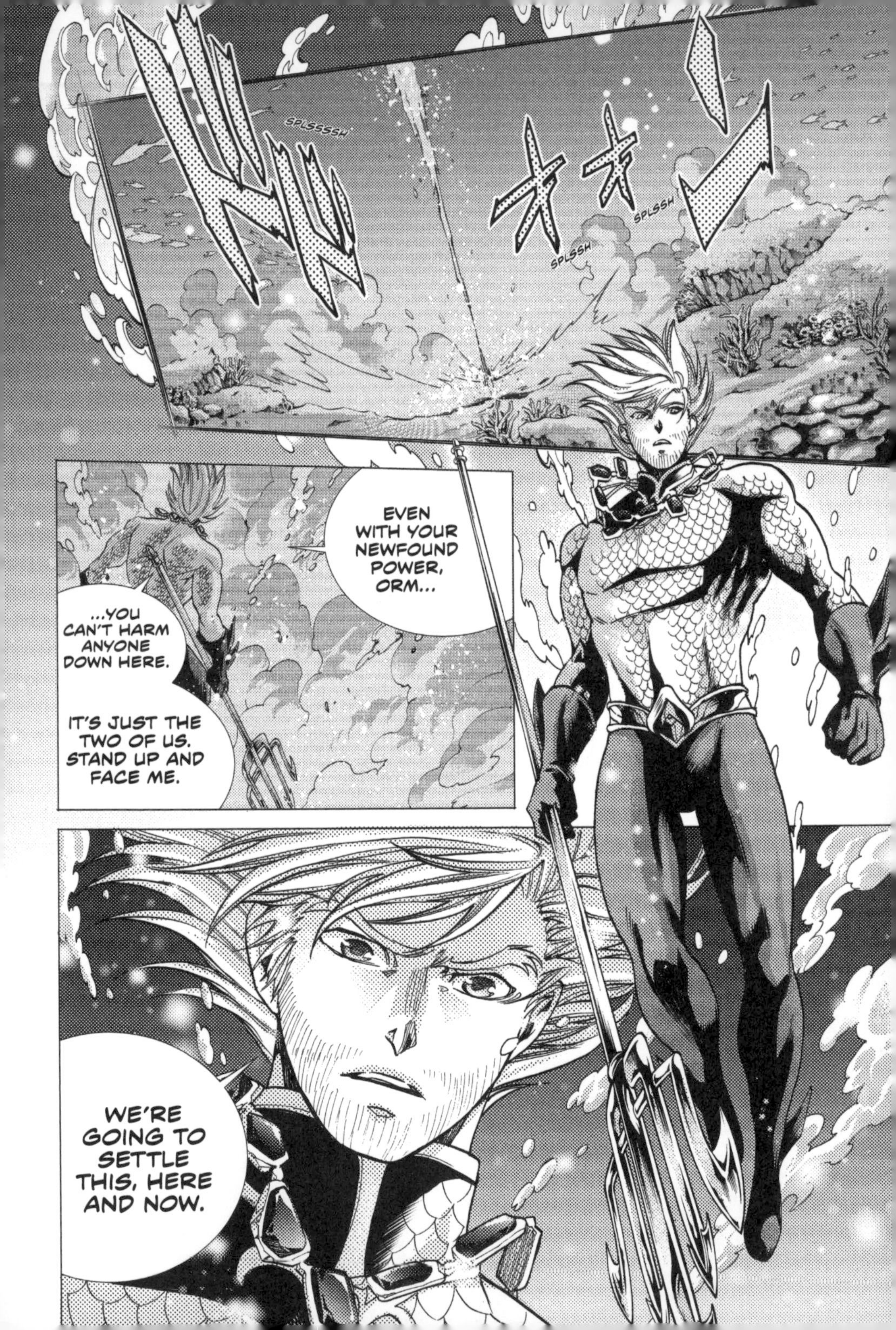
SPLSSH
SPLSSH
SPLSSSSH
EVEN WITH YOUR NEWFOUND POWER, ORM...
...YOU CAN'T HARM ANYONE DOWN HERE.
IT'S JUST THE TWO OF US. STAND UP AND FACE ME.
WE'RE GOING TO SETTLE THIS, HERE AND NOW.

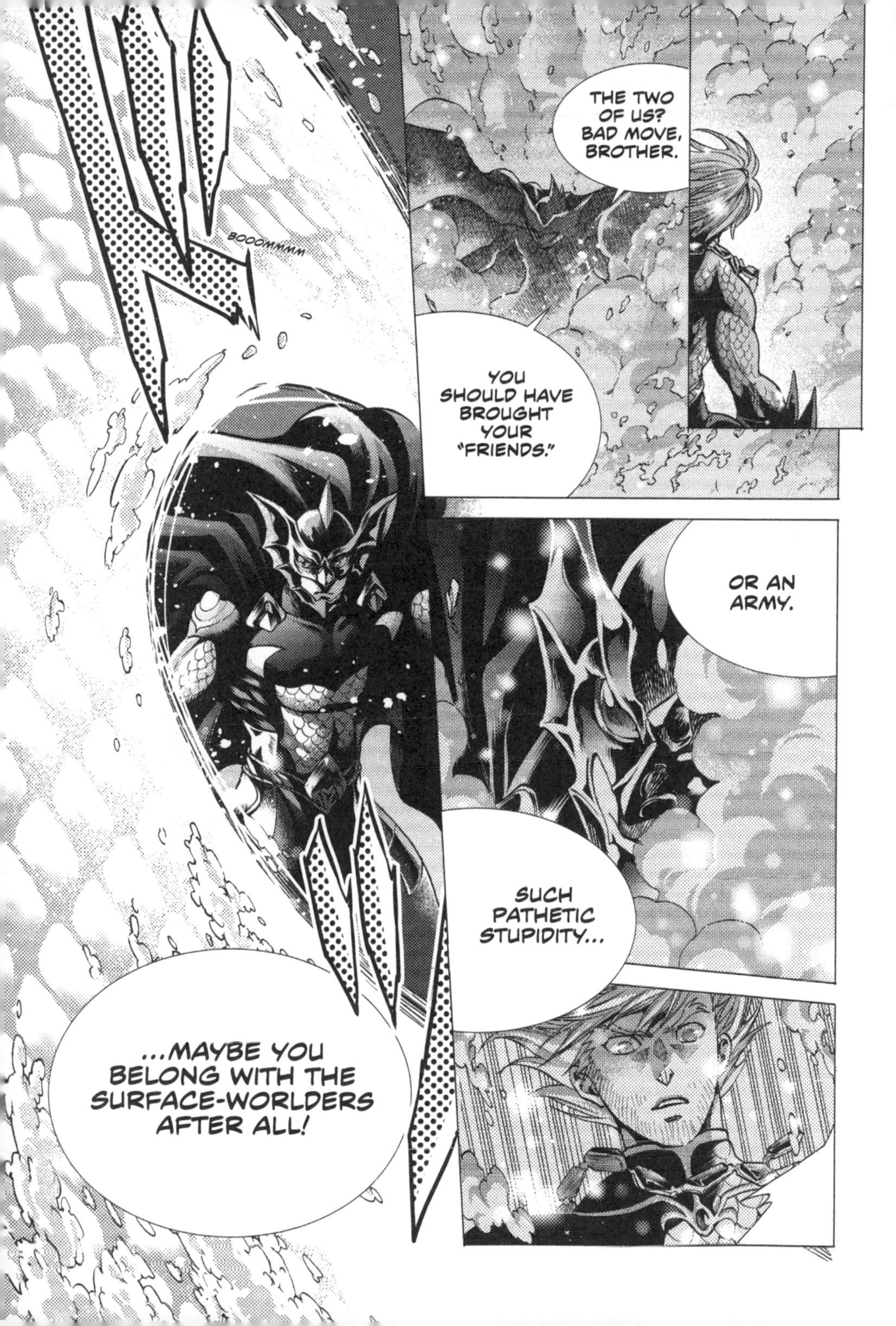
THE TWO OF US? BAD MOVE, BROTHER.
YOU SHOULD HAVE BROUGHT YOUR "FRIENDS."
OR AN ARMY.
SUCH PATHETIC STUPIDITY...
BOOOMMMM
...MAYBE YOU BELONG WITH THE SURFACE-WORLDERS AFTER ALL!

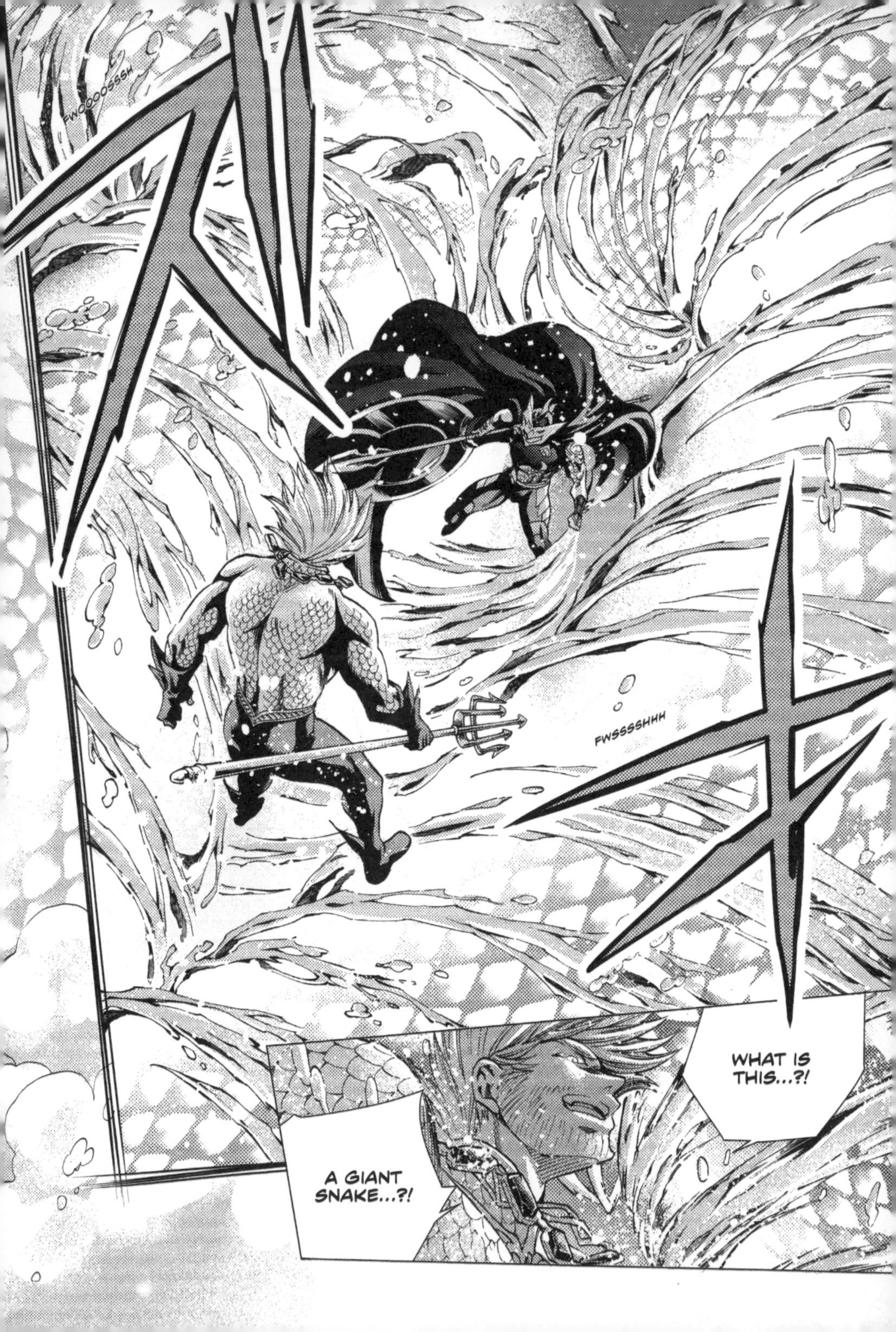
FWOOOOSSSH
FWSSSSHHH
WHAT IS THIS...?!
A GIANT SNAKE...?!

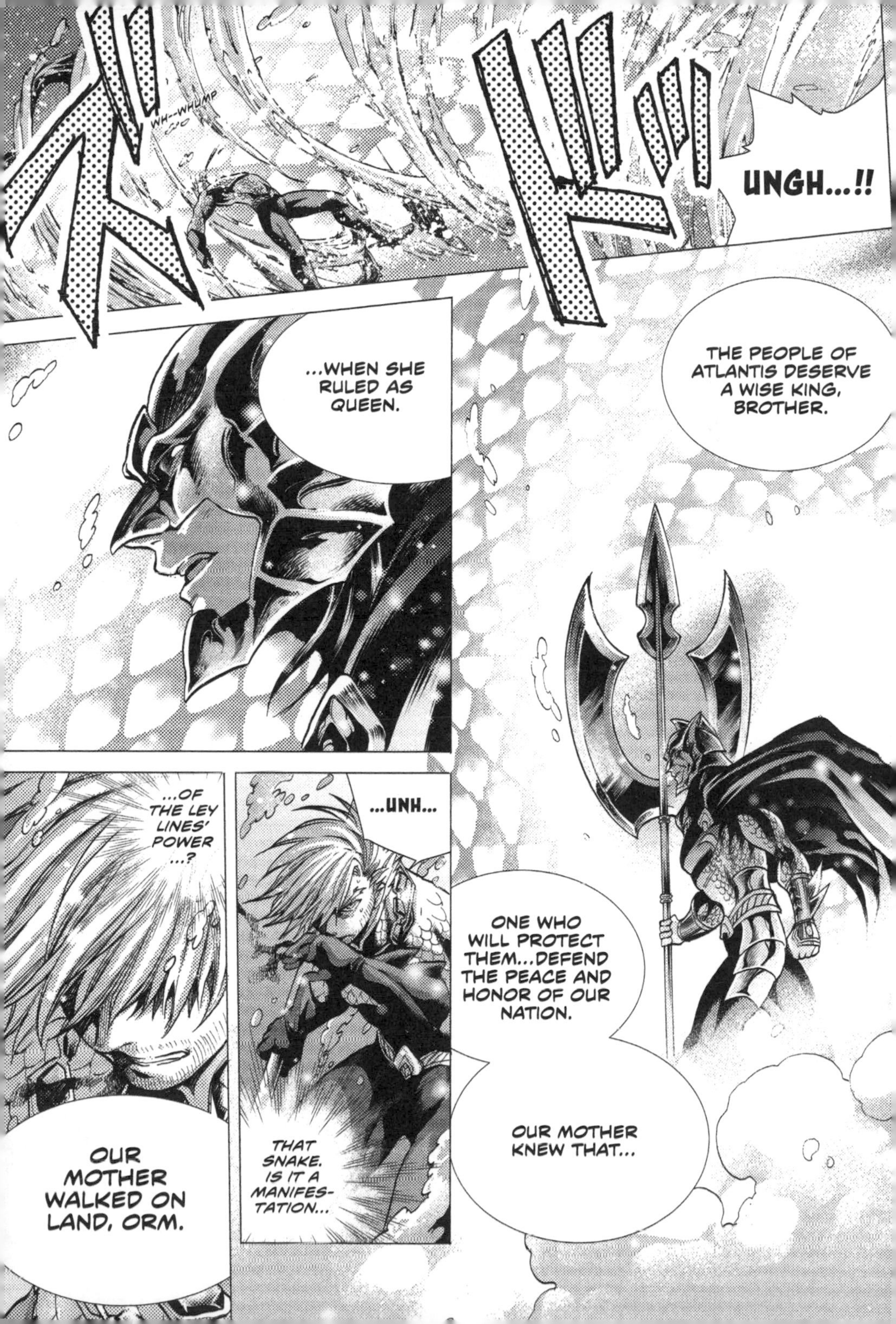
WH--WHUMP
UNGH...!!
THE PEOPLE OF ATLANTIS DESERVE A WISE KING, BROTHER.
ONE WHO WILL PROTECT THEM...DEFEND THE PEACE AND HONOR OF OUR NATION.
OUR MOTHER KNEW THAT...
...WHEN SHE RULED AS QUEEN.
...UNH...
THAT SNAKE. IS IT A MANIFESTATION...
...OF THE LEY LINES' POWER ...?
OUR MOTHER WALKED ON LAND, ORM.

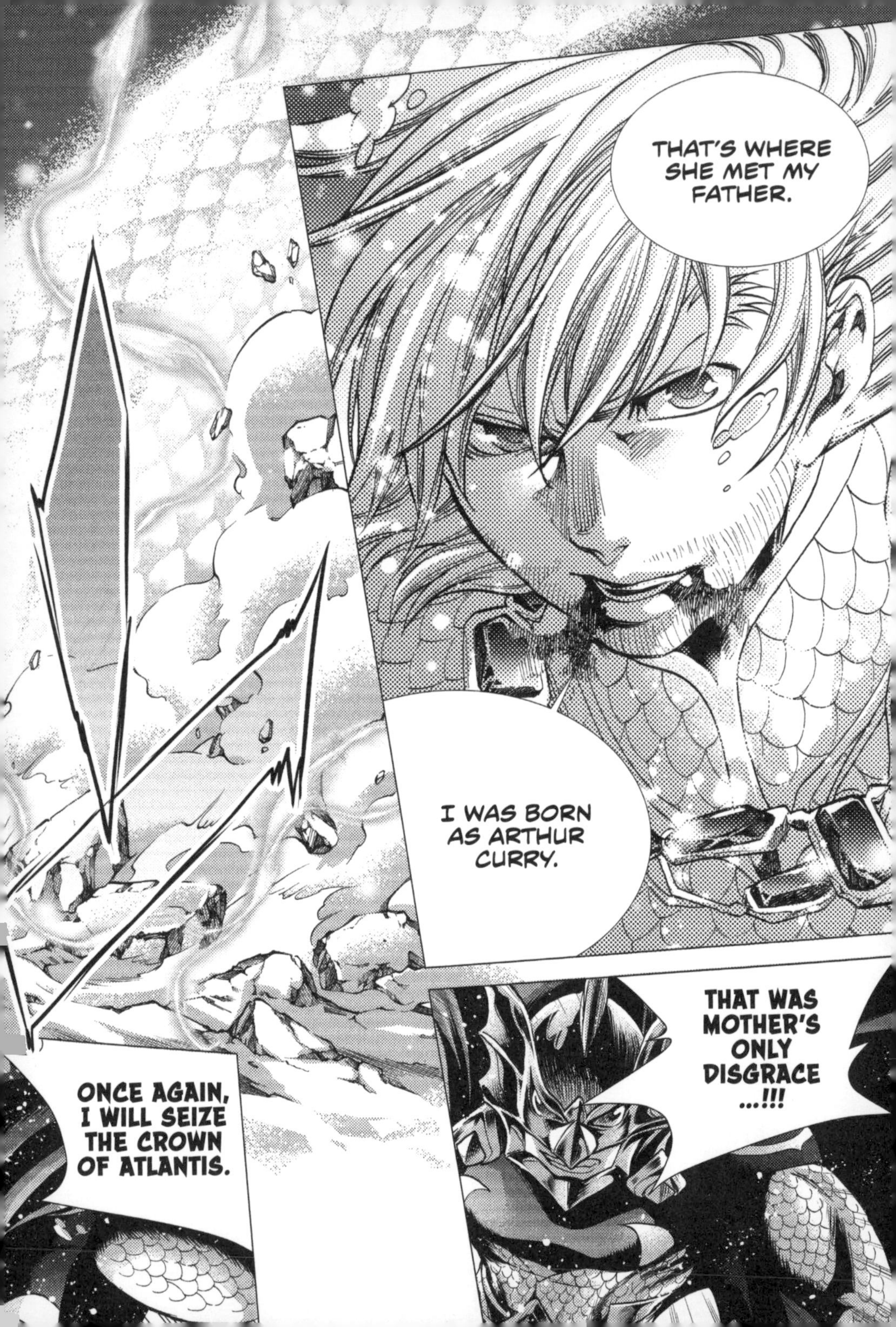
THAT'S WHERE SHE MET MY FATHER.
I WAS BORN AS ARTHUR CURRY.
THAT WAS MOTHER'S ONLY DISGRACE ...!!!
ONCE AGAIN, I WILL SEIZE THE CROWN OF ATLANTIS.

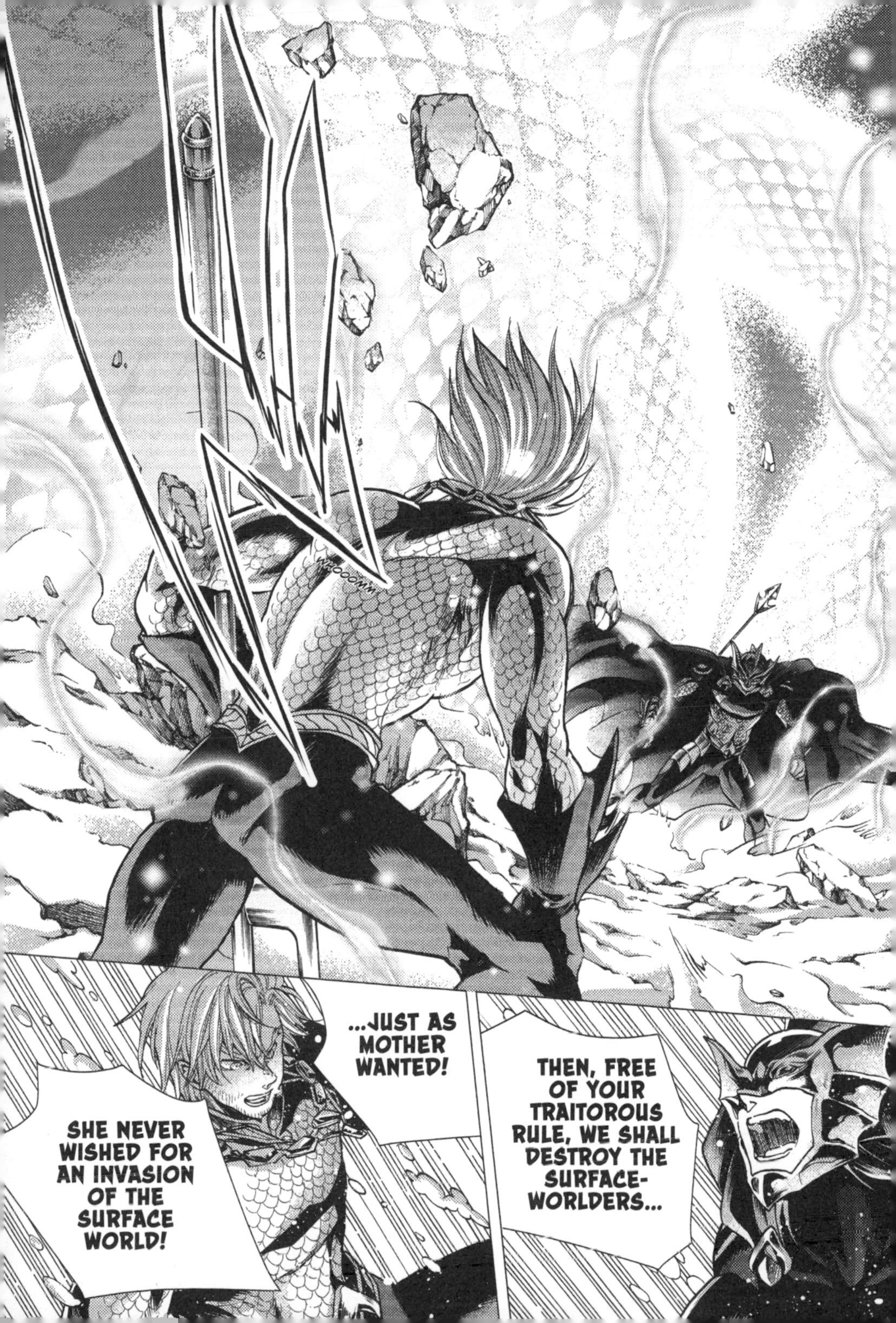
WHOOOMM
THEN, FREE OF YOUR TRAITOROUS RULE, WE SHALL DESTROY THE SURFACE-WORLDERS...
...JUST AS MOTHER WANTED!
SHE NEVER WISHED FOR AN INVASION OF THE SURFACE WORLD!

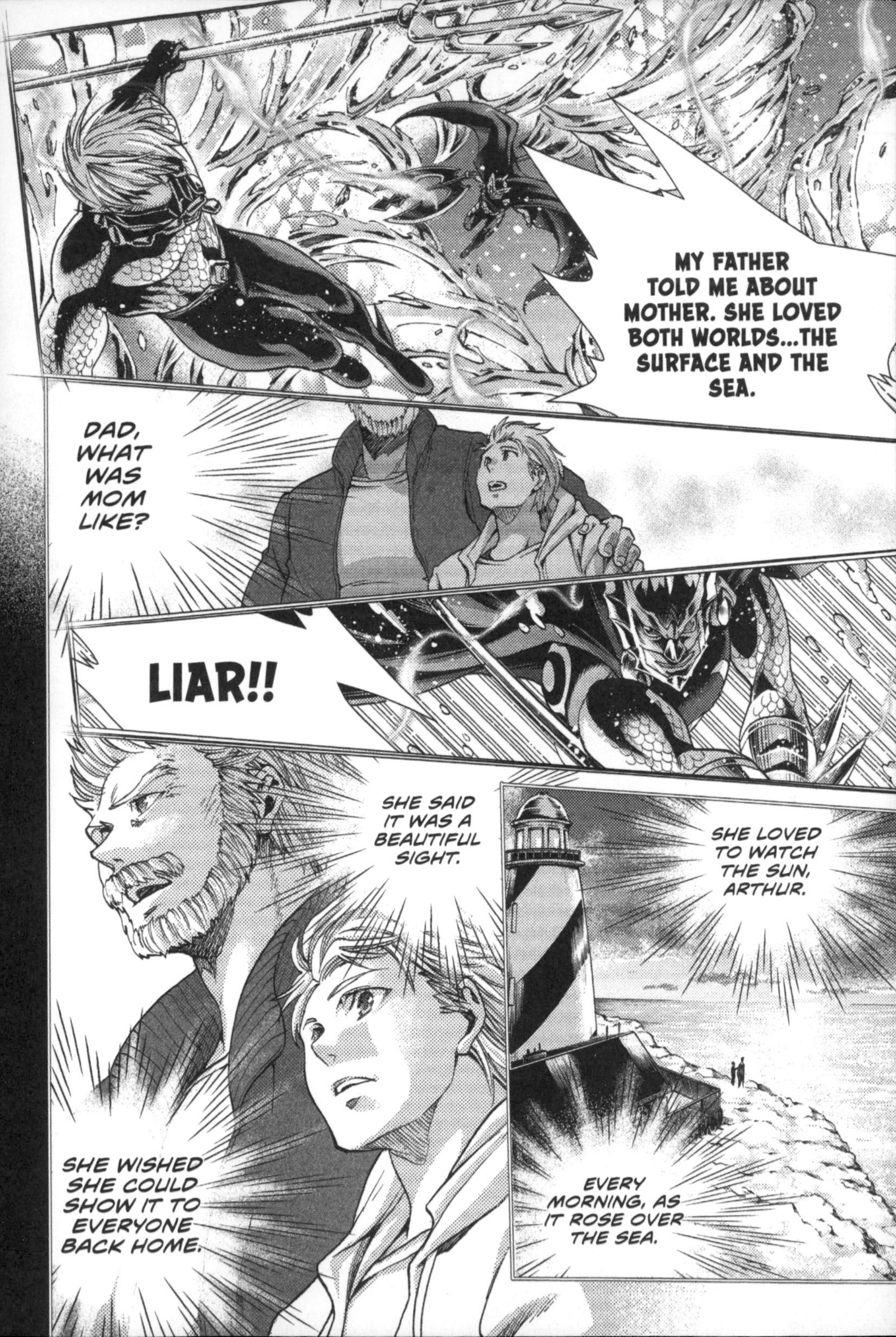
MY FATHER TOLD ME ABOUT MOTHER. SHE LOVED BOTH WORLDS...THE SURFACE AND THE SEA.
DAD, WHAT WAS MOM LIKE?
LIAR!!
SHE LOVED TO WATCH THE SUN, ARTHUR.
EVERY MORNING, AS IT ROSE OVER THE SEA.
SHE SAID IT WAS A BEAUTIFUL SIGHT.
SHE WISHED SHE COULD SHOW IT TO EVERYONE BACK HOME.

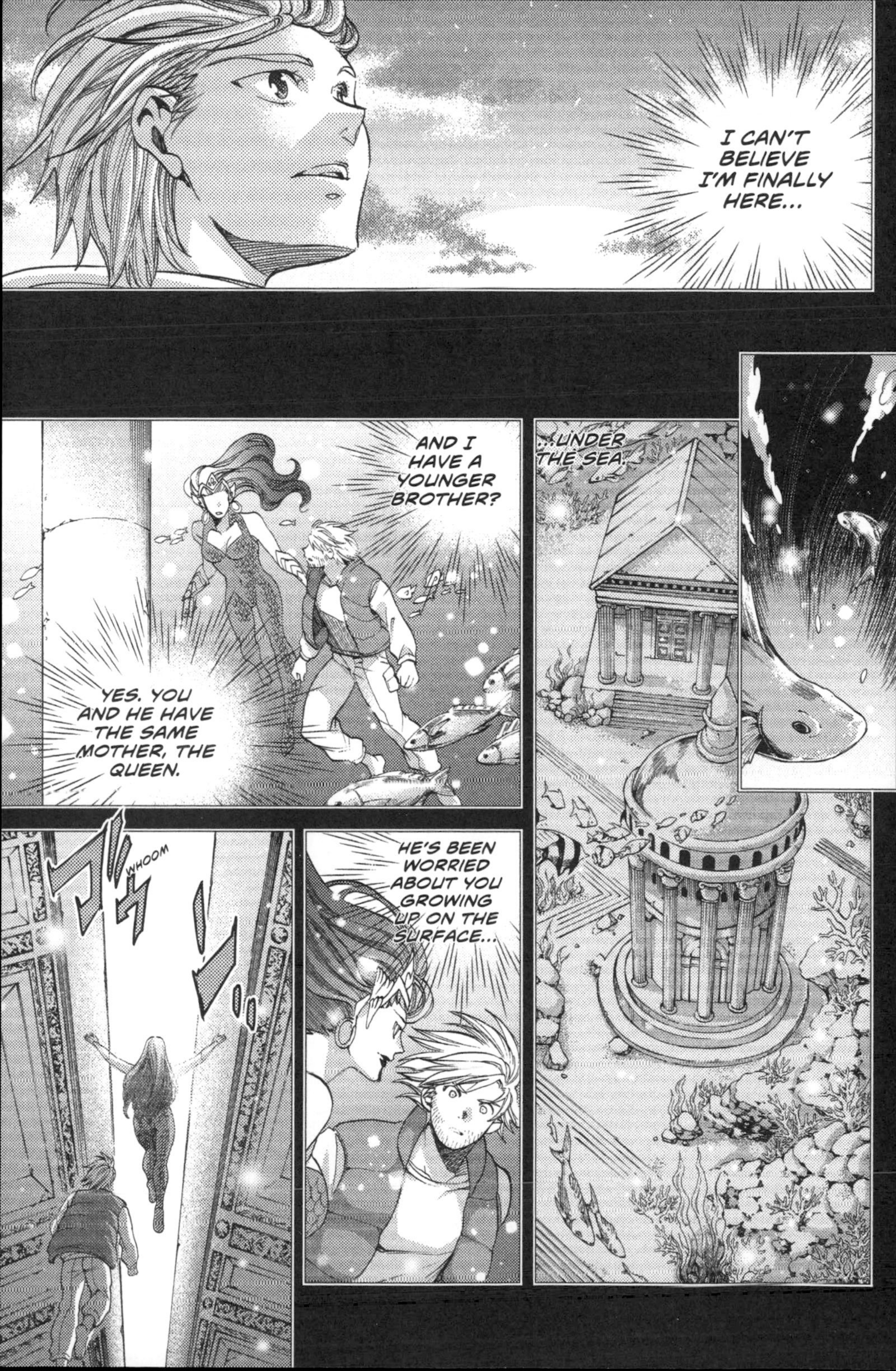

I CAN'T BELIEVE I'M FINALLY HERE...
...UNDER THE SEA.
AND I HAVE A YOUNGER BROTHER?
YES. YOU AND HE HAVE THE SAME MOTHER, THE QUEEN.
HE'S BEEN WORRIED ABOUT YOU GROWING UP ON THE SURFACE...
WHOOM

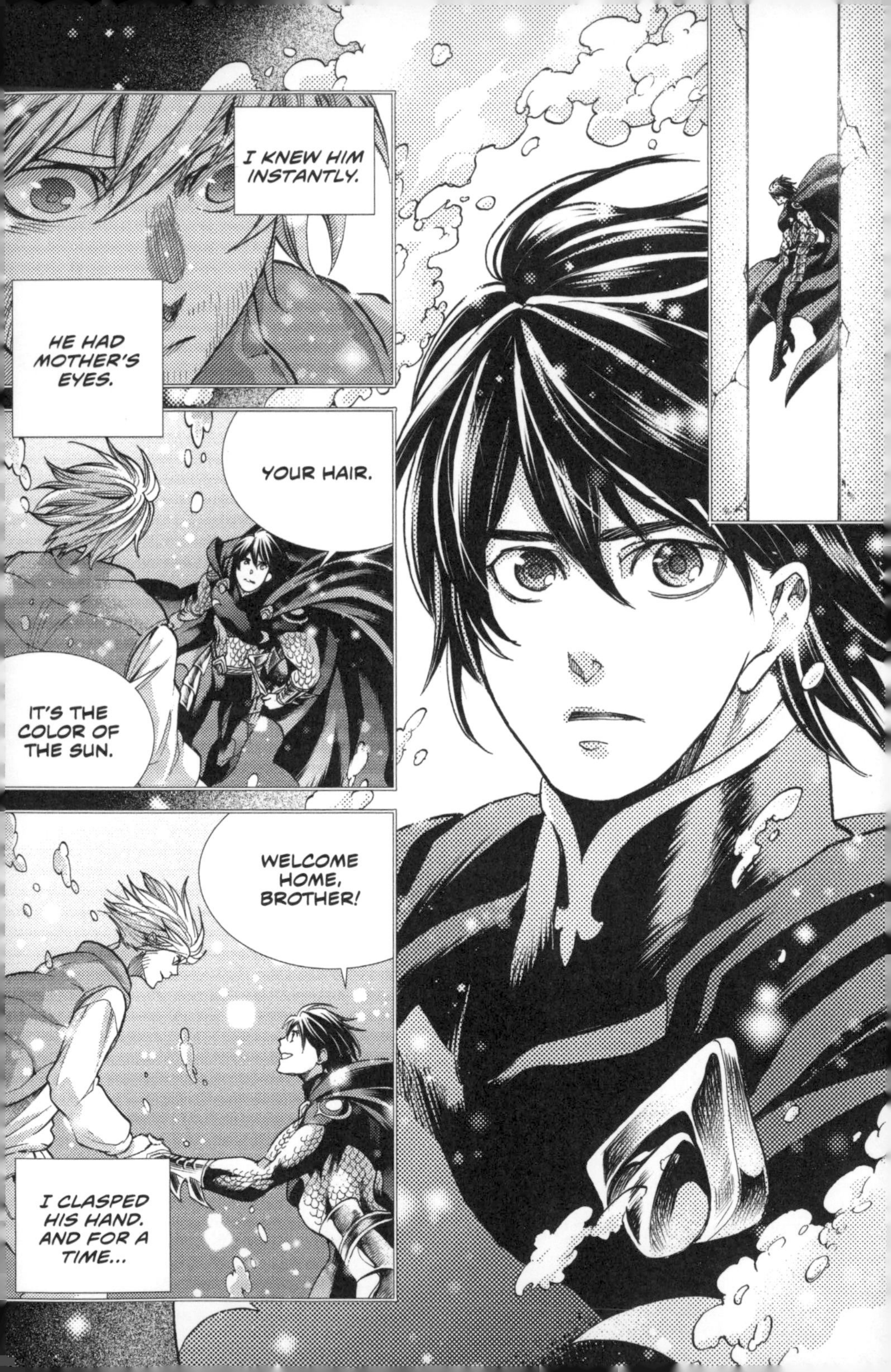
I KNEW HIM INSTANTLY.
HE HAD MOTHER'S EYES.
YOUR HAIR.
IT'S THE COLOR OF THE SUN.
WELCOME HOME, BROTHER!
I CLASPED HIS HAND. AND FOR A TIME...

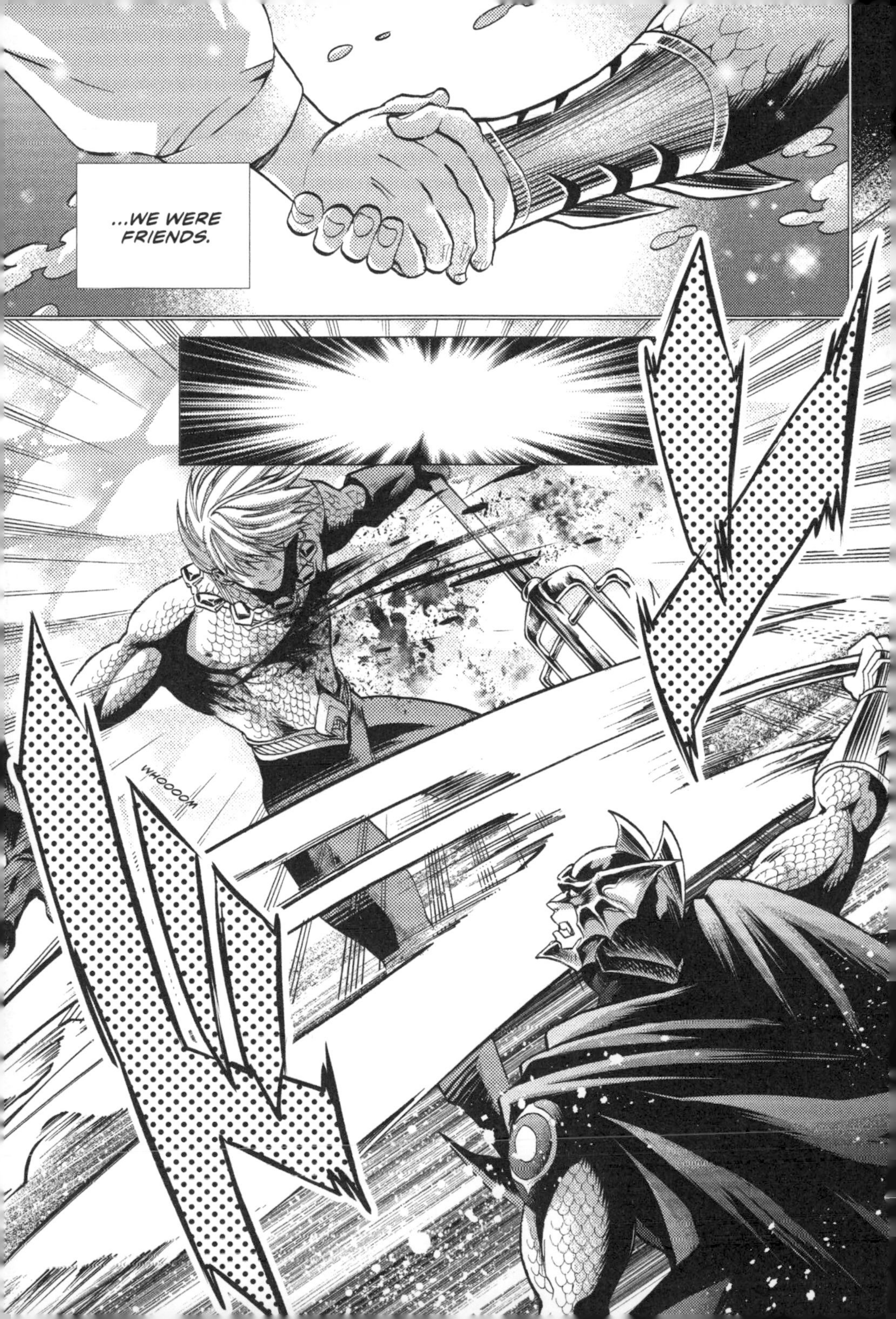
...WE WERE FRIENDS.
WHOOOOM

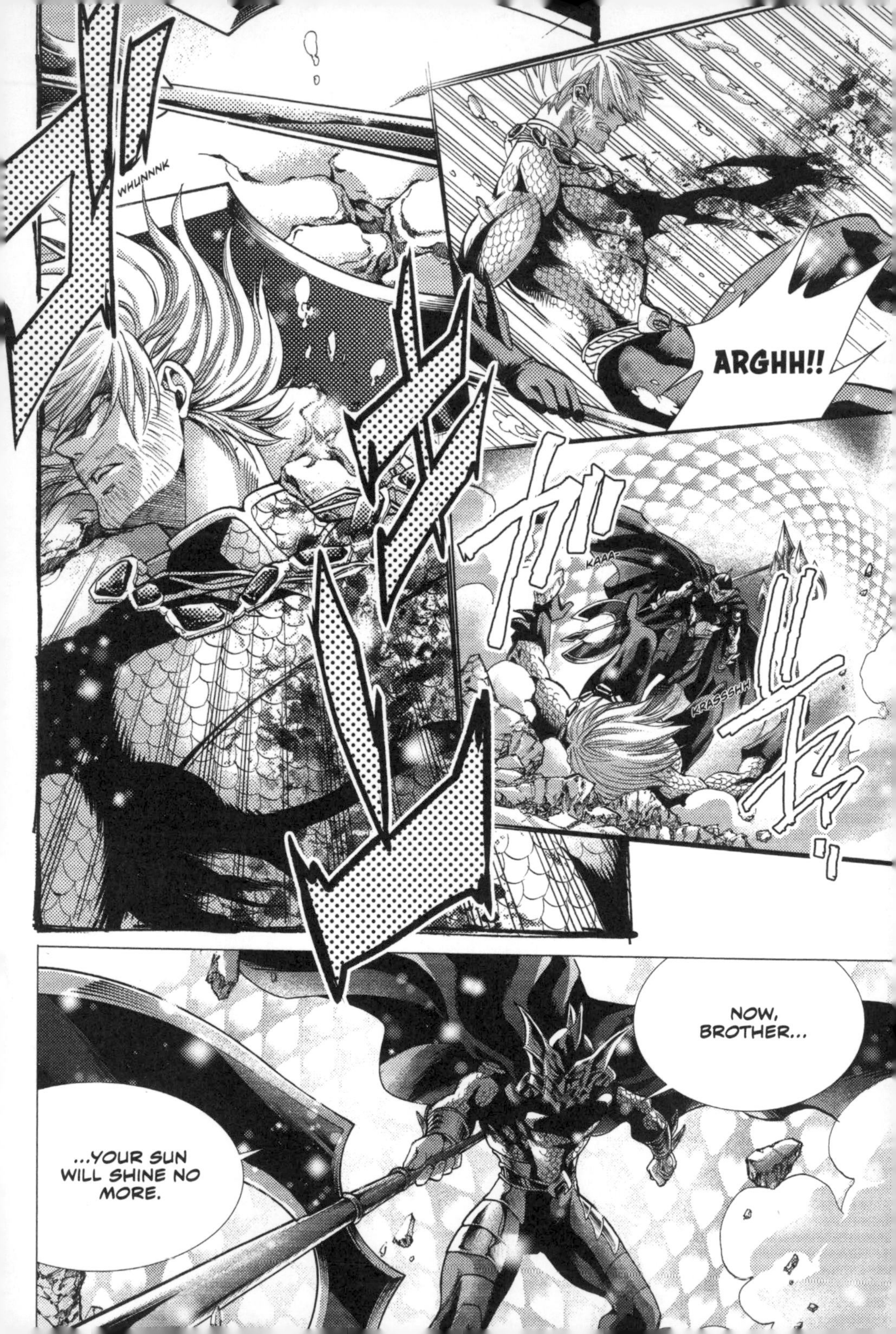
ARGHH!!
KAAA
KRASSSHH
WHUNNNK
NOW, BROTHER...
...YOUR SUN WILL SHINE NO MORE.

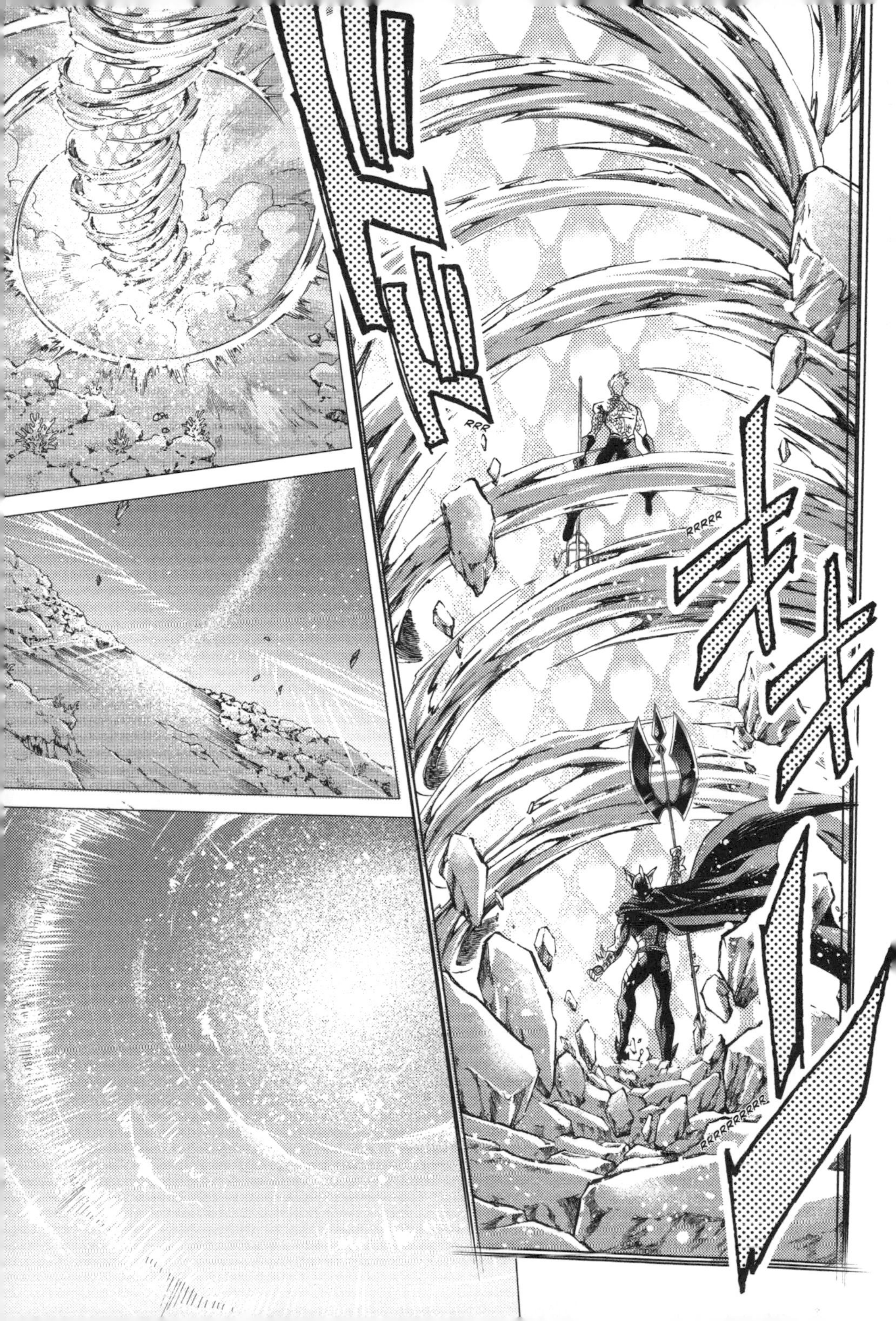
RRR
RRRRR
RRRRRRRRRRR

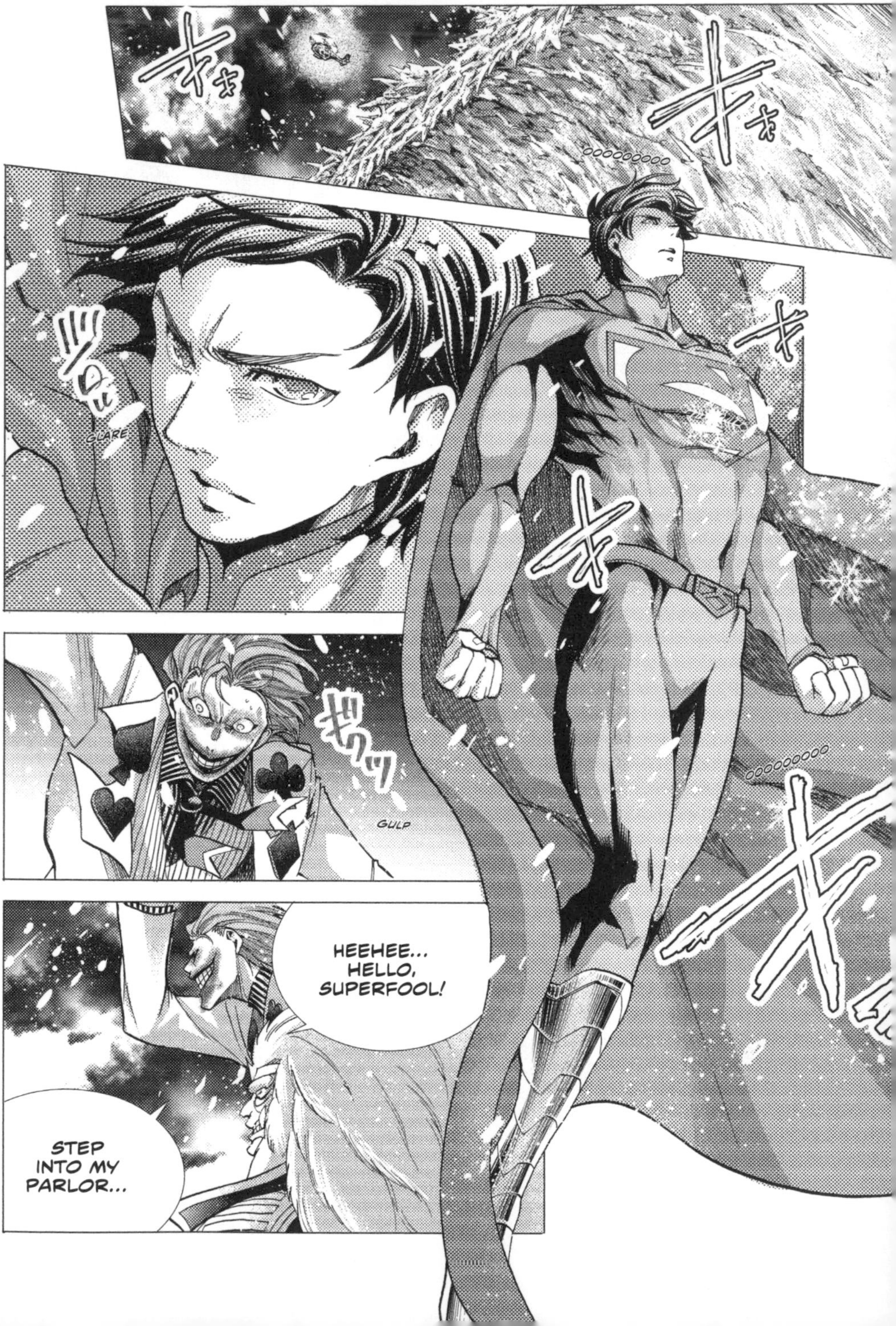
OOOOOOOOOO
OOOOOOOOOO
GLARE
GULP
HEEHEE... HELLO, SUPERFOOL!
STEP INTO MY PARLOR...

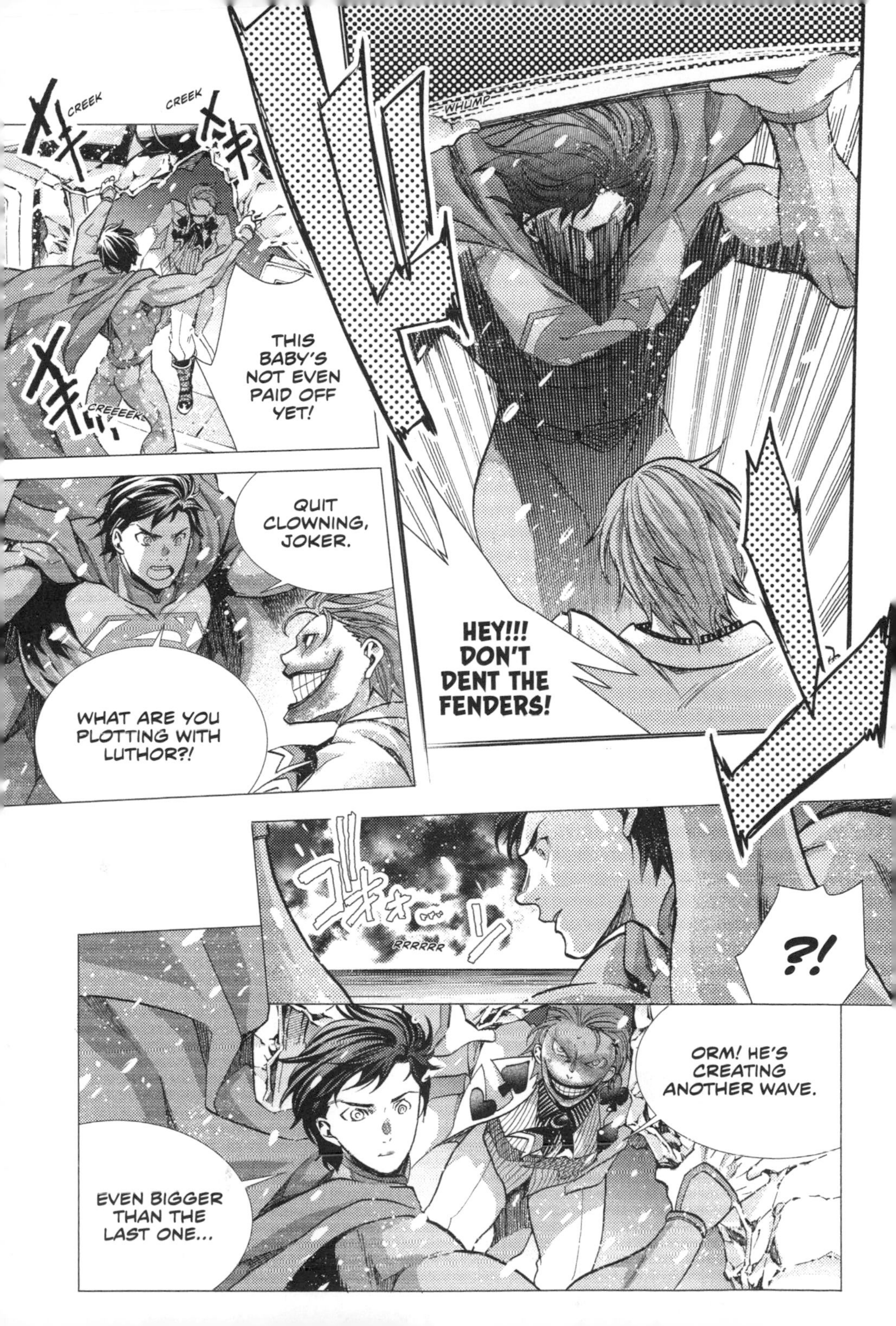
WHUMP
HEY!!! DON'T DENT THE FENDERS!
CREEK
CREEK
THIS BABY'S NOT EVEN PAID OFF YET!
CREEEEEK
QUIT CLOWNING, JOKER.
WHAT ARE YOU PLOTTING WITH LUTHOR?!
RRRRRR
?!
ORM! HE'S CREATING ANOTHER WAVE.
EVEN BIGGER THAN THE LAST ONE...

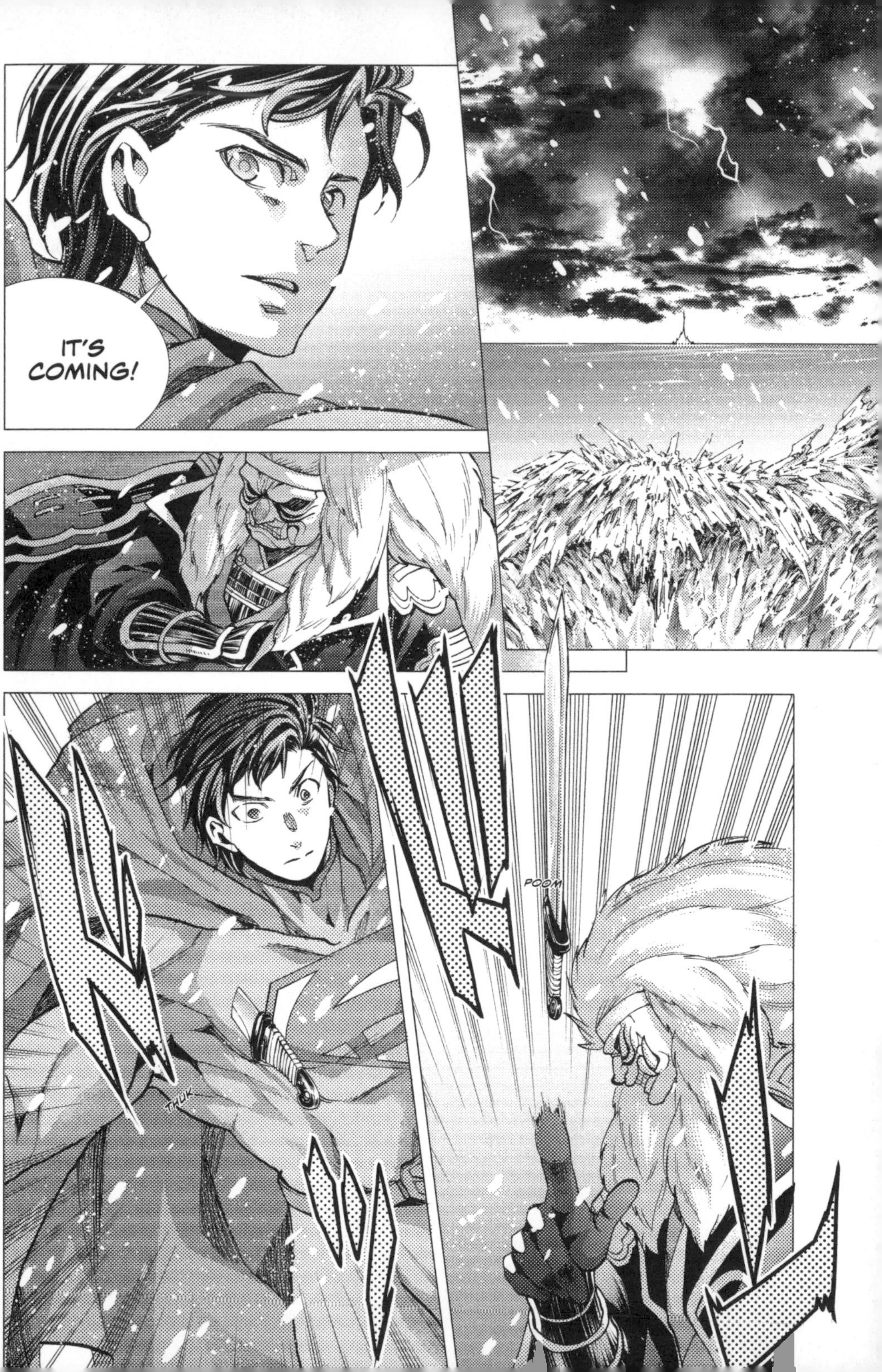
IT'S COMING!
POOM
THUK

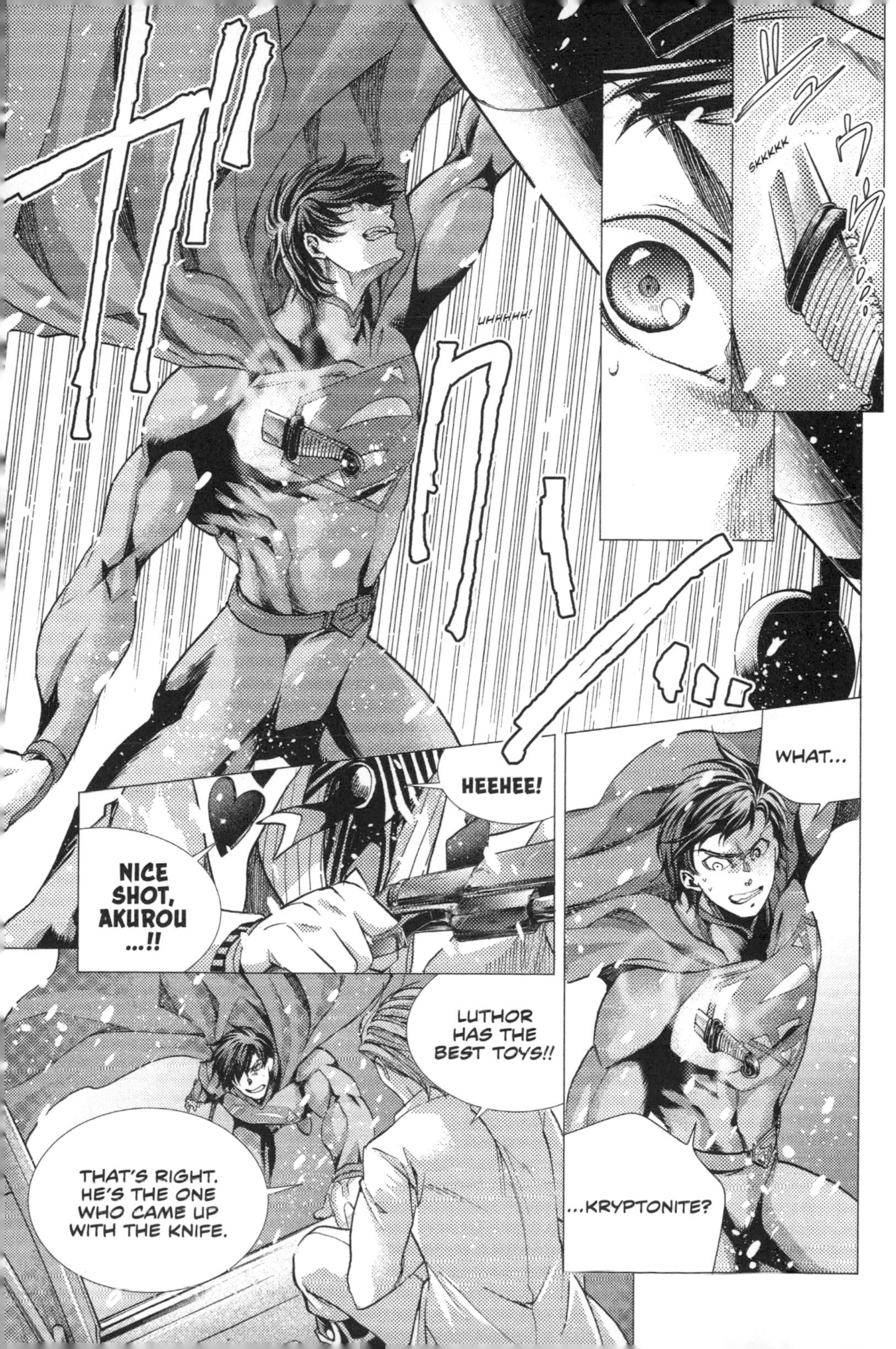
SKKKKK
UHHHHH!
...
WHAT...
...KRYPTONITE?
HEEHEE!
NICE SHOT, AKUROU ...!!
LUTHOR HAS THE BEST TOYS!!
THAT'S RIGHT. HE'S THE ONE WHO CAME UP WITH THE KNIFE.

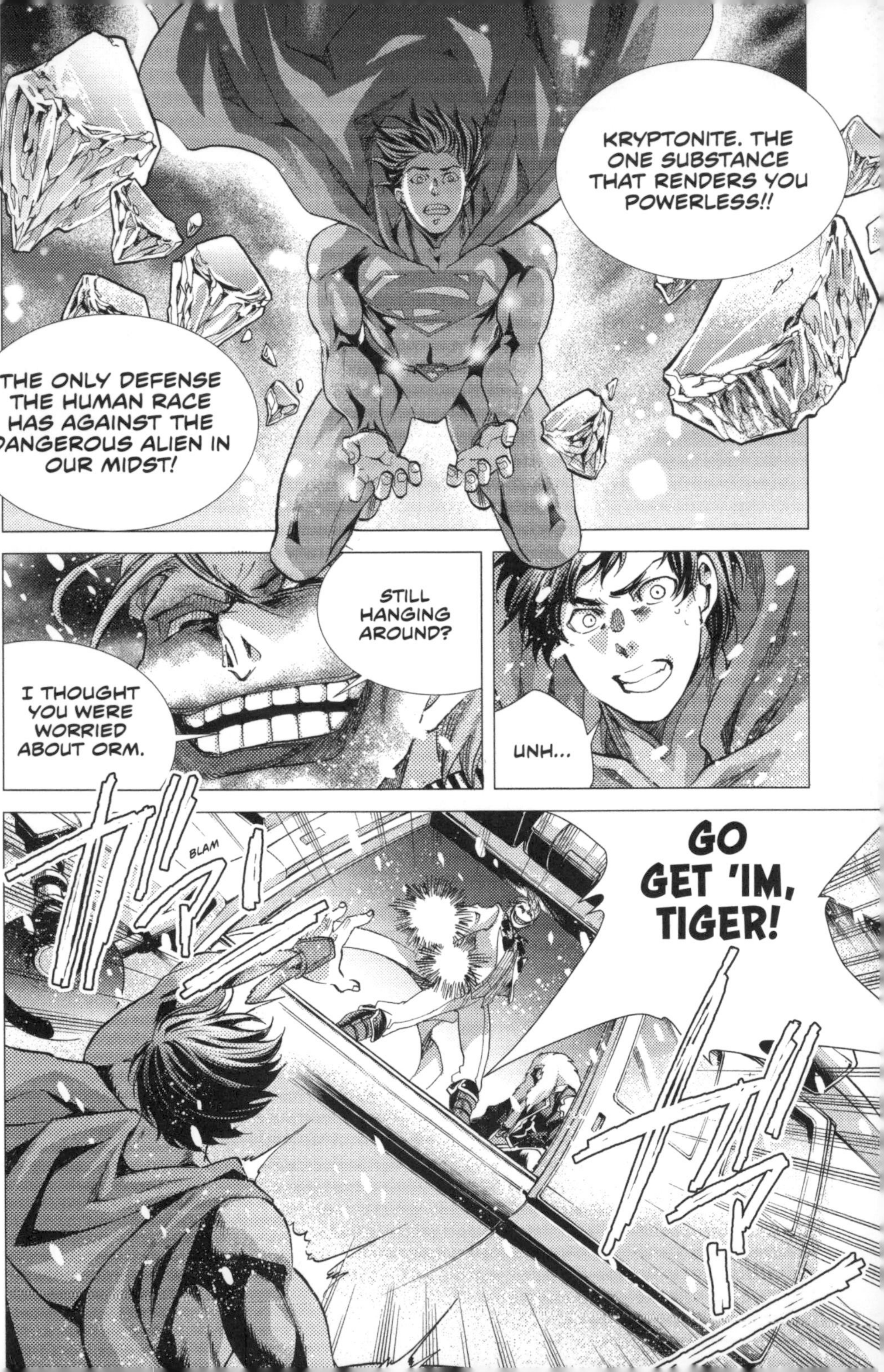
KRYPTONITE. THE ONE SUBSTANCE THAT RENDERS YOU POWERLESS!!
THE ONLY DEFENSE THE HUMAN RACE HAS AGAINST THE DANGEROUS ALIEN IN OUR MIDST!
UNH...
STILL HANGING AROUND?
I THOUGHT YOU WERE WORRIED ABOUT ORM.
GO GET 'IM, TIGER!
BLAM

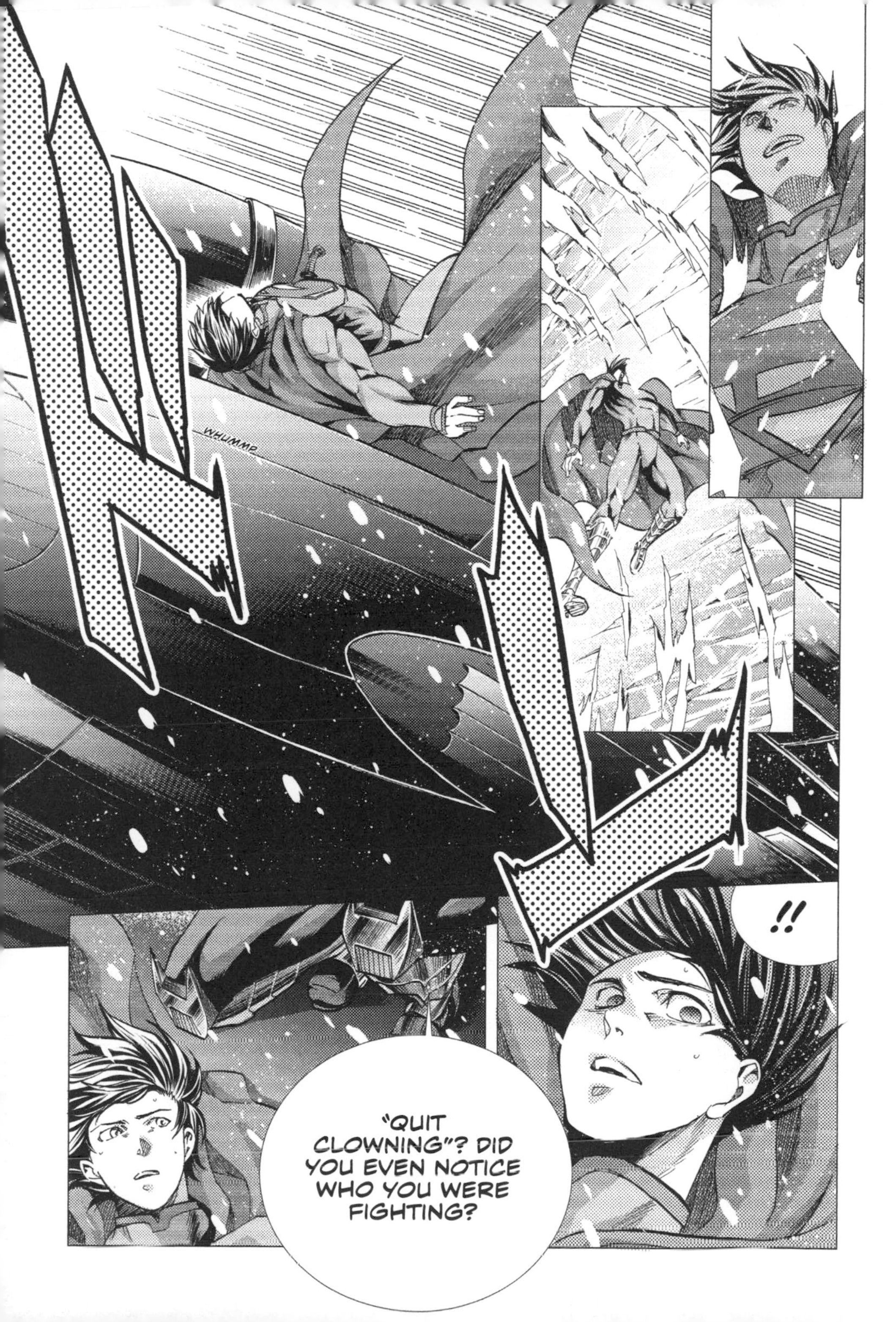
WHUMMP
!!
"QUIT CLOWNING"? DID YOU EVEN NOTICE WHO YOU WERE FIGHTING?

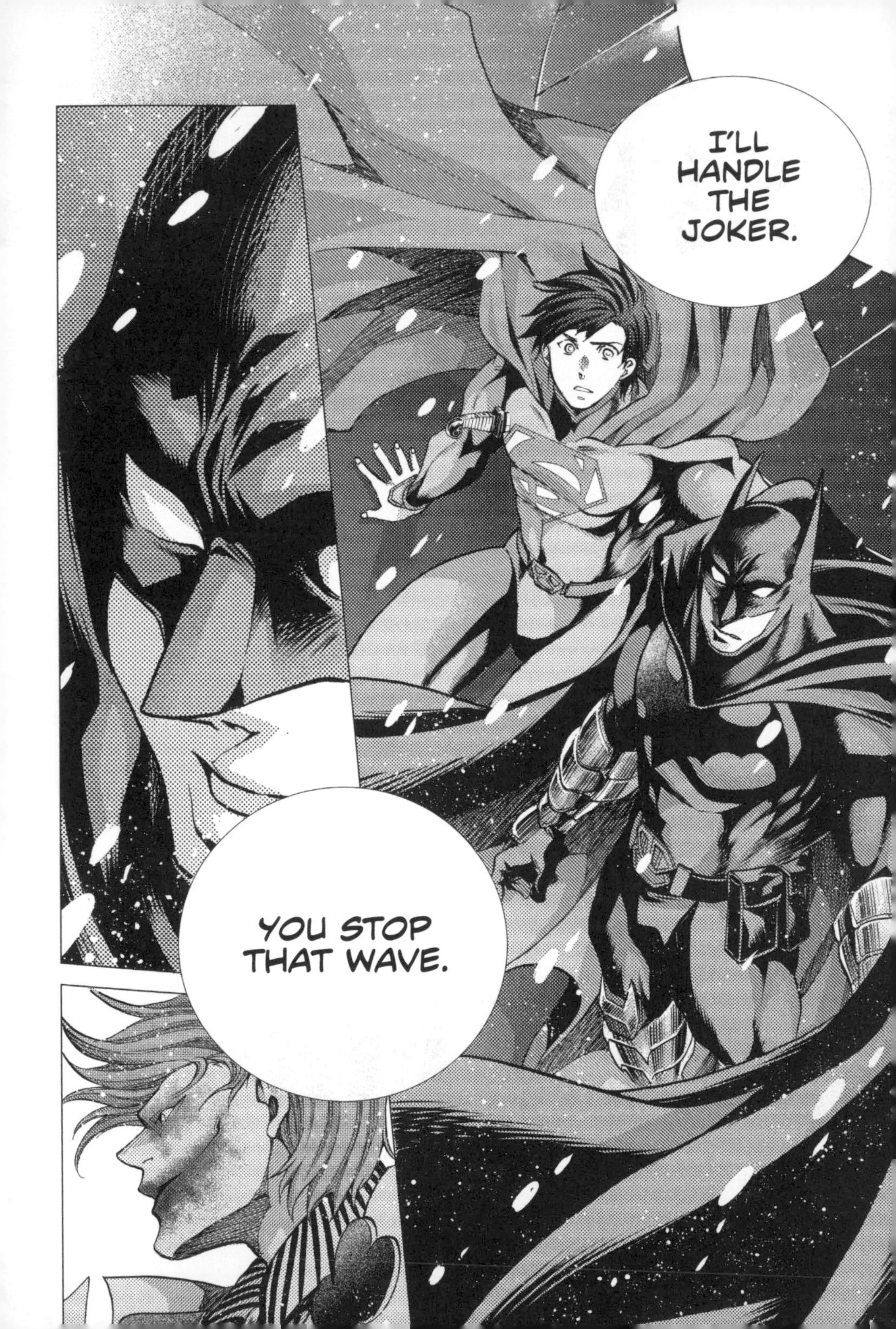
I'LL HANDLE THE JOKER.
YOU STOP THAT WAVE.

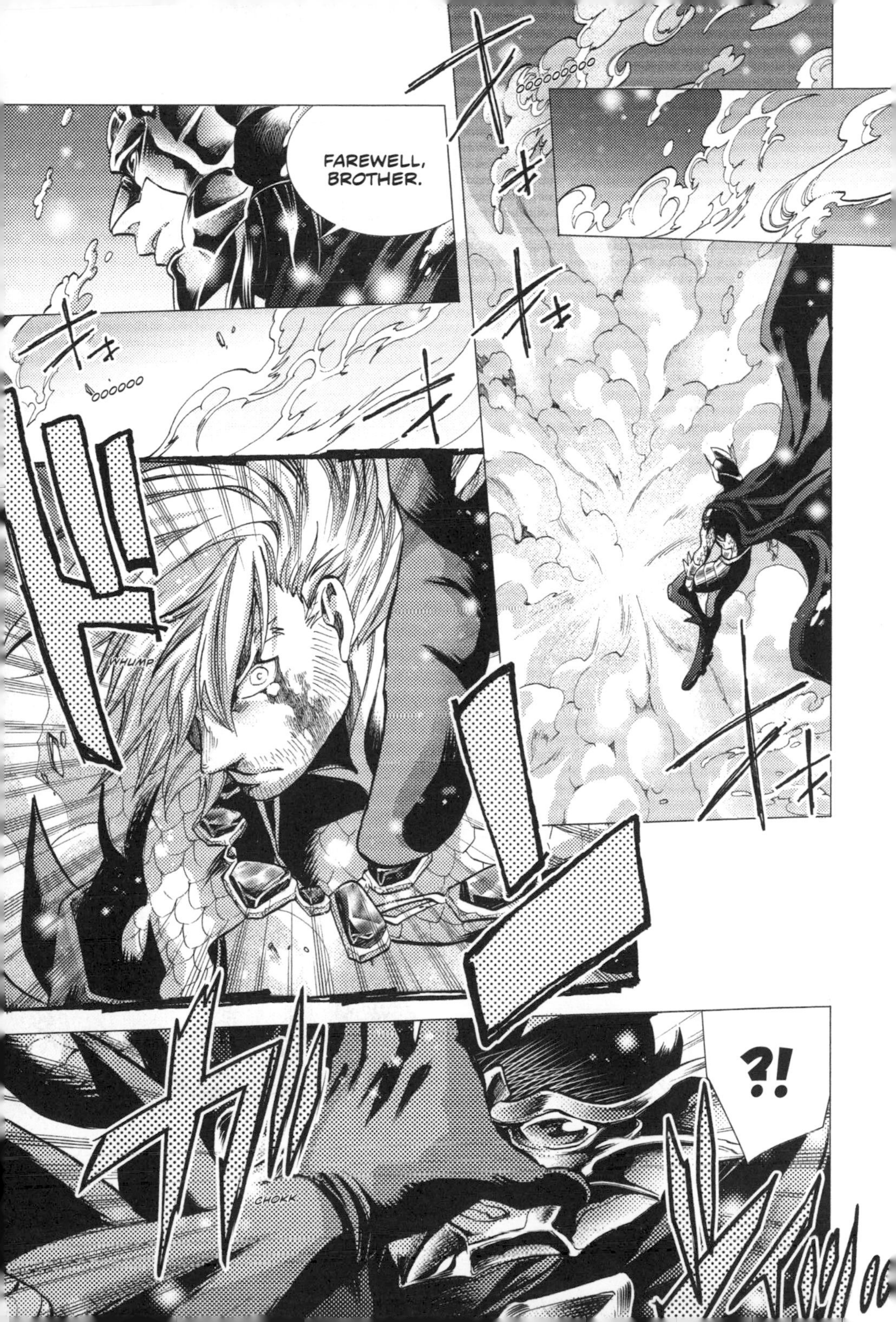

ooooooooo
FAREWELL, BROTHER.
oooooo
WHUMP
?!
CHOKK

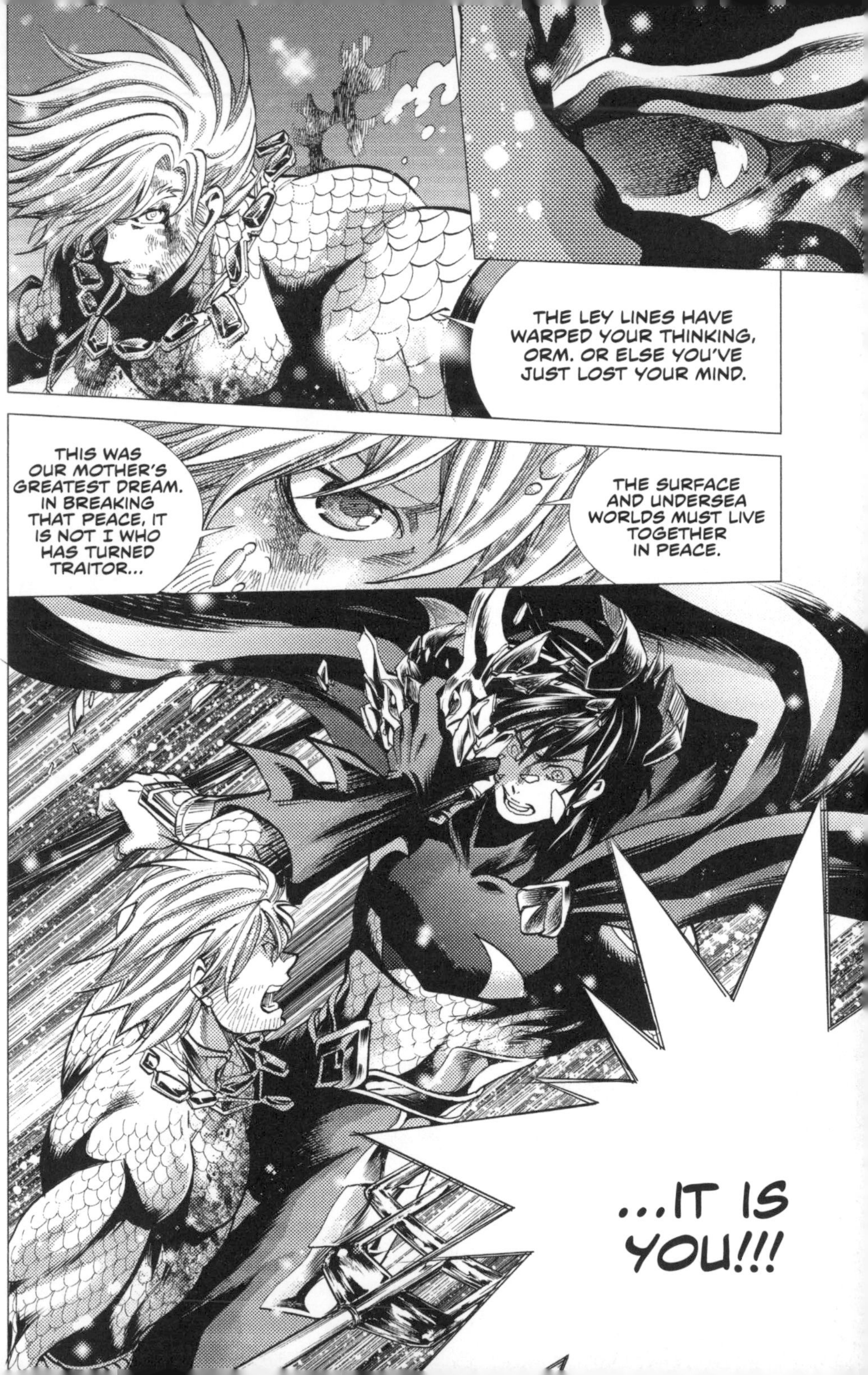
THE LEY LINES HAVE WARPED YOUR THINKING, ORM. OR ELSE YOU'VE JUST LOST YOUR MIND.
THE SURFACE AND UNDERSEA WORLDS MUST LIVE TOGETHER IN PEACE.
THIS WAS OUR MOTHER'S GREATEST DREAM. IN BREAKING THAT PEACE, IT IS NOT I WHO HAS TURNED TRAITOR...
...IT IS YOU!!!

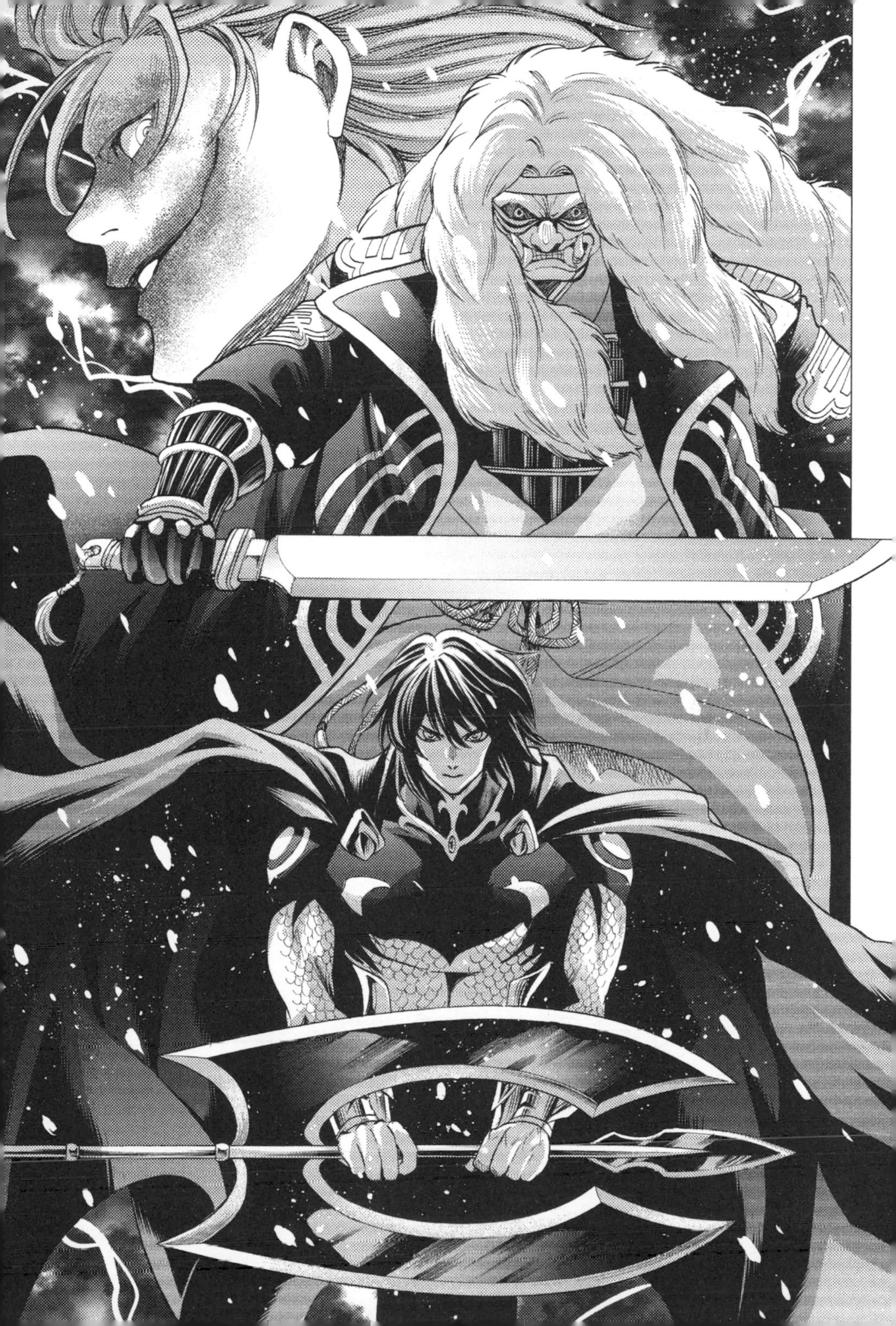

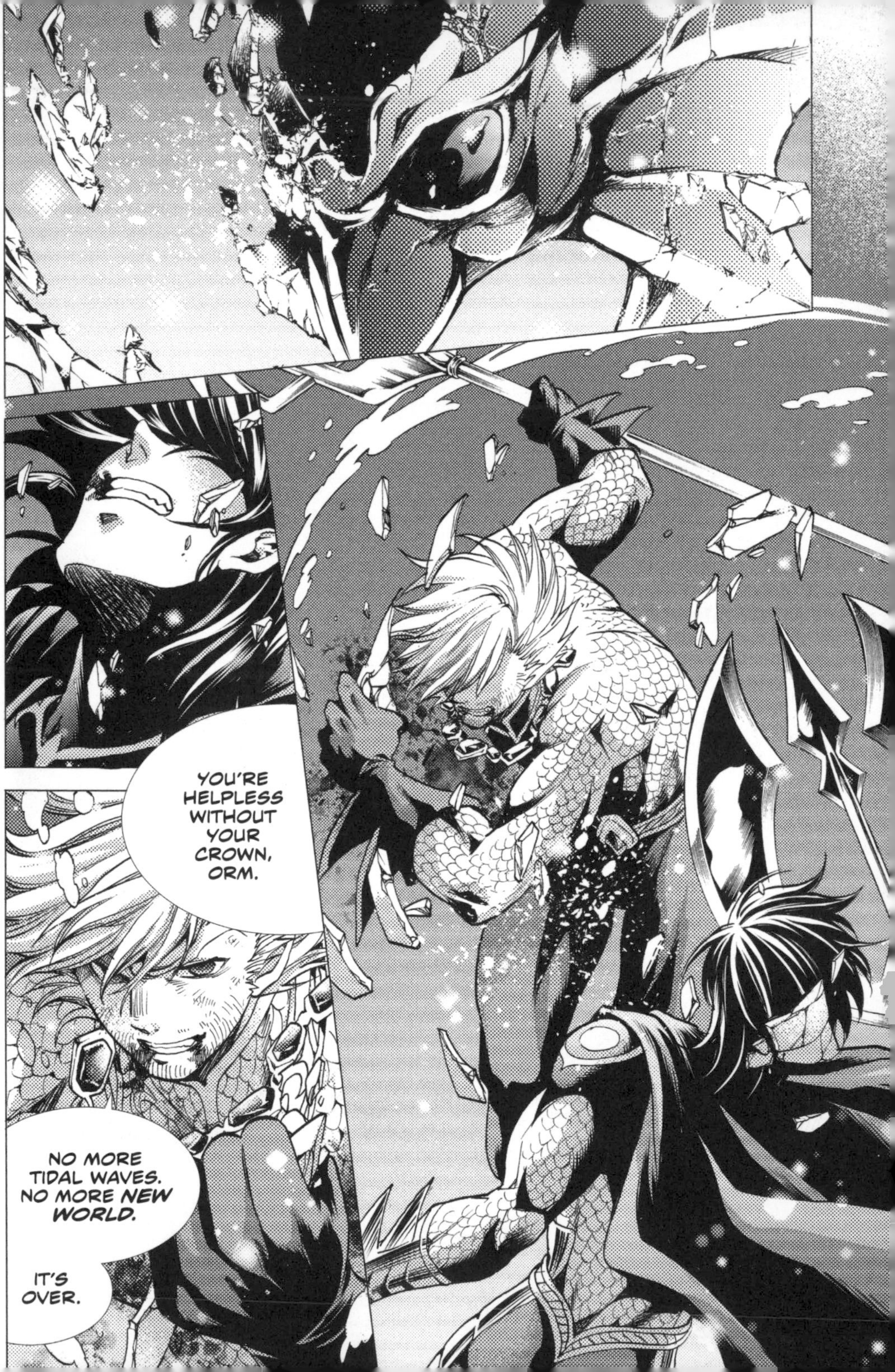
YOU'RE HELPLESS WITHOUT YOUR CROWN, ORM.
NO MORE TIDAL WAVES. NO MORE *NEW WORLD*.
IT'S OVER.

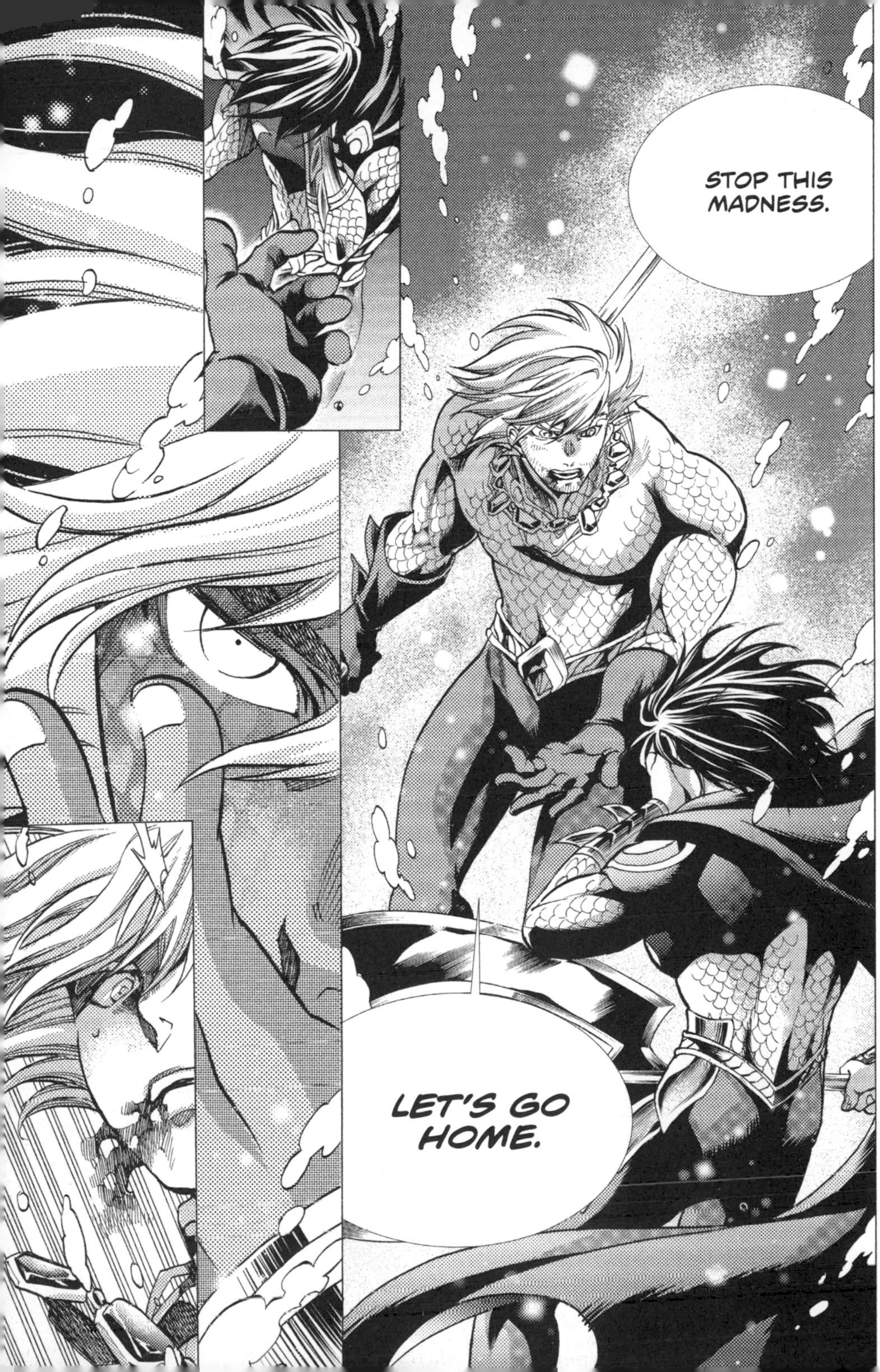
STOP THIS MADNESS.
LET'S GO HOME.

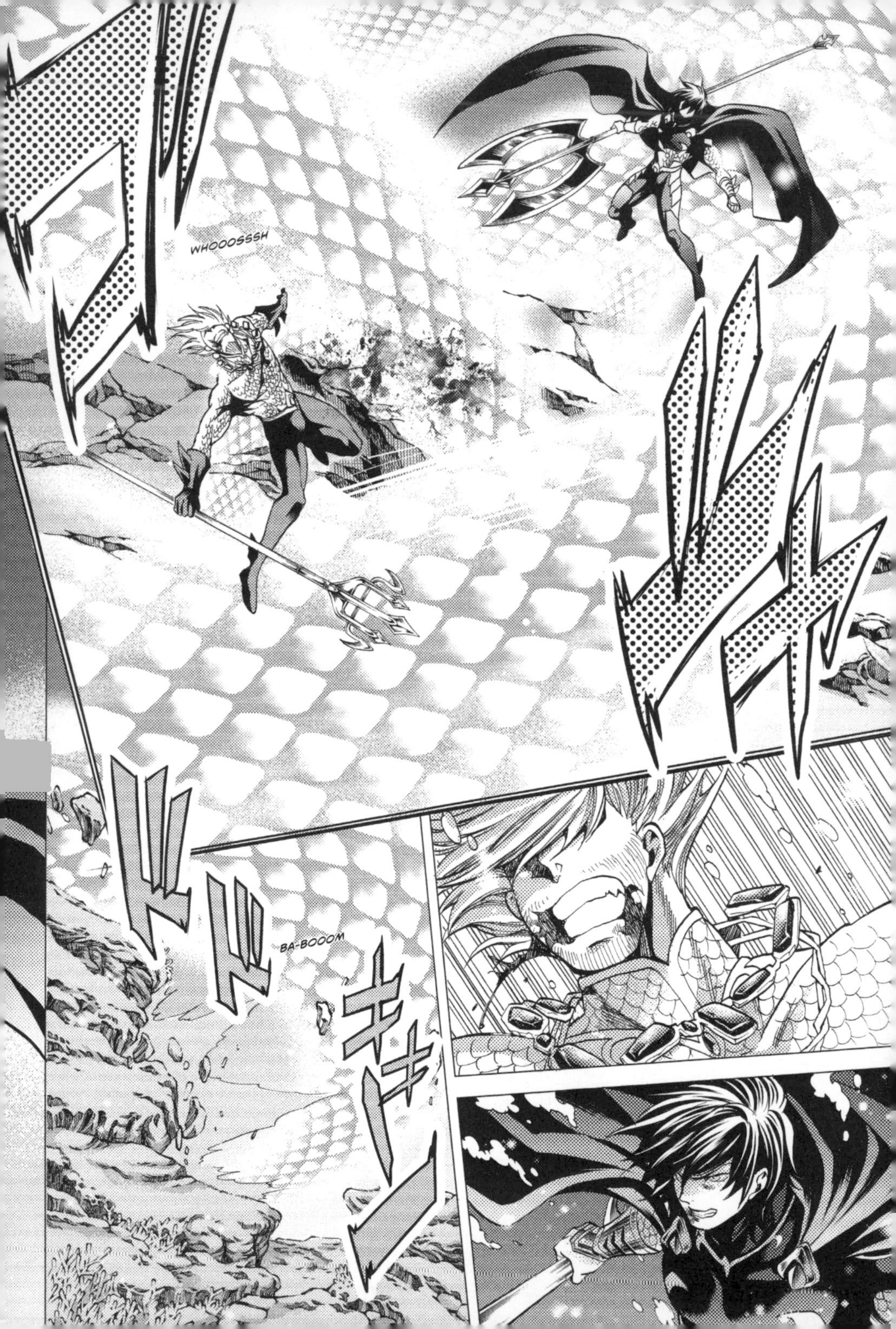
WHOOOSSSH
BA-BOOOM

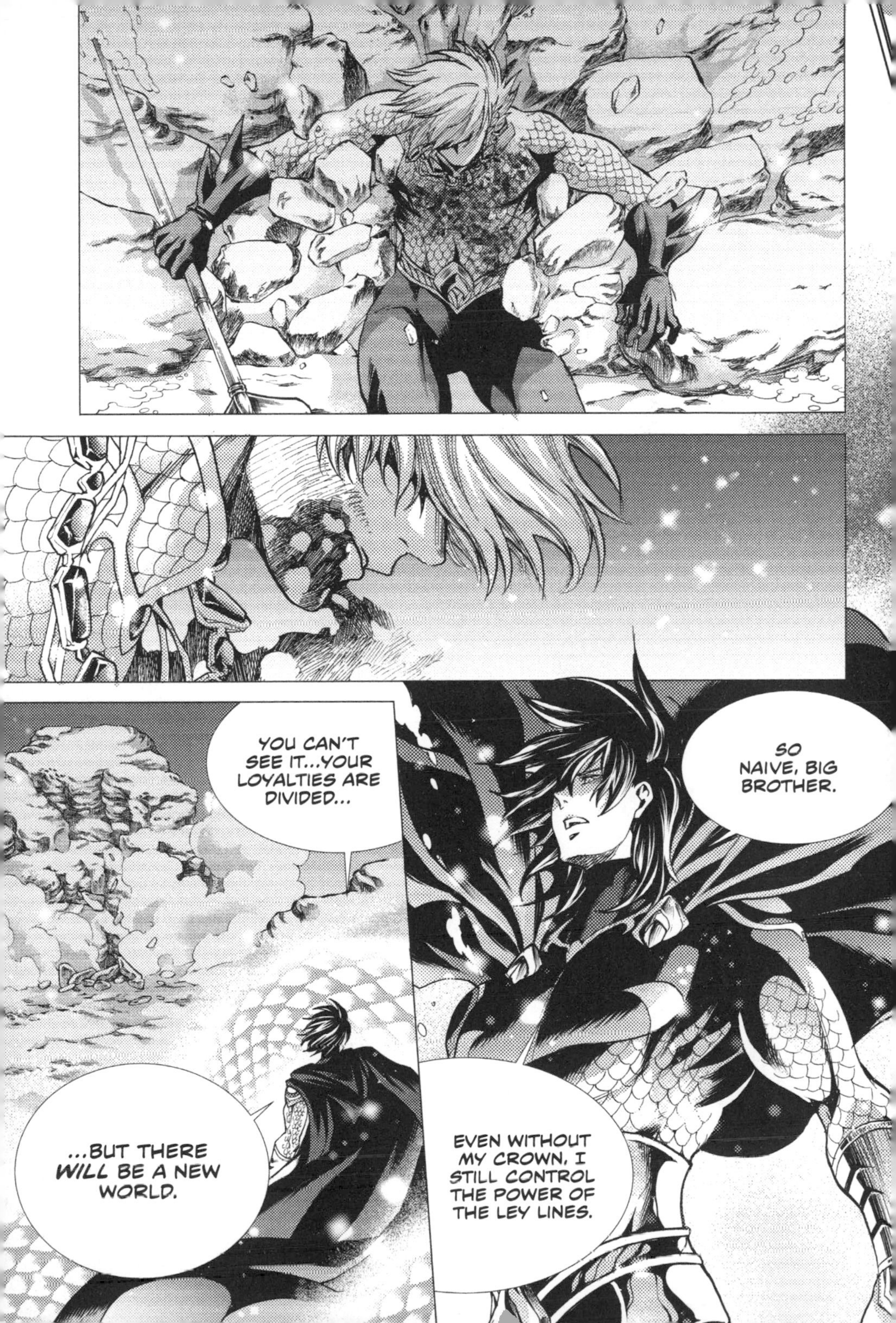
SO NAIVE, BIG BROTHER.
EVEN WITHOUT MY CROWN, I STILL CONTROL THE POWER OF THE LEY LINES.
YOU CAN'T SEE IT...YOUR LOYALTIES ARE DIVIDED...
...BUT THERE *WILL* BE A NEW WORLD.

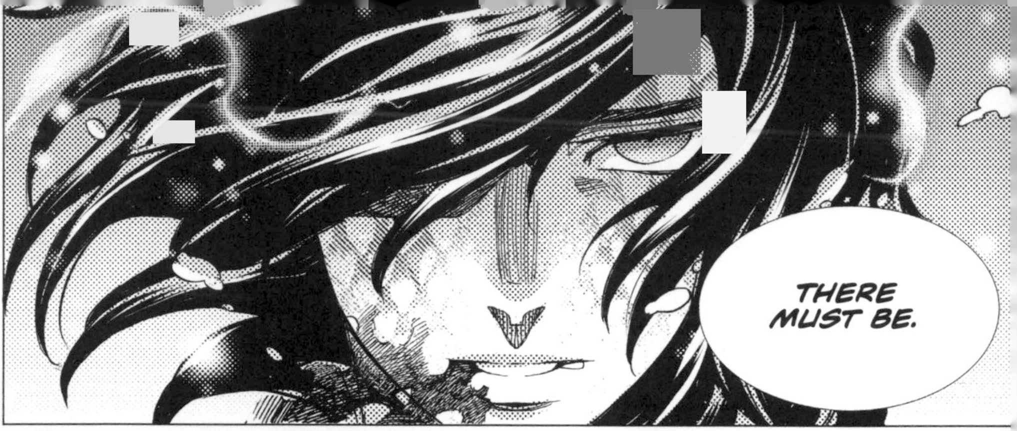
THERE MUST BE.

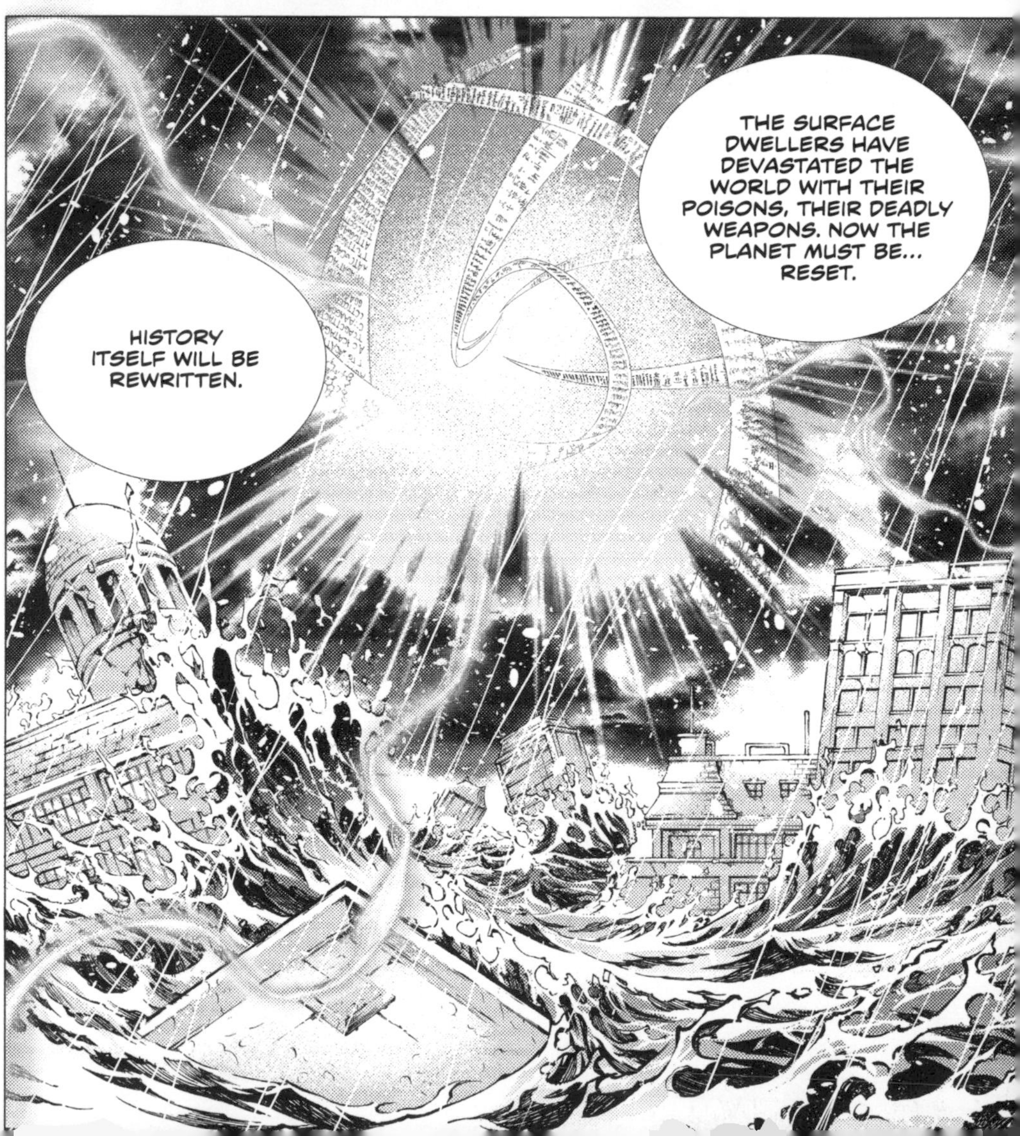
THE SURFACE DWELLERS HAVE DEVASTATED THE WORLD WITH THEIR POISONS, THEIR DEADLY WEAPONS. NOW THE PLANET MUST BE... RESET.
HISTORY ITSELF WILL BE REWRITTEN.

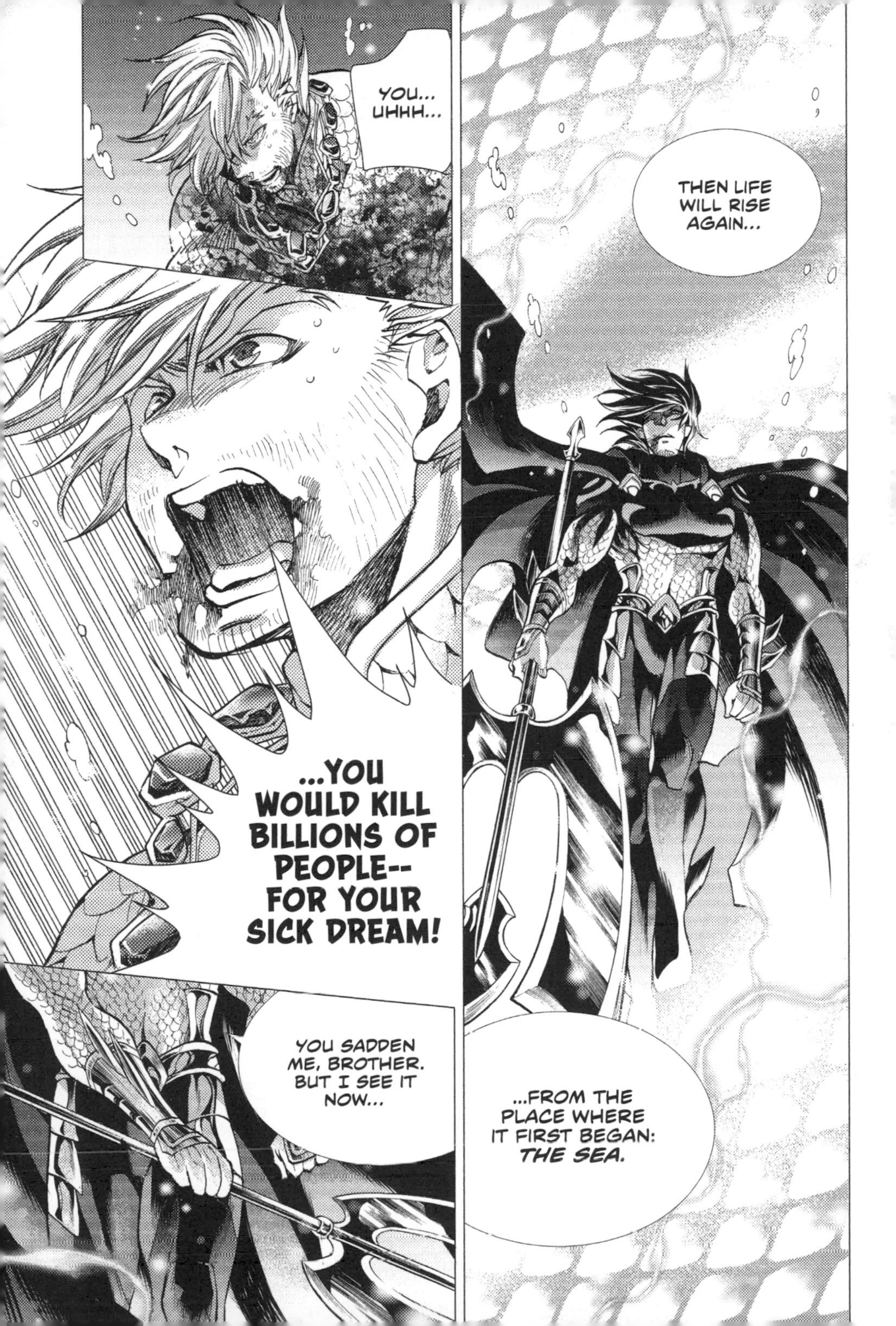
YOU... UHHH...
...YOU WOULD KILL BILLIONS OF PEOPLE-- FOR YOUR SICK DREAM!
YOU SADDEN ME, BROTHER. BUT I SEE IT NOW...
THEN LIFE WILL RISE AGAIN...
...FROM THE PLACE WHERE IT FIRST BEGAN: *THE SEA.*

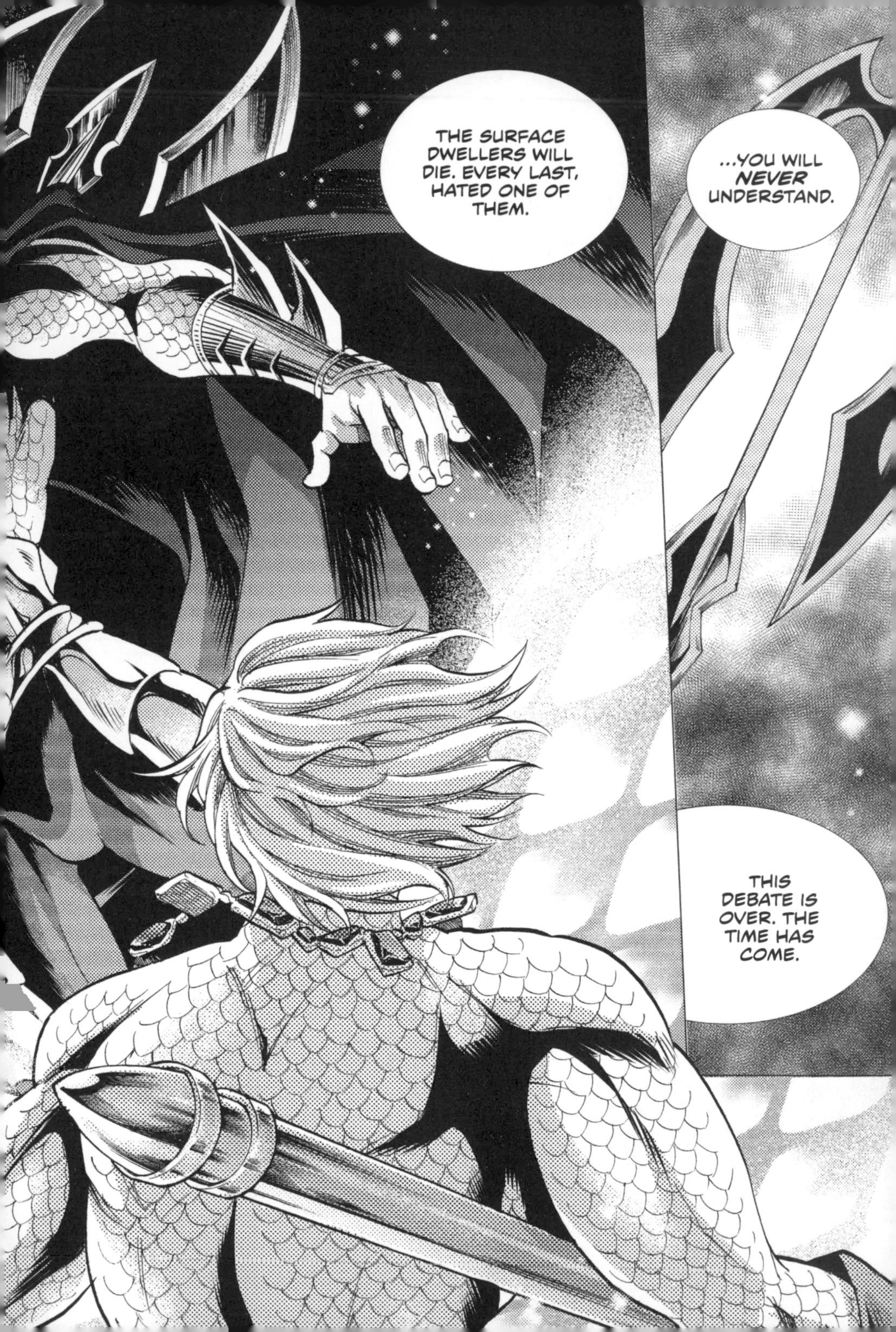
THE SURFACE DWELLERS WILL DIE. EVERY LAST, HATED ONE OF THEM.
...YOU WILL *NEVER* UNDERSTAND.
THIS DEBATE IS OVER. THE TIME HAS COME.

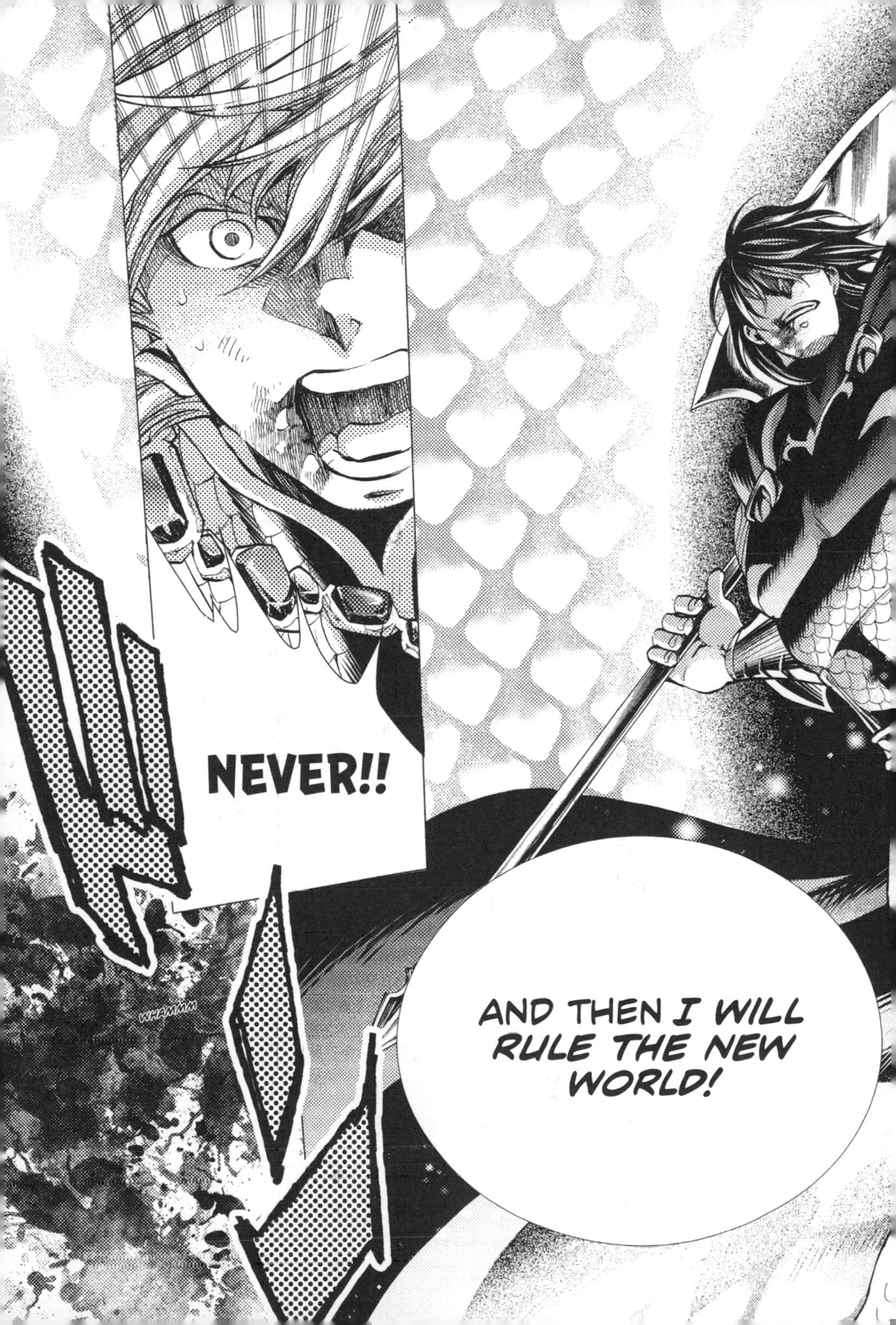
NEVER!!
AND THEN I WILL RULE THE NEW WORLD!
WHAMMM

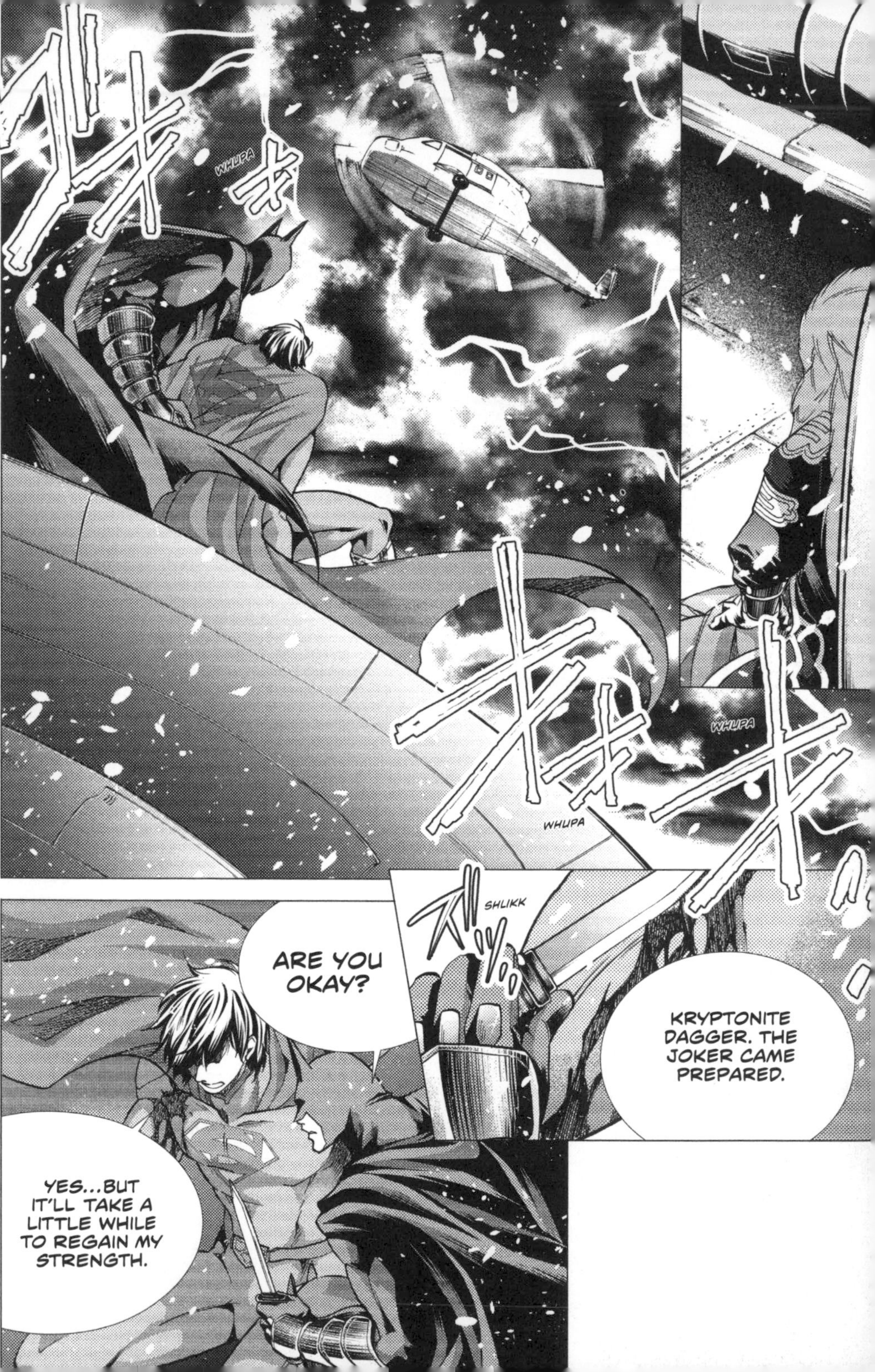
WHUPA
WHUPA
WHUPA
SHLIKK
KRYPTONITE DAGGER. THE JOKER CAME PREPARED.
ARE YOU OKAY?
YES...BUT IT'LL TAKE A LITTLE WHILE TO REGAIN MY STRENGTH.

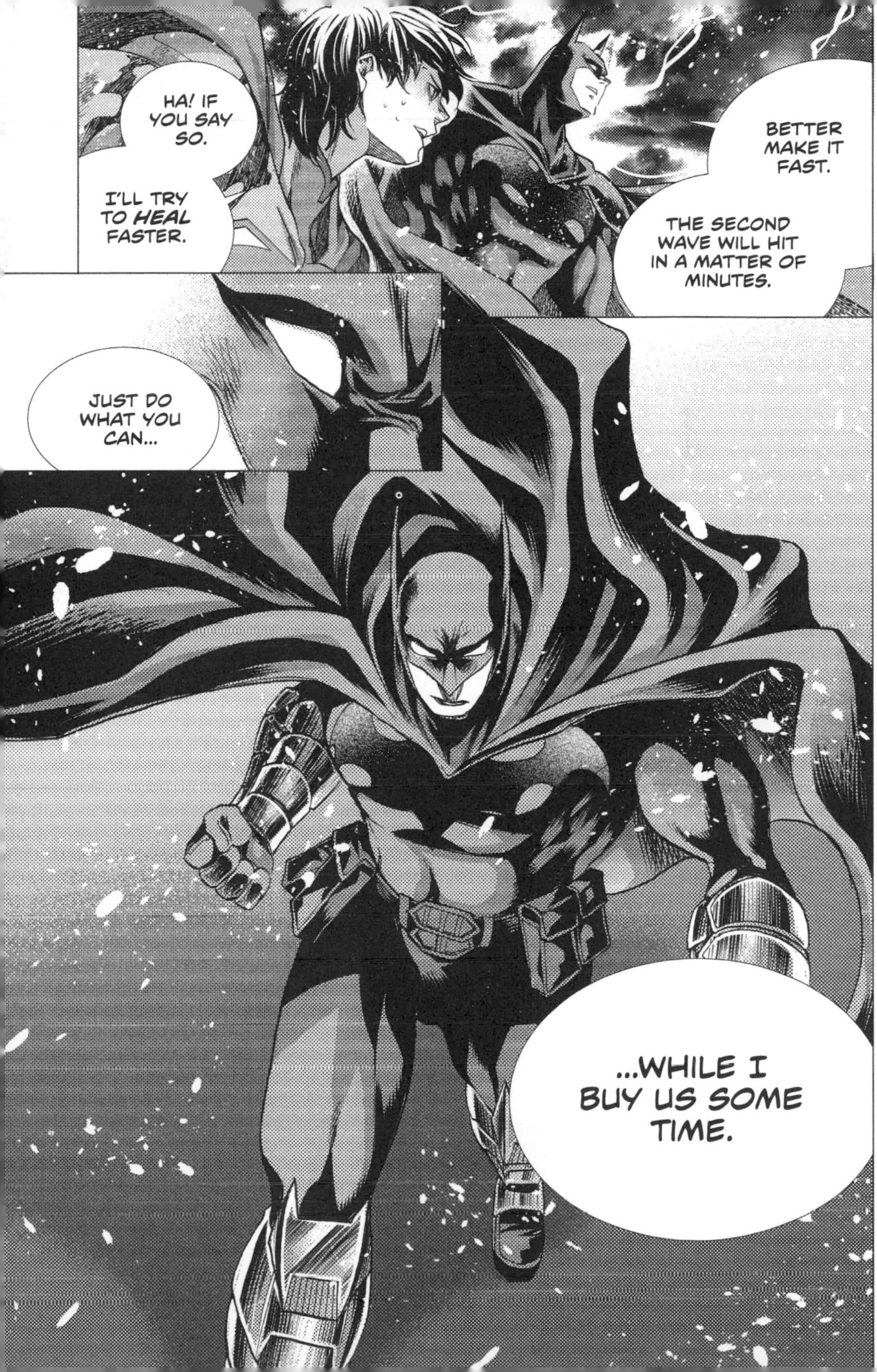
BETTER MAKE IT FAST.
THE SECOND WAVE WILL HIT IN A MATTER OF MINUTES.
HA! IF YOU SAY SO.
I'LL TRY TO *HEAL* FASTER.
JUST DO WHAT YOU CAN...
...WHILE I BUY US SOME TIME.

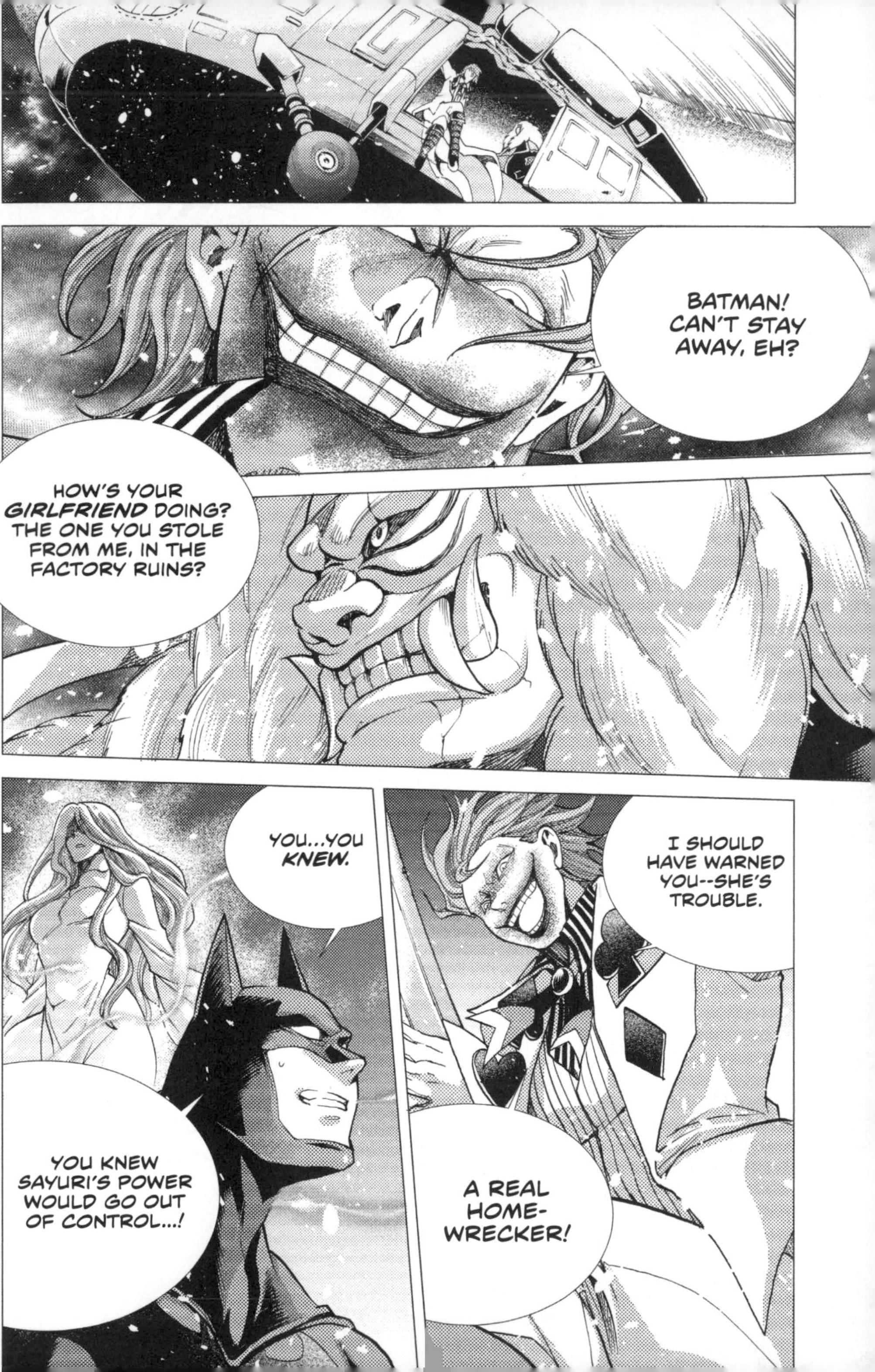
BATMAN! CAN'T STAY AWAY, EH?
HOW'S YOUR *GIRLFRIEND* DOING? THE ONE YOU STOLE FROM ME, IN THE FACTORY RUINS?
YOU...YOU *KNEW.*
YOU KNEW SAYURI'S POWER WOULD GO OUT OF CONTROL...!
I SHOULD HAVE WARNED YOU--SHE'S TROUBLE.
A REAL HOME-WRECKER!

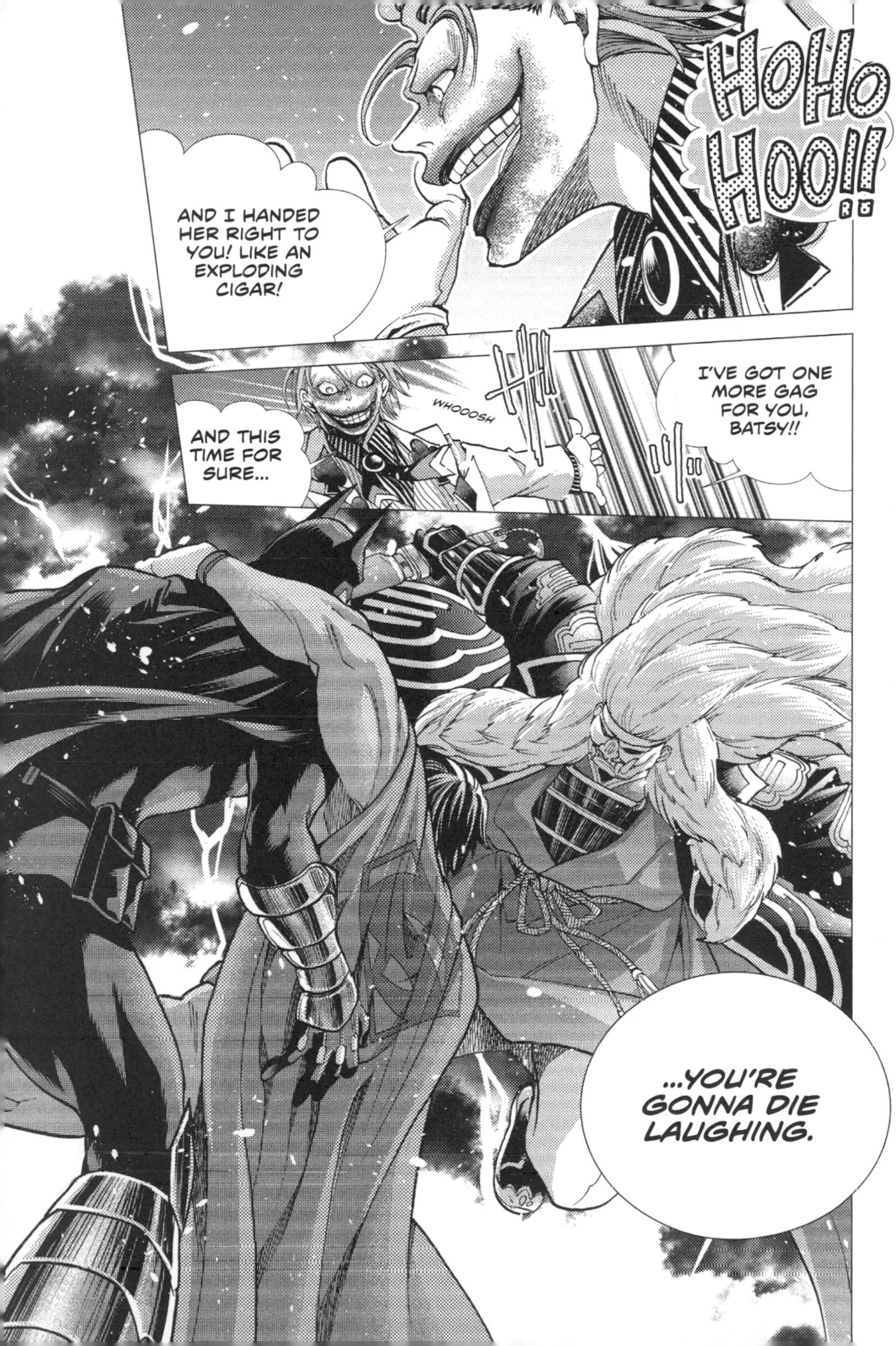
HOHO HOO!!
AND I HANDED HER RIGHT TO YOU! LIKE AN EXPLODING CIGAR!
I'VE GOT ONE MORE GAG FOR YOU, BATSY!!
WHOOOSH
AND THIS TIME FOR SURE...
...YOU'RE GONNA DIE LAUGHING.

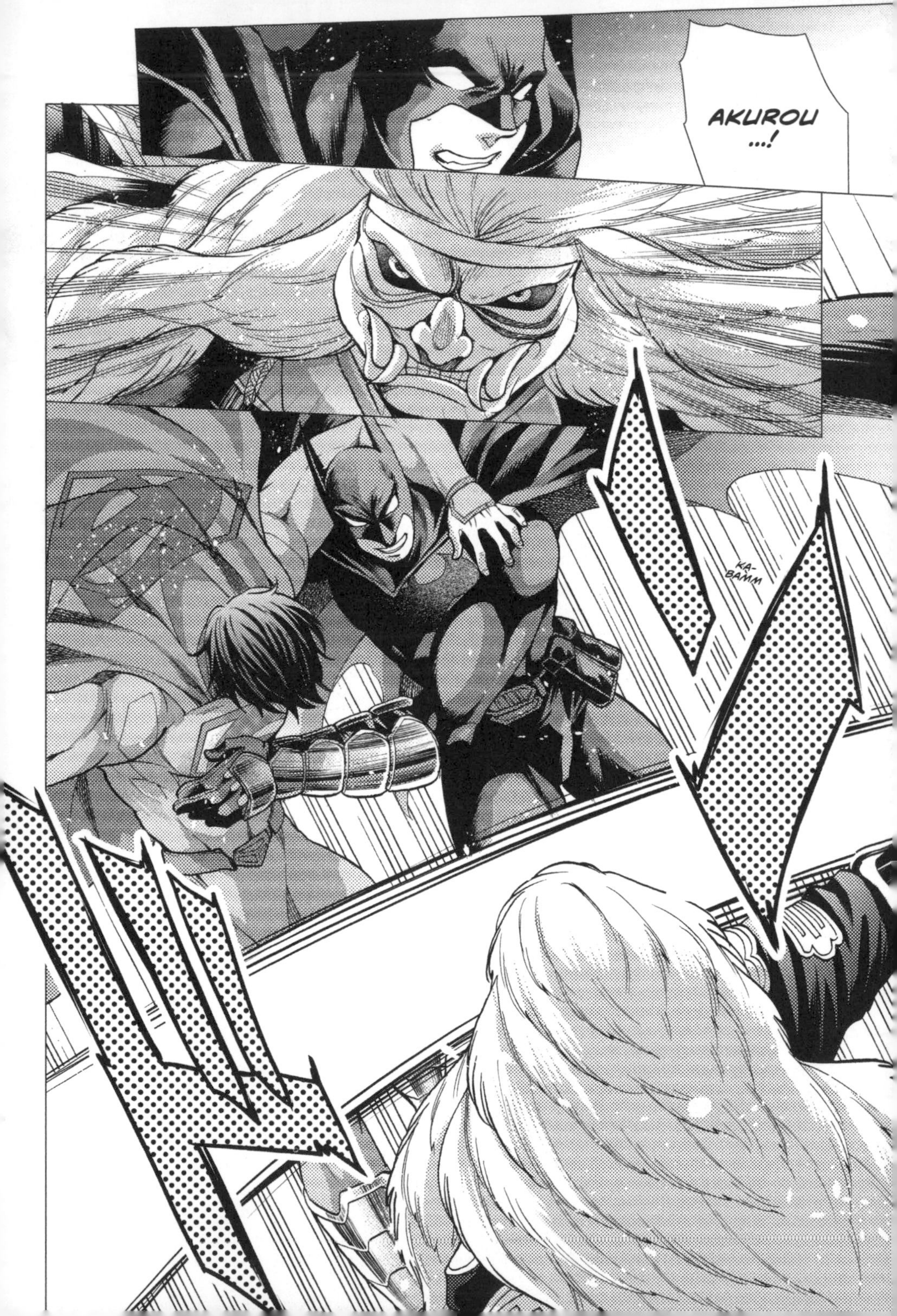
AKUROU ...!
KA-BAMM

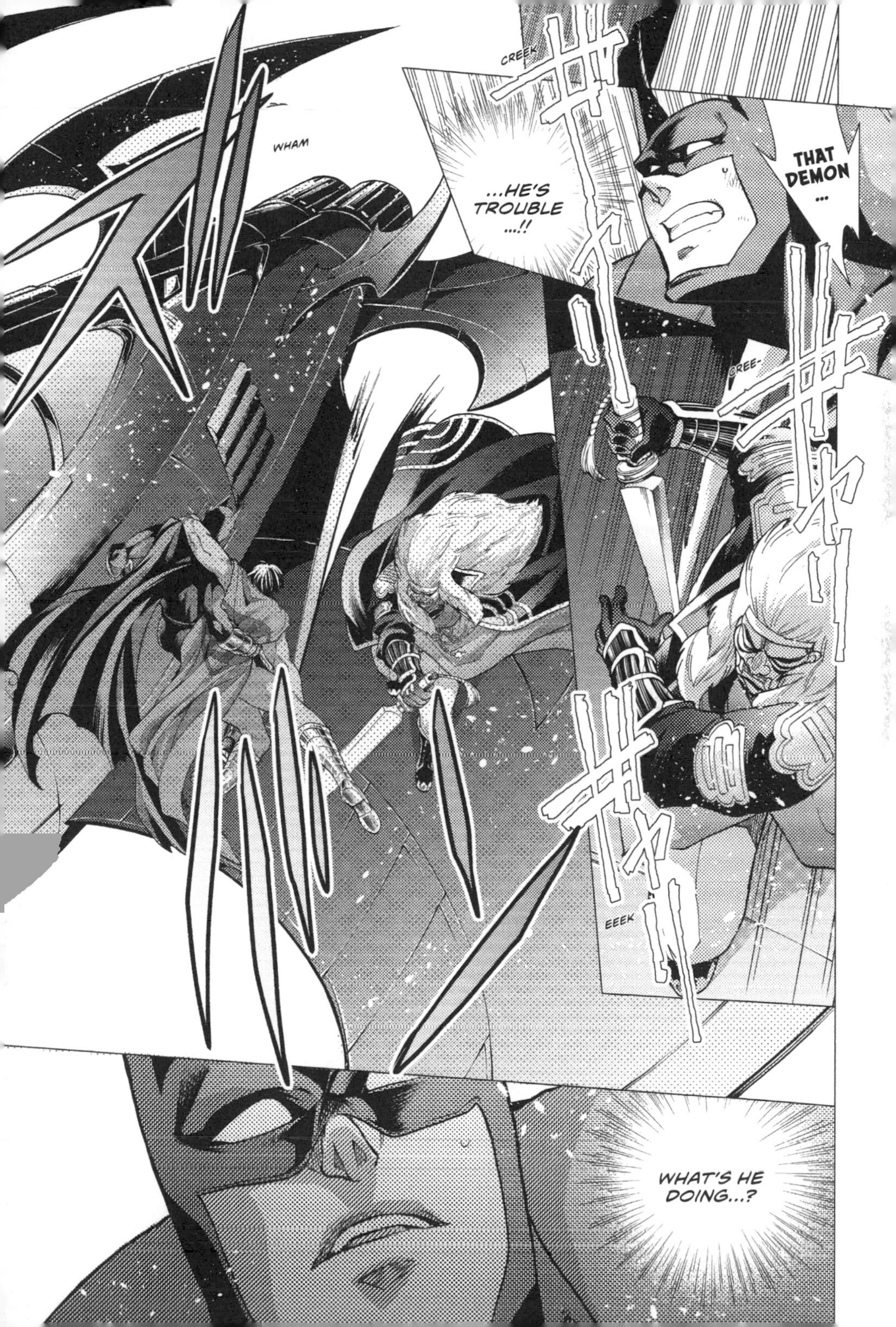
CREEK
THAT DEMON ...
...HE'S TROUBLE ...!!
CREE-
EEEK
WHAM
WHAT'S HE DOING...?

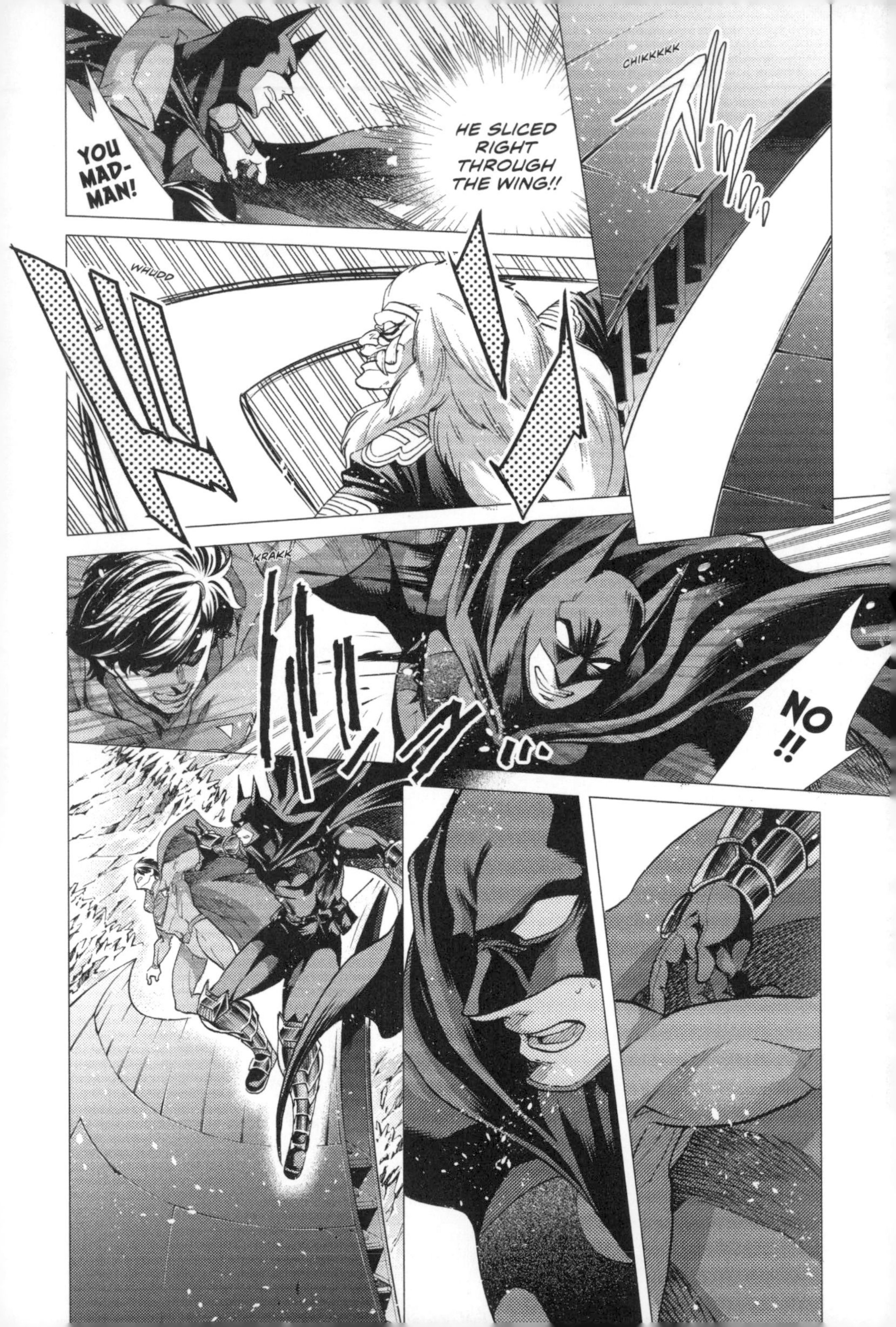

CHIKKKKK
HE SLICED RIGHT THROUGH THE WING!!
YOU MAD-MAN!
WHUDD
NO!!
KRAKK

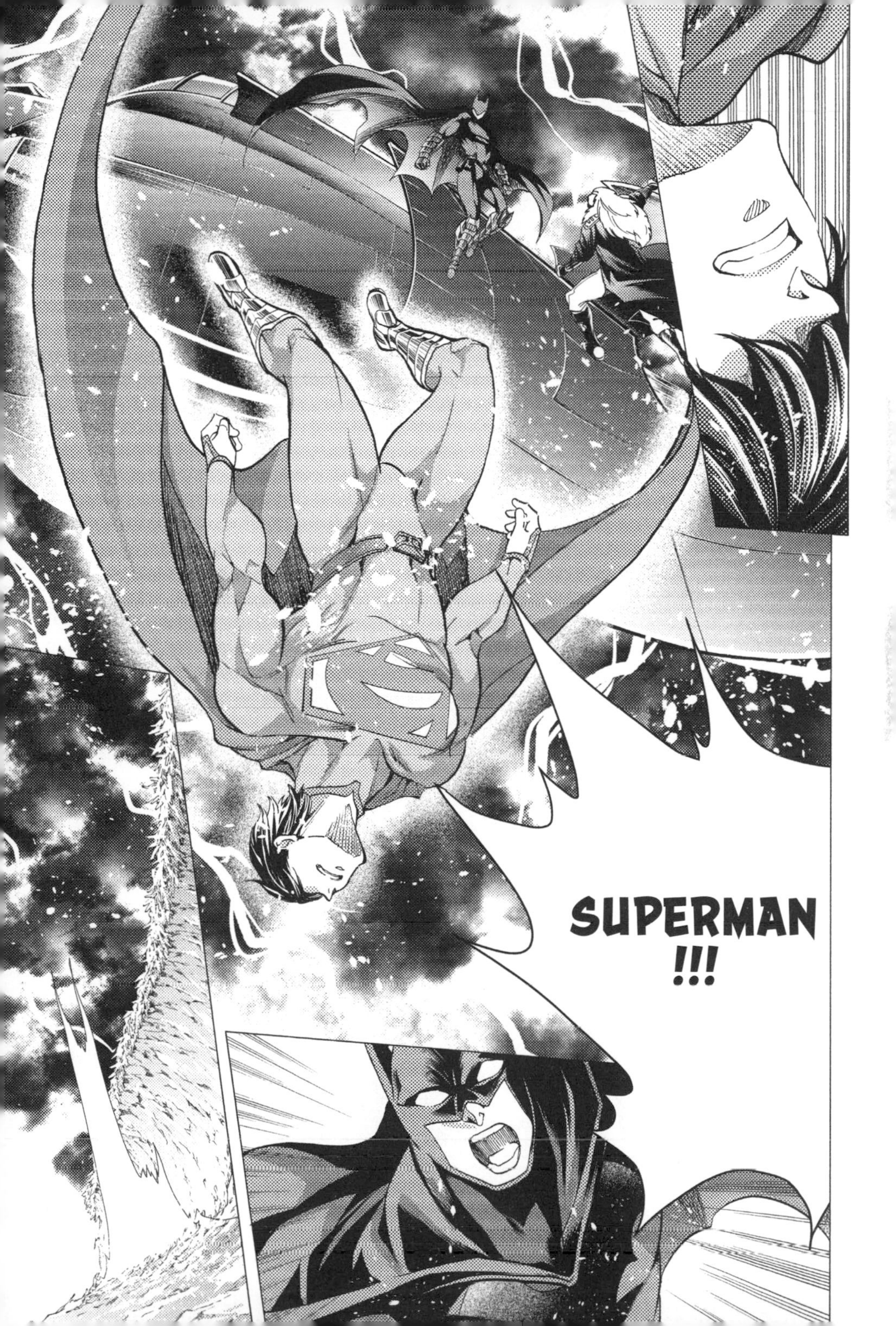
SUPERMAN
!!!

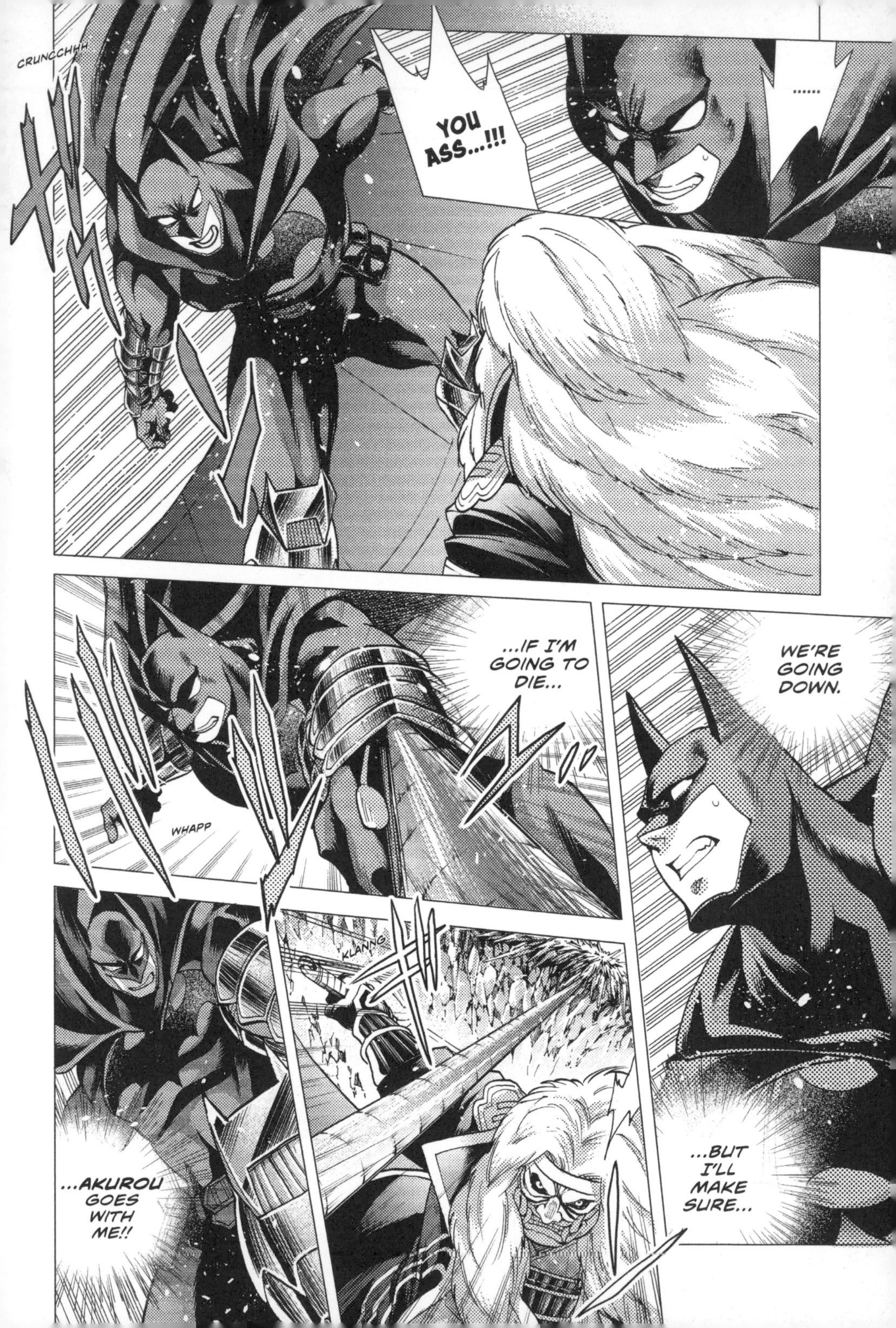
......
YOU ASS...!!!
CRUNCCHHH
WE'RE GOING DOWN.
...BUT I'LL MAKE SURE...
...IF I'M GOING TO DIE...
WHAPP
KLANNG
...AKUROU GOES WITH ME!!

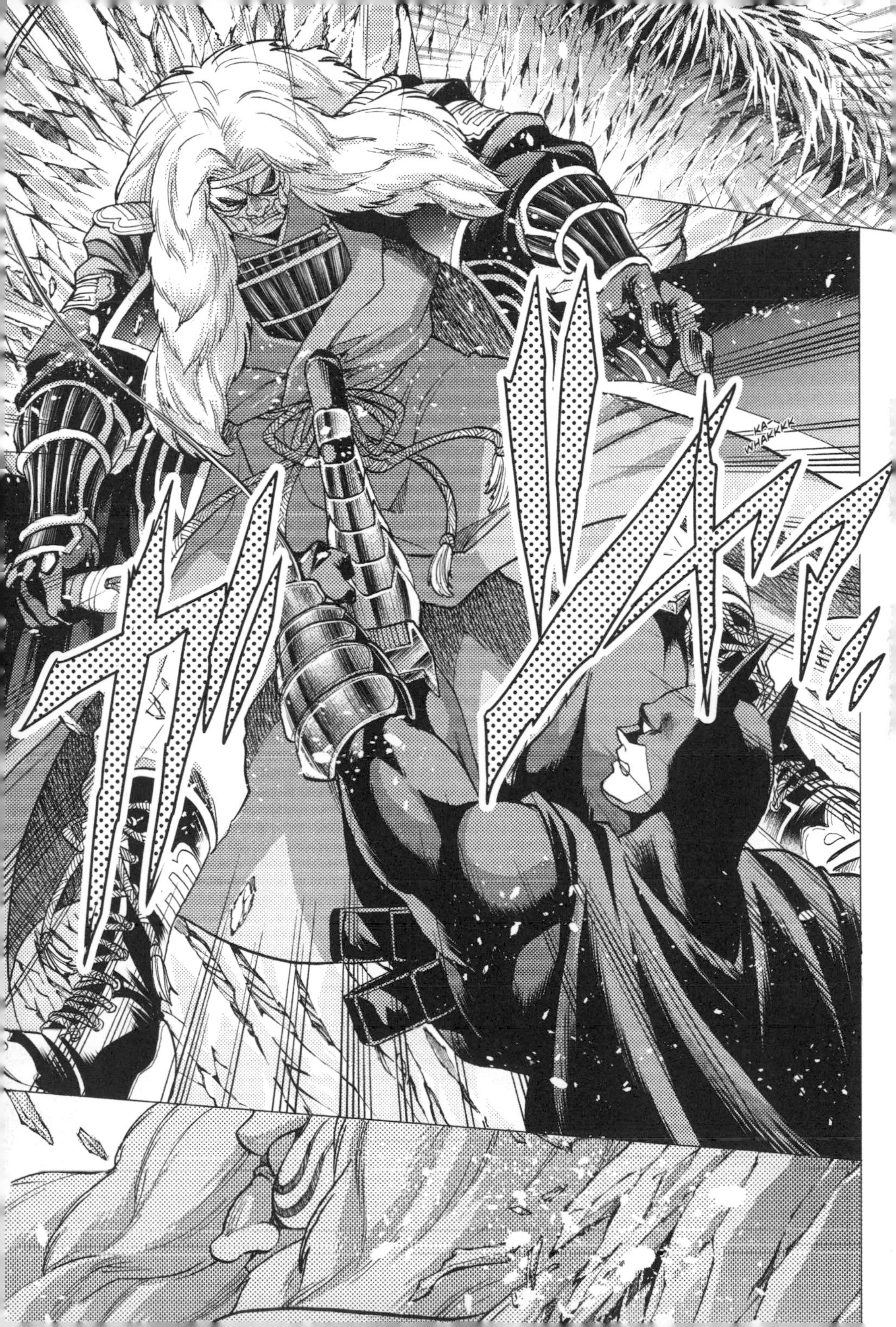
KA-WHAKKKK

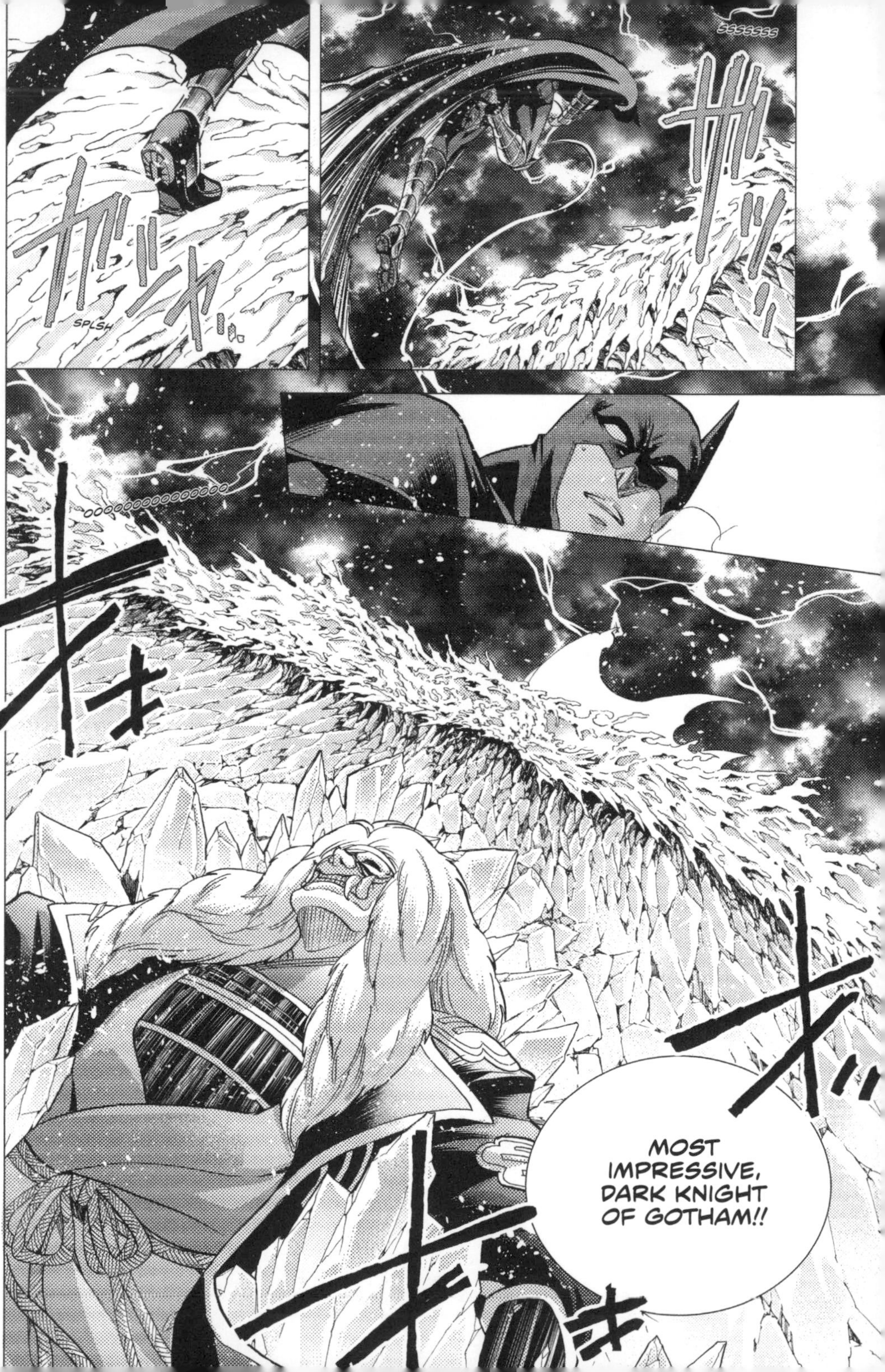
SSSSSSS
SPLSH
OOOOOOOOOOOOOOO
MOST IMPRESSIVE, DARK KNIGHT OF GOTHAM!!

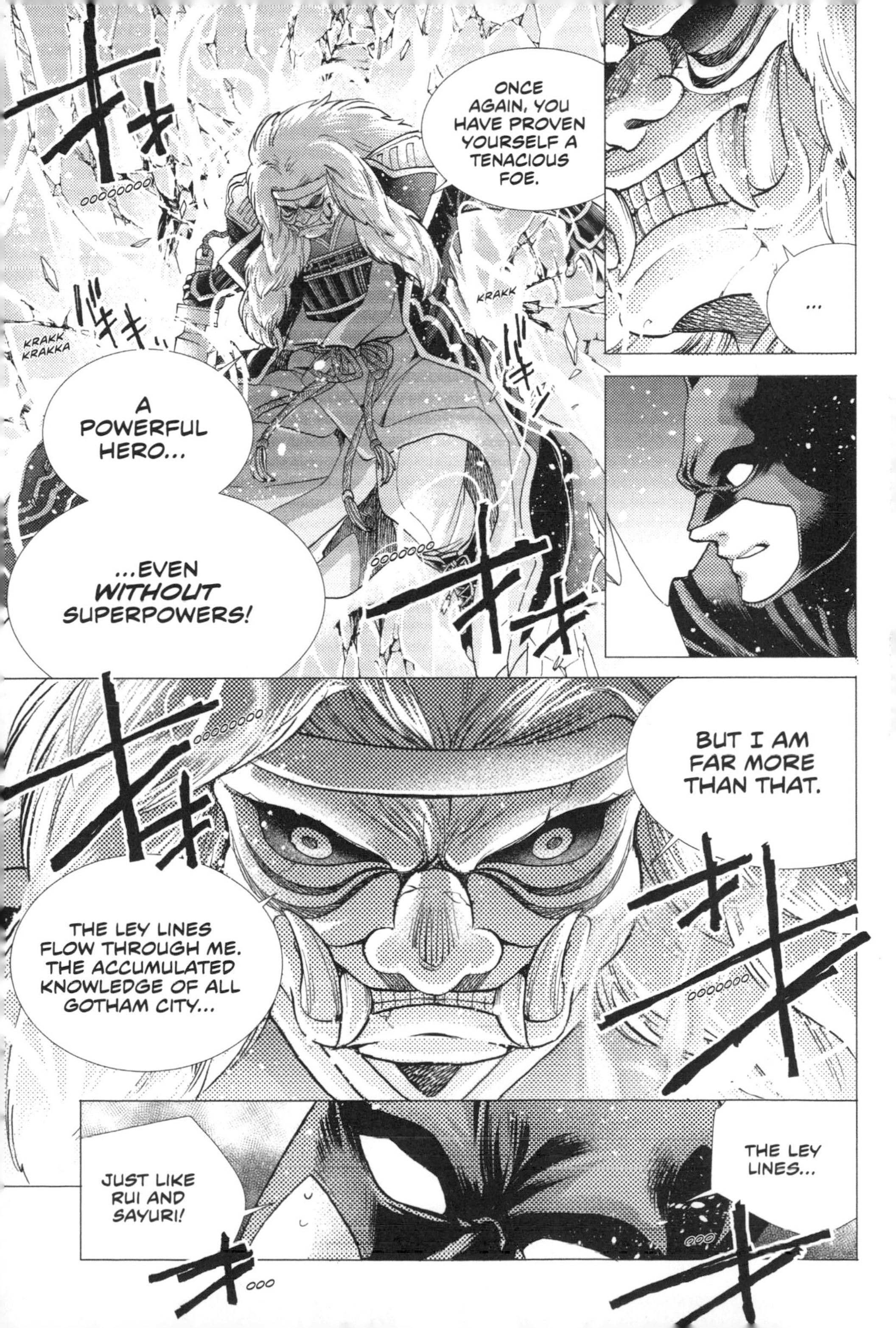
...
ONCE AGAIN, YOU HAVE PROVEN YOURSELF A TENACIOUS FOE.
OOOOOOOO
KRAKK
KRAKK KRAKKA
A POWERFUL HERO...
...EVEN *WITHOUT* SUPERPOWERS!
OOOOOOO
BUT I AM FAR MORE THAN THAT.
OOOOOOOO
THE LEY LINES FLOW THROUGH ME. THE ACCUMULATED KNOWLEDGE OF ALL GOTHAM CITY...
OOOOOOO
THE LEY LINES...
OOO
JUST LIKE RUI AND SAYURI!
OOO

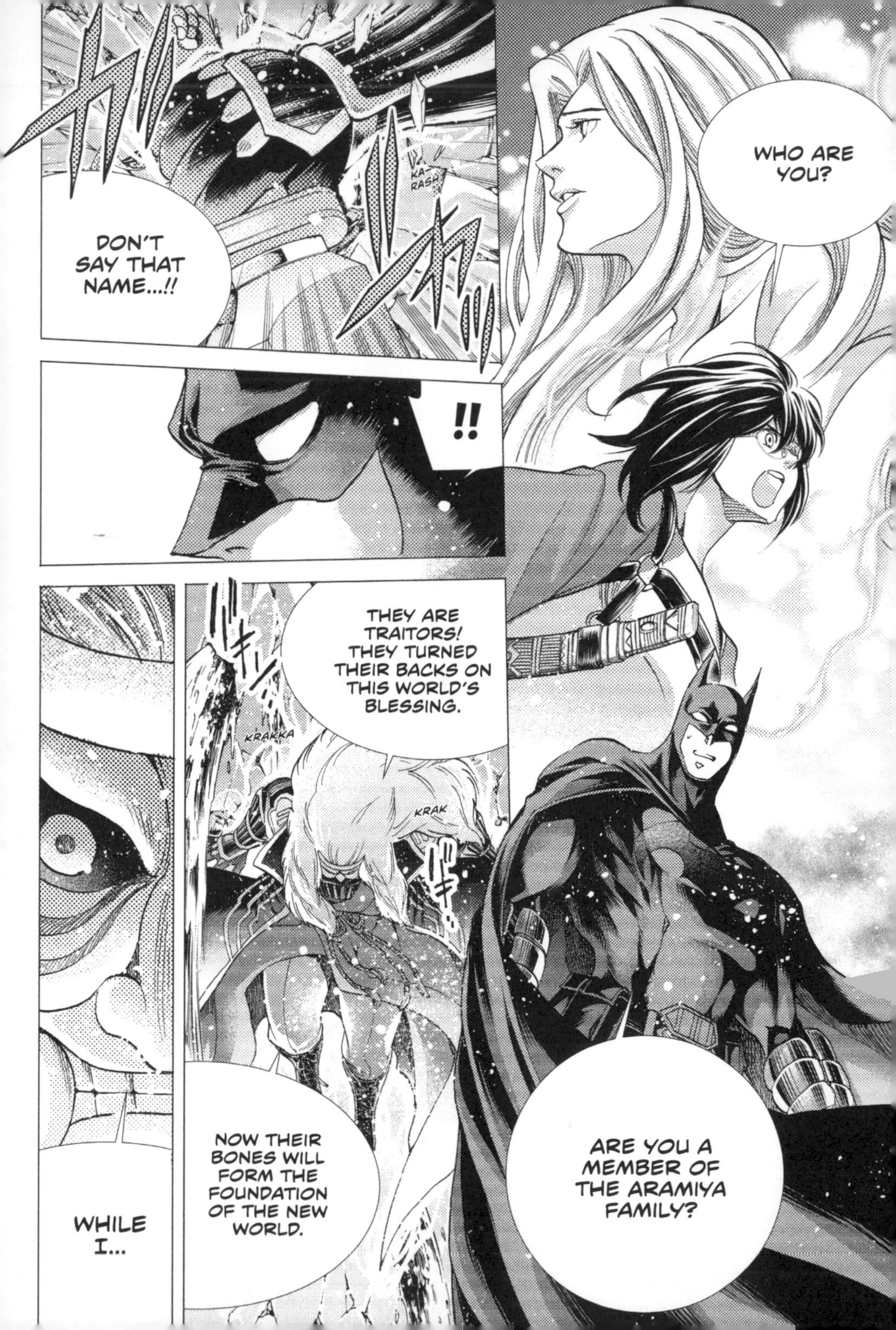
WHO ARE YOU?
ARE YOU A MEMBER OF THE ARAMIYA FAMILY?
KA-RASH
DON'T SAY THAT NAME...!!
!!
THEY ARE TRAITORS! THEY TURNED THEIR BACKS ON THIS WORLD'S BLESSING.
KRAKKA
KRAK
NOW THEIR BONES WILL FORM THE FOUNDATION OF THE NEW WORLD.
WHILE I...

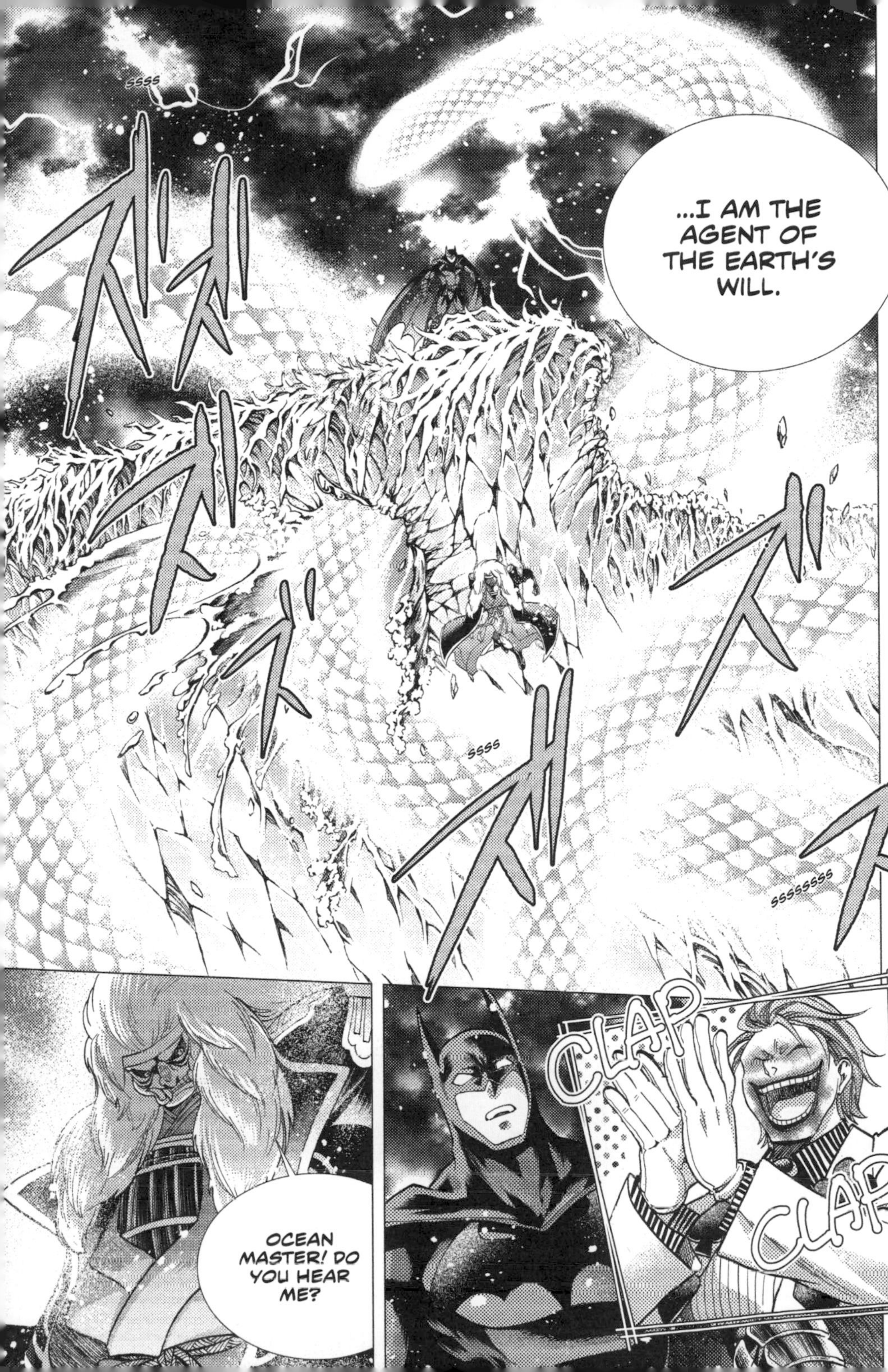
SSSS
...I AM THE AGENT OF THE EARTH'S WILL.
SSSS
SSSSSSSS
CLAP
CLAP
OCEAN MASTER! DO YOU HEAR ME?

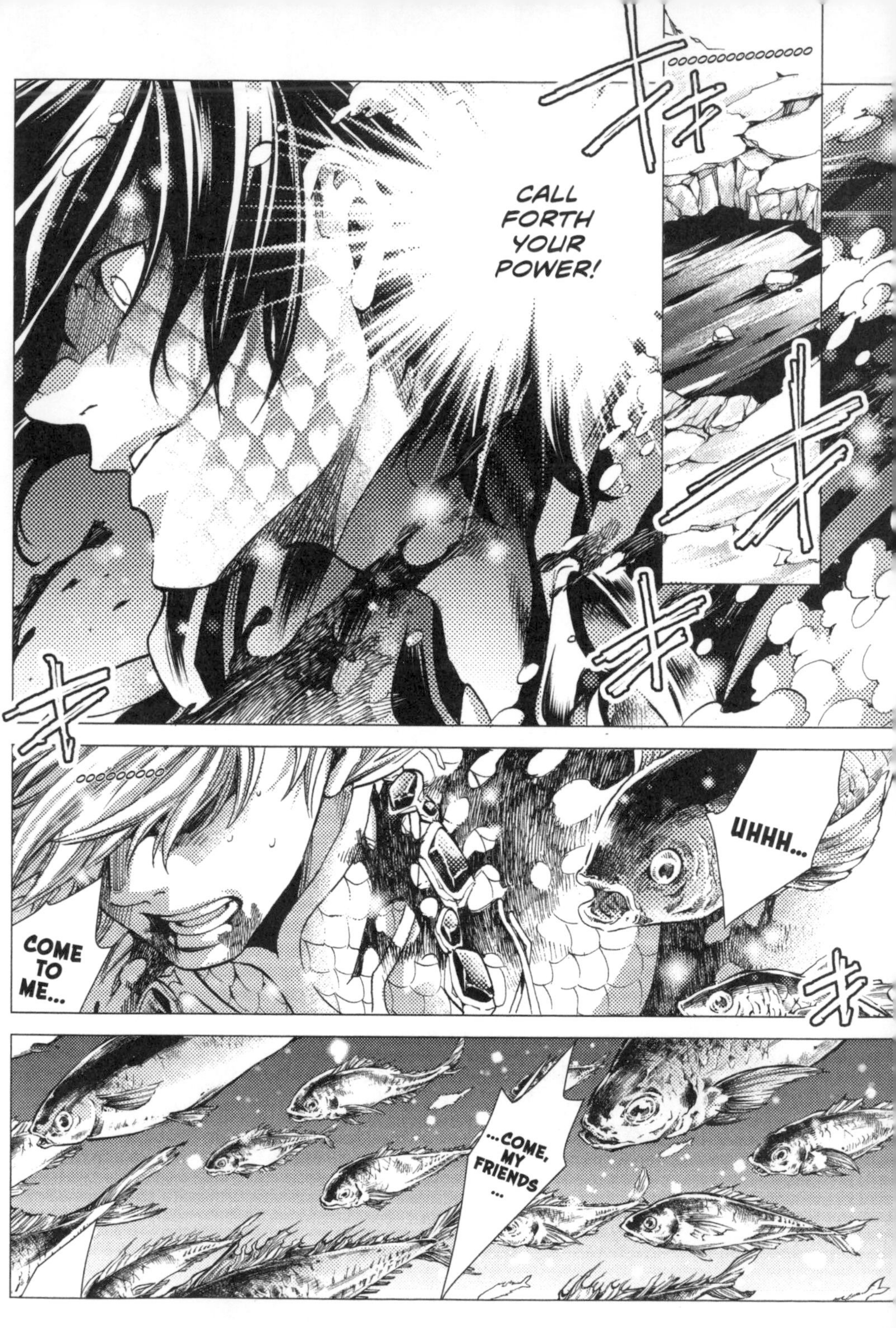

...oooooooooooooooo
CALL FORTH YOUR POWER!
...ooooooooo
UHHH...
COME TO ME...
...COME, MY FRIENDS...

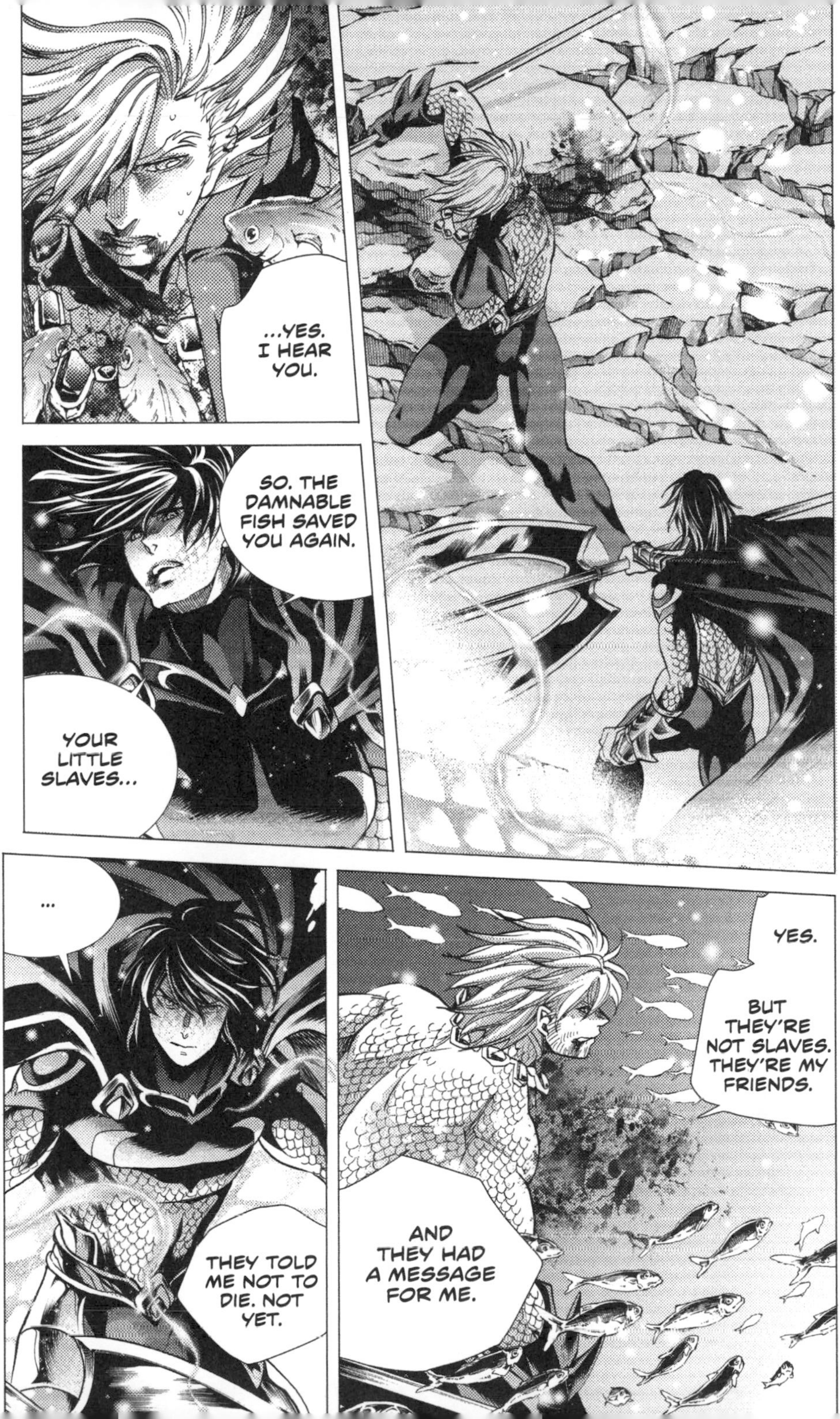
...YES. I HEAR YOU.
SO. THE DAMNABLE FISH SAVED YOU AGAIN.
YOUR LITTLE SLAVES...
YES.
BUT THEY'RE NOT SLAVES. THEY'RE MY FRIENDS.
AND THEY HAD A MESSAGE FOR ME.
...
THEY TOLD ME NOT TO DIE. NOT YET.

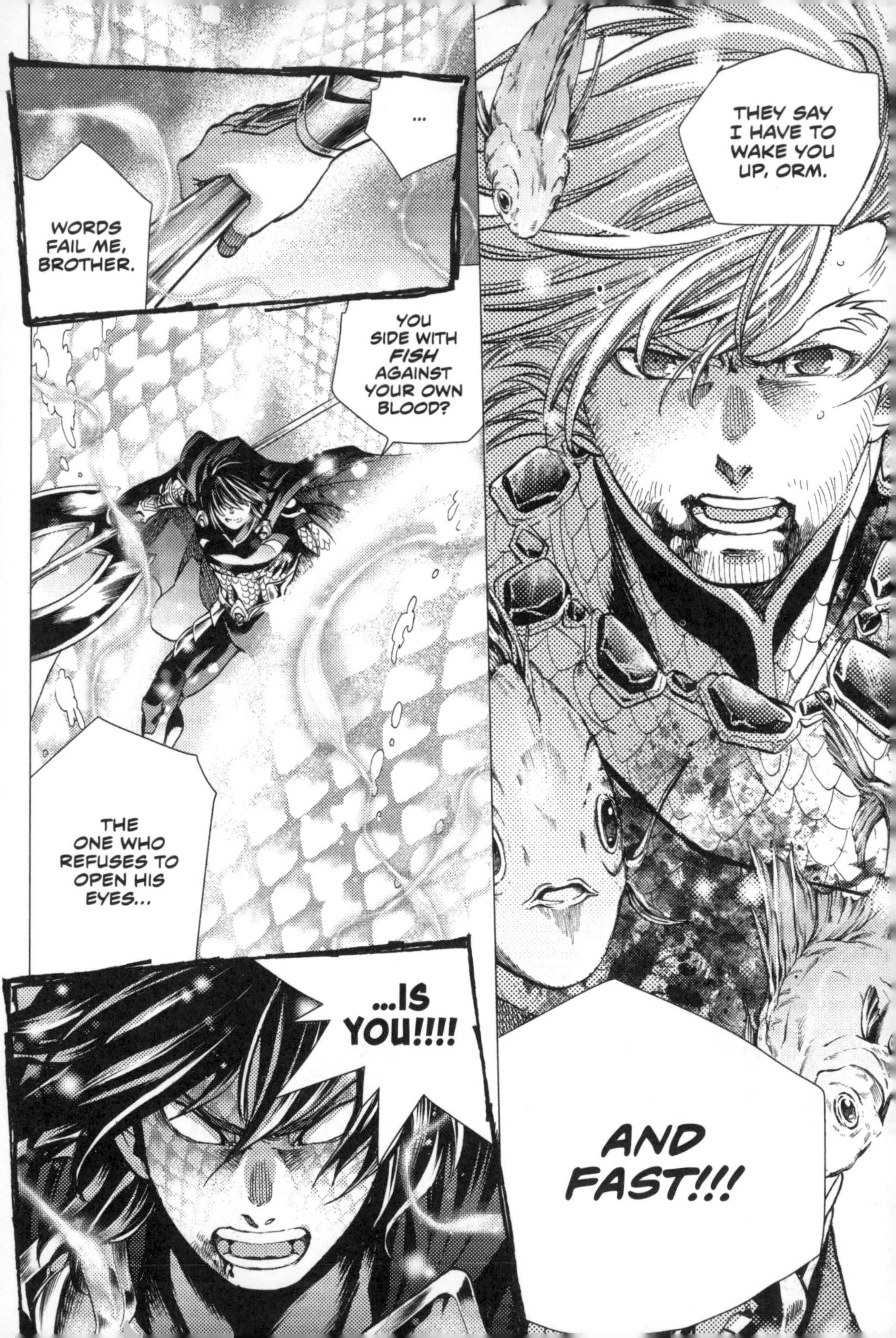
THEY SAY I HAVE TO WAKE YOU UP, ORM.
AND FAST!!!
...
WORDS FAIL ME, BROTHER.
YOU SIDE WITH *FISH* AGAINST YOUR OWN BLOOD?
THE ONE WHO REFUSES TO OPEN HIS EYES...
...IS YOU!!!!

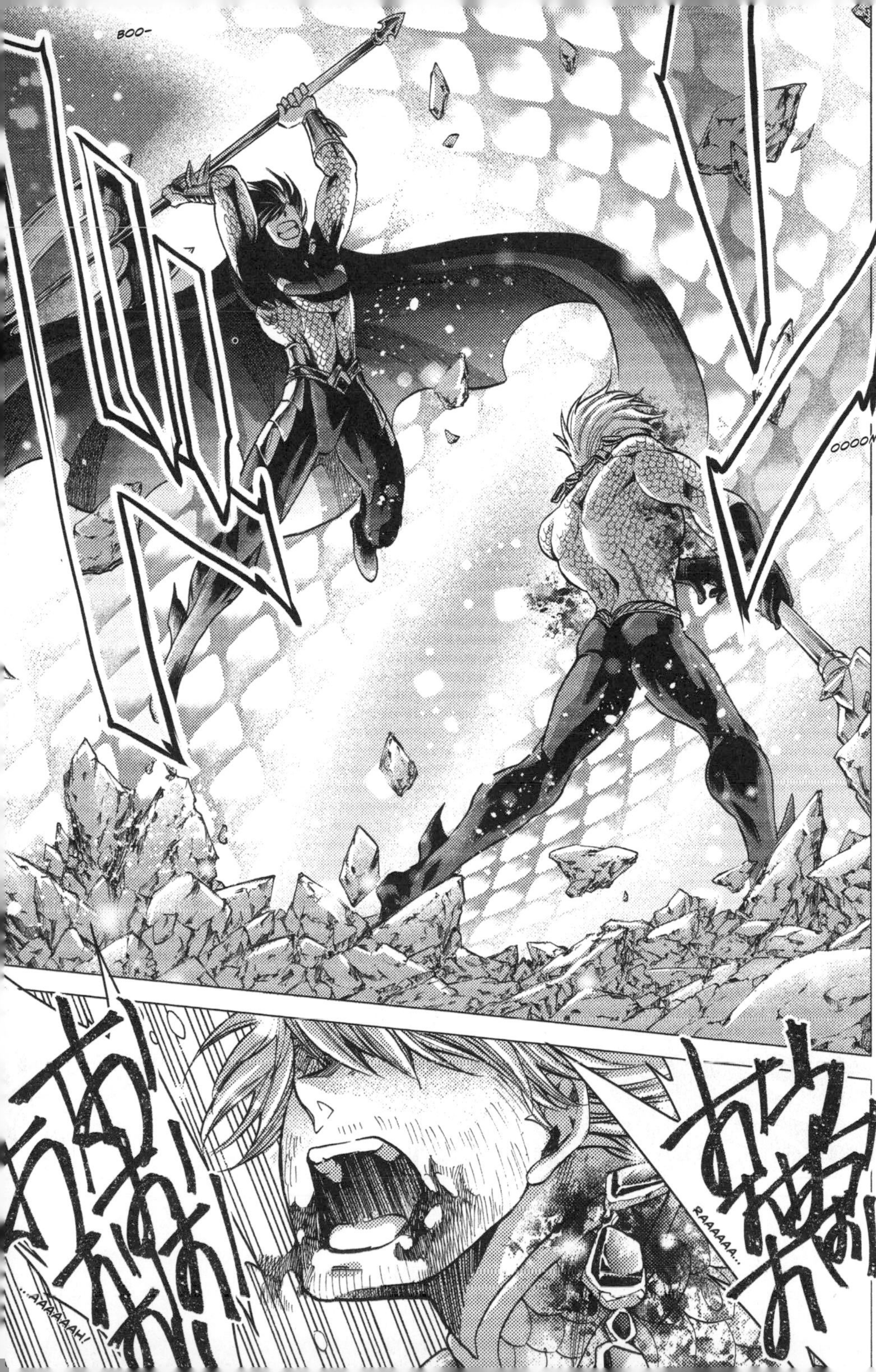
BOO-
OOOOM
RAAAAAA...
...AAAAAAH!

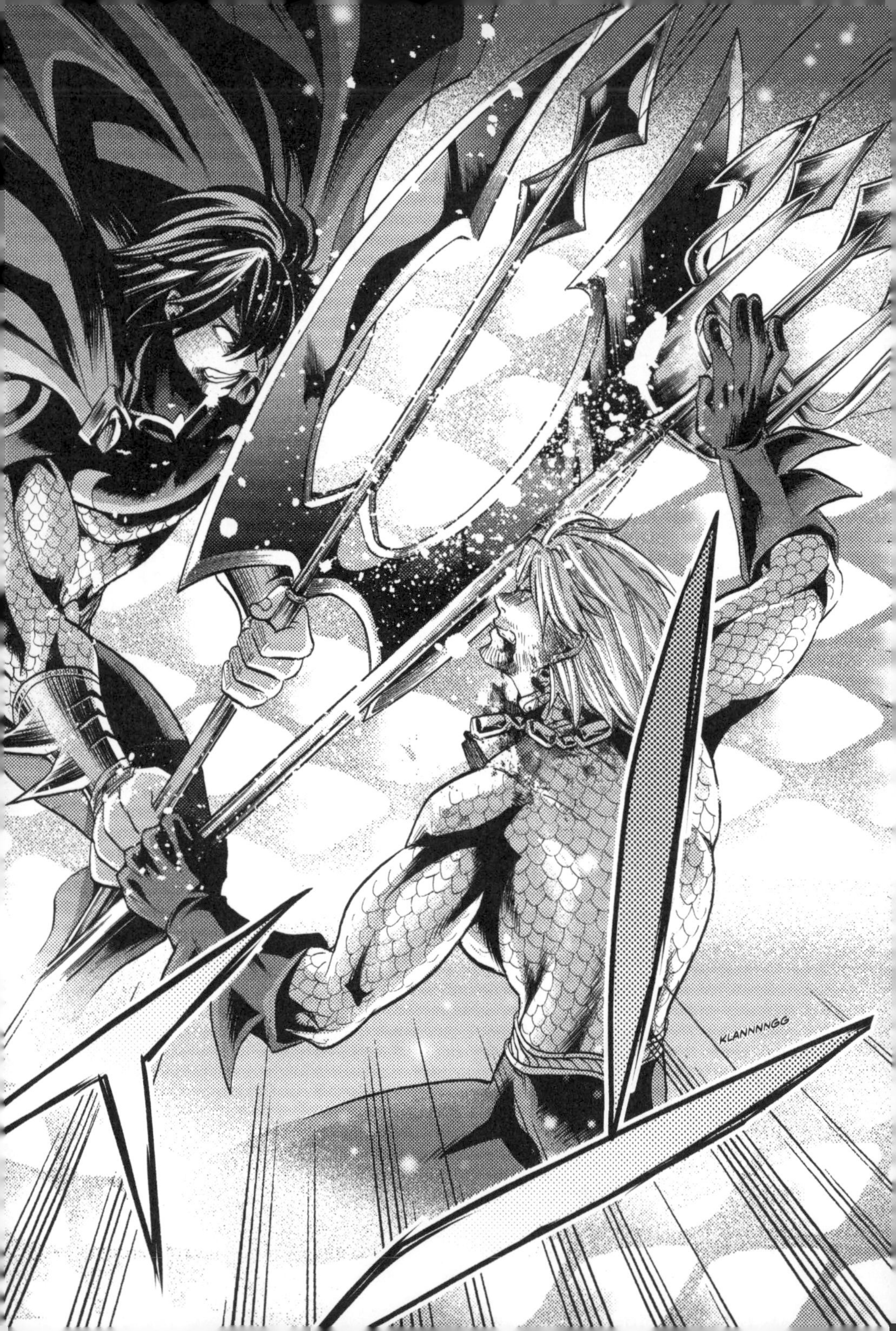
KLANNNNGG

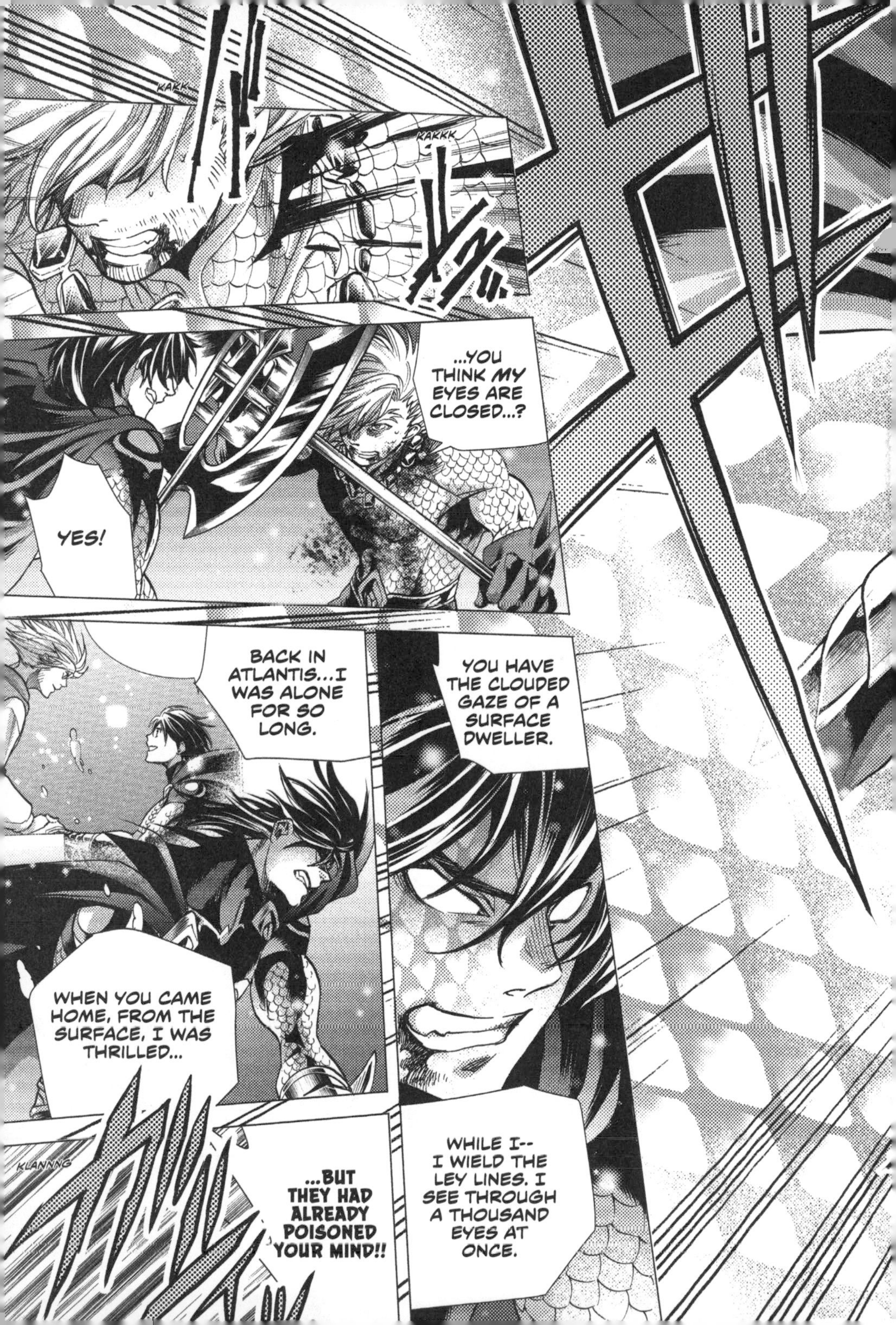
KAKKK
KAKK
...YOU THINK MY EYES ARE CLOSED...?
YES!
YOU HAVE THE CLOUDED GAZE OF A SURFACE DWELLER.
BACK IN ATLANTIS...I WAS ALONE FOR SO LONG.
WHEN YOU CAME HOME, FROM THE SURFACE, I WAS THRILLED...
WHILE I-- I WIELD THE LEY LINES. I SEE THROUGH A THOUSAND EYES AT ONCE.
...BUT THEY HAD ALREADY POISONED YOUR MIND!!
KLANNNG

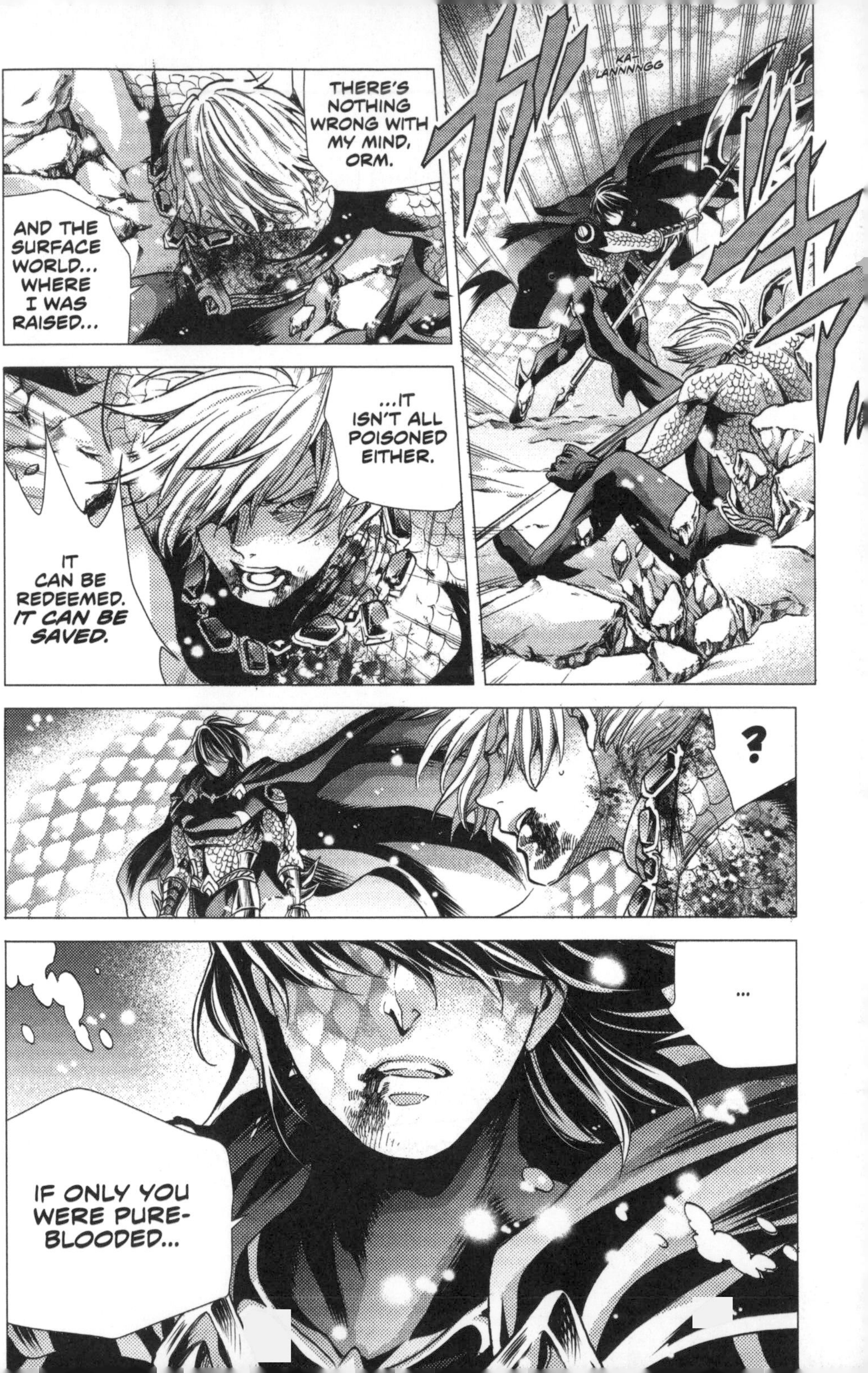
KA-LANNNNGG
THERE'S NOTHING WRONG WITH MY MIND, ORM.
AND THE SURFACE WORLD... WHERE I WAS RAISED...
...IT ISN'T ALL POISONED EITHER.
IT CAN BE REDEEMED. *IT CAN BE SAVED.*
?
...
IF ONLY YOU WERE PURE-BLOODED...

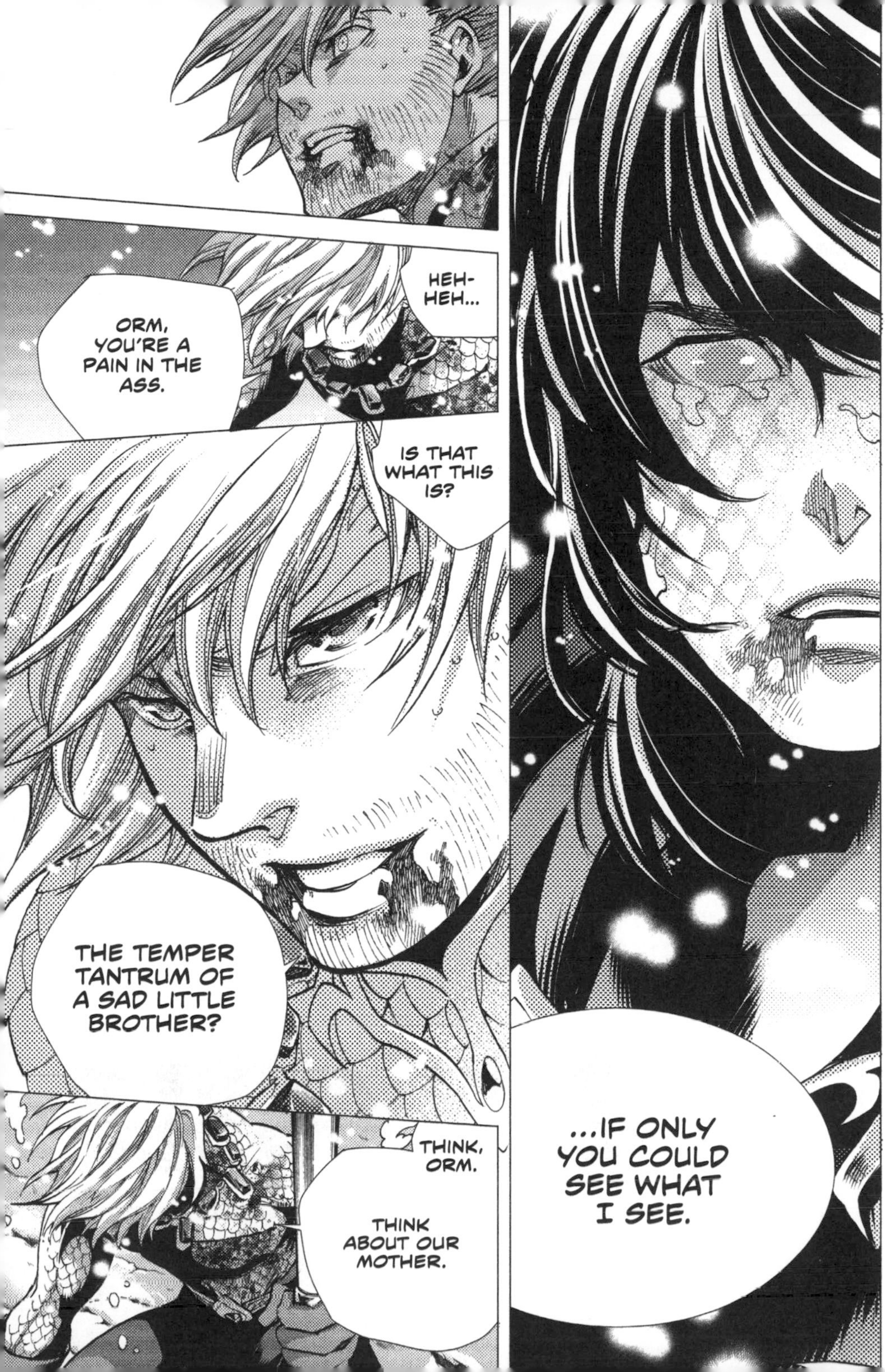
...IF ONLY YOU COULD SEE WHAT I SEE.
HEH-HEH...
ORM, YOU'RE A PAIN IN THE ASS.
IS THAT WHAT THIS IS?
THE TEMPER TANTRUM OF A SAD LITTLE BROTHER?
THINK, ORM.
THINK ABOUT OUR MOTHER.

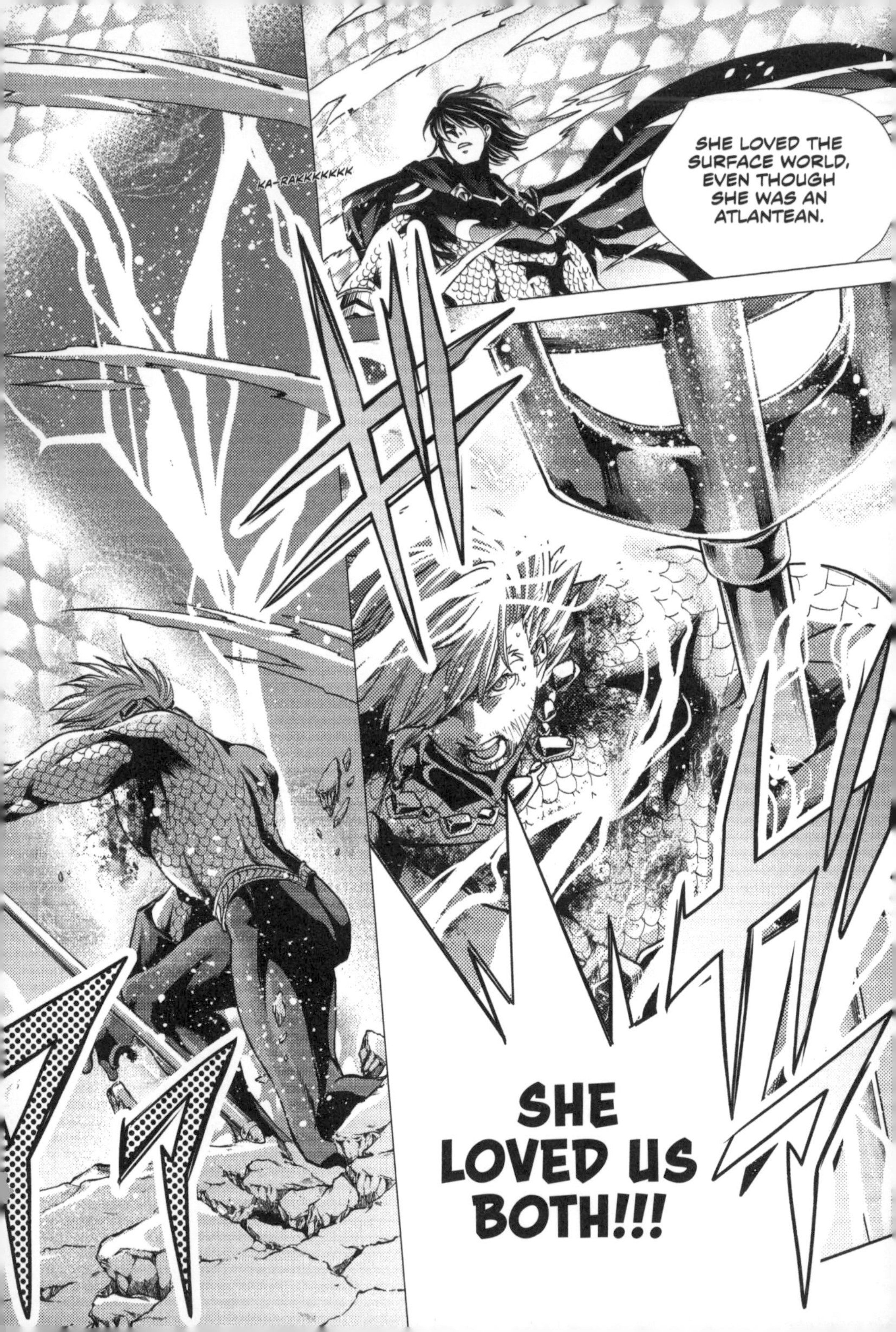
SHE LOVED THE SURFACE WORLD, EVEN THOUGH SHE WAS AN ATLANTEAN.
KA-RAKKKKKKK
SHE LOVED US BOTH!!!

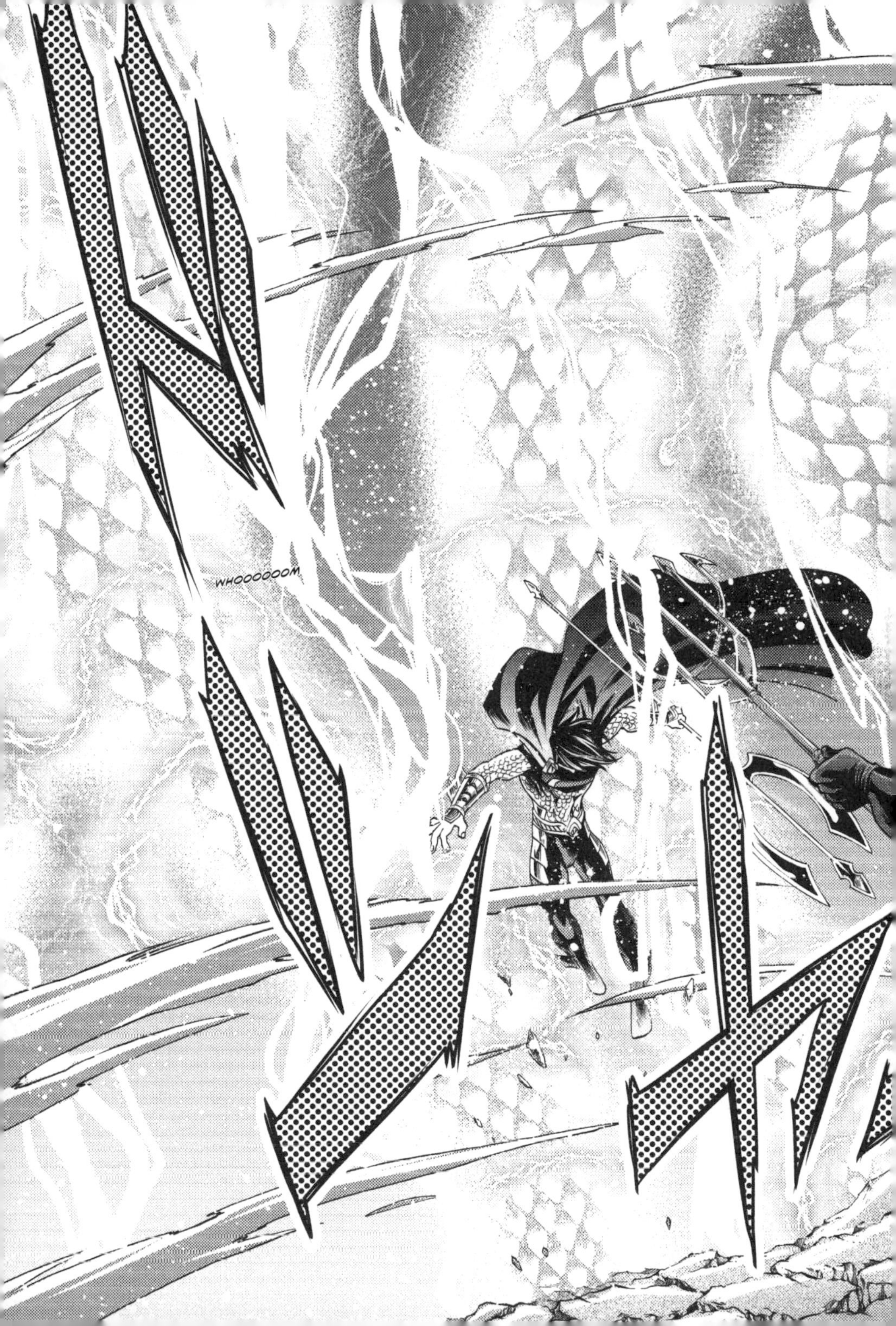
WHOOOOOOM

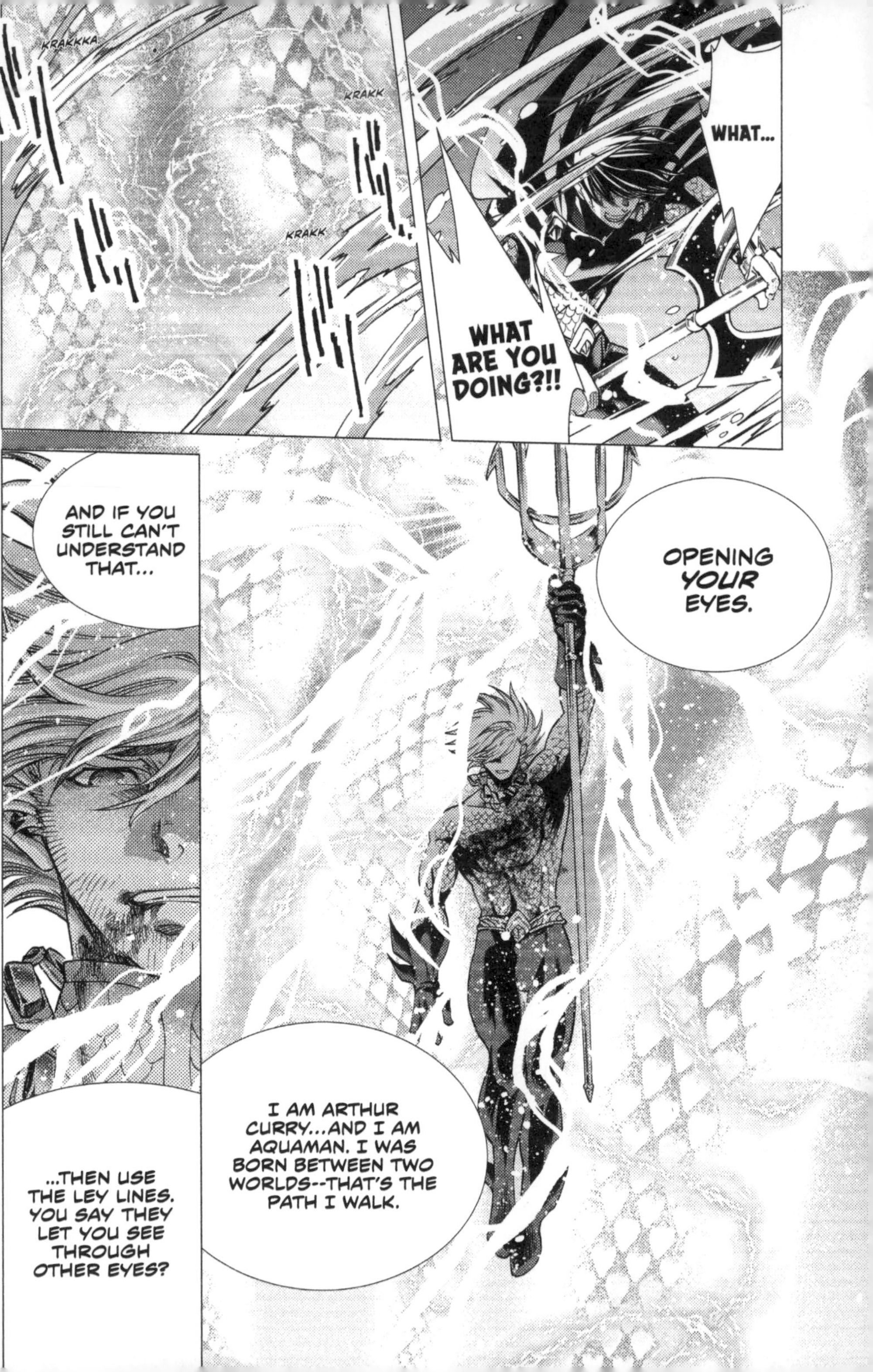
WHAT...
WHAT ARE YOU DOING?!!
KRAKKKA
KRAKK
KRAKK
OPENING *YOUR* EYES.
I AM ARTHUR CURRY...AND I AM AQUAMAN. I WAS BORN BETWEEN TWO WORLDS--THAT'S THE PATH I WALK.
AND IF YOU STILL CAN'T UNDERSTAND THAT...
...THEN USE THE LEY LINES. YOU SAY THEY LET YOU SEE THROUGH OTHER EYES?

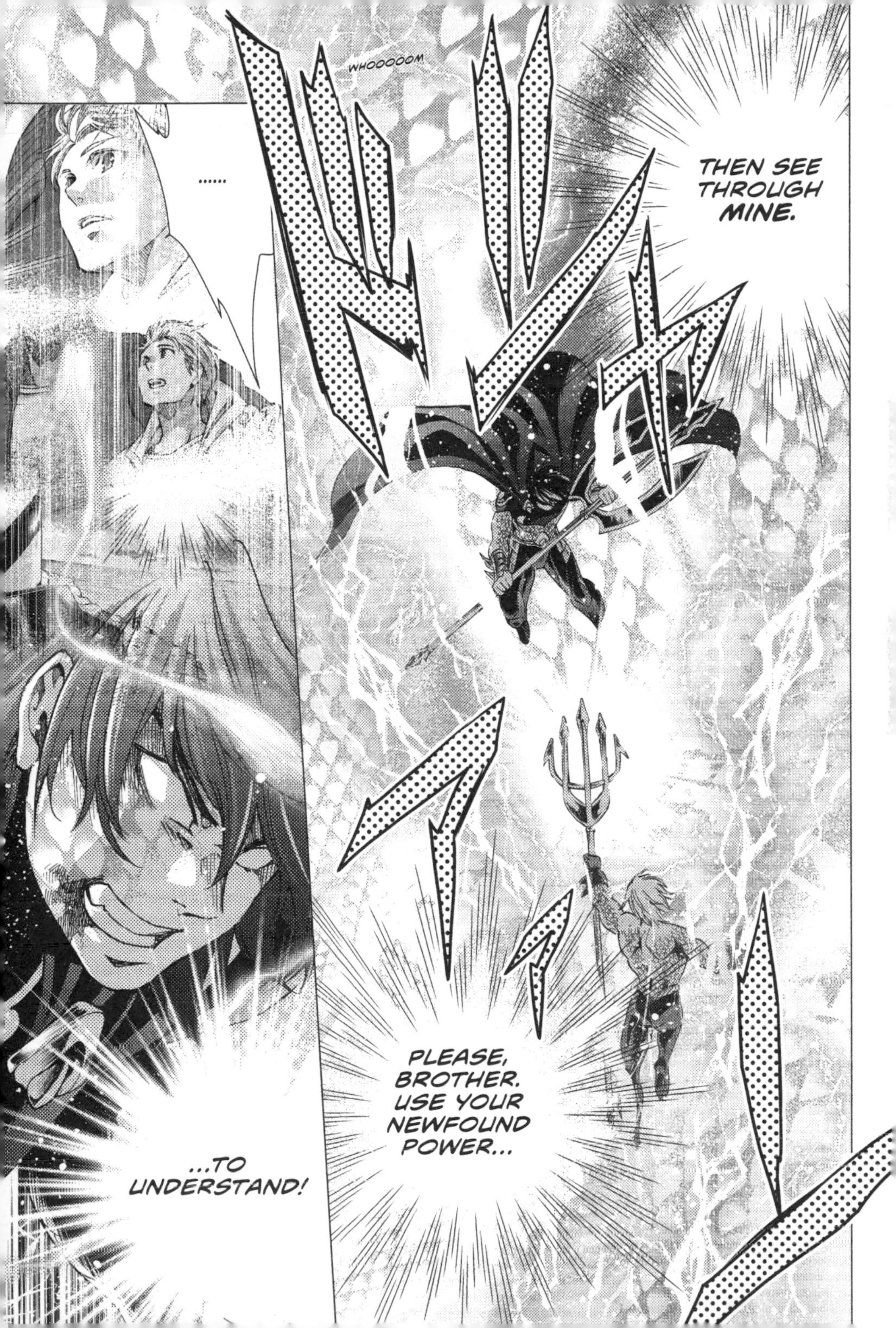
WHOOOOOM
THEN SEE THROUGH MINE.
PLEASE, BROTHER. USE YOUR NEWFOUND POWER...
......
...TO UNDERSTAND!

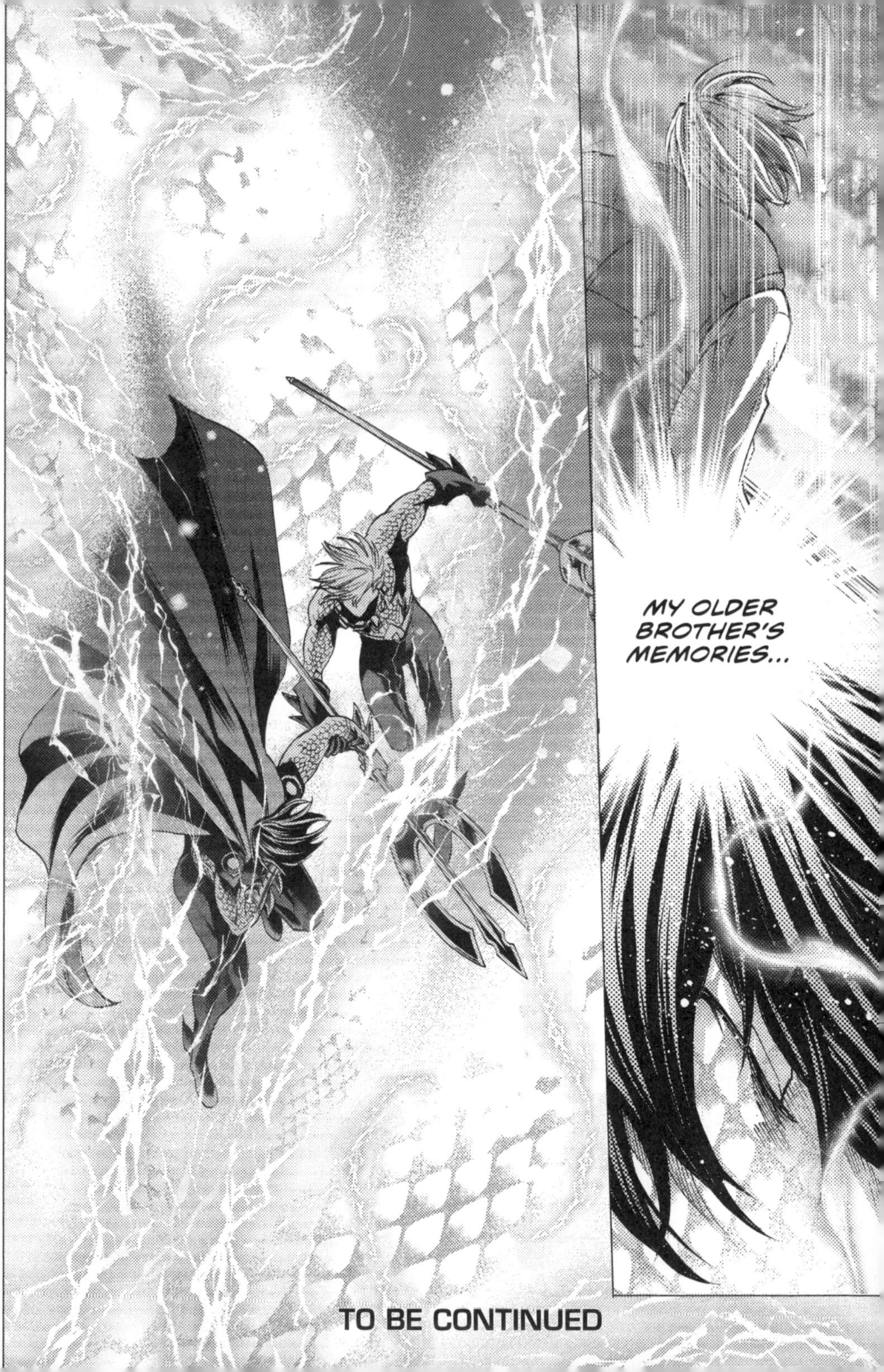
MY OLDER BROTHER'S MEMORIES...
TO BE CONTINUED

SHIORI TESHIROGI

Shiori Teshirogi is best known for writing and illustrating *Saint Seiya: The Lost Canvas–The Myth of Hades*, a spin-off of Masami Kurumada's Saint Seiya series. *The Lost Canvas* enjoyed such popularity that an anime adaptation was also produced.

Shiori lives for her pet cats, and has recently begun studying voice and practicing the Kaatsu fitness technique.

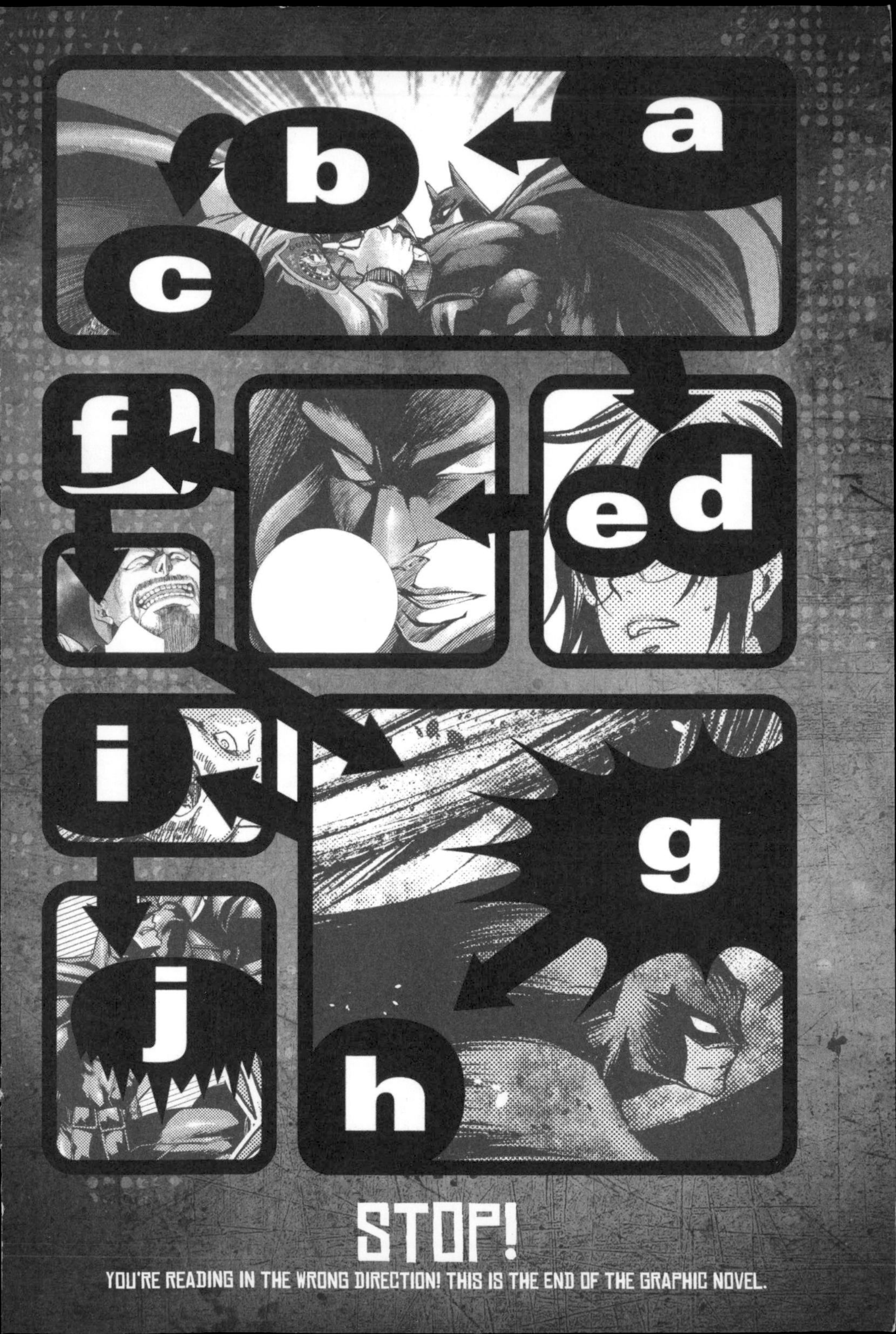
a
b
c
d
e
f
g
h
i
j

STOP!

YOU'RE READING IN THE WRONG DIRECTION! THIS IS THE END OF THE GRAPHIC NOVEL.